DUQUESNE STUDIES

PHILOLOGICAL SERIES

7

A CRITICAL ANTHOLOGY OF ENGLISH RECUSANT DEVOTIONAL PROSE, 1558 - 1603

DUQUESNE STUDIES

PHILOLOGICAL SERIES

7

A CRITICAL ANTHOLOGY OF ENGLISH RECUSANT DEVOTIONAL PROSE, 1558 - 1603

by
JOHN R. ROBERTS

DUQUESNE UNIVERSITY PRESS, Pittsburgh 19, Penna.
Editions E. Nauwelaerts, Louvain, Belgium

1966

Library of Congress Catalog Card Number 65-13006
© 1966, by DUQUESNE UNIVERSITY
Printed in the United States by
THE AD PRESS, LTD., New York, N. Y.

DUQUESNE STUDIES

Philological Series

Editorial Board: James Holly Hanford (Princeton), John F. Mahoney (Detroit), Herbert H. Petit (Duquesne), Henry J. Petit (Colorado), George Foster Provost (Duquesne).

Volume One—*Calvin Huckabay,* John Milton: A Bibliographical Supplement *1929-1957.* xi and 211 pages. Price: $6.25.

Volume Two—*Joseph A. Lauritis, C.S.Sp., Vernon F. Gallagher, C.S.Sp., Ralph A. Klinefelter,* A Critical Edition of John Lydgate's Life of Our Lady. ix and 742 pages. Price: $12.50.

Volume Three—*Waldo F. McNeir and Foster Provost,* Annotated Bibliography of Edmund Spenser, *1937-1960.* xxi and 255 pages. Price: $7.75.

Volume Four—*Dorothy Clotelle Clarke,* Morphology of Fifteenth Century Castilian Verse. vii and 233 pages. Price: $6.95. This volume is also a Modern Humanities Research Monograph.

Volume Five—*Herbert H. Petit,* general editor, Essays and Studies in Language and Literature. vi and 218 pages. Price: $6.25.

Volume Six—*Arthur Hill Cash,* Sterne's Comedy of Moral Sentiments: The Ethical Dimension of the Journey. 138 pages. $4.25.

Volume Seven—*John R. Roberts,* A Critical Anthology of English Recusant Devotional Prose, *1558-1603.* 322 pages. Price: $6.95

ACKNOWLEDGMENT

I should like to acknowledge publicly the assistance of two people without whose help and encouragement this study would never have come to be. First, I would like to express my gratitude to Professor Burton A. Milligan whose kindly guidance extricated me on numerous occasions from the many problems connected with this anthology when it was originally submitted to the University of Illinois as a doctoral dissertation. Secondly, to my wife, Lorraine, I wish to express my thanks publicly for her assistance in typing and proof-reading this work and for her continual patience and encouragement.

Thanks must also be given to Professor G. Blakemore Evans, who was instrumental in obtaining for the University of Illinois Library the many microfilms that were needed in preparing this book; likewise, I am indebted to Professor Helen C. White, who read my typescript and made valuable suggestions for improving it. A special note of thanks must be extended to Miss Eva Faye Benton of the English Library at the University of Illinois and Miss Isabelle Grant of the Rare Book Room at the University of Illinois for their kind assistance.

TABLE OF CONTENTS

ix

GENERAL INTRODUCTION

The primary aim of this anthology is to present to the scholarly reader a generous sampling of English Recusant devotional prose, written during the reign of Queen Elizabeth I (1558-1603) and printed either secretly in England at clandestine presses or on the Continent at Antwerp, Rheims, Douay, Louvain, Paris, or other centers where refugee Catholics gathered during those days of persecution. As far as I am aware, no previous anthology has given adequate representation to these important prose works. In fact, until recently the Recusants have been quite generally ignored and slighted by both literary and cultural historians. Their Protestant counterparts, on the other hand, have survived remarkably well. Most students of Elizabethan literature have some acquaintance with the names of John Jewel, Thomas Cartwright, and Richard Hooker; but how many are there who have heard of their Catholic counterparts, Stephen Brinkley, Richard Hopkins, or Robert Persons, even though these Catholic writers wrote remarkably fine English prose?[1]

In assembling these little known books, I have found A. F. Allison and D. M. Rogers' *A Catalogue of Catholic Books in English Printed Abroad or Secretly in England, 1558-1640,* 2 pts. (Bognor Regis, [England], 1956) to be an indispensable guide and certainly the most complete bibliography of English Recusant books yet compiled. The authors themselves caution, however, that "the catalogue should not be regarded as final. It represents a halting-point and taking stock in a work which we began over ten years ago and which is still incomplete."[2] No one, of course, knows how many volumes not recorded in this catalogue may be hidden away in the great public, university, and monastic libraries of England and of the Continent. Many of the books which have survived exist in only a few widely scattered copies; many of them are not listed in the *Short Title Catalogue,* and of some that are listed, Allison and Rogers have found both earlier and later editions. A complete bibliographical note on each work included in this anthology will be found in the notes to the text.

Although many of these books were written or translated by men of considerable intellectual standing and, in a few cases, by men of

---

[1] A. C. Southern, *Elizabethan Recusant Prose, 1559-1582* (London, 1950), p. ix.

[2] Allison and Rogers, I, ii.

1

European reputation for both learning and style, I have made neither brilliance of content nor excellence in style the principal basis for selecting the works represented in this anthology. In order to provide a comprehensive view of the nature of the books which the Recusants were writing, translating, printing, circulating, and reading in their desperate attempts to maintain and promulgate the Catholic religion in England against ever increasing disappointments and setbacks, and in order to show the superior works in their proper perspective, I have included in this anthology books of questionable literary merit along with works of enduring interest and stylistic excellence. For the spirit of an age cannot be properly ascertained by reading merely the best books of a period nor by concentrating on the purple passages of a handful of authors whose reputations have been perpetuated and sustained by literary historians and critics.

My intention has been to make the selections from the twenty-four books which I have chosen to represent in this anthology sufficiently complete to give the reader an adequate idea of the whole of the various books, but at the same time to keep the anthology within reasonable limits. I have eliminated several fairly well-known Recusant works which are readily available to the reader in modern reprints or editions. Likewise, psalters, primers and manuals of vocal prayers have been excluded; although these devotional works were influential in the spiritual life of Catholics during the sixteenth century, they are not distinctly products of the Recusants. Works which were printed before 1558 and were merely reprinted or brought out in new editions during the reign of Queen Elizabeth have also been excluded. The Rheims *New Testament* (1582) has been omitted also, since few readers are unacquainted with this work, which was, in a sense, the crowning glory of Recusant devotional literature. So that the reader may have a more complete view of the devotional works which were printed by the Recusants during the years 1558-1603, I have listed in the "Introduction to the Text" the devotional prose works that have been omitted in the anthology but are included in Allison and Rogers' catalogue.

Because of the vastness of Recusant prose, I have chosen to limit this anthology to devotional prose exclusively. Although the age was primarily one of religious controversy, marked by acrimonious polemics and theological abstractions, it is the devotional books of the period which "give us some glimpse, even on time-yellowed pages, of the inner life and spirit that made these half-forgotten dramas and these too often now wholly despised abstractions such burning realities in their own day."[3]

The line between controversial literature and devotional literature is, of course, very thin. First of all, devotional tracts and prayers are, whether the author intends them to be or not, partially didactic and instructional, since they are attempts on the part of the author to put into words religious concepts and emotions which he holds and feels; they have the effect of leading the reader to accept the same religious convictions and to feel the same emotions which the author has. For example, Christ in his great prayer, the *Pater Noster,* surely meant the words "forgive us our trespasses as we forgive those who trespass against us" to be instructive as well as importunate.

Secondly, in the minds of the Recusants themselves, the absolute dichotomy between the aims of controversial and devotional literature was never completely made. Argumentation having generally failed, the Recusants hoped that a return to the life of intensive prayer and penance might bring about the same result that the controversial literature had attempted to effect—namely, the conversion of heretical, obstinate England to the Catholic religion. In the last quarter of the sixteenth century as the hope faded that Catholicism might be re-established by political intrigue or through a Catholic succession to the throne, the Recusants turned their attention more and more to a spiritual revolution. The years 1587 and 1588 mark a decisive turning point in the hopes of English Catholics. In less than a year, the Catholic cause was almost shattered by three successive blows: first, the Queen of Scots, upon whom many Catholics had centered their hopes, was beheaded at the command of Queen Elizabeth; secondly, new and crushing financial penalties for Recusancy were levied; and lastly, the Spanish Armada was utterly routed and destroyed.[4] It is significant that the flourishing of Recusant devotional literature did not occur until the 1580's.

Robert Persons, the famous Jesuit missionary priest whose activities as a controversialist made him one of the men in England most despised by the Protestants, states the case this way in the preface to *The First Booke of the Christian Exercise* (1582):

---

[3]Helen C. White, *English Devotional Literature, 1600-1640,* "University of Wisconsin Studies in Language and Literature," No. 29 (Madison, 1931), pp. 11-12.

[4]Brian Magee, *The English Recusants* (London, 1938), pp. 204-205.

But the principall cause and reason [for writing this book]
was, to the ende our countrye men might haue some one sufficiēt
directiō for matters of life and spirit, among so manye bookes
of controuersies as haue ben writen, and are in writinge dailye.
The whiche bookes, albeit in thes our troublesome & quarrelous times be necessarie for defence of our faithe, againste so
manye seditious innouations, as now are attempted: yet helpe
they litle oftentymes to good lyfe, but rather do fill the heades
of men with a spirite of contradiction and contention, that for
the most parte hindereth deuotiō, which deuotion is nothinge
els, but a quiet and peaceble state of the sowle, endewed with
a ioyful promptnes to the diligent execution of all thinges that
appartayne to the honour of God.

    •   •   •   •   •   •

I am therfore of opinion (gentle reader) that albeit trew
faithe be the grownde of Christianitie, without which nothinge
of it selfe can be meritorious before God: yet that one principall meane to come to this trew faithe, and right knowledge,
and to ende all thes our infinite cōtentions in religion, were for
eche man to betake him selfe to a good & vertuous life, for
that God could not of his vnspeakeable mercie suffer suche a
man to erre lōge in religion.[5]

For, as Father Persons continues, "as loose lyfe and worldlye ambition, was the first cause of all heresye in Christian religion from the
beginninge: so is it the cōtinuance of the same."[6]

Richard Hopkins in the dedication of his translation of Luis de
Granada's *Of Prayer, and Meditation* (1582) makes the same point:

And it is nowe about foureteene yeares agoe, since the time that
Master Doctor Hardinge (a man for his greate vertue, learninge, wisdome, Zeale, and sinceritie in writinge againste heresies, of verie godlie and famous memorie) perswaded me earnestlie to translate some of those Spanishe bookes into our
Englishe tounge, affirminge, that more spirituall profite wolde
vndoubtedlie ensewe thereby to the gayninge of Christian sowles

---

[5]Robert Persons, *The First Booke of the Christian Exercise* (n.p. [actually
Rouen], 1582), pp. 2-3.
[6]*Ibid.*, pp. 3-4.

in our countrie from Schisme, and Heresie, and from all sinne, and iniquitie, than by bookes that treate of controuersies in Religion. . . .[7]

And again in his translation of Granada's *A Memoriall of a Christian Life* (1586) he remarks:

> For in my simple Iudgement, the right assured waye to reforme Christendome, beinge at this present so farre corrupted in euerie Countrey, is not by force of Armes, nor by terror, & constraint of greiuous penall lawes, forfeitures, confiscations, and executions with terrible deathes: because the Christian Commonwealth in such a general corruption of al estates cannot by anie other means be dewlie reformed, mainteyned, and preserued, but by such as it was at the first fownded, and increased. As by the Bisshoppes & Pastors preaching of Penaunce, contempt of the worlde, mortification of the flesh, & geuing themselues apparant good example thereof to the common people. . . .[8]

The primary aim of the Recusant devotional writers and translators, then, was to encourage, guide, teach, and exhort men to turn from the world, the flesh, and the devil and give themselves to God; they had no doubt that men of good will would be led by God to accept the Catholic faith once they began to live a virtuous life of prayer and penance.

Although the Recusants hoped that the devotional books they were producing under great difficulties would help effect the conversion of Englishmen to a life in conformity with God's will (to them this meant a return to Catholicism), this is not to say, of course, that these works were intended solely to be spiritual weapons in the struggles against heresy. These devotional books were produced primarily to be "dumb preachers" to English Catholics, who can be classified according to three different categories.

One group was the loyal band of the faithful who remained in England and suffered the risk, and frequently the actuality, of the grave punishments reserved by the government for those who main-

---

[7]Luis de Granada, *Of Prayer, and Meditation,* trans. Richard Hopkins (Paris, 1582), sig. avi^v.

[8]Luis de Granada, *A Memoriall of a Christian Life,* trans. Richard Hopkins (Rouen, 1586), p. 4.

tained and encouraged the old faith in England. A second group was
the many refugee Catholics who fled England for conscience' sake
and settled on the Continent, primarily in France, Spain, Italy and
the Low Countries. Though mostly loyal servants of the Queen, this
group preferred exile to what Cardinal Allen describes as "the daily
dangers, disgraces, vexations, feares, imprisonments, empouerish-
ments, despites, which they [who remain in England] must suffer:
and the railings and blasphemies against Gods Sacraments, Saincts,
Ministers, and al holies, which they are forced to heare in our Countrie."[9] The third group, probably the largest, was composed of those
Catholics who through ignorance, indifference, or fear chose to com-
promise with the new order rather than to suffer the loss of position, fame, property, or possibly life itself. These lukewarm Catholics were commonly referred to as "Demi-Catholics" or "Church
Papists," for many of them attended the Protestant church service
in order to avoid the fines levied against those who refused to com-
ply with this governmental regulation. Commenting on this group,
Father Herbert Thurston, S. J., says:

> Thousands of those who were still, in conscience and convic-
> tion, Catholics, too careless about any matter of religion to
> brave persecution in its behalf, and shrinking with a thor-
> oughly English mistrust from the taint of foreign intrigue
> which the Government astutely and successfully sought to at-
> tach to the Catholic cause, fell into an indifference very nigh
> akin to absolute infidelity. They were not Protestants . . .; they
> would not profess themselves Catholics because the practice of
> Catholicism entailed the sacrifice of goods and liberty, and
> seemed to involve some kind of fellowship in the designs of
> Spaniards and conspirators beyond the seas.[10]

It was to these three heterogeneous groups of Catholics, then,
that the Recusants primarily directed the devotional books which
they were writing and translating. To the first two groups the books
served as guides to the spiritual life, sustaining, supporting, and

---

[9]William Cardinal Allen, *An Apologie and true declaration of the institution
and endeuours of the two English Colleges* (Mounts in Henault [actually
Rheims], 1581), sig. B4.

[10]Herbert Thurston, "Catholic Writers and Elizabethan Readers. I—Father
Parsons' 'Christian Directory,'" *The Month*, LXXXII (1894), 475.

comforting them in their religious convictions. To the members of the third group, the books served as grave reminders of the faith which they had relinquished or were ashamed to espouse openly; the books also served as exhortations to return to a life of prayer and penance. Commenting on the number of Catholics in England during the reign of Elizabeth, Professor Magee states, "In the documents which have come to light, there is no suggestion that, after 1588, the Catholics formed a majority of the people. Up to the very eve of the Armada, there is abundant evidence that they did; all estimates and opinions converge in this and a Catholic proportion of two-thirds constantly recurs in estimates and statistics. . . . Nowhere after 1587 is this figure repeated or confirmed."[11] The audience which the devotional writers attempted to reach was in no sense merely a small group of religious zealots who obstinately refused to conform to the church established by the English government.

Although the Council of Trent (1545-1563) had initiated the arduous task of overhauling the vast external machinery of church government through careful and detailed legislation and definition, most Catholics realized that no amount of overhauling the machinery alone could effect the reformation that was so desperately needed if the Church was to survive the threats that menaced it from all sides, from the inside as well as from the outside. What was needed was a complete and fundamental renewal of the spiritual life of the average Catholic layman, a reformation that had to begin with the conversion and spiritualizing of the individual.[12] Therefore, the majority of the devotional books written in the second half of the sixteenth century was essentially intended for laymen, for beginners unfamiliar with the ways of going about this revitalization. Consequently, most of the books are primarily ascetical rather than mystical in their orientation, that is, they deal with the ordinary ways for the average Christian layman to approach God (vocal and discursive mental prayer, penance, the sacraments, the Rosary, spiritual reading, etc.) rather than with the extraordinary ways of approaching God reserved, for the most part, for those select few whom God favors with rare and exceptional mystical graces (infused contemplation, ecstasies, the prayer of quiet, etc.).

With moral disorder all about, with ignorance of religion the general rule rather than the exception, and with heretical doctrines

---

[11]Magee, p. 36.
[12]Gerard Sitwell, *Spiritual Writers of the Middle Ages,* Vol. XL: *Twentieth Century Encyclopedia of Catholicism* (New York, 1961), p. 108.

being preached openly in former centers of Catholic worship and devotion, it was quite natural that the spiritual writers devoted their talents to the writing and translating of books dealing with fundamental and elementary topics like how to pray, how to avoid sin, how to confess and receive the Holy Eucharist, how to say the Rosary, etc., rather than with more sublime and exalted mystical subjects. In fact, the sixteenth century, in many respects, marks the beginning of serious concern on the part of spiritual writers with the perfection of the average, sinful, ordinary Christian layman. The survival of the Catholic faith rested on the hope that the divine command, "Be ye therefore perfect, as also your heavenly Father is perfect," (Matt. 5:48) would be heeded by laymen as well as by monks and nuns. Luis de Granada, certainly one of the most popular spiritual writers of the sixteenth century among both Catholics and Protestants, was one of the first of the spiritual writers, after St. Ignatius of Loyola, to formulate a method of prayer intended for Christians living in the world.[13]

Although the last half of the sixteenth century witnessed one of the most splendid and significant flowerings of mysticism in the long history of the Catholic Church, especially in Spain under the guidance of St. Teresa of Avila and St. John of the Cross, there was, nevertheless, among Catholics, especially English Catholics, a general cold skepticism and distrust of both mystics and mysticism. I believe there are several reasons for this suspicion.

First of all, in an age when the hierarchical Church throughout Europe was being challenged and in many corners repudiated, the reluctance of Catholics to accept mysticism can be attributed to the habit, common among mystics, of seeking inspirations and rules of life in direct communion with God rather than in the directions of the hierarchical Church.[14] The mystic's union with God is a very personal affair, a mystery which he alone shares with the Almighty and for which there are no absolute standards and norms. Catholics feared that if such an approach were consciously fostered among laymen, especially among laymen who were not prepared either intellectually or spiritually to pursue a life of such extraordinary graces, the results would be a promotion of fanaticism and heresy,

---

[13]Pierre Pourrat, *Christian Spirituality,* trans. W. H. Mitchell, S. P. Jacques, and D. Attwater, 4 vols. (Westminster, Maryland, 1953-55), III, 96.

[14]*Ibid.,* II, 336.

imbued with self-deception; illusion; rejection of legitimate authority; and the seeking for extraordinary mystical phenomena such as visions, private revelations, ecstasies, divine touches, etc.—in short, results which would undermine the whole purpose of the Counter Reformation, which was to lead the Christian to find God within the well-defined, objective framework of the visible, teaching Church. If one conceives his relationship with God to be a very personal and private affair between himself and God alone, it is very easy to make the false assumption that the Church, with its rules, sacraments, and order, is merely an intermediate obstacle to the attaining of a more perfect union with God.

In fact, rejecting the hierarchical structure of the Church and seeking his inspiration and guidance from God directly or from God as He spoke through the Scriptures, Luther himself embraced a type of mysticism, false in the Catholic view, which was wholly emancipated from the authority of the Church. His frequent appeal to the mystics of the late Middle Ages as justification for his actions undoubtedly is one of the major reasons why mystics in general suffered somewhat in reputation among the leaders of the Counter Reformation,[15] who naturally were skeptical of a source which the great German Reformer felt supported his own ideas and claims. Likewise, in Spain during the first two-thirds of the sixteenth century there arose a sect of false mystics known as the Alumbrados or Illuminati.[16] This group was repeatedly condemned by the Church because it emphasized the direct action of God, in contrast to the indirect action of God through the teaching Church and the sacraments, and because it embraced a theological position concerning free will and the futility of good works quite akin to that proposed by the Protestant reformers. One of the champions of the Catholic position against the Alumbrados was Luis de Granada. His opposition to these mystics may account in some measure for his popularity among English Catholics and even Anglicans who daily witnessed in England the rise of "inner light" sects which encouraged a type of false mysticism. Since throughout the sixteenth century the Church was menaced by these movements of what it considered to be false mysticism, there is little difficulty in understanding why Catholics regarded all mystical approaches to God, the valid along with the fallacious, with reservation and suspicion.

---

[15]*Ibid.*
[16]*Ibid.,* III, 80.

Not only did the Protestant reformers espouse the mystics of the late Middle Ages as precursors of their own illuminism and rejection of the authority of the Church, but also they regarded certain early Christian humanists of the sixteenth century, especially Erasmus, Lefèvre of Etaples, and Giovanni Pico della Mirandola, as forerunners of their movement. Erasmus, for example, reacted against the nominalist theology of his time and against the too formalistic religion he saw practised about him by the masses, a religion riddled with superstition and ritual but devoid of spirit and interior conviction. One of the remedies he proposed was serious reading of the Bible, which was coupled with a belief that the Christian who reads the Bible is given a kind of inner light to enable him to comprehend it. This inspiration was not simply pious suggestion which a person arouses in himself when he reads about God; it was a direct intervention which came from God to enlighten and teach him.[17] "For," states Erasmus in *Ratio seu methodus perveniendi ad veram theologiam* (1518), "when we read the Holy Books, God speaks to us more really and efficaciously than he did to Moses in the burning bush, provided that we come to hold converse with him with a clean heart."[18] If then God instructs the pious by this direct means, it is easy to assume that there is no need for recourse to the teaching Church for an interpretation of the Scriptures. Piety becomes something inward and absolutely spiritual—a very personal matter. Although Erasmus and his followers dissociated themselves from the Protestant revolt once it became absolutely clear where the movement was leading, nevertheless, they were keenly aware that their emphases on seeking the rules of the Christian life through immediate communication with God and through the Scriptures, rather than through the theologians and the teaching Church, contributed significantly in preparing the way for the Protestant revolt and the rise of false mysticism. Writing to Erasmus after the Reformation began in earnest, Thomas More laments, "In these days in which men by their own default, misconstrue and take harm of the very scripture of God, until men better amend, if any man would now translate *Moria* [sic] [*The Praise of Folly*] into English or some works either that I have myself written ere this, albeit there be none harm therein, folk yet being (as they

---

[17]Quoted by Pourrat, III, 57-58.
[18]*Ibid.*, p. 57.

are) given to take harm of that that is good, I would not only my darling's [Erasmus's] book but mine own also, help to burn them both with mine own hands rather than folk should (though through their own fault) take any harm of them, seeing that I see them likely in these days so to do."[19] These well-intentioned Christian humanists presented the Recusants with one more reason to fear mysticism, whether genuine or false; the possibility of deception and extremism was considered too great a risk in a time when the whole Christian world was being ripped wide open by extremes.

It is significant that none of the lofty mystical writings of the great Spanish mystics and saints, in particular those of St. Teresa of Avila and St. John of the Cross, were translated into English by the Recusants during the sixteenth century. St. Teresa's *Avisos* were included in a translation of Luca Pinelli's *Briefe Meditations of the Most Holy Sacrament* (1595-1600), a fact which indicates that the Recusants were not totally unaware of the great Spanish mystics who were their contemporaries; but these short maxims of St. Teresa are certainly not comparable to her great mystical works. English Catholics, witnessing the daily rise of "inner light" movements at home and abroad, felt reluctant to present to struggling and bewildered Catholics in England esoteric material which was inappropriate for their needs. The Spanish writers who were translated—Granada, Alonso de Madrid, Francis Arias, and others—were all, in fact, attempting to curb the rise of the false mysticism of the Illuminati groups. Therefore, these writers were received with greater confidence by the Recusants, who saw a similar task to be accomplished among their countrymen.

Since the religious upheaval of the sixteenth century, Protestantism has shaped Catholic thinking considerably, primarily in a negative way. Many of the emphases of Modern Catholicism, for example, have been made to counterbalance Protestant thinking. When Protestants have placed too much emphasis on one doctrine over another or stressed one facet of a doctrine at the expense of another facet, the Church has felt obliged to take the opposite position in order to balance the extremes. For example, when Protestants began stressing Scripture as the primary and only rule of faith, Catholics began to stress tradition and to de-emphasize the role of Scripture. As Protestants began to de-emphasize the neces-

---

[19]Note in Thomas More, *Utopia,* trans. Ralph Robinson; ed. Phillip E. Hallett (London, 1935), pp. 64-65.

sity of the sacraments for salvation, Catholics stressed the absolute necessity of the sacraments in the Christian schema with renewed vigor.

Likewise, as Protestants began urging a type of illuminism and mysticism, Catholics began emphasizing a methodical asceticism to counteract it. Much of the emphasis of Catholic spiritual writers on asceticism during the sixteenth century is a reaction to the Protestant doctrine of faith alone and the denial of free will. If, as many Protestants maintained, man is saved by faith alone, irrespective of his moral conduct, then, of course, an ordered, disciplined life of penance, prayer, fasting, corporal punishment, and reception of the sacraments is rather pointless. If the corporal and spiritual works of mercy, such as almsgiving, visiting the sick, praying for the dead, etc., can in no way help to effect a man's salvation, then it is useless to encourage Christians to engage in such activities. If a man cannot choose between good and evil because he does not have the free will necessary for such a choice, then, of course, there is little need for manuals in how to avoid sin and choose virtue. In his introduction to Luis de Granada's *A Memoriall of a Christian Life,* Richard Hopkins states the following:

> And therefore let no man maruaile, that theise newe Preachers doe neuer preache to the people, to doe penaunce for their synnes, and to fast and praye for them, seinge all their doctrines beinge wholie grounded vpon their newe Heretical licentious doctrine of iustification by onelie faith, (which newe doctrine they nowe terme to be the Soule of their newe Caluinisticall Churche,) are directlie contrarie to doinge of penaunce, and vnto all kinde of spirituall exercises of an austere vertuous life, and doe breede in all their followers onelie an arrogant presumption of securitie of their owne peculiar election, predestination, iustification, and saluation, whereby they are moued to singe psalmes in their Schismaticall Congregations, and at home, onelie to thanke God for the same.[20]

Catholic theology, on the other hand, has always stressed that man has free will and thus moral responsibility. It has traditionally held that man, in order to be saved, must take the proper means to

---

[20]Granada, *A Memoriall of a Christian Life,* p. 11.

prepare himself for the grace of God. To Catholics, fasting, corporal punishment, vocal and mental prayer, reception of the sacraments, the spiritual and corporal works of mercy, and an ordered, disciplined life are means for attaining moral perfection and personal sanctification. Therefore, in reaction to Protestantism, Catholic spiritual writers of the sixteenth century tended to place more and more emphasis on the role that man plays in his own salvation while at the same time de-emphasizing (but not denying) the role that God plays. Speaking of his own spiritual writings, Luis de Granada in "The Prologve to the Christian Reader" of *The Memoriall of a Christian Life* says, "And albeit the thinge we pretēde here to doe, (which is to forme a perfecte Christian) be properlie the worke of the holie ghoste, yet neuertheles like as grace excludeth not our trauaile & industrie, but must rather of necessitie concurre therewith, euen so the inwarde instruction of almightie god excludeth not the owtwarde teachinge of men, but doth of necessitie require the same."[21]

One of the major objectives of the writer of devotional literature, therefore, was to delineate exactly what man's role was in saving his soul and to make very practical suggestions about how the man unfamiliar with the intricacies of the spiritual life was to go about reforming and revitalizing his interior life. For, as Granada points out in his prologue to *A Memoriall of a Christian Life,*

> How shall a simple vnlearned man vnderstande how much this matter importeth him, if there be not laide before him the promises and threatninges of almightie God, and the great benefites also for which he is bound to serue him? How shal he Knowe how to confesse his sinnes perfectlie, if he be not instructed in the partes of the sacramēte of pennaunce, and how he ought to behaue him selfe in euerie one of them? How shall he be sorowfull and repentant for his sinnes, if there be not declared vnto him the reasons and causes that shoulde moue him to be sorowfull for them. . . . How shall he obteine the loue of God, if he knowe not the meanes whereby it is obteined, and the impedimentes and lettes that doe hinder him from it, and the exercises wherein he ought to exercise him selfe for the obteininge thereof?[22]

---

[21]*Ibid.,* p. 8.
[22]*Ibid.,* pp. 11-12.

In other words, if the average Catholic layman was going to begin living a life of Christian perfection, he needed guidance and direction. Unlike the religious, monks and nuns, who had a rule or constitution to delineate in detail their duties and daily obligations in striving for perfection, the layman who sincerely desired to pursue a life of prayer and penance frequently had nowhere to turn for help and direction. The spiritual writers of the sixteenth century saw that their primary obligation, then, was to supply this need. For as Diego de Estella remarks in *The Contempte of the World,* "Nothing then can be more conuenient for vs [Christians who sincerely desire to lead a life of spiritual perfection] then to haue a good order and methode proposed, what is meete to be beloued and folowed, and what is meete to be detested and eschewed."[23]

One might quite reasonably wonder, of course, if this instruction and spiritual guidance were not primarily the function of the priest, especially of the preacher. Why then, one might ask, were devotional books considered absolutely essential? Luis de Granada, anticipating this obvious objection, answers in his prologue to *A Memoriall of a Christian Life* in the following manner: "although it be the office of Catholique preachers to cure this blindnes with the light of godes worde: yet notwithstandinge theise be not euerie where to be founde, neither do all preachers treat of theise so necessarie matters, nor yet can they well (speakinge generallie) descēde to such particularities, as this moral doctrine requireth . . . . for all theise causes the readinge of deuout Catholique bookes is verie profitable: for somuch as they be vnto vs as it were domme preachers. . . ."[24] Certainly in Elizabethan England, where priests were recognized quite generally by the government to be outlaws in the service of the King of Spain (one official document, referring to the Jesuits, calls them "the creatures of the Beast, the very loathesome locusts that crawl out of the bottomless pit")[25] and where their pulpits were not only forbidden them but actually occupied by Protestant ministers, the importance of these "domme preachers" became ever increasingly significant in effecting the renewal and maintenance of the Christian life among the English Catholic laity.

---

[23]Diego de Estella, *The Contempte of the World,* trans. G. C. [George Cotton] (n.p. [actually Rouen], 1584), sig. A2ᵛ-A3.

[24]Granada, *A Memoriall of a Christian Life,* p. 12.

[25]Quoted by Thurston, "Catholic Writers and Elizabethan Readers," p. 470.

Let us now turn our attention to the particular types of devotional books which the English Recusants wrote and translated in their attempts to meet the needs of their fellow Catholics. I have divided the entries in this anthology into four major categories: (1) spiritual directories and general ascetical treatises, (2) books concerned with prayer and meditation, (3) treatises on the sacraments, and (4) treatises on the Rosary. Since many of the books deal with varied subjects, this division is at times quite arbitrary.

The first type, the spiritual directory, is no more than a handbook for Christian living. It considers the details and particulars of such matters as how to make a good confession, how to receive worthily and devoutly the Holy Eucharist, how to avoid sin and its occasions, how to adorn the soul with virtue, how to pray effectively, and a host of other spiritual topics. It is, in many respects, a type of spiritual courtesy book. In fact, Luis de Granada in his prologue to *A Memoriall of a Christian Life* recognized this parallel: "Others haue endeauored . . . to forme a perfecte prince, others a captaine, others a courtier. And thus hath eche one trauailed to extolle and aduance that thinge with his penne which he most estiemed. Nowe of this are we right well assured, that emonge all the thinges of this world, there is nothing of greater price and estimation, nothinge more excellente & diuine, thā a perfecte Christian."[26]

Anyone acquainted with Elizabethan courtesy books knows that the author does not attempt to establish merely abstract rules of conduct for his courtier or prince; he endeavors rather to suggest very practical ways and means of putting into the daily life of his charge those general principles which he wishes to stress. The spiritual writers, likewise, recognized that no genuine reform could be effected among the Catholic laity unless the abstract concepts and precepts of Christian living were reduced to practical, concrete rules and directives. As Alonso de Madrid in *A Breefe Methode . . . how to serue God* points out clearly, ". . . it profiteth verie litle, if one know what is writen for seruing God, & be ignorāt in what manner and order it is to be done. And albeit arte and knowledge of euery good thinge, floweth from God the supremest artificer, & many be illuminated by his goodnes, & preuented with benedictions of delighte & sweetenes: yet for all that we must not omitt to doe what is in vs, to seke (as we are bounde) his commaundementes & will, & other thinges which be necessary for doinge perfectly whatsoeuer is

[26]Granada, *A Memoriall of a Christian Life*, pp. 1-2.

pleasing vnto him."[27] Loarte in Stephen Brinkley's translation of *The
Exercise of a Christian Life* states, "For if in case euery artisan
thinke it necessary to knowe such things as belong vnto his Arte:
how much more is a true Christian bounde to knowe what appertaineth to his profession, (beeing an Art aboue al Arts) & to be
ready (as the Apo. S. *Peter* saith) to yeeld an account of that which
he beleueth & hopeth for as also of that which he is bound to do, to
liue according to Gods holye wil and ordinance, & to obtain
euerlasting life."[28] And lastly, Granada in Hopkin's translation ex-
presses the same idea when he writes, "For like as good artificers do
endeuor to haue all such tooles and instrumētes as belonge to their
occupation, and as those that studie any arte or science do seeke to
haue some booke wherein is conteined whatsoeuer concerneth that
science, that hauinge eche thinge sette in order together in one place
their memorie might the lesse be distracted, euen so me thought it
was verie requisite to do the like in this profession, which is the arte
of artes, and science of sciences. . . ."[29]

It is important to note that the spiritual directories can be divided into two general categories. The first type, like Alonso de
Madrid's *A Breefe Methode . . . how to serue God* or Robert Persons' immensely popular *The First Booke of the Christian Exercise*
(later known as *The Christian Directorie*), deals with general and
broad religious topics such as "how necessarie a thinge it is for a man
to resolue to leaue vanities," "how willfull ignorance doeth increase,
not excuse sinne," "of seuen speciall reasons, why the deuill moueth
us to delaye," etc. The primary aim of these directories, as Persons
points out on the title page of his work, is to lay down "the causes &
reasons that should moue a man to resolue hym selfe to the seruice
of God: And all the impedimentes remoued, which may lett the
same." The second type are those, like Loarte's *The Exercise of a
Christian Life,* which attempt to delineate in detail the daily duties,
obligations, and actions of the Christian who, having decided to embrace a Christian life, needs a detailed plan to guide him in applying
general Christian concepts and precepts to his daily life. Loarte, for

---

[27]Alonso de Madrid, *A Breefe Methode or Way Teachinge all sortes of
Christian people, how to serue God in a moste perfect manner,* trans. I. M.
[John Mitchell] (n.p.d. [secretly in England, 1602-05]), sig. A5ᵛ.
[28]Gaspar Loarte, *The Exercise of a Christian Life,* trans. I. S. [pseud.
Stephen Brinkley] (n.p.d. [secretly in England, 1596-97]), pp. 287-288.
[29]Granada, *A Memoriall of a Christian Life,* pp. 2-3.

example, deals with such particular topics as the daily schedule of prayer which the Christian should follow, what he should do on arising in the morning, what he should do before meals, how he should observe holy days, what practical means can be used to overcome specific temptations to sin, etc. Of course, the dichotomy between these two general categories is never absolute.

Unlike many other types of devotional literature, spiritual directories do not aim primarily to arouse in the reader pious and edifying thoughts about the Christian life; rather they endeavor to make the Christian life appear reasonable, logical, and desirable. During the Middle Ages the average Christian was presented with a moral problem if he chose to turn away from the flesh, the world, and the devil and to turn to God, but he was hardly presented with an intellectual dilemma. Although throughout the Middle Ages there were always a few scattered sects (like the Lollards, the Hussites, and the Albigensians) which did not accept the Church's view of man and of God, these were in no way reflective of society at large. For the ordinary Christian the choice was clear and obvious; the decision was not, of course, easy to make. He could either accept and embrace the schema set up by the Church for salvation or he could reject it; but there was, generally speaking, no tenable third choice. His problem was not so much what to choose, but whether or not to choose. During the Middle Ages, therefore, much of the devotional literature was written to move and excite the lukewarm Christian to embrace the life of prayer and penance; the appeal quite frequently was primarily to his emotions, not to his intellect. With the coming of the Protestant Reformation and pagan humanism, with the coming of the breakdown of the medieval concept of man and his world, an intellectual problem was also posed. The Christian was presented during this period of religious and philosophical upheaval with an array of choices concerning the nature of man, his ultimate goals, and the means of achieving these goals. Therefore, there arose a need among Catholics to produce devotional books which strengthened intellectual conviction, which spelled out in clear terms the old values and presented the Catholic life as reasonable, logical, and desirable.[30] Spiritual directories were written partly to meet this challenge; they offered to the Catholic a rational plan for Christian living and attempted to justify the inherent wisdom and common sense of such a plan. For as Granada points out in his prologue to *A*

---

[30]Sitwell, pp. 129-130.

Memoriall of a Christian Life, "when the light of vnderstandinge is taken awaie, which gwideth all our doinges, and as it were the principall wheele of this clocke, that ruleth and moueth all the Christian life, what may be looked for els, but blindnes, and ignorance, with other great incōueniences."[31]

Commenting on the devotional books of the early seventeenth century, Miss White makes this significant point: "Pious these books are from start to finish, but one never feels, as he sometimes does with nineteenth century devotional books, that edification is offered as a substitute for thinking. True, much of the thinking in these books is along lines which no longer have any power to stimulate the interest of most of us. Many of the specific ideas and attitudes are for most readers of today definitely out-worn. In spite of that it is clear that for its own age it was neither shoddy nor superficial thinking. That alone gives these books a dignity and an enduring substance that no amount of mere timelessness can ever insure."[32]

Just as the spiritual directories were intended primarily to instruct the layman and give him practical suggestions as well as rational general principles for living the Christian life, so the books on meditation and the books of meditations (the second general category in this anthology) were intended to instruct him on prayer and give him not only an understanding of the nature of prayer but also a practical, detailed method for executing this most important aspect of Christian living. Meditation was the means by which those truths propounded in the spiritual directories as well as all theological truths were to become personally significant and relevant to the ordinary Catholic layman. In an age when the old verities were being challenged not only by the Protestant reformers but likewise by the pagan humanists, there arose a great need to re-enforce the old truths by making them come alive to the individual Christian, a need for him to apply these well-known truths to his own personal life. As Granada notes in *Of Prayer, and Meditation,*

> For like as the phisitions affirme that if we will haue a medecine to helpe a sicke man, it is necessarie, it be first wrowght and digested in the stomak with naturall heat, (because otherwise it shall not be anie profitt to him at all:) euen so also, if

---

[31]Granada, *A Memoriall of a Christian Life,* pp. 9-10.
[32]White, *English Devotional Literature,* p. 235.

we will haue the misteries of our faith to be profitable and
healthfull vnto our soules, it is requisite they be first wrought,
and digested in our hartes with the heate of deuotion and
meditation: because otherwise they shall profit vs verie littell.
And for want hereof, we see that manie Christians, which are
verie whole and sownd in matters of faith, be yet in there liues
verie licentious and dissolute. And the reason is, because they
do not consider, and weigh the holie misteries which they beleue: and so they keepe there faith, as it were fast locked in a
corner of a chest, or as a sword in the scabarde, or as a
medecine in the potticaries shoppe, and vse not the benefitt
thereof, for such purposes, as it serueth. They beleue generall-
lie, and as it were in a fardel or grosse sōme, all such thinges
as the Catholike Church beleueth. They beleue that there
shalbe a iudgment, that there shalbe paines for the wicked, and
glorie for the good: but how manie Christians shall ye finde,
that do consider after what sort this iudgment, these paines, and
this glorie shalbe, with other the like circumstances?[33]

Since few things are more elusive and inexact than the vocabulary of spirituality, it is necessary to define the term *meditation*.
First of all, there are two major types of prayer—vocal and mental.
Vocal prayer is that kind of prayer expressed by words or gestures;
mental prayer is that kind of prayer which takes place within the
soul, "a silent elevation and application of our mind and heart to
God in order to offer Him our homages and to promote His glory
by our advancement in virtue."[34] Quite frequently the terms *mental
prayer* and *meditation* are used as synonyms, whereas actually a
distinct technical difference exists between the two. Meditation,
strictly speaking, is but one part or kind of mental prayer—that part
which is discursive, involving reflection and reasoning. That prayer
in which acts of the intellect predominate is called discursive prayer;
that prayer in which the affections and will predominate is called
affective prayer. Generally speaking, meditation or mental prayer has
come to mean that kind of prayer in which both the intellect and affection operate. The characteristic element of meditation is mental discourse, i. e., the analysis of a religious proposition, a descent from a

---

[33]Granada, *Of Prayer, and Meditation,* sigs. Aiiiv-Aiiij.
[34]Adolphe Tanquerey, *The Spiritual Life, a Treatise on Ascetical and
Mystical Theology,* trans. Herman Branderis (Tournai, [Belgium], 1930),
pp. 319-320.

general truth to a particular application, a reasoning of some kind
—with the consequent variety of affection, practical conclusions, and
resolution which arises from these considerations and to which the
will gives it assent.[35] The object of such prayer, as De Guibert
notes, is "to make him who meditates know the truths of faith more
deeply. He will be more intimately and personally persuaded of the
validity of these truths. He will be attached to them, he will apply
them to himself and from them he will deduce and adopt practical
conclusions that will aid in reforming his life and in uniting it with
God."[36]

Another important distinction must be made between meditation
and mystical contemplation. The former is a systematic, methodical
kind of prayer which requires the one who prays to engage in volun-
tary acts of the will and the intellect. Mystical contemplation, on the
other hand, generally means that type of prayer in which the one
who prays remains passive while the Holy Spirit engages the soul
directly, without the one who prays being able to dispose himself to
this grace except in a negative way, primarily by removing the ob-
stacles (such as sin, distractions, etc.) that obstruct the action of
God on the soul. Contemplation is essentially dependent on a mystical grace and is generally reserved for those select few whom God
chooses to bring to an extraordinarily high spiritual level.[37]

Since most of the books on meditation written or translated by
the English Recusants were directed primarily to the laity, beginners
who were not necessarily called to the summits of mystical union,
they are almost exclusively books on methodical, discursive and
affective prayer (i. e., meditation in the general sense of the word)
rather than exalted treatises on contemplation, the prayer of the
mystics.

During the sixteenth century Catholic devotional writers were in
agreement on two important points: (1) that mental prayer or
meditation was the supreme and most necessary act of Christian
piety, summing up and vitalizing, though not excluding, all other
pious practices and devotions;[38] and (2) that mental prayer need

---

[35]Joseph De Guibert, *The Theology of the Spiritual Life,* trans. Paul
Barrett (New York, 1953), p. 195.
[36]*Ibid.,* p. 195.
[37]Giacomo Cardinal Lercaro, *Methods of Mental Prayer,* trans. T. F.
Lindsay (Westminster, Maryland, 1957), p. 2.
[38]Louis Cognet, *Post-Reformation Spirituality,* trans. P. Hepburne Scott,
Vol. XLI: *Twentieth Century Encyclopedia of Catholicism* (New York, 1959),
p. 13.

not, indeed should not, be restricted to the inhabitants of the cloisters and monasteries. It was recognized, of course, that the laity could not be expected to practice mental prayer unless it was taught the art or science of meditation. The laity would need a method, a set of rules to guide and direct it.

Although a number of methods of meditation were proposed by various spiritual writers during the Counter Reformation, they almost all reproduced in one way or another the fundamental procedures inculcated by St. Ignatius of Loyola (1491-1556), the founder of the Society of Jesus, in his *Spiritual Exercises.*[39] In fact, the movement toward methodical meditation can be said to have reached its climax in 1548, when the Pope gave full papal approbation to the *Spiritual Exercises.*

It is important, however, to realize that the *Spiritual Exercises* is but a summation and articulate synthesis of various methods of meditation that had been in existence in the Church for centuries and which still exerted a strong influence in the sixteenth century. Behind St. Ignatius lay many movements and many devotional writers and tractates, such as the Brethren of the Common Life and the Canons Regular of Windesheim, whose meditations have been preserved in Mauburnus's collection, the *Rosetum exercitiorum spiritualium et sacrum meditationum* (1494); the medieval *Life of Jesus* (c. 1350) by Ludolph the Carthusian; *Scala meditatioria* by Johann Wessel Ganfort (d. 1489); and Garcia Ximenes de Cisneros' *Spiritual Exercises* (1500), to name but a few. Thus, in many respects the *Spiritual Exercises* of St. Ignatius did not represent a unique or radical break with the past; rather they merely reduced to a precise and exact order and technique many earlier approaches to meditation. Because of the increasingly important influence which the Jesuit Order exerted over the devotional life of the Church during the sixteenth century, the Ignatian method of meditation came to predominate over all others.

Of those books which I have included in this anthology, approximately half were written or translated either by Jesuits or by persons like Thomas Worthington and Stephen Brinkley, who were very closely associated with the Society of Jesus. Many of the books not written or translated by Jesuits exhibit, nonetheless, signs of strong Jesuit influence.

---

[39]*Ibid.*

It is also important to note that not only were the Jesuits and their immediate friends influenced by the method of prayer advanced in St. Ignatius's *Spiritual Exercises,* but also that the whole devotional life of the Catholic Church was pronouncedly influenced. As Louis Martz notes, "During the latter half of the sixteenth century and the first half of the seventeenth, all the important treatises on meditation show a remarkable similarity in fundamental procedure. A large part of this similarity is directly due to the widespread influence of the *Spiritual Exercises* of St. Ignatius Loyola, disseminated throughout Europe by religious counselors and by dozens of Jesuit treatises."[40] In 1958 when Pope Paul III gave full papal approbation to the Exercises, he commended them to the universal Church, stating that "all the faithful of both sexes throughout the world, each and every one [were] to be instructed . . . and to profit by such holy lessons."[41] The Jesuits immediately began to carry out this challenge, for, as Martz again notes, "In the middle of the sixteenth century, under the stimulus of the Counter Reformation and its spearhead, the Jesuit order, new treatises on meditation began to appear by the dozens, and after the opening of the seventeenth century, by scores and by the hundreds."[42] Few spiritual writers of the time were left entirely uninfluenced. For example, Luis de Granada, the famous Spanish Dominican, whose devotional books were unquestionably the most popular and most widely disseminated of all devotional works translated into English during the second half of the sixteenth century, was admittedly influenced by the *Spiritual Exercises*: this influence is most readily recognized in his *Libro de la Oracion y Meditacion,* translated into English under the title *Of Prayer, and Meditation,* in which the method of prayer recommended presents few radical or essential variations from the Ignatian method. It is interesting also that when Father Robert Persons, S. J., came to England in 1580 (accompanied by the eminent Edmund Campion), one of his primary aims was to establish a secret press for the printing of Catholic books. This press, known as the Greenstreet House press, was placed under the direction of Stephen Brinkley; significantly, one of the first books to issue from this clandestine press was a small manual of prayers and meditations

---

[40]Louis Martz, *The Poetry of Meditation* (New Haven, 1954), p. 25.
[41]See unpubl. diss. (University of Illinois, 1955) by George Tade, "A Rhetorical Analysis of the *Spiritual Exercises* of St. Ignatius of Loyola," p. 13.
[42]Martz, p. 5.

entitled *A Manuall, or Meditation,* a work which exhibits on nearly every page, and especially in the meditations, the influence of the *Spiritual Exercises.*

Although in the *Spiritual Exercises* we find a complete embodiment of the methodical, systematic approach to mental prayer, nevertheless, it must be remembered that the *Spiritual Exercises* is essentially a manual of asceticism and considers, in addition to prayer, many other matters. Describing what the Exercises are, St. Ignatius says, "Under the name of Spiritual Exercises is understood every method of examination of conscience, of meditation, of contemplation, of vocal and mental prayer, and of other spiritual operations, as shall be afterwards declared: for as to go for a walk or a journey, and to run, are bodily exercises, so is the name of spiritual exercises applied to any method of preparing and disposing the soul to free itself from all inordinate affections, and after it had freed itself from them, to seek and find the will of God concerning the ordering of life for the salvation of one's soul."[43] It would also be incorrect to think of a single Ignatian meditation; St. Ignatius, in fact, suggests in the *Spiritual Exercises* several different kinds of meditations of varying complexity. Nevertheless, that method of prayer employing the three faculties of the soul—memory, understanding, and will—is the one which is most readily associated with the Jesuits and their founder.

The Ignatian meditation consists basically of four parts: (1) a preparatory prayer, (2) three preludes (sometimes two), (3) three or five points or parts of the meditation proper, and (4) a colloquy and a short vocal prayer. In the preparatory prayer, the exercitant asks God for the grace that all his "intentions, actions, and operations may be ordained purely to the service and praise of His Divine Majesty."[44] The first prelude is to recall the history of the mystery being considered (this prelude is excluded if the subject is some abstract truth). The second prelude consists of the "composition of the place" or the "seeing the spot" where the mystery being contemplated took place, such as "the Temple or the mountain, where Jesus Christ or our Lady is found."[45] If the subject being considered is totally or partially abstract and not historical (such as a meditation on hell, heaven, a virtue, sin, or creation), then the

[43] St. Ignatius of Loyola, *The Spiritual Exercises,* trans. and ed. John Morris (4th ed. rev.: Westminster, Maryland, 1943), p. 1.
[44] *Ibid.,* p. 20.
[45] *Ibid.*

exercitant uses his imagination as best he can to construct the scene or to "see" God. In the third prelude the exercitant petitions God for the particular graces he wishes to obtain from the meditation; generally the mystery being considered will determine, to some extent, the exact nature of the petition. ". . . if the contemplation [St. Ignatius does not use this term in the more modern sense of mystical prayer] is on the Resurrection, the petition ought to be to ask for joy with Christ rejoicing; if it be on the Passion, to ask for grief, tears, and pain in union with Christ in torment."[46] Next comes the meditation proper, which generally consists of three or five stressed points of the mystery proposed for meditation; that is, the exercitant divides the subject into manageable segments. To these points he directs his memory, his understanding, and his will—generally in that order; the memory recalls the facts of the mystery, the understanding intervenes to make inferences from the facts, and the will arouses the affections. The meditation concludes with the colloquy, which "is made properly speaking as one friend speaks to another, or as a servant to his master,"[47] followed by a short vocal prayer such as the *Pater Noster* or *Anima Christi.* Slight variations of this schema, of course, are permissible.

In the meditation (or that specific kind of meditation called a contemplation by St. Ignatius) on the Nativity of Christ, we see these directives applied and somewhat amplified. Since the method proposed by St. Ignatius is the embodiment of the fundamental procedure of sixteenth century approaches to mental prayer, it is to the point to reproduce this meditation in its entirety here:

The usual preparatory prayer.

The first prelude is the history. It will be here to think how our Lady already with child for about nine months, as it may piously be thought, seated on an ass, left Nazareth, together with St. Joseph and a serving-girl, leading an ox, in order to go to Bethlehem to pay the tribute which Caesar imposed on these countries.

The second prelude is a composition of place, seeing the spot; it will be here to see with the eyes of the imagination the road from Nazareth to Bethlehem; considering its length, breadth,

---

[46]*Ibid.,* p. 21.
[47]*Ibid.,* p. 23.

and whether the way be level or through valleys and over hills; and likewise seeing the spot or cave of the Nativity, how large or small, how low or high, and how it is prepared.

The third prelude will be the same, and in the same form, as it was in the preceding contemplation [i. e., "to ask for what I want: it will here be to ask for an interior knowledge of our Lord, Who for me is made Man, that I may the more love Him and follow Him."][48]

The first point is to see the persons; that is to say, to see our Lady, and St. Joseph, and the serving-maid, also the Infant Jesus, after His birth, accounting myself a poor and unworthy servant, looking at and contemplating them and tending them in their necessities as though I were present there, with all possible homage and reverence; and after that to reflect on myself in order to derive some profit.

The second point is to see and notice and contemplate what they are saying; and by reflecting on oneself to derive some profit.

The third point is to see and consider what they are doing: that is to say, the journey and the labour that they undergo in order that our Lord may be born in extreme poverty; and in order that after such toils, after hunger, thirst, heat, cold, insults, and affronts, He may die on the Cross, and all this for me; and then by reflecting to derive some spiritual profit.

Finish with a colloquy, as in the preceding contemplation, and with a *Pater noster.*[49]

The *Spiritual Exercises,* it should be noted, is not so much a book about the ascetical life as it is the embodiment of a method or technique for acquiring spiritual union with God. It is primarily an outline, ever so specific and ordered, but still merely an outline, which the exercitant or the spiritual director must amplify and apply. As Pourrat points out, "If, from the time of its composition till our own day, the booklet has continued to be an inestimable means of sanctification, that is because the sons of St. Ignatius have always managed to adapt it to the needs of every age."[50]

The majority of the works represented in this anthology exhibit strong Ignatian influences; many of them are essentially adaptations

[48]*Ibid.,* pp. 36-37.
[49]*Ibid.,* pp. 38-39.
[50]Pourrat, III, 41.

and amplifications of that method proposed in the *Spiritual Exercises.*
It is noteworthy that an English translation of the *Spiritual Exercises* did not appear until 1736,[51] yet it is not surprising. Since the
majority of Catholic devotional books written in English during the
sixteenth and seventeenth century were intended primarily for laymen, it would have been rather pointless to translate the exercises
themselves, for they are too sketchy and too abbreviated to make
much sense to one not directed in their use; what the Jesuits and
their associates did, however, was to adapt the exercises, to enlarge
the mere outlines into full-blown meditations which would be meaningful and helpful to the layman who did not have the advantage of
a spiritual director to lead him and to develop the meditations in some
detail for him.

One of the most distinctive and admirable features of methodical
prayer as it was developed during the sixteenth century, and especially
the Ignatian meditation as it was adapted throughout the Counter Reformation, was the intimacy and personal involvement which it fostered
toward the supernatural—especially towards the persons of Christ and
His Mother. Prayer, though possibly rendered somewhat less spontan-
eous and less individualistic in many respects than it had been during
the Middle Ages, did not become, as might reasonably be expected, a
mere mechanical, routine exercise of piety which demanded little of
the one who prays. In fact, the movement towards methodical prayer,
which was initiated during the late Middle Ages in the great monasteries and religious houses of the Continent to reform and revitalize the
interior life of the religious, was begun precisely to make prayer more
meaningful, more personal, and less mechanical.[52] Quite naturally,
when the need was felt acutely to effect a similar reform among the
laity during the Counter Reformation, that means which had proven
successful among a large segment of the clergy and religious was
adapted—methodical prayer.

If we consider the meditations in the *Spiritual Exercises* of St.
Ignatius as proto-types of the kinds of methodical prayer which
flourished during the second half of the sixteenth century (and beyond,
of course), and I think it is quite valid to make such an assumption,
we immediately recognize that the method proposed there has many

---

[51]St. Ignatius, p. ix.
[52]Lercaro, p. 25.

inherent features designed to encourage the person meditating to gain intimacy with the supernatural.

First of all, it is important to note that St. Ignatius himself was quite concerned that if the meditations were too completely developed and explained by the spiritual director, they would cease to be prayer and would become merely pious instructions. In the second annotation in the *Spiritual Exercises,* he cautions the giver of the exercises to beware of leaving too little opportunity for development by the exercitant:

> He who gives to another the method and order of a meditation or contemplation ought faithfully to narrate the history of the contemplation or meditation, going through the points however only briefly, and with a short explanation: because when the person who contemplates, takes the true groundwork of the history, discussing and reasoning by himself, and meeting with something that makes the history clearer and better felt (whether this happen through his own reasoning, or through the enlightenment of his understanding by Divine grace), he thereby enjoys greater spiritual relish and fruit than if he who gives the Exercises had minutely explained and developed the meaning of the history; for it is not to know much, but it is to understand and savour the matter interiorly that fills and satisfies the soul.[53]

In other words, the meditations were to be guides which would leave plenty of opportunity for the person meditating to develop his own ideas, arouse his own emotions, and make his own applications and resolutions.

The devotional writers represented in this anthology (who were, for the most part, adapting and taking their inspiration from the *Spiritual Exercises*) seem to have observed this injunction of St. Ignatius quite faithfully. Most of the meditations they propose to their readers are not fully and completely developed; they are, in a sense, very careful and detailed prompt books. However, they are more developed than the meditations in the *Spiritual Exercises,* but then the spiritual exercises, unlike the books of meditation written or translated by the Recusants, were outlines of spiritual retreats for members of the Society of Jesus, men well acquainted with Scripture and the spiritual life. Laymen, quite understandably, needed more direction, more de-

---

[53]St. Ignatius, pp. 1-2.

tail, than the experienced religious. Loarte in *The godly garden of
Gethsemani* justifies his expansions of the meditations in the following way:

> Herein also are declared the poyntes to discourse on, and so to
> proceede with more deuotion in thy meditation. Or if thou
> knowe not howe of thy selfe to make these or the like talkes or
> speeches with God, then I say, this may teache thee the order
> and maner howe, because herein is shewed thee howe to geue
> thanks to thy Redeemer for that which thou shalt meditate or
> call to minde he hath suffred for thee: and also what thou
> oughtest to praye for, conformable to that poynt and parte of the
> passion thou hast to meditate vpon.[54]

Secondly, the very method of meditation embodied in the *Spiritual
Exercises,* which, for the most part, makes extensive use of visual
images, encourages the person meditating to become intimate and
passionately involved with the subject proposed. The contemplation on
the Nativity, for example, which we have already considered above,
exhorts the one meditating to put himself imaginatively into the scene
of the mystery as if he were actually and physically present. He is to
see "the spot or cave . . . how large or small, how low or high, and
how it is prepared" and "to see the persons . . . accounting [himself] a
poor and unworthy servant, looking at and contemplating them and
tending them in their necessities as though [he] were present there."
He is encouraged to "see and notice and contemplate what they are
saying," and lastly "to see and consider what they are doing." The
final prayer of the meditation or colloquy in which one speaks freely
and personally with Christ, His Mother, or the saints is to be made
"as one friend speaks to another, or as a servant to his master." The
whole effect of such a meditation is to render the divine and histori-
cally remote events of Christianity immediate, real, and personal. The
person meditating uses these imaginative devices to gain an intimacy
with the Divine.

Again Loarte, in *The godly garden of Gethsemani,* merely one example of the many adaptations of the Ignatian method represented in
this anthology, encourages the same kind of immediacy and intimacy in
the first and most essential manner of meditation on the passion

---

[54]Gaspar Loarte, *The godly garden of Gethsemani,* trans. anon. (n.p.d.
[actually London, c. 1576]), sigs. Avii^v-Aviii.

"whiche [he states] consisteth in knowing wel the letter and historie of that mysterie which thou purposeth to haue in minde and contemplation: the which thou must as freshly remember and consider of, as it were presently set before thine eyes."[55]

Despite, then, the emphasis on method and the rigidity of form in the books on meditation written during the sixteenth century (stressed with such vigor that many have mistaken it to mean that meditation cannot be effective unless faithful in every minor detail to the schema), anyone who reads this anthology must realize that the methodical approach to prayer left plenty of room for adaptation by the individual who employed it. Nearly all of the spiritual writers during the period emphasized and re-emphasized, like Loarte, that they did not desire to impede or encumber the individual with methodology, but rather they wished to teach a practical, detailed way that all could follow according to their dispositions.[56]

Another important feature of the books of meditation is the stress placed on the humanity of Christ and on his person over his divinity and official role as Redeemer. (This centering of attention on the personality of Christ, it should be noted, is found throughout the Catholic devotional books represented in this anthology and not limited to just those few that I have specifically classified under the heading "Prayer and Meditation.") There is almost a psychological probing of Christ in an attempt to understand him as a person and to know him as a personal friend. Catholic devotion has always centered on the Incarnation, on the fact that the Creator became a man in all respects but sin, that he had been born of a Mother, that he had suffered and was tempted, and that when he was scourged and nailed to the cross his flesh recoiled like that of any other man. Consider, for example, the nailing of Christ on the cross as presented by Luis de Granada in *Of Prayer, and Meditation:*

> Consider . . . how our Sauiour was nailed vpō the Crosse, and how passinge great griefe, and tormente, he suffered at that time, when those great, and square nailes were driuen in, and pearced through the most sensible, and tender partes of his most blessed bodie, which was of all bodies most tēder, and delicate. And consider also, what an extreme grieffe it was to the blessed virgin, when she sawe with her eies, and hearde with her eares,

---

[55]*Ibid.,* sig. Bii.
[56]John Roothaan, *How to Meditate,* trans. Louis Puhl (St. Meinrad, Indiana, 1957), p. iv.

the mightie, and cruell harde strokes, which were so often, and so thicke laied on, and iterated one after an other vpon his diuine members. For certainlie those hammers, and nailes, as they passed throwghe the handes of the sonne: so did they also pearce the verie harte of his most tender, and louinge mother.

Consider moreouer, how they lifted vp the Crosse on highe, and how when they went about to ramme it in the hole, which they had made for that purpose (such was the crueltie of those tormentinge raginge ministers) that at the verie time of rearinge it vp, and placinge it therein, they let it falle furiouslie from them, with a iumpe into the hoole, with all the weight thereof: and so all his blessed bodie was sore shaken, and iogged vp and downe in the aier, and thereby his woundes were wydened and enlarged, and his paines, and grieffes more encreased.

.   .   .   .   .   .

I see thee ô my kinge fastened to a tree, and there is nothinge to susteine thy bodie, but onelie three iron nailes, wherevpon thy sacred fleashe hangeth, without anie other staie or comforte. When the weight, and swaie of thy bodie staieth vpon thy feete, then are the wounds of thy feete the more torne, and enlarged, with the nailes wherewith they are pearced. Againe, when the weight of thy bodie staieth vpon thy handes then are the woundes of thy handes the more rente, and enlarged also, with the poyce of thy bodie. One of thy members cannot succour an other, but with equall preiudice, either of the one, or of the other.[57]

In the sixteenth century with the rise of Puritanism and other like sects such as the German Anabaptists, the need to re-emphasize the humanity of Christ became ever increasingly important in order to counter-balance the emphasis being placed on Christ's official role, his Mediatorship, by these groups. Baxter, the great Presbyterian divine, for example, declared, "Christ as Mediator is not the Ultimate End, but the Way to the Father."[58] Before him Melanchthon, explaining what it means to know Christ, said, "[It] means to know his blessings, and not, as [the Scholastics] assert, to meditate on his natures and the possible modes of his Incarnation."[59] As Louis Martz points out,

---

[57]Granada, *Of Prayer, and Meditation*, sigs. Niiij-Nv.
[58]As quoted by Martz, p. 163.
[59]As quoted by Pourrat, III, 69-70.

"Students of English Puritanism have often remarked upon the small part which the person and humanity of Christ played in Puritan writings of the sixteenth and seventeenth centuries. Of Christ the Redeemer and Mediator we hear much ... but of the man, the babe in the manger, the suffering servant on the Cross, we hear remarkably little, in comparison with the kinds of Catholic devotion which have been discussed [i. e., the continental devotional books]."[60] Miss White also stresses this point: "This concentration [by the Puritans] on the redemptive aspect of Christ's life in this world inevitably resulted in more attention being paid to his official role than to his personality. Indeed, the human aspects of Christ's nature, now the object of the most widespread interest in the modern world, were for the most part neglected. That is one reason why continental writing of the time on the life and personality of Christ seems so much livelier, so much richer."[61]

(By continental books, Miss White means, of course, Catholic continental devotional works, those works which found such a warm reception among English Recusants.)

This contrast between the Catholic and Puritan traditions in their approaches to Christ can possibly be seen more readily and compactly in poetry than in prose. Let us, for example, compare Robert Southwell's "New Heaven, New Warre"[62] with Milton's "On the Morning of Christ's Nativity"[63]—two poems which treat the same subject and which stand as almost archetypes of the two traditions.

In Southwell's poem the awesome Almighty appears as "our little Tobie." In fact, the most significant feature of the poem is its intimacy and concentration on the Christ Child as a child. Great solicitude is shown for the person of the Child: "His chilling could doth heate require," "this little ark no cover hath," "Come, Raphiell, this babe must eate,/ Prouide our little Tobie meate," "Let Gabriell be nowe His groome," and "Let Graces rocke, when He doth crye,/ And angells singe His lullybye." Likewise, the person of Christ is examined with a loving tenderness and care for detail that reminds one of a mother examining her new-born son: "He Him self for cold do shake," "With teares He fightes and wynnes the feild," "His naked breste

---

[60]Martz, p. 163.

[61]White, *English Devotional Literature*, p. 195.

[62]Robert Southwell, *The Complete Poems of Robert Southwell, S. J.*, ed. Alexander Grosart (The Fuller Worthies Library: Blackburn, Lancashire, 1872), pp. 110 112.

[63]John Milton, *John Milton: Paradise Regained, the Minor Poems, and Samson Agonistes*, ed. Merritt Hughes (New York, 1937), pp. 150-167.

standes for a sheilde," "His battering shott are babishe cryes," "His
arrowes, lookes of weepinge eyes," and "feeble flesh, His warrier's
steede." Thus, in Southwell's poem we feel a personal involvement
with a child, a real child, that shakes with cold, that cries and demands
attention. "The same yow sawe in heavenly seate,/ Is He that now
suckes Mary's teate." Significantly, the whole poem is in the present
tense.

In Milton's "On the Morning of Christ's Nativity," "Our little
Tobie" becomes "Son of Heav'n's eternal King." Milton's poem, as
Martz notes, "deals with all the world except the manger scene."[64]
The manger is mentioned in the first stanza and again in the last it is
visualized.[65] The intimate concern with the Child as a child is practically absent from the poem. I am not, of course, suggesting that
Southwell's poem is a better poem than Milton's, but it is undeniable
that the warmth and intimacy of Southwell's presentation of the Infant
is remarkably different from the cold, detached presentation of Milton,
who stands in awe at a great mystery and a remote historical event that
spelled a release from "our deadly forfeit," i. e., original sin; nearly all
of the poem is in the past tense. Southwell, on the other hand, expres-
ses a real love for the humanity of Christ; his intimacy, appreciation,
and sensitivity toward things divine, I would suggest, were in a great
part a direct result of his training as a Jesuit, a training which had at
its core the Ignatian method of meditation.

The works in this anthology which I have included under the title
"The Sacraments" are essentially books of instruction—advising the
Christian how to make a good confession or how to receive Holy
Communion with devotion and merit. The intention of these books
has been effectively summarized by the unknown translator of Arias's
*The Litle Memorial, concerning the Good and Frvitfvll Vse of the
Sacraments* in "The Preface to the Reader," in which he states that
the principal object of these books is:

> to inflame all with the loue of the Sacraments, and to stir vp our
> dull spirits, often to repaire vnto those diuine fountaines of
> grace, from which so many and rare benefittes doe flowe: to dis-
> couer also the vsuall disorders, into which not only those that be
> carelesse, but euen the deuoute servants of God doe sometimes

---

[64]Martz, pp. 164-165.
[65]*Ibid.*, p. 165.

fall, when they goe to confession, and to receaue the blessed
Sacrament, togither with singular remedies, how we may auoid
al such inconueniences, and so free our selues, more & more
from sin, purchase greater abundance of grace in this world,
and eternall felicitie in the worlde to come: . . . and like a diuine
phisition search out the secret and lurking diseases of our soule,
and prescribe such sweet and heauenly receits, that there is
almost none so voide of spiritual sence, but by reading, shal
finde theire conscience touched. . . .[66]

These books are, however, generally more than merely instructional
guides in the proper use of the sacraments; they intend to arouse in the
reader a love and need for these traditional aids to salvation. They are,
unlike catechisms, directed to the will as well as to the intellect.
Granada in the preface to *A Memoriall of a Christian Life* makes this
important distinction: "And albeit that the Catholique Catechismes
(which are sommes or abrigementes of the Christiã doctrine) do treate
of euerie thinge that appertaineth to the same, yet for so much as these
haue respecte to declare the substance of thinges, an such as belonge to
the vnderstãdinge thereof, the doctrine of such Catechismes apperteineth rather to speculation, than to practize: I meane hereby, that such
doctrine tendeth rather to giue light to the vnderstandinge, than to
moue the wil vnto the exercise and vse of vertue."[67]

As we have noted previously, much Catholic thinking and writing
during the sixteenth century was, quite understandably, influenced neg-
atively by Protestant theology. And that theology, stressing the direct
working of the Divine in the human soul and putting its faith in the
power of preaching to arouse the subjective dispositions of faith in the
believer, soon relegated to the background the necessity of the sacraments, reducing them in number and altering their character. Different
parties among the various Protestant sects held widely divergent views
about the sacraments: some, like the Anabaptists and Zwinglians, regarded them as little more than badges of their Christian faith, but
others, like the Anglicans and Lutherans, maintained more conserva-
tive and traditional but widely varying interpretations.[68] Certainly those

---

[66]Francis Arias, *The Litle Memorial, concerning the Good and Frvitfvll Vse of the Sacraments,* trans. anon. (Rouen [actually secretly in England], 1602), sigs. ¶ 3ᵛ-¶ 4.

[67]Granada, *A Memoriall of a Christian Life,* pp. 3-4.

[68]Henry Symonds, *The Council of Trent and Anglican Formularies* (London, 1933), p. 29.

sacraments most frequently attacked or altered by the Protestant Reformers were Penance and the Holy Eucharist, those two sacraments
which are, according to Catholic teaching, the channels through which
the grace of God flows into the daily lives of men. Catholic writers,
therefore, felt called upon to defend these sacraments, to explain their
use, and to encourage among men a love and reverence for them. John
Fowler, in *A Brief Fourme of Confession,* states:

> Wheras in this great corruption of Faith and good life, there
> is also great want of good instruction for the amendmēt of both
> the same: & wheras yet the blindnes or malice of some mē is so
> great, that the very same meanes leaft by Christe and his
> Apostles in the Church for that end, they make so smal account
> of, that they both contemne, and condemne the same, & without
> al reason raile therat with full vncomely termes: it hath semed
> to many good and vertuous men right necessary, to set forth
> some such Treatise, wherein briefly is conteined bothe the right
> vse and ende of Shrift or Confession and also the due order
> that eche Christian man ought to kepe and obserue in the
> same.[69]

Although the Protestant reformers during the reign of Elizabeth
struck hard at all the surviving devotional practices of the Catholic
Church—the Rosary, auricular confession, pilgrimages, etc.—nothing
was more abused and more savagely attacked than the Mass and the
Holy Eucharist. For, as Evelyn Waugh has noted:

> the Mass was recognised as being both the distinguishing sign
> and main sustenance of their opponents. The objects specially
> connected with it, the vestments, plate and missals, were singled
> out for destruction; the altar stones were taken for paving and
> cheese presses; they ridiculed the Host in broadsheets and bur-
> lesques, called it by derisive names, "Round Robin," "Jack in
> the Box," and "Wormes Meat." "Massing priests" is the phrase
> constantly used in Cecil's correspondence to designate the
> Marian priests; the right to have Mass said in a private chapel
> was one of the main questions at issue in the negotiations for
> Elizabeth's marriage with her Catholic suitors; one of the terms

---

[69] John Fowler, *A Brief Fourme of Confession* (Antwerp, 1576), sigs.
a5ᵛ-a6.

suggested for peace with Mary Stuart was that she should "abandon the Mass in Scotland and receive Common Prayer after the form of England."[70]

With the closing of Queen Elizabeth's first Parliament on May 8, 1559, the Mass was outlawed in England, and it became a criminal offense either to hear or say it on or after June 24, 1559. By a legislative gesture, the real presence of Christ in the Blessed Sacrament was denied officially.[71] In actuality the Mass and the dispensation of the sacraments continued in England, no longer publicly but secretly. All sorts of evasions of the law were conceived and executed. Frequently priests would say Mass in their own homes before proceeding to the parish church; some would even bring consecrated Hosts with them to the service and distribute them to their Catholic parishioners.[72] Thomas Wright in his dedication to the Mistress S. H. and her son in *The Disposition or Garnishmente of the Sovle* comments, "I know parte, but he onlye knowethe all, whom there you participate, What hazard you put your selues into, to come by it [i. e., the Blessed Sacrament]. . . ."[73] The fascinating stories of the many missionary priests like Robert Southwell, Edmund Campion, John Gerard, Jaspar Heywood, and Robert Persons, who risked their lives to bring the sacraments to the Catholic laity of England during those days of persecution, make most modern mystery thrillers appear insipid. Especially noteworthy among these accounts is Evelyn Waugh's *Edmund Campion* and the autobiography of John Gerard, S. J., recently edited by Father Philip Caraman, S. J., and entitled *The Autobiography of a Hunted Priest*. Gerard, incidently, is one of the writers whose work is included in this anthology.

The years that saw the immense upheavals of the Renaissance and the Protestant Reformation were, as we have seen, quite fertile in new expressions of Catholic devotional writing, but we would be quite mistaken if we expect to find a complete rejection of or radical break with the Middle Ages. In fact, medieval tendencies and works flourished throughout the sixteenth century, new ideas and approaches generally being grafted onto them without violence. Even the reformers did not

---

[70]Evelyn Waugh, *Edmund Campion* (Boston, 1946), pp. 21-22.

[71]Henry N. Birt, *The English Religious Settlement* (London, 1907), p. 502.

[72]Waugh, p. 25.

[73]T. N. [pseud. Thomas Wright], *The Disposition or Garnishmente of the Sovle* (Antwerp [actually secretly in England], 1596), sig. A3.

hesitate to espouse what they considered to be the best of the Middle Ages; Luther, for instance, as we have noted, championed the late medieval German mystics as precursors of his own ideas.[74] Likewise, even the Ignatian meditation, as we have seen, was merely a perfection and culmination of many tendencies which were certainly underway by the fourteenth century. Primers and psalters, both popular medieval forms of devotion, also continued being printed and re-issued throughout the sixteenth century as did the greatest of medieval books of devotion, the *Imitation of Christ*. In 1585 the Recusants at Rouen brought out an edition of Richard Whitforde's translation of the *Imitation* made in 1531; in 1567 Edward Hakes published his translation, and in 1580 Thomas Rogers' well-known translation issued from the press, a work which was to run to some fourteen editions before 1640.[75] These last two translations were, of course, Protestant editions; Part Four on the Eucharist was carefully omitted.

But of all the medieval devotional practices which continued into the sixteenth century, none was more popular nor more generally encouraged among Catholics than devotion to Mary, the Mother of God, especially the recitation of the Rosary. There are several possible explanations for the number of books on the Rosary which issued from the secret presses of England or were smuggled into the country from the Continent by the Recusants. First of all, the Rosary was unquestionably the devotion *par excellence* of the Middle Ages, and as Martz has suggested, "Since England had fully participated in this devotion during the fourteenth and fifteenth centuries, it seems that a fertile ground must have remained in this area for the emissaries of the Counter Reformation to work upon."[76] And as Conrad Pepler, O. P., notes, "Long before 'methods of mental prayer' were devised this method [i.e., the Rosary] had brought hosts of Christians to the threshold of contemplation."[77] It is important to remember, likewise, that in medieval England devotion to Mary was particularly fervent; in fact, England was piously called "Our Lady's Dowry." The Archbishop of Canterbury, Thomas Arundel, noted in 1399, "The contemplation of the great mystery of the Incarnation has drawn all Christian people to revere [Mary], from whom came the first beginnings of our redemp-

---

[74]Cognet, p. 9.
[75]Helen White, "Some Continuing Traditions in English Devotional Literature," *PMLA*, LVII (December, 1942), 976-977.
[76]Martz, p. 96.
[77]Conrad Pepler, *The English Religious Heritage* (St. Louis, 1958), p. 91.

tion. But we [the English], being the servants of her own inheritance and liegemen of her especial dowry, as we are commonly called, ought to surpass others in the warmth of our praise and devotion."[78] One has only to glance at the long list of Marian shrines of medieval England in *A Dictionary of Mary* to be assured that devotion to the Virgin most certainly did not falter during the era immediately preceding the Reformation.[79] The Recusants were then merely re-enforcing a devotion which was particularly dear to the English. So entrenched, in fact, was devotion to Mary that even many Anglicans of the period were reluctant to relinquish their service of her. For example, at least three of the major Protestant poets of the early seventeenth century felt moved to praise the Virgin: Donne in the "Litany," Herbert in "To All Angels and Saints," and Vaughan in "The Knot."[80] In the *Book of Common Prayer* there are many references to Mary; her feastdays—the Annunciation, the Purification, the Visitation, her Nativity and Conception—are all listed. And instructions are given that the *Magnificat* be sung each day at Evensong.[81] It is interesting to note, incidentally, that in the bull of Pope Gregory XIII, which made special arrangements for the persecuted Catholics of England to gain the Jubilee Year indulgence of 1575, it was stipulated that in order to receive the indulgences the Rosary or Corona of the Blessed Virgin Mary was to be recited.[82] It was apparently assumed that this devotion was sufficiently widespread and known that it could be made an essential requirement for gaining the indulgence.

Secondly, Mary has been traditionally invoked by the Catholic Church against heresies. As Garnet states in *The Societie of the Rosary,* "she is in speciall maner a rainbow against Heretickes: wheras the Church generally singeth, she hath destroid all heresies in the wholle world, and therfore is a perticuler signe and aboade of the ceassing thereof. . . ."[83] In fact, in the lessons for the Feast of the Holy Rosary in the Roman Breviary we learn that when the Albigensian heretics of Toulouse threatened the Church in the thirteenth cen-

---

[78]Quoted in *A Dictionary of Mary,* comp. and ed. Donald Attwater (New York, 1956), p. 70.
[79]*Ibid.,* pp. 75-76.
[80]Martz, pp. 97-99.
[81]*A Dictionary of Mary,* p. 230.
[82]Herbert Thurston, "Our Popular Devotions. The Rosary," *The Month,* XCVI (1900), 635.
[83]Henry Garnet, *The Societie of the Rosary* (n.p.d. [actually secretly in England, 1596-97]), sig. A3.

tury, St. Dominic sought the help of the Blessed Virgin and was instructed (so tradition asserts) to preach the Rosary among the simple people as an antidote to sin and corruption of faith.[84] Apart from the signal defeat of the Albigensians at the Battle of Muret in 1213, which legend attributes to the devout recitation of the Rosary by St. Dominic, it is generally believed among Catholics that devotion to the Rosary has on many occasions won Divine favor against heresy and schism. For example, the great naval victory at Lepanto on the first Sunday of October, 1571, by which Christendom was delivered from the threat of Turkish invasion, was attributed to the processions and prayers offered up at Rome by the members of the Rosary Confraternity while the battle raged.[85] After the victory Pope St. Pius V declared: "By the Rosary the darkness of heresy has been dispelled, and the light of the Catholic Faith shines with all its brilliancy."[86] To commemorate this great event, the Pope established an annual feast to be held in Rome on the first Sunday of October; and at the request of the Dominican Order, Pope Gregory XIII in 1573 extended the feast to all churches throughout Christendom which possessed an altar especially dedicated to Our Lady of the Rosary.[87]

It is quite understandable, therefore, that English Catholics of the sixteenth century, daily witnessing the suppression of the Catholic Church in their homeland and the increase of numerous Protestant sects, would turn to the Rosary. For as Garnet advises them, it is "an auncient meanes euen from *S. Domincks* time of rooting out of heresie."[88] As the hope faded more and more during those last years of the reign of Queen Elizabeth for establishing once again the Catholic faith in England by political means, Catholics quite naturally turned to spiritual weapons to effect a solution, especially to the Rosary, for as Garnet again notes, ". . . the beades must be to our afflicted brethren, . . . all maner of armour or weapons. . . ."[89]

Thirdly, to the many thousands of simple laymen to whom formal mental prayer as outlined in the books of meditation which we have previously considered would have appeared too complicated and too demanding, the Rosary served as a guidebook for mental prayer.

---

[84]Herbert Thurston, "The Rosary," *The Catholic Encyclopedia* XIII (New York, 1912), p. 184.
[85]*Ibid.,* p. 189.
[86]Lawrence Lovasik, *Our Lady in Catholic Life* (New York, 1957), p. 195.
[87]Thurston, "The Rosary," p. 189.
[88]Garnet, sig. A5.
[89]*Ibid.*

Garnet notes, ". . . the beades are the vnlearned mans booke. . . ."[90]
It is important to remember that although the Rosary consists of a
number of vocal prayers, its essence is meditation on the chief events,
or mysteries as they are more generally called, of the lives of Christ
and His Mother; the vocal prayers are meant to be merely accompani-
ment to the meditation. Yet apparently in the sixteenth century the
practice of meditating on the mysteries was either not well-known or
was generally ignored: nearly all the books on the Rosary in this anthology are attempts to explain and suggest practical ways of encour-
aging this practice. As Loarte notes in *Instrvctions and Advertisements, How to Meditate the Misteries of the Rosarie,* "Howbeit,
because al knowe not how to meditate these Misteries (as it bohoueth)
and by this lacke they loose a great part of the fruit which might wel
be gathered thereby, for their helpe this present Treatise hath bene
composed; wherin is shewed, in what maner they ought to meditate
with greatest profite and consolatiō of their soules."[91] Of course, one
reason why the layman may not have known about meditating on the
mysteries is that this practice did not become commonly associated
with the Rosary until the fifteenth century; Dominic of Prussia, a
Carthusian monk, is generally accredited with having introduced this
practice.[92] Likewise, without such guidebooks as we are considering,
the average layman may have felt at a loss as to how to exercise
himself in this manner.

But what was "the fruit which might wel be gathered" by meditating on the mysteries? In other words, why did the devotional writers
so generally agree on the merit of this practice? First of all, by meditating on the chief events of the lives of Christ and Mary, the Christian would make the Rosary a more meaningful prayer, disarming the
critics who saw it as merely a monotonous repetition of a set number of
prayers. By meditating on the mysteries, he would review with personal application the major events in the drama of Redemption—the
Nativity, the Crucifixion, the Resurrection, etc. It should be remembered that the average Catholic of the sixteenth century could not turn to
a Catholic English translation of the Scriptures for his source of inspiration; even though the Catholic translation of the New Testament

---

[90]*Ibid.*

[91]Gaspar Loarte, *Instrvctions and Advertisements, How to Meditate the
Misteries of the Rosarie of the most holy Virgin* (n.p.d. [actually London,
1579]), sig. iiij[v].

[92]William O'Shea, *The Worship of the Church; a Companion to Liturgical
Studies* (Westminster, Maryland, 1957), p. 554.

was printed at Rheims in 1582, it is highly unlikely that many laymen could have obtained a copy. The Rosary was then, in a sense, the average layman's Bible. As Loarte states, "... I determined with my selfe to write onely vpō the misteries of the Rosarie of the moste blessed virgin Mary; sithens, besides that it is so godly, renowned, and approued, a deuotiō as is abouesaid in the Prologue; therein, in my fancie, are the chief points of the life of Christ cōteined, frō the time of his incarnatiō, vntil the sending doune of the holy Ghost; in-somuch as, who-soeuer he be that shal meditate these wel, may assure him-selfe to haue meditated the greater and the more principal part of his most sacred life."[93] Garnet states the same idea in the following terms: "... in this deuotion of the Rosary is daily with great fruit remembred the principall pointes of the life of our Sauiour, and of his holy Mother, ... by this deuout exercise of Christian duety, ... euery deuout Catholicke, dailye when he saieth his beades, doth as it were in a booke read and reuerentlye laieth before his eies, Christ our Sauiour. ... Wherof what gratitude, what humilitie, what charitie, what spurres vnto all vertue may be ingendered in Christian mindes. ..."[94]

The treatises on the Rosary, therefore, which are represented in this anthology were, as we have already noted, written primarily to serve as guidebooks to the simple, unlearned layman; they were at-tempts to introduce him to the practice of mental prayer, which was considered more and more to be an essential of the spiritual life, by engrafting onto the most common and appreciated of popular devo-tions, the Rosary, a system of mental prayer. The object of the devo-tional writers in these books, like those of the books of formal mental prayer, was to make the mysteries of Christianity, and especially the persons of Jesus and Mary, more meaningful, more immediate, and more personal.

One problem which faced the devotional writers was how com-pletely and how fully the meditations should be developed by them. They recognized that a treatment which was too developed and too amplified would hinder the personal reflections and affections of those persons who had the ability and insight to amplify the points of the meditation themselves; on the other hand, they realized that a barren, sketchy presentation of the meditations would be insufficient to the less

---

[93]Loarte, *Instrvctions and Advertisements,* sigs. Avi-Aviᵛ.
[94]Garnet, pp. 8-10.

learned or less able layman, and would, therefore, alienate him from the practice of mental prayer. Gasper Loarte recognized this dilemma and attempted a solution:

> But because the pointes which I noted in the other meditations of the sacred Passion [*The godly garden of Gethsemani*] were no whitt amplified and dilated, but onely a bare text set downe of the matters that were to be meditated vpon (the which was done, supposing that eche one would them-selues, according to their deuotion haue dilated and amplified the same) vnderstanding since, that if some doo make this discourse and dilatatiō, yet, al for lack of capacitie doo it not; for this cause haue I done mine indeuour in this booke, to content both th'one and th'other; acknowledging my selfe, as S. Paule saith, to be indebted both to the learned and the ignorāt. For the lerned therfore, I haue thought good, after a text wise, first to set downe that which they maye meditate vpon in euerye misterie, leauing eche one to pause therein, and to dilate the same, according to their capacitie and deuotion: nowe for the ignorant, that knowe not howe to doo this, without some further helpe, I haue shewed thē the maner, how to interteine thē-selues, and to discourse vpon eche point. . . .[95]

Therefore, as in the books of methodical meditation which we have already considered, the devotional writers who composed meditations on the mysteries of the Rosary attempted to walk the very thin tightrope between overdevelopment and underdevelopment in the presentation of their material. Most of the books, however, are quite elementary and simple, as might be expected; although they frequently are quite detailed, giving each point of the meditation with scrupulous care, their style is unpretentious and plain. Almost all of the books contain quite elaborate woodcuts of the mysteries, which, far from being purely ornamental, serve as pictorial reminders to the reader of the great Christian events being presented. These woodcuts, once more, indicate that these books, in contrast to the more formal books of methodical meditation, were directed to an unsophisticated audience.

It is extremely difficult, in fact, to appraise in terms of ordinary literary criticism the twenty-four devotional books included in this

---

[95]Loarte, *Instructions and Advertisements*, sigs. Aviᵛ-Aviiᵛ.

anthology, books which were, after all, written primarily to stir up devotion in the average Catholic layman or to give him directions and a plan for living the Christian life. Although I do not intend to give an analysis of each work since such an analysis would be unrewarding in many cases and certainly far beyond the scope of this present study, I do believe, nevertheless, that a few valid generalizations can be made about the stylistic merits of these books.

Although some of the works included in this anthology, like Persons' *The First Booke of the Christian Exercise* and the various translations of Luis de Granada made by Richard Hopkins, deserve to rank among better pieces of Renaissance prose, it is true that many of these books were written in haste by men who had neither the natural ability nor the background to produce fine prose. Even these lesser works, however, as Southern notes, call "for sympathetic understanding rather than cold-blooded analysis,"[96] for they were written with an intense faith and conviction which make them worthy of the attention of anyone who respects sincerity and conviction.

Sincerity and conviction—these two words summarize the prime qualities of Recusant devotional writing in general. The books represented in this anthology were written with earnest and serious purpose; the survival of the Catholic faith was, after all, no light matter to Catholics of the sixteenth century. We moderns frequently make the mistake of assuming that an author who uses ornate diction, alliteration, precariously balanced sentences, and other elaborate rhetorical devices is not sincere and that his work is merely a literary *tour de force*. Especially does the author become suspect if he treats religious themes. I would suggest that the religious writers were merely taking advantage of the literary trends of the day. This was the age of ornate, elaborate prose, and as is pointed out by Bernard de Fresneda in the introduction of Granada's *Of Prayer, and Meditation:*

> because the Awthor vnderstode right well howe farre the mouthes of men now adayes are owt of tast, and how much they are more affectionate vnto the fleshe pottes of Egypt, than to the breade of Angels, I meane hereby, rather to the readinge of prophane bookes, by reason of the pleasant stile wherewith they thinke they are written, than to the bookes of spirituall doctrine, which are commonly written with more simplicitie, he hath

---

[96]Southern, p. 215.

therefore dressed this meate in suche wise, and hath written this doctrine in such a sweete and pleasant stile, that it maie prouoke an appetite vnto this boke, euen in such persons as doe otherwise lothe good and holesome foode: besides, that the verie matters them selues are exceedingly well chosen, and of great profite.[97]

Commenting on the popularity of Granada, Underhill makes this significant point:

In England, where affectation in style became so common in the last quarter of the century, they [the qualities of his style] procured for him a unique welcome. His reputation rose with that of Lyly, and was based upon the same fundamental grounds. It was three years after the appearance of *Euphues* that a work of Granada appeared in English. Lyly became the leader of a fashion, and Granada the most popular peninsular author translated during the closing reign of Elizabeth. One was animated by a strong moral sense, the other by a religious ecstasy; but the preëminent vogue of both was due to the cultivation of an exaggerated style.[98]

The practice of converting secular literature into religious in order to make religion more pleasing and palatable was fairly widespread during the sixteenth century. C. H. Firth, for instance, has pointed out that even the broadside ballads, which traditionally have been associated with amatory and even salacious subject matter, were moralized.[99] "Ladie Greene sleeves answere to Donkyn hir frende" became "Green Sleeues moralized to the Scriptures"; "Row well, ye Mariners" became "Row well, Christ's Mariners"; and "Dainty, come thow to me" was revised to "Jesus, come thow to me."[100] In 1549 Sternhold and Hopkins rendered into verse fifty-one psalms so that they might be sung "in priuate houses, for godly solace and comfort, and for the laying apart all ungodly songs and ballads."[101] In 1600

---

[97]Granada, *Of Prayer, and Meditation,* sigs. bvii-bvii^v.

[98]John G. Underhill, *Spanish Literature in the England of the Tudors* (New York, 1899), p. 207.

[99]C. H. Firth, "Ballads and Broadsides," *Shakespeare's England,* ed. William Winter (New York, 1916), II, 518.

[100]*Ibid.,* p. 515.

[101]Quoted by Hyder Rollins, "The Black-Letter Broadside Ballad," *PMLA,* XXXIV (1919), 259.

Robert Chambers wrote an allegorical romance on the gospels, *Palestina* (Florence), in which a heavenly king sends out his only princely son to rescue his daughter, who, having eaten of some magical fruit, lost her beauty. Also, the frequent employment of the dialogue was a means of popularizing religious subject matter; as Southern remarks, an "author's resort to this particular literary form [was] common eough in the sixteenth century as a device for sugaring the didactic pill."[102]

Although some of the authors represented in this anthology resorted to an euphuistic and exaggerated style in order to "prouoke an appetite" for their devotional books, many others disdained these devices "for sugaring the didactic pill" and chose the plain style as their medium of expression. Diego de Estella, for example, in his dedicatory epistle to *The Contempte of the Worlde* states the case for unadorned, unpretentious style as follows: "Lastlie the booke it selfe is such as asketh no outwarde settinge out, nor glorious shew of wordes, the whole argument therof, entreatinge of nothinge els, but onely of the contēpt of the world, and the vanitie thereof, so as it were neither agreeable with the matter, nor conuenient for the persons, to come either richelie arrayed, or any better then meanlie appareled. If the letter it selfe be trulie expressed, and the authors minde faythfullie delyuered, I haue that I sought for. . . ."[103] Especially those books which were addressed to the less sophisticated reader, like the books on the Rosary, or those books like the spiritual directories which attempted to inform, clarify, and suggest practical ways of living the Christian life, tended to follow the plain style.

It is important to note that approximately one half (14) of the books represented in this anthology are translations: six are translations from Italian, six from Spanish, and two from Latin. There are several reasons why the English Recusants borrowed so heavily from continental sources. First and possibly most significant is the fact that many of the Recusants were living abroad, in France, Italy, Spain, and the Low Countries, where much great devotional literature was being produced. In Spain, for example, the Counter Reformation took a much different turn than it did in England. Protestantism made very few important inroads in Spain; the government rigorously suppressed even the slightest tendency toward Protestantism.

---

[102]Southern, p. 323.
[103]Diego de Estella, sig. A4.

There was no need to write lengthy and detailed confutations of Protestant theology, for to most Spaniards the issues were not ever known; the Counter Reformation in Spain attempted to revitalize and strengthen the interior lives of the clergy and laity, thereby making them impervious to possible Protestant propaganda. There was produced to meet this need an abundance of devotional writings, which the English Recusants found quite attractive and practical. They hoped, by presenting these works in English, to effect the same results among the English laity.

Secondly, the Recusants were primarily men of action. There were so many battles to be waged both by pen and by sword, and there was so much active missionary work to be accomplished with few priests and little money that there was simply not the time nor the leisure needed for composing books of devotions, which are the products of contemplation and silence, especially when a rich harvest of continental devotional works was readily at hand.

Thirdly, Catholic books of devotion, whether written in English, Spanish, or Italian, are essentially alike in doctrine, although the temperament of the people is quite different. What a Spaniard said about prayer and meditation or what an Italian said about the good use of the sacraments was perfectly valid for an Englishman. The Protestants, on the other hand, were not so fortunate. Anglicanism, for example, although it was very early impregnated with many Calvinistic and Lutheran theological concepts, was essentially a different religion from German Lutheranism or Swiss Calvinism. This difference was theological and not merely a difference of temperament. Miss White notes, "In spite of the enormous debt of the English Church to the continental leaders of the Protesant Reformation, particularly to Calvin and his followers, all the evidence points to very much less borrowing from continental Protestant sources for the books of devotion than one would suppose."[104]

Despite the fact that the Anglicans regarded the Catholic religion as a grave perversion and corruption of the original Christian message and considered the Pope as the very incarnation of the Anti-Christ, this did not in the least hinder them from borrowing rather wholesale from Catholic devotional books; the Protestants adapted and expurgated those works written by English Catholics and printed abroad or secretly in England and translated into English the great Catholic continen-

---

[104]White, *English Devotional Literature*, p. 89.

tal devotional works. Helen White notes, "As usually happens in the
age that succeeds a revolution, not a little of the fresh progress of the
opening of the seventeenth century consisted in a recovery of elements
too hastily discarded in the first heat of innovation and a recognition
of neglected elements that had unobtrusively weathered the storms of
revolution. Nowhere is this fact more apparent than in the devotional
literature of the time."[105] The question which immediately arises is,
why did the English Protestants resort to Catholic devotional books for
their inspiration and models?

First of all, it might be argued that the Protestants, like the Catholics, in those early hectic days of the Reformation had little time to
engage in the writing of spiritual books. The age, as we have noted
previously, was one primarily of controversy and of active propagan-
dizing. But as the sixteenth century wore on, Protestants, like their
Catholic counterparts, grew weary of the eternal theological bickerings
and scurrilous apologetics; they recognized that if the Protestant religion was to grow and prosper it would need an inner spirit, a devotional life of its own. But the immense problem which faced the
Anglicans was where to turn for their devotional tradition. The
Catholics, of course, had a long tradition of devotional literature that
they could easily build on and modernize to meet the demands of the
day; also they had a rich continental tradition which was at that
moment flourishing. The Protestants, though, were not as fortunate;
they had no tradition and, as we noted, the Protestant literature of
the Continent was significantly barren of good devotional works.

The first attempts to compensate for this lack of tradition were the
Protestantizing of the old books of devotion like the *Imitation of
Christ,* the primers, and psalters. Also, various collections of prayers
were gathered and published in an effort to supply the Anglican laity
with inspirational matter—the most important of these being, of course,
the *Book of Common Prayer.* Still others attempted to espouse the
early Christian fathers as their own, seeing the English Church as a
return to primitive Christianity. But as Miss White points out, "One
may scorn fifteen hundred years of corporate experience, and even forget it, but he cannot escape its influence. So even the most optimistic
of the sixteenth-century primitivists found it impossible to start at
scratch as if those fifteen hundred years had never been."[106] All of

---

[105]*Ibid.,* p. 69.
[106]Helen C. White, *Tudor Books of Private Devotion* (Madison, 1951),
p. 11.

these attempts, then, were not sufficient; and as Martz notes, "set beside the continental books . . . these English books are dull and dry."[107] Therefore, the Protestants turned to the Catholic books of devotion for their inspiration and spiritual guidance.

It was not until the 1580's that original Anglican devotional books began to be written and published in any significant numbers.[108] In fact, in 1585, when Robert Persons published the second edition of *The First Booke of the Christian Exercise* under the new title *A Christian Directorie guiding all men to their Saluation,* he felt sufficiently safe to challenge the Rev. Edmund Bunny, an Anglican divine, who had published a bowdlerized edition of his book in 1584, in the following terms: "But here I would demande of M. Buny in sinceritie where or when, any of his religion did either make or set forthe (of them selues) any one treatise of this kinde of subiect? I meane, of deuotion, pietie, and contemplation?"[109] And even in 1626, when Protestant devotional works were flourishing, Daniel Featley, in his preface to the reader of *Ancilla Pietatis: Or Hand-Maid of Priuate Deuotion,* admits that "the Romanists for the most part exceed in bulke, but our Diuines in weight. The Church of *Rome* (like *Leah*) is more fruitfull; but her Deuotions (like *Leah* in this also) are *bleareyed* with superstition. But the mother of our faith (like *Rachel*) is not altogether so fruitfull, yet she is more comely, and beautiful, and I hope will be also hereafter as fruitfull."[110]

Another possible explanation for the dearth of Anglican devotional literature during the sixteenth century may be that such an emphasis was placed by the early Reformers on the primary role which the Scriptures played in forming the true Christian that other spiritual writing was looked upon as extraneous, if not with suspicion. Later in the century when the English Church itself was theatened by the excesses of the "inner light" movements, the Anglican clergy recognized that the laity needed guidance and direction in the spiritual life if these abuses were to be avoided.

Not all Catholic books of devotion, of course, appealed to the Protestants. Books on the use of the sacraments of penance or Holy Eucharist and books on the Rosary, for example, were not adapted or

---

[107]Martz, p. 8.
[108]Maria Hagedorn, *Reformation und Spanische Andachtsliteratur. Luis de Granada in England,* "Kölner Anglistische Arbeiten," XI (Leipzig, 1934), p. 7. White, *English Devotional Literature,* p. 64.
[109]Quoted by White, *English Devotional Literature,* p. 64.
[110]*Ibid.,* p. 65.

translated by the Protestants. The most popular ones were Persons'
The First Booke of the Christian Exercise and certain books of meditation written by Luis de Granada. Persons appealed to Protestants because the subject matter, which is no more than a plea for sinners to be
converted and to return to God, is general enough to avoid specific
theological entanglements. Granada's meditations appealed for various
reasons: first, they were written in the style of Lyly at a time when
that exaggerated style was most popular; and secondly, his meditations
on the life of Christ, once more, were not controversial in nature.

The subject of Protestant adaptations of Catholic devotional literature is one of the most interesting, and, at times, one of the most
amusing aspects of the religious literature of the sixteenth century, but
neither space nor appropriateness allows for a fuller discussion of the
subject in this study. In fact, two excellent studies have already been
done: Miss Maria Hagedorn in a long monograph entitled "Reformation und Spanische Andachtsliteratur. Luis de Granada *(Kölner
Anglistische Arbeiten,* III [Leipzig, 1934]) has studied several of the
adaptations of Granada, and Robert McNulty in an unpublished dissertation entitled "Robert Parsons. *The First Booke of the Christian Exercise.* An Edition and Study," (Columbia University, 1956) has made
an interesting comparison of Persons' original and Bunny's famous
bowdlerized version. Such studies show in detail that Recusant devotional literature had a far-reaching influence on Protestant devotional
literature as well as on later Catholic writing.

Also, the influence that the tradition of meditation introduced by
the Recusants had on the religious poets of the late sixteenth and early
seventeenth century has recently been the object of several first-rate
studies. Most noteworthy among these is Louis Martz's *The Poetry of
Meditation* (New Haven, 1954). Mr. Martz remarks: ". . . English
religious poetry of the seventeenth century represents the impact of the
continental art of meditation upon English poetical traditions. That impact was exerted to some extent through the example of continental
religious poetry: Southwell and Crashaw make this plain. But funda-
mentally, I shall argue, the Counter Reformation penetrated to English
literature through methods of religious meditation that lay at the heart
of the century's spiritual life and provided a radiant center for religious
literature of every kind."[111] Martz also suggests that the influence of
the meditative style and method "forms a tight link between the seven-

---

[111]Martz, p. 13.

teenth and the twentieth centuries; for the art of meditation appears fundamental to the achievement of Yeats and Eliot, and is certainly fundamental to the achievement of Hopkins, whose delayed publication has made him a twentieth-century poet. For these three poets, at least, the kinship with the seventeenth century is more than a matter of the local texture of their poetry: more than a style that can fuse the natural and the supernatural, the common and mysterious. One can find in their poems a total movement, a total structure, that shows a remarkable resemblance to the threefold method [of meditation suggested by St. Ignatius]. . . ."[112]

Because of this recent rediscovery and appreciation of the influence of devotional Catholic literature of the sixteenth and early seventeenth centuries and because of the inherent merit of much of this prose, it seems appropriate and necessary to make readily available to the scholarly reader a generous sampling of the books of devotion which were written or translated by English Catholics during the reign of Elizabeth I. Also it is hoped that by bringing to light these Catholic works and authors, which have been for too long ignored or slighted, a renewed interest will be generated in a major segment of English social, religious, and literary history. It is true that many of the ideas expressed in these works hold little inherent interest to many modern readers; but as Miss White has so astutely noted, "If it be true that a man who today confined his attention strictly to religious reading would find himself in possession of but a partial and indirect view of a very large portion of contemporary life and thought, it is equally true that any one who out of modern prejudice disregards the religious literature of the first half of the seventeenth century [and I would add the latter half of the sixteenth century] will find himself quite as much outside of some of the most important and characteristic movements of thought and feeling of that age."[113]

---

[112]*Ibid.*, p. 325.
[113]White, *English Devotional Literature*, pp. 10-11.

INTRODUCTION TO THE TEXT

The primary intention of this anthology is to offer to the reader a large sampling of English Recusant devotional prose, printed either secretly in England or on the Continent during the reign of Elizabeth I. No attempt has been made to collate various editions or to record variant readings. The difficulty and expense of obtaining copies of every edition of each work, together with the time that collation would have required, explain why I made no attempt to produce definitive texts. However, I have been particularly careful to note editions being used and to indicate other Catholic editions that were printed during the years 1558-1603. With few exceptions (all of which are indicated in the notes to the text) I have used first editions when these were accessible. In all matters of bibliography, I have relied on the work of A. F. Allison and D. M. Rogers entitled *A Catalogue of Catholic Books in English Printed Abroad or Secretly in England, 1558-1640*, 2 pts. (Bognor Regis, [England], 1956).

Elizabethan spellings have been generally maintained with care; the only modernizations are *w* for *vv, s* and *ss* for ∫ and ∫∫, and *th* for the thorn. No attempt, however, has been made to represent ligatures (*æ*, for example has been standardized to *ae*) ; likewise, the various abbreviations for the relative pronouns, the preposition *with,* and the article *the* have been expanded. Capitalization, especially in titles, half-titles, etc., has been generally standardized; and no effort has been made to indicate black-letter type or other peculiarities of sixteenth-century printing. Punctuation in the original works has generally been kept, except in a few cases of end punctuation and periods within sentences, when to do so would have been impractical. All marginal glosses in the original works have been placed in the margins. Archaic words of unusual difficulty have been glossed in the notes to the text.

Omission of parts in an individual work has been indicated by square brackets, and a very brief summary of that which has been omitted is given in order that the reader may obtain a better idea of the whole work.

So that the reader may have a bibliography of all the Catholic devotional prose works published in English during the years 1558-1603, I have attached to this introduction the following list of books which are not included in this anthology but which are found in Allison and Rogers' catalogue:

Bruno, Vincenzo.

The second parte of the meditations of the passion and resurrection of Christ our Sauiour . . . Translated. n.p.d. [1599?] Pr. [secretly in England.] Not in *STC.* Allison and Rogers, I, Entry 173.

The third parte of the meditations of the passion and resurrectiō of Christ our Sauiour . . . Translated. n.p.d. [1599?] Pr. [secretly in England.] Not in *STC.* Allison and Rogers, I, Entry 174.

The fourth part of the meditations of the passion & resurrectiō of Christ our Sauiour . . . Translated. n.p.d. [1599?] Pr. [secretly in England.] Not in *STC.* (I have chosen to represent only *The first part of the meditations* in this anthology, Entry XIV.)

A short treatise of the sacrament of penance. With the maner of examination of conscience for a generall confession. Wherunto is added another treatise of confession. n.p. 1597. A translation. Pr. [secretly in England.] Not in *STC.* Allison and Rogers, I, Entry 176.

[Anr. ed.] n.p. 1597. Pr. [secretly in England.] *STC* 3942. Allison and Rogers, I, Entry 177.

Certaine deuout and godly petitions, commonly called Iesus Psalter. 2 pts. Antuerpiae, apud Iohan. Foulerum, 1575. Pt. 2 contains *Godly contemplations for the vnlearned.* Not in *STC.* Allison and Rogers, I, Entry 413. (This and other psalters have been excluded from this anthology since they are, generally speaking, merely reprints or editions of earlier works.)

[Anr. ed.] 2 pts. Antuerpiae, apud Iohan. Foulerum 1575 [1576?] Pt. 2 contains, in place of the *Godly contemplations, The psalter of Sainct Hierome,* bearing the date 1576. *STC* 14565 and 14506. Allison and Rogers, I, Entry 414.

[Anr. ed] Antuerpiae, 1575 [1579?] Imprint false; pr. [London, William Carter.] Not in *STC.* Allison and Rogers, I, Entry 415.

[Anr. ed.] n.p.d. [c. 1580,] Pr. [Rouen, George L'Oyselet.] *STC* 14564. Allison and Rogers, I, Entry 416.

[Anr. ed.] [1580-81.] Part of *Manual or Meditation*. *STC* 14568. Allison and Rogers, II, Entry 520.

[Anr. ed.] 1583. Part of *STC* 17263. *STC* 14566. Allison and Rogers, II, Entry 495.

[Anr. ed.] n.p.d. [1595-1600?] Pr. [secretly in England.] Not in *STC*. Allison and Rogers, I, Entry 417.

[Anr. ed.] n.p. 1596. Pr. [secretly in England.] *STC* 14567. Allison and Rogers, I, Entry 418.

Fisher, John.

A spirituall consolation, written by Iohn Fyssher . . . to hys sister Elizabeth, at suche tyme as hee was prisoner in the Tower of London. n.p.d. [c. 1578.] With *A Sermon . . . preached vpon a good Friday, by the same Iohn Fissher.* Pr. [London, Thomas East.] *STC* 10899. Allison and Rogers, I, Entry 304. (This work was first published in 1535.)

Godly contemplations for the vnlearned. n.p. [1575.] Pr. [Antwerp, John Fowler.] Not in *STC*. Allison and Rogers, I, Entry 359. (This work is a collection of pious woodcuts.)

A manual of prayers newly gathered out of many and diuers famous authors aswell auncient as of the tyme present. 2 pts. n.p. 1583. Compiled and tr. G. F. [George Flinton.] Pr. [Rouen, Fr. Persons' press.] This and subsequent editions include the *Jesus Psalter* (followed by the *Golden Litany*) generally with its own separate title page. *STC* 17263 and 14566. Allison and Rogers, II, Entry 495.

[Anr. ed.] *Where vnto is addid* [*sic*] *a sommarie of the Christian belefe. More certaine litanies.* 2 pts. n.p. 1589. Pr. [Rouen, George L'Oyselet.] *STC* 17264. Allison and Rogers, II, Entry 496.

[Anr. ed.] 2 pts. n.p.d. [c. 1593.] Pr. [secretly in England.] The wording of the title follows *STC* 17263. Not in *STC*. Allison and Rogers, II, Entry 497.

[Anr. ed.] *Whereunto is added a newe callender, & a summary of the Christian beleefe, with the litanies.* 2 pts.

n.p.d. [c. 1595.] Pr. [secretly in England.] *STC* 17265. Allison and Rogers, II, Entry 498.

[Anr. ed.] 2 pts. n.p.d. [1596.] Pr. [secretly in England.] The wording of the title follows *STC* 17265. Not in *STC.* Allison and Rogers, II, Entry 499.

[Anr. ed.] *A manuall of praiers, gathered out of many famous & good authors . . . Distributed according to the daies of the weeke. Whereunto is added a newe calender, with the order to helpe at Masse.* Printed at Calice, 1599. Imprint false; Pr. [secretly in England.] *STC* 17266. Allison and Rogers, II, Entry 500.

[Anr. ed.] *A manual of prayers. Gathered out of manie famous authors.* n.p.d. [c. 1602-05.] Pr. [secretly in England.] Not in *STC.* Allison and Rogers, II, Entry 502.

[A manual or meditation.] 9 pts. Printed at Doway by I. R. [1580-81.] Imprint false; pr. [secretly at the "Greenstreet House" press.] The general title page is unknown; the imprint is taken from the *Jesus Psalter,* no. (9). The nine opuscules, each with its own signatures, are listed in *STC* respectively as (1) 17776a; (2) 14107; (3) 25131; (4) 20194; (5) 14108; (6) 5183; (7) 11182; (8) 20199; and (9) 14568. Allison and Rogers, II, Entry 520.

[Anr. ed., entitled:] *A manual o* [*sic*] *meditation, and most necessary prayers: with a memoriall of instructions right requisite. Also a summarie of Catholike religion: and an absolute order of confession: with direction for receauing. & other necessary thniges* [*sic*]. 9 pts. n.p.d. [1580-81.] Pr. [secretly at the "Greenstreet House" press.] Not in *STC.* Allison and Rogers, II, Entry 521.

[Anr. ed.] n.p.d. [c. 1596.] Pr. [secretly in England.] With one continuous set of signatures. Not in *STC.* Allison and Rogers, II, Entry 522.

More, Thomas.

A dialogue of cumfort against tribulation. Antuerpiae, apud Iohannem Foulerum, 1573. *STC* 18083. Allison and Rogers, II, Entry 549. (This work was first published by Tottel in 1553.)

N., C.

Our Ladie hath a new sonne. Printed at Dowaie, 1595. Init. C. N. Imprint false; pr. [secretly in England.] *STC* 18326. Allison and Rogers, II, Entry 558.

The New Testament of Iesus Christ, translated faithfully into English, out of the authentical Latin . . . In the English College of Rhemes, Rhemes, Iohn Fogny, 1582. *STC* 2884. Allison and Rogers, II, Entry 567.

[Anr. ed.] Set forth the second time, by the same college now returned to Doway. Antwerp, Daniel Vervliet, 1600. *STC* 2898. Allison and Rogers, II, Entry 568.

Peryn, William.

Spirituall exercyses and goostly meditations, and a neare way to come to perfection and lyfe contemplatiue. Neulye imprynted at Caen by Peterle Chandelier, 1598. *STC* 19785. Allison and Rogers, II, Entry 643. (There is an earlier edition of this work published in 1557.)

Peter of Lucca.

A dialogue of dying wel. First written in the Italian tongue . . . Translated first into French, and now into English. Antwerp, by A. C., 1603. Tr. R. V. [Richard Verstegan.] Pr. [Arnout Conincx.] *STC* 19815 and 6802. Allison and Rogers, II, Entry 645.

The primer, or office of the blessed Virgin Marie, in Latin and English: according to the reformed Latin: and with lyke graces priuileged. Antwerp, Arnold Conings, 1599. ed. R. V. [Richard Verstegan.] *STC* 16094. Allison and Rogers, II, Entry 680. (This primer is merely an edition of an earlier work.)

Southwell, Robert.

A short rule of good life. To direct the deuout Christian in a reguler and orderly course. 2 pts. n.p.d. [1596-97.] Anon. Pt. 2 consists of *An Epistle of a religious priest vnto his Father,* signed R. S. [Robert Southwell.] Pr. [secretly in England.]

Not in *STC*. Allison and Rogers, II, Entry 787. (Richard M. Loomis did an edition of this work [diss. Cornell University, 1959].)

    [Anr. ed.] n.p.d. [1597?] Anon. With *An Epistle, etc.* Pr. [secretly in England.] *STC* 22969. Allison and Rogers, II, Entry 788.

    [Anr. ed.] n.p.d. [1602-05.] Anon. With *An Epistle, etc.* Pr. [secretly in England.] Not in *STC*. Allison and Rogers, II, Entry 789.

Suso, Henry.

Certayne sweete prayers of the glorious name of Iesus, commonly called, Iesus Mattens. n.p.d. [1575-78] Tr. from the Latin. Pr. [London, William Carter.] Not in *STC*. Allison and Rogers, II, Entry 801.

Thomas à Kempis.

The following of Christ, translated out of Latin into Englishe, newlie corrected and amended. Whereunto is added the golden epistle of sainct Bernarde. And now lastelie the rules of a christian lyfe, made by Iohn Picus the elder earle of Mirādula. n.p. 1585. An edition of [William Whytford's] translation. Pr. [Rouen, George L'Oyselet.] *STC* 23968 and 23960a. Allison and Rogers, II, Entry 814.

W., P.

An exercise of spirituall recollection. By a Catholic priest. n.p.d. [c. 1602?] Init. P. W. [Philip Woodward?] Pr. [secretly in England.] Not in *STC*. Allison and Rogers, II, Entry 868. (I was unable to obtain a copy of this work.)

I.

The Exercise of a
Christian Life.

Written in Italian by the Reuerend Father Iaspar Loarte
D. of Diuinity, of the holy Societie of Iesus.

Newely perused and corected by
the Translatour.

With certaine verie deuout Exercises & Praiers added therunto, more than were in
the first Edition.

[Woodcut of the dead Christ in the arms of His Mother]

With Privilege[1]
[trans. Stephen Brinkley[2]]

---

[1]n.p.d. [1596-97.] Pr. [secretly in England.] Allison and Rogers, I,
Entry 464. *STC* 16642.

Earlier editions:

The exercise of a Christian life. Written in Italian . . . And newly
translated into Englishe. by I. S. [Stephen Brinkley's pseudonym.] n.p.d.
[1579.] Pr. [London, William Carter.] Allison and Rogers, I, Entry 462.
This edition does not appear in the *STC*.

[Anr. ed.] *Newly perused and corected by the translatour. With cer-*
taine very deuout exercises and prayers added therunto, more then were
in the first edition. n.p. 1584. Pr. [Rouen, Fr. Persons' press.] Allison and
Rogers, I, Entry 463. *STC* 16643.

Gaspar Loarte was a Spanish theologian who entered the Society of Jesus
in 1552. He lived nearly all his life in Italy. He died at Valencia in 1578
(Augustin and Aloys de Backer, *Bibliothèque de la Compagnie de Jésus*, ed.
Carlos Sommervogel, 2 pts., 10 vols. [Bruxelles, 1890-1909], pt. 1, V, 1879).
Loarte's original is entitled *Essercitatio della vita christiana. Composto per il*
R. P. D. Gaspar Loarte and was published at Barcelona in 1569 (Southern,
p. 389).

[2]Stephen Brinkley (fl. 1584) was a law student and printer. As a young
man he joined an association of young Catholic gentlemen, founded by George

[♥2]   To the Most Reverend
                        Fathers and Bre-
                     thren of the Holy Socie-
              tie, of the name of Iesus: the Trans-
                latour wisheth all increase of
                        Spirituall graces.

For so much as from you I haue receiued so singular benefits, as
needs I must more than to any other earthlie Creatures, acknowledge
my selfe indebted vnto you: & for that I haue receiued from you the
Copie, the Counsaile, and other commodities, to Translate this worthie
Treatise into our Englishe tongue: I coulde doe no lesse, as wel in
respecte of your former merits, as of the encouragement & other meanes
which you gaue vnto me to finishe this pore *Christian Office,* but make
you the Patrons of my small paines, and vowe the coate & simple attire
to them, who gaue the Paterne and excellent subiect to me. Voutsafe
therefore (I beseeche you) most Reuerend Fathers & Brethren, to accept at my hands a Birde of your own broode, pluckt out of her na-
[♥2ᵛ] tural plume, & according to my simple skill decked vppe with
forraine feather. Voutsafe (I praye you) to take in good part this fruit
of my poore endeuour, as a testimony of the reuerent zeal which (by
your merit) I bear vnto your whole Society, and as a recognisance of a
farder debt which I owe vnto you, and am not able to discharge but by
the bountifull goodnesse of my sweete Redeemer: who as he hath giuen
his word vnto you on my behalfe, so will he not faile in due time to
performe the same, to your inexplicable contentation: whō I most

---

Gilbert, which had as its aim the preparation of Protestants for reception into
the Catholic Church and the conducting of priests to them. The association,
which was solemnly blessed by Pope Gregory XIII on April 14, 1580, also
procured alms for a common fund, out of which missionary priests were
supported (Joseph Gillow, *A Literary and Biographical History, or Biblio-*
graphical Dictionary, of the English Catholics, from the Breach with Rome,
in 1534, to the Present Time, 5 vols. [New York, 1885-1902], I, 298). Brinkley
became friends with Fr. Edmund Campion, S. J., and Fr. Robert Persons, S. J.,
and at the suggestion of the latter, he operated a secret press near London,
known as the Greenstreet House press. On August 8, 1581, Brinkley and
four associates were arrested for operating a private press and committed
to the Tower. Brinkley, however, was released on June 24, 1583, and proceeded
immediately to Rome to visit Fr. Persons and to seek his counsel (Southern,
p. 356). Later he settled in Rouen in order to assist George Flinton, a printer,
who was engaged in the printing of Catholic books under the direction of
Fr. Persons (Southern, p. 356). For an interesting biographical account of
Brinkley, see Gillow (I, 298-300), and for a critical discussion of Brinkley's
translation, see Southern (pp. 192-197).

humbly beseeche to preserue, increase, and strengthen you for euer, and to giue me and all others grace to followe your good Instructions. At Paris, the 20. of Iune. 1579.[3]

Your most bounden Beads-
man and dutifull poore
seruant for-euer.
Iames Sancer.[4]

[9 3]

The Author to the
deuout Reader.

Concerning *the necessity of many men, who hauing a good will, haue not for all that the capacity or meanes, to seeke out and reade such bookes, as intreat of the Exercises, wherin euery good Christian ought to occupy himselfe. I haue for this cause thought good to gather togither in this short Treatise, the principall exercises which euerie Christian man is bound to vse: that by spending his time laudably therein, he may haue hope to obtaine the grace of God Almighty, and by meanes thereof, come afterwardes to enioy eternal felicity, which is the end whervnto wee are created. And albeit this treatise may generally helpe all men, yet is it principally intended to those persons which vnderstanding (the ende wherunto they are created, & the rigorous account which they must render of their whole life yea of euery idle worde) desire in such sort to spende and gouerne their temporal life that they may afterwards come to obtaine euerlasting life. Such persons as are thus* [9 3ᵛ] *affected shall (I hope) make their auaile of those thinges whereof I shall heere intreat, and will (I doubt not) with good will and plaine meaning receaue that which is with the like afforded vnto them. There are also annexed vnto this excellent Treatise, certaine deuout and Godly Praiers, wherein euerye good Chris-*

---

[3]Southern suggests that the reference to Paris is meant to mislead the authorities. There is no evidence, he maintains, that Brinkley was in Paris before 1583 (p. 390). In the later editions of the work, the subscription was apparently preserved as it had appeared in the first edition.

[4]James Sancer or Sanker was the pseudonym of Stephen Brinkley (Southern, p. 192). The 1610 edition of the work is signed S. B. (Allison and Rogers, I, Entry 465).

tian may exercise himselfe on Mornings and Euenings: which are the two special times wheron the whole course of a well ordered life dependeth. These (gentle Reader) I deemed most necessary, I heere thought good to present vnto thee: which I beseech thee to vse to thine auaile, whiles thou shalt want better means to helpe thy selfe.

[Here follow a "sonnet" to the reader and Chapter one, entitled "What thing he ought to doe, that purposeth to begin a new life . . .," which deals with the subject of general confession, pp. 1-7.]

[7]

Certain General Ad-
uertisements, necessary for such as minde
to serue God sincerely.

CHAP. II.

Having thus made a generall Confession, who so had not (as I haue already sayde) made the same before, thy soule being nowe cleansed [8] from all Mortal sinne, it behoueth thee to haue a most steedfast purpose neuer to offend Mortally againe, but rather to suffer any affliction, or worldly contempt: yea, death it selfe, if neede required. For if a chaste wife ought to cary this minde, rather to loose her life, than to betray the trouth she hath once plight vnto her husband, how much more oughtest thou to be of the same minde, rather to loose a thousand liues (if thou haddest so many) than to play the traitour towardes God, who is thy Husbande, thy Father, thy   2. Cor. 11. Lord, and Maker. When thou hast once thus fully determined, take then a zelous & feruent desire to liue a-newe hereafter, & striue to get other newe behauiours, & to liue farre otherwise than thou hast donne before, reputing thy selfe to be nowe a newe man, farre changed from that thou erst was, seeing all the time thou hast hitherto liued hath beene but lost, & as it were a death. For the better doing whereof this shall helpe thee greatly, in any wise, to eschew al occasions of sin, especially the company of [9] wicked men, but much more of women   1. Cor. 5. such as may prouoke thee to naughtinesse, and giue thee loose & lewde example. For albeit thou art bounde to loue euery one, and to pray for euery one (as Charity commaundeth) yet art thou not bounde to company and conuerse with euery one, but onely such as may helpe to doe thee good, and with their good wordes and vertuous examples, serue to edifie thee.

Secondly, thou must flye such places where God is customably offended, as be *Dising-houses, Tauernes, Daunsing schooles*, and such like: not onely foreseeing thou doe no euell thy selfe, but also not to be present there where it is done, for looke howe much more thou standest a-loofe from the fire, and so much more secure art thou, not to be burned therewith.

Thirdly, thou must take great heede to be at no time *Idle*, for that (as holye Scripture telleth) many men haue receiued much harme through Idelnesse. See therfore thou followe S. Ieroms counsaile saying: *It behoueth vs to be al-*[10]*waies doing of some good, that when the fiende shall come to tempt vs, he may finde vs well and vertuously occupied.*

Eccle. 33.
S. Ierom.

Fourthly, thou must take heede of all excesse in Eating, Drincking, Sleeping, and Cloathing, and indeuour thy selfe to obserue a Mediocrity and Temperance in each of them: yea, rather to decline to some rigour and austeritye, than to anye superfluitye and delicate pampering of thy fleshe: for looke by howe much the more thou tamest and bridelest it, and by so much the lesse shalt thou be troubled with the temptations and disordinate desires, that proceede thereof: yea, so much the more apte shalt thou finde they selfe to serue God, and to performe all spirituall Exercises.

Luc. 21.

As touching corporal punishments and Penance, as Fasting, Discipline, Haire-Cloath, and other chastisementes, it behoueth thee herein to vse good discreation, taking such as helpe to represse the assaultes and temptations of the fleshe, and leauing others that may be hurtfull, not yeeld-[11]ing herein to the heates, which some *Nouices* are wonte to haue in their beginning, who through indiscreet mortifying and dompting[5] of their fleshe, fall into some such infirmity, as afterwardes they must needes pamper and cherishe it too much. It shall be good therefore that thou gouerne thy selfe in these thinges by thy Ghostlye Fathers aduise, if he be practised in spirituall Exercises.

---

[5]*dompting*, subduing

Fiftly, it shall greatly profite thee to set before thine eies the good examples, Workes, & Life, that others haue ledd and still continue in, but chiefely of such as be like vnto thy selfe, animating thee by their good examples, and procuring as much as thou maiest to imitate them in euery thing: yea, forgetting the good which thou hast already donne, thou oughtest to striue euery day to become better than other, & alwaies to aduaunce forwarde in the seruice and feare of God.

2. Cor. 4.

Sixty, make none account of the tediousnesse and temptations which they commonlye feele, that beginne first to [12] leade a Godly and Spirituall life. Bee not thou, I say, dismayed therewith at all, but march on forwarde, and fight manfully against all such temptations comforting and confirming thy selfe with this vndoubted trueth which thou must haue firmely fixed in thy minde to witte, that nowe thou hast taken in hande the highest and most happy enterprise that may be thought of in this worlde, and howe this is an affaire of more weight and importance than any other, & whereby more certaine gaine, greater aboundance of Treasure, more Honour and Dignitye, and finallye the most blessed happes of all the happye and good thinges that may be founde or desired in this worlde, shall redound vnto thee: yea, there is no good thing that is good indeede, but onely this, neither any other important affaire, but this alone, this beeing the one onely thing, which our Sauiour himselfe said, to bee necessarye. And therefore, no toiles, temptations, or disquietnesse, no backe-bitings, slaunders, and persecutions, which may and must befal thee [13] in this life, ought to seeme any whitte grieuous for the gaining of so pretious a pearle and rare iewell, as thou lookest for. Heerewith must thou eftsoones animate & encourage thy selfe, calling ofte to minde that saying of the Apostle, *How all the afflictions & crosses of this worlde are not to be compared to the future glory that shall be giuen vnto vs.* Persuade thy selfe likewise least thou mightest happily faint in resisting the toiles and temptations which may befall thee in this straight waye that bringeth to Heauen: persuade thy selfe (I say assuredly, that as herein there be worldely toyles and temptations, so be there Heauenly comfortes and consolations, and that to ouercome these crosses & ouerthwartes of nature, there are helpes and succours of grace giuen withall, which in power doe farre surpasse nature. And with this consideration maiest thou remaine a vanquisher, & doe all thinges, (as did Saint Pavl) in him that shall comforte thee, which is Iesvs Christ our Lorde and Captaine.

1. Cor. 9.

Luc. 10.
Rom. 8.
2. Cor. 4.

Rom. 8.

Phil. 4.

[14]

Of the Particular Or-
der which we ought euery day to ob-
serue in our daily Exercises.

Chap. III.

Descending now to more particularity, for that things orderly disposed, be both more durable & profitable also, I haue thought good to
aduertise thee, what order thou oughtest euery day to keepe. Which let
be this: first, to *Rise* in the *Morning* so early as thou maiest, hauing
before refreshed thy selfe sufficiently with sleepe, that is, the space of
Sixe, or *Seauen* houres, little more or lesse, according to the diuersity
of complexions. So soone as thou art a-wake, it is a good and Godly
deuotion, before thou settle thy minde to any other thing, to offer vp to
God, the *First Fruites* of all thine actions, & powers of thy whole
body: as for example, thy Heart, thinking of thy Creator, & sighing
after him: thine Eies, casting them vpon some Godly Picture, or [15]
to Heauen: thy Legs, kneeling humbly before his Presence: thy Hands,
lifting them vp to adore and thanke him: thy Mouth saying some short
Praiers, as the *Pater noster, Aue Mary,* and the *Creed*: & then maiest
thou afterwardes, according as thy deuotion shall teache thee,
briefely giue him thankes for hauing preserued thee the night
past, desiring him likewise to defend thee that present day from all
sinne, and to giue thee grace to spende it fruitefully in his diuine seruice.

*The or-
der of
our mor-
ning ex-
ercise.*

After this, if thou be at leisure, and haue no great businesse, reade a
little of some deuoute Treatise, or make a little Meditation, whereof I
shall intreate hereafter. For doing thus, thou doest as our Sauiour himselfe aduised thee, saying: *Seeke first the kingdome of God, and his
iustice, and all other thinges shall be giuen vnto you.* It were very good
also, after thou hast donne thus, to goe to the Chvrch, if thou mightest
conueniently, & there to heare Masse, or at least to see & adore thy
Saviovr in his most holye Sacrament: but [16] if thy neede & pouerty
could not well afforde thee such leaue as to go thither it shal then
suffice on working daies, to doe the same with heart & good desire.

Mat. 6.

Hauing now recommended thy selfe to God in maner aforesaid, thou maiest with his holy blessing attende to thine occupation or temporall businesse, referring all thinges, yea, temporall also to his diuine seruice, choosing rather to doe them for his loue, than for thine owne lucre. And therefore oughtest thou often-times to thinke vpon him whiles thou labourest, or art busied in any kind of temporall affaires, & to recommende thy selfe to his diuine mercy, offering vp thine heart with all thy doings vnto him.

All our actions to be directed to. Gods glorie.

And in any wise beware of one thinge that neither in thine occupation, or other temporall doings, thou vse anye guile, or exercise any vnlawfull trade, and against conscience: for so shoulde thy building laide on such a foundation be very faulty. Thou must likewise take heed of Swearing, Lying, vsing of Idle Wordes and impertinent speeches, so [17] must as may be, yea, not to heare any such, if it were possible for thee.

Vprightnesse & iust dealing. Iac. 5. 1. Cor. 15.

Thus hauing spent the day til *Dinner* time, see when thou goest thereto, that beeing nowe at *Table,* either thou, or some other say *Grace* before thou eate, or at least-wise, say a *Pater noster* and *Aue Mary.* And beware thou feede not too greedily, nor of too dainty and delicate *Meate*: take heede also of all such excesse and superfluitye as might make thee vnlifting, and lesse apte to Reade, Pray, or doe any other Worke: take therefore so much as thou maiest well thinke necessarye for thee and no more, remembring that Meate is rather to be receiued as a medicine or refection, to susteine the Body, and intertaine this temporall life of ours, than to satisfie the sensuall delightes and desires of our fleshe. And therefore must thou force thy selfe not to feede with the whole man, but to eleuate thy minde vp to God, and to listen to some holy & spiritual lessons, if there were any read. And if thou finde thy selfe disposed to gluttonye, thou must seeke to represse [18] the same with some good thought: for example, remembring that through thy sins thou deseruest not that, which God of his meere liberallity bestoweth vpon thee: and how others that merit more, lacke what thou leauest. Calling also to minde the toiles, tormentes, & sorrowes of our Sauiour, & how for thy sake he tasted *Gaule and Vineger*: with these and such like good cogitations maiest thou, as with a wholsome sauce delay, the too sweete and pleasaunt sauour of thy meate.

Meate to bee vsed as a medicine.

Meanes to repres Gluttony.

Mat. 27. Luc. 23. Psal. 68.

After Dinner see thou rise not from *Table,* before thou hast thanked thy Maker, who in such wise hath vouchsafed to susteine and refreshe thee with his most bountifull hand, thou deserueing rather through thy sinnes, to suffer eternall tormentes, and say some *Pater noster* & *Aue Mary* for the Liuing & the Dead: and thus maiest thou at thy pleasure returne again to thy businesse demeaning thy selfe therein, as is afore saide in the Morning.

At Euening it should be very good (if thou couldest conueniently) to say [19] some fewe deuotions before Supper, or to reade a little, as I shall hereafter instruct thee, that by this meanes thy soul might receiue some refreshing before thy body: howe-beit if thy trade & businesse* would not giue thee leaue so to doe, then maiest thou get thee to Supper on Gods name, behauing thy selfe herein, as is saide at Dinner-time.

The residue of time from Supper, till thou goe to Bed, thou maiest bestowe on some honest talke, or other good Exercise and recreation, alwaies taking heed of occupying thy selfe in any such thing as may hinder and disturbe the quietnesse of thy minde.

Afterwardes (hauing thus reposed thy selfe some time) see thou prepare thy self to Bed-ward, cōsidering that euery good christiã ought in such wise to dispose himselfe therunto, as if he were that Night to depart out of this life.

Exercise to Bed-warde.

The maner how to prepare thy selfe, for this, first kneeling downe deuoutely before some picture of Christ, or of our Lady (which thou oughtest alwaies to haue in thy Chamber) say the [20] *Creede, Pater noster,* and *Aue Mary* afterwardes 1 giue God most humble thankes for hauing preserued thee that Day: 2 & require the light of his grace to vnderstand and knowe thy faultes but chiefely those which thou hast committed that present Daye: 3 Examine afterwardes thy conscience at leisure and with good deliberation, discussing howe, and in what thinges thou hast bestowed the same. And where thou findest thee gilty of anye offence, 4 be sorrowefull for it, and aske God hartily mercy: purpose also to Confesse the same in due time, & to amende thy life hereafter: but finding not thy conscience gilty of any great offence, yeeld him humble thankes, who hath preserued thee: and finally be-seeche him to defend thee the Night following, from all the deceites and illusions of the diuell, graunting thee conuenient rest for the health of thy Soule & Body. And thus maiest thou goe to Bedde, making the signe of the holy Crosse vpon thee as thou layest thee downe: and see thou dispose thy whole Body in honest and [21] decent wise, re-

1

2

Foure principal points to be consi-dered.

3

4

---

*businesse] *ed.;* bunesse

membring that God, and his holy Angel thy Gardian doe looke vpon
thee: to whome thou must not fail to recōmend thee. It shalbe like
wise very good to remēber otherwhiles that euen as thou nowe layest
thy selfe downe in Bed, so shall others one day couche thee downe in
thy *Graue*: and ponder well, that this must needes bee the ende of all
the riches, pompes, and honours, and of all the whole pride and glory
of this worlde. Say therefore, as thou art laid some short Praier,
Hymne, or *Pater noster* ouer thee, crauing Gods good helpe and assistance for that last houre of so great dread & importance. And beware
in any wise of louing too dainty & softe a Bed, calling to minde that
narrowe and harde couche of the Crosse, which for thy sake our Sauiour lay vpon, and thus maiest thou fall asleepe either with this, or such
other like Godly thought: & looke that when thou chancest at any time
to wake, that thou haue God by and by in thy mind, & let thy Mouth
be filled with his praises, saying some verse to thanke and [22] blesse
him, or to recommende thy selfe to his diuine mercy: & when thou
riseth againe in the Morning, behaue thy selfe as is a fore-saide.

Mat. 18.
Psal. 33.

Our Bed
not vnlike
to our
graue.

[Here follow discussions on how to observe holy days and on the
necessity and method of mental prayer, pp. 22-40.]

[40]

Meditations of the
*blessed Passion of our Sauiour, for eue-
ry day in the weeke, especially on
Mornings.*

Chap. VII.

The Meditations wherein I thinke most profitable for thee to exercise thy selfe, especially on Morning, ought to be of the Passion of
Christ, which thou maiest dispose in this order.

[41]

Mvnday.

On Munday Morning at thine appointed houre, thou shalt thinke
of the last Supper of our Lord & Sauiour: wherein amongest other

thinges which thou shalt Meditate conformably to the story of the Gospel: cal chiefly to minde these three points: to witte, that most profound humility wherwith He washed his Disciples Feet: the institution of the most Holye Sacrament: those most sugred speeches which hee lastly preached vnto them.

Ioh. 13.
Mat. 26.
Marc. 14.
Luc. 22.

About the first: consider that woonderfull humilitye wherewith that most high and puissant Prince (into whose hands his eternall Father had giuen the rule of al things) bowed himselfe down to washe & cleanse his Disciples Feete, & amongest the rest, those filthy feete of Iudas, the Traitour: neither yet did his puissance, wisedome, holinesse, nor his greatnesse, (euery one being incomprehensible) let him to doe this so base a worke: that we should followe the example which he lefte vs therein, not onely to humble ourselues to our bet-[42]ters, but also to our equals & inferiours.

Ioh. 13.

Touching the second point: consider that most feruent loue our sweete Redeemer bare vnto vs, *In the ende*, whereby (he being now departed from vs) deuised this ineffable meanes howe to remaine still with vs, for our consolation, profit, and refection, in this most holy Sacrament. And like as he could now leaue vs any gifte more pretious than this, so ought we not to seeke or desire any other than this, disposing our selues often-times to receiue this most Sacred foode: that being often-times vnited to Him, we may be made partakers of the inestimable fruits, which are by means thereof imparted to vs.

Ioh. 13.

Concerning the third: amongest the other wordes of that long and most excellent Sermon which he made to his Disciples: take for thee that his newe precept of Charity, so highly commended of him: wherein he saide, that his Disciples should be discerned: & withall, note the patience thou must haue in the manifolde tribulations and persecutions which thou must needes suffer [43] this worlde, wherewith the soule is purged, and gaineth great & inspeakeable Meede.

[Here follow the remaining meditations for both mornings and evenings, meditations on the mysteries of the Rosary, remedies for problems in prayer, directions on receiving the sacraments of confession and Holy Communion, a discourse on temptations and suggested remedies against the various sorts of sin, a discourse on preparation for death, and a discussion of the temptations at the time of death, pp. 43-283.]

[284]

A conclusion & brie fe rehersal of al that
hath bin said in this little Treatise, & of
the things that euery good Christian is
bound to learne & haue by hart.

Chap. XXIX.

In this little Treatise (Christian Reader) haue beene hitherto as
brieflye, as might well be) shewed vnto thee, the rules & aduises,
whereby thou oughtest to guide thy selfe, as wel on working, as on
holy daies : and howe thou maiest exercise thy selfe in Praier, & frequent very profitably the Sacraments of confession and Communion.
And because this our mortall life cannot be passed ouer without the
temptations & greeuous assaultes of such our aduersaries as heere in
this worlde doe enuirone vs, there are weapons and remedies giuen
vnto thee to vanquishe them, & to preserue thee from sinne, by meanes
wherof thou maiest also obtaine such vertues as be needful for thee.
Againe, for so much as this our temporal life is subiecte to many infirmities, and in fine to the dint of deathe, (which no man can [285]
auoide) for this cause I haue in this third Impression annexed 2. Chapters more thã there was before : wherin is shewed vnto thee, in what
sort thou must gouern thy selfe in time of sickenesse, whẽ it shall
please God therewith to visite thee, as also howe thou oughtest to
behaue thy selfe in the hour of death, whẽ our Lord shal through his
holye prouidence vouchsafe to bring thee to that time. This haue I
thought to be sufficiẽt for thee : that in case of the giuer of al goodnes
thou hast receaued a good wil & desire to amend thy life, & to liue like
a true Christian man, thou maiest by perusing this pamphlet, learne
how to obtaine thine intent, and to haue a firme trust and confidence to
enioye eternal life (which is the onely ende for which thou wast created.)

It resteth now, that for conclusion & knitting vp of this litle worke,
I admonishe thee, beseech thee, & exhort thee, as much as posibly may
lie in my power to do, that if thou hast once laide thy hande to the
plough, & begonne to exercise thy selfe in diuine seruice, taking [286]
the rules & aduises which in this Treat. are prescribed vnto thee for

The sum of the whole booke.

Luc. 9.

thy guide and gouernment, that in no wise thou looke backe againe, nor let thy selfe by any troubles & toiles, which may crosse thee in this life, be ouercome and vanquished. And if at any time it should so chāce, (as wel it may do oftētimes) that by reason of certaine lets & hindrances thou shouldst be for some space forced to intermit thine ordinary & woonted exercises, be not (I say) any whitte dismaide therewith, but when this time of trouble is once ouershot, renue againe thy course, & followe it as if thou hadst neuer failed, perseuering till the ende, as it is needful if thou minde to obtaine the Crowne of life, & to winne euerlasting happines. For in doing thus, I dare on the behalfe of our Lord and Sauiour assure thee, that this perseuerance shall ease the pain which at the first seemeth to be so great : & loke how much more thou shalt perseuere therein, so much more comfort, helpe, consolation, and heauenly light shalt thou receaue of his most bountiful liberallitye. Thou must [287] not therefore, content thy selfe with once reading ouer of this litle Treatise, but it behooueth thee often to read the same. For seing the things that are treated of in this Booke, are the rules & documentes by which thou must gouerne thy self in thy spiritual life, it shal be necessary for thee to reade them ouer at al times, whensoeuer thou meanest to put them in practise. And besides, that the bare reading thereof shal be a laudable & meritorious exercise, and after a sort stand in steede of praier : the reiterating & often reading ouer of the same, shall helpe thee to learne by heart, what in actiō thou are bound to execute : & thus maiest thou afterwards exercise thy self in euery point with a great deale more facility. Now albeit this litle labor may profit eury one that with good & godly intēt wil voutsafe to read the same, yet was it principally framed for the simple & more ignorant sort : & for that cause I haue also thought good to annexe here in the ende such things as many of thē wot not, & yet are bound to know. For if in case euery artisan thinke it ne-[288]cessary to knowe such things as belong vnto his Arte : how much more is a true Christian bounde to knowe what appertaineth to his profession, (beeing an Art aboue al Arts) & to be ready (as the Apo. *S. Peter* saith) to yeeld an account of that which he beleueth & hopeth for as also of that which he is bound to do, to liue according to Gods holye wil & ordinance, & to obtain euerlasting life. Wherfore, for such as be in this behalfe blame worthy & negligent, I haue here set downe such things, as without danger of their own wel doing, they nether ought, nor cā be ignorāt of, that by reading these notes & short remēbrances they may both

Mar. 15.
Mat. 24.
Luc. 12.
Apoc. 16.

This booke should be read aftentimes.

1. Pet. 3.

vnderstande what they knowe not, as also haue commodity to learne
the same, without farder seeking of other bookes. Nowe as for the
textes both of the *Creed,* the *10. Com.* & of the rest, I haue here set
thē forth, both in the latine & vulgar toungs, for euery one to learne
them, as they shal thinke it best. Neither ought any man so much to
regard the words therof, as the substance and doctrine conteined in the
same.

[This book concludes with a variety of prayers, explanations of
prayers, instructions, and meditations, pp. 289-441.]

II.

The First Booke of
the Christian Exer-
cise, appertayning to re-
solution.

Wherein are layed downe the
causes & reasons that should moue
a man to resolue hym selfe to the
seruice of God: And all the impedimentes remoued, which may lett
the same.

Psal. 62. vers. 4.

Vnam petii a domino, hanc requiram:
vt inhabitem in domo domini omni-
bus diebus vitae meae: vt videam vo-
luntatem domini.

One thing haue I requested at
gods hādes, & that will I demaunde
still: which is, to dwell in his house
all the daies of my life: to the
ende, I maye knowe and doe his will.

Anno. 1582.
With Privylege.[1]
[Robert Persons, S. J.[2]]

[A1ᵛ]

The Svmmarie of the Chri-
stian exercise, as it is intended.

For that three thyngs are necessarie to a man in this lyfe, for the attayning of saluation: that is, to resolue hym selfe to serue God in

---

[1]n.p. Init. R. P. Pr. [Rouen, Fr. Persons' press.] Allison and Rogers, II, Entry 619. *STC* 19353. In 1584, there was published a pirated edition of this book at Rouen (Allison and Rogers, II, Entry 620), and in the same year Edmund Bunny, the Anglican vicar of Bolton Percy, published a bowdlerized, Protestant edition, which before 1600 had run to nine issues (Southern, pp. 184-5). When Persons published the second edition in 1585, he changed the title to *Christian Directorie*. For accounts of the early history of this work and of the controversy that surrounded it, see Southern (pp. 183-186) and Herbert Thurston, "Catholic Writers and Elizabethan Readers," (pp. 467-469).

[2]Robert Persons (or Parsons) (1546-1610) was unquestionably one of the most remarkable and influential persons connected with the English Recusant Movement. He was a fellow of Balliol College in 1568 and received the M. A. degree in 1572. Later he was made bursar and dean at Balliol. In 1574, however, he resigned his fellowship and proceeded to Padua with the intention of studying medicine there. Stopping at Louvain on his way, he made the Spiritual Exercises of St. Ignatius under the direction of Fr. William Good, S. J., and was reconciled to the Catholic Church. In 1575, he was received into the Society of Jesus at Rome and was ordained a priest in 1578. At the urgent request of Pope Gregory XIII, Persons set off for his native England to engage in missionary work, accompanied by the famous Fr. Edmund Campion, S. J. They arrived in England on June 12, 1580, Persons being disguised as a soldier to avoid detection by the authorities. He made numerous converts among his countrymen and established the secret press at Greenstreet House for the publication of Catholic books (Southern, pp. 353-356). In 1581, he retired to the Continent, thereby escaping the fate of Edmund Campion. Persons was one of the most agile controversialists of his day; during his life time he wrote some thirty books and pamphlets in English, Latin, Spanish, and Italian. For a bibliography of his English works, see Allison and Rogers (II, Entries 611-642). Persons' phenomenal zeal for the Catholic cause in England led him to urge the Spanish succession to the throne of England, thereby incurring the disfavor of many Catholics as well as his Protestant adversaries. In 1588, he became the rector of the English College at Rome, and in 1589 and 1592, he aided in the establishing of English seminaries at Valladolid and at Seville. Likewise, he was virtually master of Douay College through his influence on Dr. Worthington, the president, who had taken secretly a vow of obedience to the Society of Jesus. Persons died in Rome on April 15, 1610. Although he was such an impressive figure, no modern biography of him has been written; however, the accounts of his life and activities in the *D. N. B.* (XV, 411-418) and in Gillow (V, 273-287) are quite full and interesting.

deed: to begynne a right: and to perseuere vnto the ende: therfor this whole treatise shalbe deuied vnto three bookes.[8]

The first booke shalbe of resolutiō, deuided into two partes. And in the first parte shalbe layed downe all the principall reasōs that ought to moue a man to this resolutiō. In the second shalbe remoued all impedimētes that commonlie doe hynder men from the same.

The seconde booke shall treate of the waye how to begynne well, and shall lykewyse be deuided into two partes: wherof the fyrst shall shew the waye how to delyuer ourselues from sinne, and from the custome, bondage or delectation therof. The second shall open the meanes, how to ioyne our selues perfectlie to God, and to make a right entrāce into his seruice.

The thirde booke shall hādle the meanes of perseuerance, so farre forthe as it concerneth our habilitie, for thogh this gyft be onelie of god: yet are there two thinges left by his grace to be performed of vs: the one, to aske his ayde: the other, to ioyne our endeuour with the same. According to which two pointes, this booke shalbe deuided also into two partes: The first wherof shall intreate of all kynde of prayer, bothe mētall and vocall. The secōd shall declare the wayes & meanes, how (by help of gods grace) we may resist & ouercome all sortes of sinne, & tēptatiōs therof.

[A2]

An Advertisement to the Reader.

I *hadde purposed (gētle reader) at the beginning, to haue printed againe, the Exercise of a Christian lyfe, composed by D. loartes, & trāslated (not lōg since) into our tōgue:[4] as may appeare by the preface foloweing. And albeit I minded to adde certaine matters and treatises vnto the same: yet ment I not, but to retayne so muche as therin was*

---

[8]Only the first of the three books originally intended was ever published.

[4]Persons is referring to Stephen Brinkley's translation of Gaspar Loarte's *The Exercise of a Christian Life* (1579). Persons' book has been considered for many years to be a very liberal translation of Loarte (Southern, p. 186; White, *English Devotional Literature*, p. 144); and Maria Hagedorn in her study of the influence of Granada on English devotional literature entitled *Reformation und Spanische Andachtsliteratur. Luis de Granada in England* (pp. 110-120) has attempted to show the influence of Granada on Persons. Both of these positions have been recently challenged by J. P. Driscoll in his "The Supposed Sources of Persons' 'The Christian Directory,'" (*Recusant History*, VI [1955], 235-243). Driscoll states, "A study of the *Christian Directory* and its contents, however, reveals that Persons did not borrow from Loarte at all, and if he borrowed from Granada, it was only in a minor way." (p. 236)

done before, esteeming it so well done (as in deed it is) as no altera-
tion needed therein. But yet notwithstanding, when I had sett downe
an other order & method to my selfe, than that booke foloweth: and
had begūne this first booke of resolution: wherof no parte is handled
in that treatise: I founde by experiēce, that I could not well ioyne that
with this: to satisfie, ether the order or argument by me cōceyued: &
therfore was I inforced, to resolue vpon a further labour, than at the
first I intended: whiche was, to drawe out the whole three bookes
myselfe: not omitting any thing, that is in the sayd Exercise, or other
like bookes, to this effect. Which thing by gods holy assistance, I meane
to doe, as time, healthe & libertie shall permit me.[5]

Now I am constrayned to breake of, for the presēt, & to send thee
onelie this first booke of resolutiō: which I beseeche our Lord may so
[A2ᵛ] worke in thy hart by his heauenlie grace, as I maye be īcouraged
therby the sooner to dispache the other two. God for our better triall
permitteth many difficulties, disturbances, lettes, & hynderāces, in
euerie thing that is takē in hād for his seruice: but yet, alwayes after,
he helpeth vs out agayne: as I know he will doe from tyme to tyme:
the cause being his: and much more importing hym than vs. The onelie
thing that he desireth at our hādes is, that we should once resolue our
selues throughelie to serue hym in deede: & consequētlie cast our
selues wholie īto his holy armes: without reseruatiō of any one iote
that we haue, vnto our selues: & then should we see, how good and
mercifull a lord he is: as now also we proue dailie beyond all desertes,
or expectatiō. Our lord blesse & preserue thee (gētle reader) & en-
riche thee with the guyftes of his holie grace: & when thou art amid-
dest thy deepest deuotiōs, I beseeche thee to haue some memorie of me
also, poore sinner: as I shall not be forgetfull of thee. But aboue all
others, lett vs bothe be myndfull to praye for our persecutors: who
finallie will proue to be our best freēdes: being in deed the hammers
which beate and polish vs, for makyng vs fytt stones, for the buylding
of gods new Ierusalem in heauen.

[Here follows the table of contents for the First Book, Sigs. A3ʳ-
A6ᵛ.]

---

[5]Southern suggests that the reason Persons decided against merely adapting
Brinkley's translation was that its appeal was too narrowly confined for his
purposes. Persons wanted to reach the unconverted masses and to set out
logical reasons why men should turn to God, whereas Loarte's book is primarily
intended to direct faithful Christians who merely needed a guide to the spiritual
life (p. 183).

[1]

To the Cristian
Reader Towchinge
two editions of this booke.

Abowt three yeres past (good reader) a certaine learned and de-uout gentilman, consideringe the greate want of spirituall bookes in Englande, for the direction of men to pietie & deuotiō (whiche ought to be the cheefest point of our exercise in this lyfe) tooke the paines to translate a godlye treatise to that effect, named, *the exercise of a Christian life,* writen in the Italian toung, by a reuerende man of the societie of Iesus, named Gasper Loartes, Doctor in diuinitie, and of greate experience in the handlinge and managinge of sowles to that purpose. Whiche booke because I vnderstande of certaintie, to haue done greate good, & to haue wrought forcebly in the hartes of manye persons, towards the foresayed effect of pietie and deuotion: I was moued to cause the same to be printed againe, and that in muche more ample manner than before, hauinge added vnto it, two partes of three, which were not in the former booke.

The reason of this so large an additiō shall [2] appeare in the Induction followinge, where shalbe shewed the partes of this booke, with the causes and cōtentes therof. But the principall cause and reason was, to the ende our countrye men might haue some one sufficiēt direc-tiō for matters of life and spirit, among so manye bookes of controuersies as haue ben writen, and are in writinge dailye. The whiche bookes, albeit in thes our troublesome & quarrelous times be necessarie for defence of our faithe, againste so manye seditious innouations, as now are attempted: yet helpe they litle oftentymes to good lyfe, but rather do fill the heades of men with a spirite of contradiction and contention, that for the most parte hindereth deuotiō, which deuotion is nothinge els, but a quiet and peaceble state of the sowle, endewed with a ioyful promptnes to the diligent execution of all thinges that appartayne to the honour of God. In respect wherof, S. Paule geeueth this counsayle to his scholer Timothie: *contende not in wordes, for it is profitable to nothinge, but to subuert the hearers.* The lyke counsayle he geuethe in diuers other places, in respect of this quiet deuotion, whiche is trowbled by contention.

But yet (as I haue saide) these bookes of controuersies are necessarie for other considerations, especialie in thes our tymes, when euerye man almost is made of a fancie, and apte to esteeme the same

A descrip-tion of deuotiō.

2. Ti. 2.

Bookes of cōtro-uersie ne-cessarie,

greate wisdome, except it be refuted. Suche are our dayes, most vnhappie truelye in respect of our fo-[3]refathers, whoe receauinge the grownde of faithe peaceably, & without quarelinge from their mother the Churche,* did attend onlye to builde vppon the same, good woorkes and Christian life, as their vocation required. But we spendinge all the tyme in ianglinge abowte the foundation, haue no leysure to think vpon the building, and so we wearye out our spirites without cõmoditie, we dye with muche adoe and litle profit, greate disquiet & small rewarde. For whoe knoweth not, that what faithe so euer a man hathe, yet without good lyfe it helpeth hym litle?

I am therfore of opinion (gentle reader) that albeit trew faithe be the grownde of Christianitie, without which nothinge of it selfe can be meritorious before God: yet that one principall meane to come to this trew faithe, and right knowledge, and to ende all thes our infinite cõtentions in religion, were for eche man to betake him selfe to a good & vertuous life, for that God could not of his vnspeakeable mercie suffer suche a man to erre lõge in religion. We haue a cleare exãple of Cornelius a Gentile to whome God in respect of his religious lyfe, prayer and almes deedes, (as the scripture affirmeth) sent his Apostle S. Peter to instruct him in the right faithe. So mercifull is God to those whiche applye thē selues to vertue and pietie, albeit they erre as yet in pointes of faithe.

And on the contrarie side, as loose lyfe and worldlye ambition, was the first cause of all heresye in Christian religion from the be-[4]ginninge: so is it the cõtinuance of the same,[6] and it is verie harde for him that is so affected to be recalled from his error. For that (as the scripture saithe) *the wisdome of God will not entre into a malitious minde, nor dwell in a bodye subiect to sinne.* And our Saueoure in the gospell askethe a question of certaine ambitious worldlynges, whiche geeuethe great light to the thinge we talke of: *how* (sayeth he) *can you beleeue, which seeke glorye one of an other?* as whoe woulde saie, that this worldly ambition and euill life of theirs, did make it impossible for them to come to the trewe faithe.

Wherfore (gentle reader) if thow be of an other religiõ than I am, I beseeche the most hartelye, that layenge a side all hatred, malice and wrathfull contention, let vs ioyne together in amendmēt of our lyues,

---

[6]The idea of reforming morals and improving the spiritual life of Christians as means of stemming and correcting heresy was a prevalent one among Catholics of the Recusant Movement. See pp. 7-8 of the introduction.
*Churche] *ed.;* Chuche.

and prayeng one for an other: and God (no doubt) will not suffer vs to perishe finallye for want of right faithe. And to Catholiques I must saye further withe S. Paule and S. Iames, that all their faith will profitt them nothinge, except they haue charitie allso, bothe towardes God and man, and therby doe directe their lyues accordinglye. Whiche God of his holye mercye geeue them grace to doe, to his honour and their eternall saluation. And I most humblye request the (good Christian reader) to praie for me allso, (if thow take any commoditie by this booke) that I be not like the Conduit pipe whiche bringeth water to the citie, without drinkinge anye it selfe, or as [5] S. Paule withe muche lesse cause than I haue, feared of hym selfe, to witt, lesse that after preachinge to other, I become perchaunce a reprobate my selfe. Remēbre allso I beseeche the, that most vertuous good gentilman, whoe by his first translation, was the cause of this labour now taken againe. He hathe suffered much sence for the cause of his conscience, and is at this present vnder indurāce for the same,[7] and by that meanes, so muche the more in disposition to receaue fruite by thy prayer, by howe muche the more he hathe suffered for righteousnes sake, and is nearer ioined to God by his separation from the world. Our lorde blesse him and the allso (good reader) and sende vs all his holy grace, to doe his will in this woorld, that we maye raigne with him in the world to come. Amen.

1. Co. 13.
Iaco. 2.

1. Cor. 9.

Thy hartie welwiller and seruant in Christ.

R[obert] P[ersons]

[Here follows "An Induction to the three bookes followinge," pp. 6-9; page 10 is blank.]

[11]

The First Booke
and First Parte.

*Of the end and partes of this booke, withe
a necessarie aduertissement to
the reader.*

Chap. I.

The first booke (as I haue shewed before) hathe for his proper end, to perswade a Christian by name, to become a trewe Christian

The en-
de of this
booke.

---

[7]Stephen Brinkley (as noted above) was imprisoned in the Tower from 1581-1583 after the seizure of his press.

Two partes of this booke.

in deed, at the leaste, in resolution of mynde. And for that there be two principall thinges necessarie to this effect: therefore this first booke shalbe deuided into two partes. And in the first shalbe declared important reasons and strong motyues, to prouoke a man to this resolution. In the second shalbe refuted all the impedimentes, whiche our spirituall enymies (the fleshe the world & the deuyll) are wont to laye for the stoppinge of the same, knowinge very well, that of this resolution dependethe all our good in the life to come. For he that neuer resolueth hym selfe to doe well and to leaue the dangerous state of synne wherin he lyuethe, is farof from euer doynge the

The necessitie of resolution.

same. But he that sometymes resolueth to doe it, althoughe by frayltie [12] he performethe it not at that tyme, yet is that resolution much acceptable before God, and his mynd the rediar to returne after to the like resolution againe, and by the grace of God, to putt it manfully in execution. But he that willfully resistethe the good

Act. 7. Apoc. 3.

motions of the holly ghost, and vncurteouslie contemnethe his Lorde, knockinge at the doore of his conscience, greatly prouokethe the indignation of God agaynst hym, and cōmonlye growethe harder &

Rom. 1.

harder daylye, vntill he be giuen ouer into a reprobate sense, which is the next doore to damnation it selfe.

An aduertisement.

One thinge therfore I must aduertyse the reader before I goe any further, that he take greate heede of a certayne principall deceyt of our ghostlye aduersarie, whereby he drawethe many millions of soules into hell daylye. Whiche is, to feare and terrifie them from hearinge or readinge any thinge contrarye to theyre present humor or resolution. As for example, a vsurer, from readinge bookes of restitution: a lecherer, from readinge discourses against that synne: a worldlinge, from readinge spirituall bookes or treatyses of deuotion. And he vsethe commonlye this argumēt to thē for his purpose: Thow seest how thow art not yet resolued to leaue this trade of lyfe,

The deuyles argument.

wherin thow art: & therfore the readinge of these bookes will but trouble & afflict thy conscience, and caste the into sorrowe and melancholye, and therfore reade them not at all. This (I saye, is a cunninge sleyght of Satan, wherby he [13] leadethe manye blyndfolded to perdition, euen as a faulkener carriethe many hawkes quyetly beinge hooded, whiche other wyse he could not doe, yf they hadd the vse of their sight.

Wilfull ignoran-

If all ignorance dyd excuse synne, than this might be some refuge for thē that would lyue wickedlye: But this kinde of ignorāce, (beinge voluntarie and willfull) increasethe greatlye bothe the sinne & the synners euell state. For of this man the holye ghost speakethe in great dysdayne. *Noluit intelligere vt bene ageret. He would not vnderstande to doe well.* And agayne: *quia tu scientiam repulisti, repellam te. For that thou hast reiected knoledge, I will reiect the.* And of the same men in an other place the same holye ghost sayethe: *they doe leade their lyues in pleasure, and in a moment goe downe vnto hell, whiche saye to God, goe frome vs, we will not haue the knowledge of thy wayes.* Let euery man therfore be ware of this deceyt, and be contente at the least, to reade goode bookes, to frequent deuoute companye and other lyke goode meanes, of his amendment, albeit he were not yet resolued to follow the same: yea althoughe he should fynde some greeff & repugnaunce in hym selfe to doe it. For these thinges can neuer doe hym hurte, but maye chaunce to doe hym very muche goode: and perhappes the very contrarietie and repugnance which he bearethe in frequentinge these thinges against his inclination, may moue our mercifull lorde, whiche seethe his harde case, to [14] gyue hym the victorye ouer hym selfe in the ende, and to send hym much more cōforte in the same, than before he hadd dislyke. For he can easelie doe it onelie by alteringe our taste withe a litle droppe of his holye grace, and so make those thinges seeme most sweet and pleasant, whiche before tasted bothe bitter and vnsauerye.

Wherfore as I would hartelye wyshe euery Christian soule, that comethe to reade these cōsiderations folowinge, should come with an indefferent mynde, layed downe wholly into godes handes, to resolue & doe as it should please his holy spirite to moue hym vnto, althoughe it were to the losse of all worldlye pleasures what so euer: (whiche resignation is absolutlie necessarye to euery one that desirethe to be saued:) so yf some can not presentlye wynne that indifferencie of them selues: yet would I counsayle thē in any case to cōquer theyr myndes to so much patience, as to goe throughe to the ende of this booke, & to see what maye be sayde at leaste to the matter, althoughe it be withoute resolution to followe the same. For I doubt not, but God maye so pearse these mennes hartes before they come to the ende, as their myndes maye be altered & they yealde them selues vnto the humble & sweete seruice of theyr lorde and sauiour, and that the Angells in heauen (whiche will not ceasse to praye for theym whyle they are readinge, maye reioyce and triumphe of theyr regayninge, as of sheepe most dangerouslye loste before.

ce increasethe sinne.
Psal. 35.

Ose. 4.

Iob. 21.
See. S. Austen of this sinn: de gra. & lib. arbi. cap. 3. & S. Chrisostome. homi. 26 in epist. ad Rom.

What mynde a man should bringe to the readinge of this booke.

Luc. 15.

[Here follow Chapters II-X, a discussion of the necessity to meditate on one's state in life, of the end of man, and of man's need to yield to God, a consideration of the nature of sin, a consideration of God's judgments and our demerits, a treatise on death, a discussion of the pains appointed for sin after this life, and a consideration of the rewards for the just, pp. 15-184.]

[185]

The Second Part
of This First Booke

Of impedimentes that lett men from this reso-
lution: and first, of the difficultie or hard-
nesse, whiche seemeth to many to
be in vertuouse lyfe.

Chap. I.

Notwithstanding all the motiues and consideratiõs before sett downe, for inducing men to this necessarie resolution of seruing God, for their saluatiõ: there want not many Christiãs abrode ĩ the world, whose hartes, ether intangled with the pleasures of this lyfe, or geuen ouer by God to a reprobate sense, doe yeeld no whit at all to this batterie, that hath bene made, but sheweing them selues more hard than adamant, doe not onelie resist and contemne, but also doe seek excuses for their slothe and wickednesse, and do alleage reasons of their own perdition. Reasons I call them, according to the cõmon phrase, though in deede, there be no one thing more against reason, than that a man shoulde become enemye to his own soule, as the scripture affirmeth obstinate sinners to bee. But yet (as I say) they haue their excuses. And the first and [186] principall of all ys that, vertuouse lyfe is painfull and harde, and therfore they can not endure to folow the same: especiallie such as haue bene brought vp delicatlye, and neuer were acquainted with such asperitie, as (they saye) we require at their hands. And this is a great, large, and vniuersall impedimẽt, which stayeth infinite men from embracinge the meanes of their saluation. For which cause yt is fullie to be answered in this place.

First then supposing that the way of vertue were so hard in deede, as the enemie maketh it seeme yet might I well saye with S. Iohn

Margin notes:
Ep. Iud.
Rom. 1.

Pro. 18.
& 20.
Psa. 140.

Tob. 12.
Pro. 29.

Lib. de

Chrisostom, that seeyng the rewarde is so great and infinite as now we haue declared: no labour should seeme great for gayning of the same. Agayne, I might say with holy S. Austen, That seeing we take dayly so great payne in this worlde, for auoyding of small incōueniences, as of sicknes, imprysonemētes losse of goodes and the lyke: what paynes should we refuse for auoyding the eternitie of hell fyre sett downe before? The first of these cōsideratiōs S. Paul vsed when he sayd, *the sufferinges of this lyfe are not worthie of the glorie which shall be reuealed in the next.* The second, S. Peter vsed, when he sayed, seeing the heauenes must be dissolued, and Christ come in Iudgement to restore to euery man according to his woorkes: what maner of men ought we to be in holy conuersation? As whoe wold say: No labour, no paynes, no trauayle ought to seeme hard or greate vnto vs, to the ende we myght auoyde the terrour of [187] that daye. S. Austen asketh this question: what we thinke the riche gloutton in hell wolde doe, yf he were now in this lyfe again? wolde he take paynes or no? wolde he bestyrre hym selfe, rather than turne into that place of torment againe? I might adde to this, the infinite paynes that Christ tooke for vs: the infinite benefites he hathe bestowed vpon vs: the infinite sinnes we haue cōmitted against hym: the infinite examples of Sainctes, that haue trooden this pathe before vs: in respect of all whiche, we ought to make no boones at litle paynes and labour, yf it were true that gods seruice were so trauailsome as many doe esteeme yt.

But now in verie deede the matter is nothing so, and this is but a subtile deceate of the enemie for our discouragemēt. The testimonie of Christ hym selfe is cleare in this poynte: *Iugum meum suaue est, & onus meum leue:* My yooke is sweete, and my burden light. And the dearlie beloued disciple S. Iohn, who had best cause to know his maisters secret herein, sayeth playnlie. *Mandata eius grauia non sunt,* hys commaundements are not greeuouse. What is the cause then why so many men doe conceaue suche a difficultie in this matter? surelie, one cause is, (besyde the subtilitie of the deuill which is the cheefest) for that men feele the disease of concupiscence in their bodies, but doe not consider the strengthe of the medicine geuen vs against the same, they crye with S. Paul, *that they fynde a law in their members repugning* [188] *to the law of their mynde,* (whiche is the rebellion of concupiscence left in our flesh by originall synne:) but they confesse not, or cōsider not with the same S. Paul, *that the grace of God, by Iesus Christ, shall delyuer them from the same.* They remember not

cōpunct. Cordis.

Hom. 16. ex 50.

Rom. 8. 2. Pet. 2.

Luc. 16.

The waye of vertue is not hard.

Mat. 12.

1. Ioh. 5.

The cause of pretended difficulti <e>.

Ibidem.

the comfortable sayeing of Christ to S. Paul, in his greatest tēptations:
Sufficit tibi gratia mea: My grace is sufficient to strengthen thee
against them all. These men doe as Helizeus his discipie dyd, whoe
casting his eyes onelye vpon his enemies, that is vpon the huge armie
of Syrians redie to assault hym, thought hym selfe lost & vnpossible to
stand in their sight, vntill by the prayers of the holye prophet he was
permitted from God, to see the Angels that stoode there present to
fyght on his syde, & then he well perceaued that his parte was the
stronger.

So these men, beholding onelye our miseries & infirmities of
nature, wherby daylie, tentations do ryse against vs: doe account the
battaill paynfull, and the victorie vnpossible, hauing not tasted in
deed, nor euer proued (through their own negligence) the manifold
helpes of grace and spirituall succours, which God all wayes sendeth
to them, who are content (for his sake) to take this conflict in hand.
S. Paul had well tasted that ayde, whiche hauing reckned vp all the
hardest matters that coulde be, addeth: *Sed in his omnibus super-*
amus propter eum qui dilexit nos: But we ouercome in al these
combates, by his assistance, that loueth vs. And then falleth he to
that woun-[189]derful protestatiō: that nether death, nor lyfe, nor
Angels, nor the lyke, should separate him: & all this vpon the cōfi-
dence of spirituall ayd frō Christ, wherby he sticketh not to avouch
that he could doe all things. Dauid also had proued the force of this
assistance, whoe sayde, *I dyd runne the way of thy cōmaūdemētes,*
when thou dyddest enlarge my hart. This enlargemēt of hart, was by
spirituall consolation of internall vnction, wherby the hart drawen
together by anguishe is opened and enlarged: when grace is powred
in, euen as a drye purse ys softened and enlarged by annoynting it
with oyle. Which grace being present, Dauid sayed, he dyd not
onelye walke the way of gods commaundements easilie, but that he
ranne them: Euen as a carte wheele whiche crieth and cōpleyneth,
vnder a small burden being drye, runneth merilye and without
noyse, whē a litle oyle is put vnto it. Which thinge aptlye expresseth
our state and condition, whoe without gods help, are able to doe
nothing, but with the ayde thereof, are hable to conquere and ouercome any thing.

And surelie I wolde aske these men that imagine the waye of
Gods law to be so hard and full of difficultie, how the prophet could
saye, *I haue taken pleasure (o lord) in the waye of thy com-*

2. Co. 12.

4. Re. 6.

1. The for-
ce of gra-
ce for the
easing of
vertuous
lyfe.

Rom. 8.

Phil. 4.

Psa. 118.

maundementes as in all the riches of the worlde. And in an other
place: *That they were more pleasant and to be desyred, than golde
or pretious stone, and more sweter than hony or the hony combe?*
by which woordes he yeeldeth to vertuouse lyfe, not onely due estimation [190] aboue all treasures in the world: but also pleasure,
delyte, and sweetnesse: therby to confound all those that abandone
and forsake the same, vpon ydle pretensed and feyned difficulties.
And yf Dauid could say this muche in the olde law: how muche
more iustlie may we say so now in the new, when grace is geuen
more abundantlie, as the scripture sayeth? And thow poore Christian whiche deceauest thy selfe with this imagination: tell me, whye
came Christ into this worlde? whye laboured hee and tooke he so
much paines heere? whie shed he his bloode? whie praied he to his
father so oftē for thee? whie appointed he the sacramētes as cōduites
of grace? whie sent he the holye ghoste into the worlde? what signifieth gospell or good tydings? what meaneth the woord grace and
mercie broght with him? what importeth the cōfortable name of
Iesus? is not all this to delyuer vs frō sinne? frō sinne past, (I say)
by his onlye deathe: frō sinne to come, by the same deathe and by the
assistance of his holy grace bestowed on vs more abundantlie
than before by all these meanes? was not this one of the principall
effectes of Christ his coming as the prophet noted: that *craggie
wayes should be made streight, and hard wayes playne?* was not this
the cause whie he indewed his churche with the seuen blessed gyftes
of the holie ghoste? and with the vertues infused, to make the yooke
of his seruice sweete, the exercise of good lyfe easye, the walking in
his commaundementes pleasant, in such sort, [191] as men might now
sing in tribulations, haue confidence in periles, securitie in afflictions, and asseurance of victorie in all tēptations? is not this the
begynnyng, mydle, & ende, of the gospell? were not these the promises of the prophetes, the tydinges of the euāgelistes, the preachinges
of the Apostles, the doctrine, beleefe, and practise of all saincts? and
finallie is not this *verbum abbreuiatum:* The woord of God abbreuiated, wherein doe consist all the riches and treasures of Christiantie?

If any man will be contentiouse and aske me how God doeth this
maruailous woorke: I answere hym (as I haue done before) that he
doeth it by the assistance of his holie grace, poured into the soule of
man, wherby it is beautified and strengthened against all temptations
as S. Paul was in particular against temptations of the fleshe. And
this grace is, of suche efficacie and force in the soule where it en-

Right margin notes:

Psa. 118.

Psa. 18.

Ioh. 10.
Rom. 5.
Heb. 6.

Matt. 1.

Esa. 40.
Esa. 11.
Et vide
Ier. ibi.
Amb. lib.
1. de <.> sp.
S. c, 20 Au.
ser. 209.
de temp.

Matt. 5.
Luc. 6.
Act. 4.

2. Co. 4.

Esa. 10.

Of the
force of
grace.

2. Co. 12.

tereth, that it altereth the whole state thereof, making those thinges
cleare which were obscure before: those thinges pleasant, which
were bytter before: those thinges easie, which were hard & difficult
before. And for this cause also it is sayed in scripture, to make a
new spirit and a new hart. As where Ezechiel talking of this matter

Exo. ca.
11. & 36.

sayeth in the persone of God: *I will geue vnto them a new hart, and
will put a new spirit in their bowelles that they may walke in my
preceptes and keepe my commaundementes.* Can any thing in the
worlde bespoken more playnlie? Now for mortifyeing and conquer-
ing of our passions, [192] whiche by rebellion doe make the way of
gods commaundementes vnpleasant: S. Paul testifieth clearlie, that
abundāt grace is geeuē to vs also by the deathe of Christ, to doe the

Rom. 6.

same: for so he sayeth: *This we know that our olde man is crucified
also to the ende that the bodie of sinne may be destroyed, and we
serue no more vnto sinne.* By the olde man and the bodie of Sinne
S. Paul vnderstandeth our rebellious appetite and concupiscence,
which is so crucified and destroyed by the most noble sacrifice of
Christ, as we may by the grace purchased vs in that sacrifice, resist
and conquer this appetite, and so keepe our selues from seruitude of

So pro-
ueth S.
Au. li. 2.
de pec-
ca. merit
cap. 6.

Esa. 41.

sinne: that is from any consent or taste of sinne, yf we will our
selues. And this is that noble and intire victorie, whiche God promised so long agoe to euerie Christian soule by the meanes of Christ,
when he sayd: Be not a feard for I am with thee: stepp not aside,
for I thy God haue strengthened thee, and haue assisted thee: and
the right hand of my iust (man,) hathe taken thy defence. Beholde
all that fight against thee shalbe confounded and put to shame: thow
shalt seeke thy rebelles, & shalt not find thē: they shalbe as thoughe
they were not, for that I am thy Lord and God.

Loe heere a full victorie promised vpon our rebelles, by the helpe
of the right hād of gods iust man, that is vpon our disordinate passions by the ayde of grace frō Iesus Christ. And albeit these rebelles
are not heere promised to be taken cleane awaye, but onelye [193] to
be conquered and confounded: yet is it sayed *that they shalbe as
thoghe they were not.* Wherby is signified, that they shall not

A simili-
tude.

hynder vs in the way of our saluation, but rather further the same,
yf we will. For as wilde beastes which of nature are fearse, and
wold rather hurt thā profitt mankinde, being maistred and tamed,
become verie cōmodiouse & necessarie for our vses: so these rebel-
liouse passions of ours, whiche of them selues wold vtterlie ouer-

throwe vs, being once subdued and mortified by gods graces and our owne diligence: doe stand vs in singular steade to the practise and exercise of all kynde of vertues: as choler or angre to the inkyndeling of zeale: hatred to the pursewinge of sinne: a hautie mynde, to the reiecting of the world: loue, to the embracing of all great and heroicall attemptes in consideration of the benefites receaued from God. Beside this the verie conflict and combate it selfe, in subdewing these passions is left vnto vs for our greate good: that is, for our patience, humilitie, and victorie in this lyfe: and for our merit, glorie, and croune in the lyfe to come: as S. Paul affirmed of hym selfe, and cōfirmed to all others, by his* example. The vse of passiōs moderated. 2. Tim. 4.

Now then lett the slothefull Christian *goe putt his handes vnder his gyrdle,* as the scripture sayeth, and saye: *There is a lyon in the waye, and a lyonesse in the pathe, redie to deuoure hym,* that he dare not goe furthe of doors. Let him saye: *It is colde, and therefore he dareth not goe to plowe.* Let hym saye, it is vneasie to [194] labour: *& therfore he can not purge his vyneyarde of nettles and thystles, nor buyld any wall about the same.* That is, let hym saye his passions are strong, & therfore he can not conquere them: his body is delicate, and therfore he dare not put it to trauayle: the way of vertuouse lyfe is hard and vneasie, and therfore he can not applye hym selfe therunto. Let hym saye all this, and muche more, which ydle and slothefull Christians doe vse to bryng for their excuse: let hym alleage it (I say) as muche and as often as he will: it is but an excuse, and a false excuse, and an excuse moste dishonorable & detractorie to the force of Christ his grace, purchased vs by his bytter passion: that now his yoke should be vnpleasant, seing he hathe made it sweete: that now his burden, shoulde be heauie, seing he hathe made it light: that now his commaundementes should be greeuous, seinge the holie ghoste affirmeth the contrarie: that now we should be in seruitude of our passions, seinge he hathe by his grace delyuered vs, and made vs truelie free. *If God be with vs,* whoe will be against vs,* sayeth the Apostle? *God is my helper and defender* (sayeth holie Dauid,) *whome shall I feare, or tremble?* If whole armies should rise against me: yet will I allway hope to haue the victorie. And what is the reason? *for that thow art with me* (o lord:) thow fyghtest on my side: thou assistest me with thy grace: by helpe whereof I shall haue the victorie, thoghe all the squadrones

Pro. 26.
Pro. 20.
Pro. 24.
Mat. 11.
1. Ioh. 5. Ioh. 8. Rom. 7.
Rom. 8. Psal. 26. 27.
Psal. 22.

---

*his] *ed.;* <. .>s
**with vs,] *ed.;* with, vs

of my enemies, that is, of the fleshe, the world, and the deuill, should [195] ryse against me at once: and I shall not onelie haue the victorie, but also shall haue it easilie, and with pleasure and delite.

1. Ioh. 5. For, so muche signifieth S. Iohn in that (hauing saied that the commaundementes of Christ are not greeuous:) he inferreth presētlie, as the cause thereof: *Quoniam omne quod natum est ex deo vincit mundum.* For that all whiche is borne of God, conquerith the worlde: that is, his grace and heauenlie assistance sent vs from God doeth bothe cōquer the world, with all difficulties and temptations therof: and also maketh the commaundements of God easie, and vertuous lyfe most pleasant and sweete.

An obiection, answered. But perhappes you will saye: Christ him selfe confesseth it to be a yoke, and a burden: how then can it be so pleasant and easie as you make yt? I answer, that Christ addeth that it is a sweete yoke and a light burden. Wherby your obiection is taken away: and also is signified further, that there is a burden whiche greeueth not the bearer, but rather helpeth and refresheth the same: as the burden of fethers vppon a byrdes backe beareth vpp the byrd, and is nothinge **Psa. 118.** at all greeuous vnto her: So also thoghe it be a yoke, yet is it a sweete yoke, a comfortable yoke, a yoke more pleasant than hony or hony combe, as sayeth the prophet. And whie so? because we drawe therin, with a sweete companion, we drawe with Christ: that is, his grace at one end, and our endeuour at the other. And because when a great oxe & a litle doe drawe together, the weight lyeth all vppon the [196] greater oxe his necke, for that he beareth vp quite the yoke from the other: therof it cometh, that we draweing in this yoke together with Christ, whiche is greater than we are: he lighteneth vs of the whole burden, & onelie requireth that we should goe on with hym comfortablie, and not refuse to enter vnder the yoke with hym, for that the payne shalbe his, and the pleasure oures. This he signi- **Mat. 11.** fieth expresselie when he sayeth: *come you to me all that labour and are heauie loden and I will refreshe you.* Heere you see that he moueth vs to this yoke, onelie therby to refreshe and disburden vs: to disburden vs (I saye) and to refreshe vs, and not any waye to loade or agreeue vs: to disburden vs of the heauye loadinges and yokes of this world: as from the burden of a guiltie conscience, the burden of care, the burden of melancholie, the burden of enuye, hatred, and malice, the burden of pryde, the burden of ambition, the burden of couetousnes, the burden of wrathe, the burden of feare, the burden of wickednesse, and hell fire it selfe. From all these burdens and miserable yokes, Christ wold delyuer vs, by coueringe our neckes onelie with his yoke and burden, so lightned and sweetned by his holy grace, as the bearinge therof is not trauailsome, but most easie, pleasant, and confortable, as hathe bene shewed.

An other cause why this yoke is so sweete: this burden so light, and this waie of gods commaundemētes so pleasant to good men, is loue: loue (I meane) towards God, whose [197] commaundementes they are: for euery man can tell, and hathe experienced in hym selfe, what a strong passion, the passion of loue is, and how it maketh easie the verie greatest paynes that are in this world. What maketh the mother to take suche paynes in the bringing vpp of her child, but onelie loue? what causeth the wyfe to sytt so attentyue at the bedde syde of her sycke husbande, but onelie loue? what moueth the beastes and byrdes of the ayer, to spare from their owne foode, and to endaunger their own lyues, for the feedinge and defendinge of their litle ones, but onelie the force of loue? S. Austen doeth prosecute this pointe at large by many other examples, as of Marchantes that refuse no aduenture of sea, for loue of gayne: of huntars, that refuse no season of euill weather, for loue of game: of soldiers that refuse no daunger of deathe, for loue of spoyle. And he addeth in the end: that yf the loue of man can be so great towardes creatures heere, as to make labour easie, & ī deede to seeme no labour, but rather pleasure: how muche more shall the loue of good men towardes god make all their labour comfortable, whiche they take in his seruice.

This extreme loue was the cause whie all the paynes & afflictiōs which Christ suffered for vs, seemed nothing vnto hym. And this loue also was the cause why all the trauailes & tormentes whiche many Christianes haue suffered for Christ, seemed nothing vnto them. Imprisonmētes, tormentes, losse of ho-[198]nour, goodes, and lyfe, seemed tryfles to diuers seruantes of God, in respect of this burning loue. This loue droue infinite virgines, and tender children to offer them selues, in tyme of persecutiō, for the loue of him which in the cause was persecuted. This loue caused holye Apollonia of Alexandria, beinge broght to the fyre to be burned for Christ, to flypp out of the handes of suche as ledde her, & ioyfullie to runne into the fire, of her selfe. This loue moued Ignatius, the auncient Martyre to saye (being condemned to beastes, & fearing leste they

2. Loue maketh the waye pleasant.

The force of loue.

Ser. 9. de verbis domini.

The loue of Christ to his saintes, & of his saintes* to hym.

Euseb. li. 6. c. 34.

Ierom in catalogo.

---

*saintes] *ed.;* saites

wolde refuse his bodie, as they had done of diuers Martyres before) that he wolde not permitt them so to doe, but wolde prouoke and styrre them to come vpō hym, and to take his lyfe from hym, by tearing his body in peeces.

These are the effectes then of feruent loue, which maketh, euen the thinges that are most difficult and dreadfull of them selues, to appeare sweete and pleasant: and much more the lawes and com-maundementes of God, whiche in them selues are moste iust, reason-able, holye and easie. *Da amantem* (sayeth S. Austen speaking of this matter,) *& sentit quod dico: Si autem frigido loquor, nescit quid loquar:* Geue me a man that is in loue with God: and he feeleth this to be true, whiche I saye: but yf I talke to a colde Christian: he vnderstandeth not what I saye. And this is the cause whie Christ talking of the keeping of his cōmaundementes, repeateth so often this woorde *loue,* as the onelye sure cause of kee-[199]ping the same: for wāt whereof in the world, the world keepeth them not, as there he sheweth. *If you loue me, keepe my commaunde-mentes:* sayeth he: and againe: *He that hathe my commaunde-mentes, and keepeth them, he is he, that loueth me.* Agayne: *He which loueth me, will keepe my commaundement: and he that loueth me not: keepeth not my cōmaundemētes.* In which last woordes, is to be noted, that to the louer, he sayeth *his cōmaundement* in the singular number: for that to suche a one all his commaundementes are but one commaundement, according to the sayeing of S. Paul: *That loue is the fullnesse of the lawe:* For that it comprehendeth all. But to hym that loueth not, Christ sayeth *his commaundementes* in the plurall number: signifyeing thereby, that they are bothe many and heauie to hym: for that he wanteth loue, whiche should make them easie. Whiche, S. Iohn also expresseth, when he sayeth: *this is the loue of God, when we keepe his commaundementes, and his com-maundementes are not heauie.* That is, they are not heauye to hym, whiche hathe the loue of God: otherwyse no maruaile thoughe they be moste heauie. For that euerie thing seemeth heauie whiche we doe against our lyking. And so by this also (gentle reader) thow mayest gesse, whether the loue of God be in thee, or no.

And these are two meanes now, wherby the lyfe of good men is made easie in this worlde. There folow diuers other to the end that these negligent excusers may see, how vniust and vntrue this excuse of theyrs is cō-[200]cerninge the pretended hardnes of vertuous

Psa. 6 &
18.
Mat. 11.
1. Io. 5.
Tra. 26.
in Iohā.

Ioh. 14.

Marke
this ob-
seruatiō.

Rom. 13.

1. Io. 5.

3. Pecu-
liar light
of under-
standing.

lyuing: whiche in verie deede is indewed with infinite priuileges of
comfort, aboue the lyfe of wicked men, euen in this world. And the
next that I will name for example sake after the former, is a certaine speciall and peculiar light of vnderstanding, pertayning to the   Prou. 9.
iust, and called in scripture *prudentia sanctorum.* The wisdome of
Saintes: which is nothing eles but a certayne sparkle of heauenlie
wisdome, bestowed by singular priuilege vpon the vertuouse in this
lyfe: wherby they receyue moste comfortable light, and vnderstanding in spirituall matters, especiallie towching their owne saluation, &
thinges necessarie therunto. Of whiche the prophet Dauid meant,
when he sayed, *notas mihi fecisti vias vitae.* Thow hast made the   Psal. 16
wayes of lyfe knowen to me. Also when he sayde of hym selfe.
Super senes intellexi. I haue vnderstoode more than olde men. And   Psa. 118.
agayne in an other place: *Incerta & occulta sapientiae tuae mani-*   Psal. 50.
festasti mihi: Thow hast opened to me the vnknowen and hydden
secretes of thy wisedome. This is that light wherwith S. Iohn sayeth
that Christ lighteneth his seruantes: as also that vnction of the holye   Ioh. 1.
ghoste, whiche the same Apostle teacheth to be geuen to the godlie,
to instructe them in all thinges behoofefull for their saluation. In   I. Io. 2.
like wyse this is that writing of gods lawe in mennes hartes, whiche
he promiseth by the prophet Ieremie: as also the instruction of men   Iero. 31.
immediatlye from God him selfe, promised by the [201] prophet   Esa. 54.
Esaye. And finallie this is that soueraigne vnderstanding in the lawe,
commaundementes, and iustificationes of God, whiche holy Dauid so
muche desired, and so often demaunded in that most diuine psalme,
whiche begynneth: *Blessed are the vnspotted in the waye:* That is,   Ps. 118.
in this lyfe.

By this light of vnderstandinge, & supernaturall knowlege & feeling from the holie ghost, in spirituall thinges, the vertuouse are
greatlie holpen in the waye of rightetousnes for that they are made
able to discerne, for their owne direction in matters that occurre,
accordinge to the sayeing of S. Paul: *Spiritualis omnia iudicat:* A
spirituall man iudgeth of all thinges: *Animalis autem homo non*   1. Co. 2.
percipit quae sunt spiritus dei: But the carnall man conceaueth not
the thinges whiche appertayne to the spirit of God. Doeth not this
greatlie discouer the priuiledge of a vertuous lyfe? the ioye comfort
and consolation of the same? with the exceeding great miserie of
the contrarie parte? for yf two should walke together, the one
blynde, and the other of perfect sight, which of them were lyke to be
wearie first? whose iourney were like to be more paynfull? doeth not

a litle grownde wearie out a blynde man? consider then in howe
wearysome darkenesse the wicked doe walke: Cōsider whether they
be blynde or no. S. Paul sayeth in the place before alleaged, that
they can not conceaue any spirituall knowlege: is not this a great
darkenesse? Agayne, the prophet Esay describeth their [202] state
further, when he sayeth in the persone of the wicked, *we haue
grooped lyke blynde men after the walles, and haue stumbled at
myddaye, euen as yf it had beene in darkenesse.* And in an other
place, the scripture describeth the same, yet more effectuouslie, with
the paynfullnesse therof, euen from the mouthes of the wicked them
selues, in these woordes: *The light of Iustice hathe not shyned vnto
vs, and the sunne of vnderstanding hathe not appeared vnto our
eyes: we are wearyed out in the waye of iniquitie & perditiō etc.
This is the talke of sinners in hell.* By which woordes appeareth, not
onelye that wicked men doe lyue in great darkenesse: but also that
this darkenesse is most paynefull vnto them: and consequently that
the contrarie light, is a great easement to the waye of the vertuous.

An other principall matter which maketh the waye of vertue
easye and pleasant to them that walke therein, is a certaine hidden
and secret consolation, which God poureth in to the hartes of them
that serue hym. I call yt secret: for that it is knowen but of such
onelye as haue felt it: for which cause, Christ hym selfe calleth yt,
hydden manna knowen onelye to them that receaue it. And the
prophet sayeth of yt, *greate is the multitude of thy sweetnes (o
Lord,) which thou haste hydden for them that feare thee.* And
againe, in an other place, *thou shalt laye asyde (o Lord) a speciall
chosen rayne or dewe for thyne inheritance.* And an other prophet
sayeth in the persone of god, talking of the deuoute soule that
serueth hym: *I will* [203] *leede her a side into a wildernesse, and
there I will talk vnto her harte.* By all which woordes, of *wildernesse, separating, choyse,* and *hydden,* is signified, that this is a
secret priuilege bestowed onelie vppon the vertuouse, and that the
carnall hartes of wicked men, haue no parte or portion therein. But
now, how great and inestimable the sweetenesse of this heauenlie
consolation is, no tongue of man can expresse: but we may coniec-
ture by these woordes of Dauid, whoe, talking of this celestiall
wyne, attributeth to yt suche force, as to make all those drounken
that taste of the same: that is, to take from them, all sense and
feeling of terrestriall matters, euen as S. Peter hauing drounke a

1. Cor. 2.

Esa. 65.

Sap. 5.

4. Inter-
nall con-
solation.

Apo. 2.

Psa. 30.

Psal. 67.

Ose. 2.

Psal. 35.
& 64.

litle of yt vppon the mounte Thabor, forgate hym selfe presentlie, and talked as a man distracted, of building tabernacles there, and resting in that place for euer. This is that *torrens voluptatis,* that sweete streame of pleasure, as the prophet calleth yt, which comming from the mountaynes of heauen, watereth (by secret wayes and passages) the hartes, and spirites of the godly, and maketh thē drounken with the vnspeakable ioye which it bringeth with yt. This is a litle taste in this life of the verie Ioyes of heauen, bestowed vpon good men, to comfort them withall, and to encourage them to goe forwarde. For as Marchātes desirous to sell their wares, are content to let you see and handle, and some times also to taste the same, therby to induce you to buy: so God almightie willing, to sell vs the ioyes of heauen, is cōtent to [204] imparte a certaine taste before hand to such as he seeth are willing to buye: thereby to make them come of roundlye with the price, and not to stycke in payeinge so muche, and more, as he requireth. This is that exceding ioye and iubilie in the hartes of iust mē, which the prophet meaneth, when he saieth: *The voyce of exultation and saluation is in the tabernacles of the iust.* And agayne, *Blessed is that people that knoweth iubilation*: That is, that hath experienced this extreeme ioye and pleasure of internall consolation. S. Paul had tasted it when he wrote these woordes, amiddest all his laboures for Christ. *I am filled with consolation, I ouerflowe or superabounde in all ioye, amyddest our tribulations.* What can be more effectually sayd or alleaged, to proue the seruice of god pleasant, than this? Surelye (good reader) yf thow haddest tasted once, but one droppe of this heauēlie ioye: thou woldest geue the whole worlde to haue an other of the same, or at the least-wise, not to leese that one agayne.

But thou wilt aske me perhappes, whye thow being a Christian as well as other, hast yet neuer tasted of this consolation? to which I answere, that (as it hath bene shewed before) this is not meate for euerye mouthe: but *a chosen moysture layed asyde for gods inheritance onelye.* This *is wyne of gods owne seller, layed vp for his spouse,* as the Canticles declare: That is, for the deuoute fowle dedicated vnto gods seruice. This is a teate of comfort, onelye for the chylde to sucke, & fill hym selfe withall, [205] as the prophet Esaye testifieth. The soule that is drouned in synne & pleasures of the world can not be partaker of this benefite: nether the harte replenished with carnall cares and cogitations. For as gods Arcke and the Idole dagon could not stand together vppon one Aultar: so

Mat. 17.
Marc. 9.
Luc. 9.
Psal. 35.
Esa. 29.

A similitude.

Apoc. 3.

Psa. 117.

2. Cor. 7.

The waye to come to spirituall cōsolation.
Psa. 67.

Can. 1.

Esa. 66.

1. Re. 5.

Io. 8. 14.

15. 16.
1. Io. 2.
Exo. 16.

can not Christ and the world stand together in one harte. God sent not the pleasant Manna vnto the people of Israell as long as their flower and chyboles[8] of Egipt lasted: soe nether will he send this heauenlie consolation vnto thee, vntill thou haue rydde thy selfe of the cogitations of vanitie. He is a wyse marchant, thoughe a liberall. He wil not geue a taste of his treasure, where he knoweth there is no will to buye. Resolue thy selfe once in deede to serue God, & thow shalt then feele this ioye, that I talke of, as many thousandes before thee haue done, and neuer yet any man was herein deceaued.

Exod. 2.

Moyses first ranne out of Egypt, to the hilles of Madian, before* God appeared vnto hym: and so must thy soule goe* owt of worldlye vanitie, before she can looke for these consolations. But thou shalt no sooner offer thy selfe thorowglye to gods seruice, than thou shalt fynde entertaynement aboue thy expectation. For that, his loue is more tender in deede vpon them that come newlye to his seruice, than vpon those whiche haue serued hym of olde: as he sheweth playnelye by the parable of the prodigall sonne: whome he

Luc. 15.

cheryshed with much more dalyance and good cheere, than he dyd the elder brother, [206] which had serued hym of long tyme. And

Begyn-
ners chee-
felie che-
rished
with spi-
rituall
consola-
tion.
Exo. 13.

the causes hereof are two: the one, for the ioye of the new gotten seruant, as is expressed by S. Luc in the text: the other, lest he fynding no consolation at the begynnyng, should turne back to Egypt agayne: as God by a figure in the children of Israell declareth manyfestlie in these woordes: *When Pharao had lett goe the people of Israell out of Egypt: God brought them not by the countrie of philistines, whiche was the nearest waye, thinking with hym selfe, lest perhappes it might repent them, yf they should see warres streight waye ryse agaynst them, and so should returne into Egypt agayne.* Vpon which two causes thow mayest assure thy selfe, of singular consolations and comfortes in the seruice of God (yf thou wooldest resolue thy selfe therunto) as all other men haue founde before thee, and by reason therof haue proued the waye not harde, as worldlye men imagine yt, but most easie: pleasant, and comfort-

Matt. 11.

able, as Christ hathe promised.

---

[8]*chyboles,* (commonly spelled *chibol*), a species of Allium known as Stone Leek, Rock Onion, and Welsh Onion, in appearance intermediate between the onion and the leek.

*before] *ed.;* hefore

*goe] *ed.;* doe

After this priuilege of internall consolation enseueth an other, making the seruice of God pleasant, which is the testimonie of a good conscience, wherof S. Paul made so great accounte, as he called it *his glorie*. And the holie ghoste sayeth of it further, by the mouthe of the wyse mā: *Secura mens quasi iuge conuiuium*: a secure mynde, or good cōsciēce is as a perpetuall feaste. Of which we may inferre, that the vertuous man hauing allwayes this secure mynde and peace of conscience, lyueth allwayes, in festiuall glorie, and glo-[207]riouse feasting. And how then is this lyfe harde, or vnpleasant, as you imagine? In the contrary syde, the wicked man, hauing his conscience vexed with the priuitie of synne, is always tormented with in it selfe: as we reade that Cayn was, hauing killed his brother Abel: & Antiochus for his wickednesse done to Ierusalem: and Iudas for his treason against his maister: and Christ signifieth it generallie of all naughtie men, whē he saieth that they haue a worme whiche gnaweth their conscience within. The reason wherof, the scripture openeth in an other place, whē it sayeth: *All wickednesse is full of feare, geuing testimonie of damnation against it selfe: and therfor a troubled cōsciēce alwaies presumeth cruell matters.* That is, it presumeth cruell thinges to be imminent ouer it selfe, as it maketh accoūt to haue deserued. But yet further, aboue all other, holie Iobe most liuelie setteth furth this miserable state of wiked men, in these woordes: *A wicked man is prowed all the dayes of his lyfe, though the tyme be vncertaine howe long he shall playe the tyrant: the sounde of terroure is allwayes in his eares: and althoughe yt be in time of peace, yet he alway suspecteth some treason against hym: he beleeueth not that he can ryse againe from darknesse to light: expecting on euery syde the swoorde to come vppon hym: when he sitteth downe to eate, he remembreth that the day of darkenesse is redy at hand for him: tribulation terrifieth hym, and anguishe of mynde enuironeth hym, euen as a king is enuironed with soldiers, when he goeth to warre.*

[208] Is not this a maruailous description of a wicked cōscience, vttered by the holy ghoste hym selfe? what can be imagined more miserable than this man, which hathe suche a boucherie, and slaughterhouse with in his, owne harte? what feares, what anguishes, what desperatiōs are heere touched? S. Chrisostome discourseth notablie vpō this point: Suche is the custome of sinners, (sayeth he) that they suspect* all thinges, they dowte their owne

5. The quiet of cōsciēce.
2. Cor. 1.

Pro. 15.

Gen. 4.
1. Ma. 6.
Mat. 27.
Act. 1.
Marc. 9.

Sap. 7.

Iob. 15.
The trouble of an euill conscience.

Hom. 8.
ad pop.
Antiochenum.

*suspect] *ed.;* supect

shadowes, they are afeard at euery litle noyse, & they think euery
mā that cometh towardes them, to come against them. If men talke
together, they think they speak of their sinnes: suche a thyng sinne
is, as it bewrayeth it selfe, though no man accuse yt: It condemneth
it selfe, though no man beare witnesse against it: It maketh always
the sinner fearfull, as Iustice doeth the contrarie. Heare howe the
scripture doeth describe the sinners feare, and the iust mans libertie.

Pro. 28.
The wicked man flyeth though no man pursue hym (sayeth the
scripture.) Whie doeth he flye yf no man doe pursue him? Mary,
for that he hathe within his conscience an accuser pursueing hym,
whome always he carieth aboute with hym. And as he can not flye
from hym selfe: so can he not flye from this accuser within his
conscience, but where souer he goeth, he is purseued and whipped
by the same, and his wounde is incurable. But the iust man is noth-
Pro. 28.
ing so: *The iust man* (sayeth Salamon) *is as confident as a lyon.*
Hitherto are the woordes of S. Chrisostome.

[This chapter continues with a discussion of further difficulties
to be overcome in the spiritual life, pp. 209-238; hereafter follow
Chapters II-VI, on remedies to overcome impediments to serving
God, pp. 239-426.]

The con-
clusiō of
this who-
le booke.
Pag. 9.
[426] And thus now hauing sayd so muche as time permitted me,
concernynge the fyrst generall point required at our handes for our
saluation: that is, concerning resolution, appointed by my diuisiō in
the beginning, to be the subiect or matter of this first booke: I will
ende heere: deferring for a tyme the performance of my purpose for
the other two bookes, vpon the causes and reasons sett downe in an
aduertisement to the reader at the verie first entrance vnto this
booke: nothinge dowtynge but yf God shall vouchesafe to woorke in
any mans hart by meanes of this booke, or otherwise, this first point
of resolution, the moste hard of all other: then will he also geue
Phil. 2.
meanes to perfite the worke begunne of hym selfe, and will supplie
by other wa-[427]yes the two pointes foloweing: that is, bothe right
beginning, and constant perseuerance, wherunto my other two
bookes promised, are appointed. It will not be harde for hym that
were once resolued, to fynde helpers and instructours enoughe, beside the holye ghoste, whiche in this case will always be at hāde:
there want not good bookes, and better men (God be glorified for
it) in our owne countrie at this daye, whiche are well able to guyde
a zealous spirite, in the right way to vertue: and yet as I haue

promised before, so meane I (by gods most holie helpe and assist-
āce) to send thee (gentle reader) as my time and habilitie will permitt, the other two bookes also: especiallie, yf it shall please his
diuine Maiestie to comforte me therunto, with the gayne or good of
any one soule by this whiche is alredie done: that is, yf I shal
conceiue or hope, that any one soule so dearlie purchased by the
pretiouse bloode of the sonne of God, shalbe moued to resolutiō by
any thing that is here sayd: that is, shalbe reclamed frō the bondage
of sinne, and restored to the seruice of our maker and redemer:
whiche is the onelie ende of my writing, as his maiestie best
knoweth.

And surelie (gentle reader) thoughe I must confesse that muche
more might be sayde for this point of resolution, than is heere
touched by me, or than anye man can well vtter in any competent
kinde of booke or volume: yet am I of opinion, that ether these
reasons heere alleaged are sufficient, or els [428] nothing will suffice,
for the cōquering of our obstinacie, and beating downe of our rebellious disobedience in this pointe. Heere thou mayest see the principall argumentes inducing thee to the seruice of God, and detesta-
tion of vice. Heere thou mayest see the cause and ende whye thou
was created: the occasion of thy cōming hyther: the things required
at thy handes in particular: the account that will be demaunded of
thee: the iustice and seueritie of God therein: his goodnes towardes
thee: his wachefullnes ouer thee: his desire to wynne thee: his rewarde, yf thou doe well: his infinite punishement, yf thou doe euill:
his calles: his baytes: his allurementes to saue thee. And on the
contrarie parte, heere are discouered vnto thee, the vanities, and
deceytes of those impedimentes, hynderances, or excuses, whiche any
waye might lett, staye, or discourage thy resolution: the faigned
diffyculties of vertuous lyfe are remoued: the conceyted feares of
gods seruice are taken awaye: the alluringe flatteryes of worldlie
vanitie are opened: the foolyshe presumption vpon gods mercye: the
daunger of delaye: the dissimulation of slothe: the desperate perill
of careles and stony hartes are declared. What then wilt thou desire
more to moue thee? what further argument wilt thou expect, to
drawe the from vice and wickednes, than all this is?

If all this styrre the not, what will stirre thee (gentle reader?)
yf when thou hast read this, thou laye downe the booke againe, and
[429] walke on in thy careles lyfe as quietlye as before: what hope
(I beseeche thee) maye there be conceiued of thy saluation? wilt

Marginal notes:

The ef-
fecte of
that whi-
che hath
bene said
in this
booke.

In the
first par-
te.

In the se-
cōd par-
te.

thou goe to heauen liuing as thow doest? it is impossible: as soone
thow maiest driue God owt of heauen as gett thither thy selfe, by
this kind of lyfe. What then? wilt thow forgoe heauen, and yet
escape hell too? this is lesse possible, what soeuer the Atheistes of
this world doe persuade thee. Wilt thow perhappes deferre the
matter, and think of yt heerafter? I haue tolde thee my opinion
heerof before. Thou shalt neuer haue more abilitie to doe it than
now, and perhappes neuer halfe so muche. If thou refuse it now: I
maye greatlie feare, that thou wilt be refused hereafter thy selfe.
There is no waye then so good (deare brother) as to doe it presentlie whiles it is offered. Breake from that tyrant, whiche de-
tayneth thee in seruitude: shake of his chaynes: cutt a sunder his
bandes: runne violentlie to Christ, whiche standeth redye to em-
Luc. 15. brace, thee with his armes open on the crosse. Make ioyfull all the
Angels, and court of heauen with thy conuersion: strike once the
stroke with God agayne: make a manlye resolution: saye with that
A nota-
ble saye-
ing of S.
Ierome. olde couragious souldier of Iesus Christ S. Ierome, If my father
stoode weeping on his knees before me, & my mother hanging on
my necke behynde me: and all my bretheren, sisters, children, and
kynsefolkes howling on euery syde to retayne me in synfull lyfe with
them: I wolde fling of my mother to the grounde: dispyse all my
[430] kynred, runne ouer my father & treade hym vnder my feete,
therby to runne to Christ when he calleth me.

Oh that we had suche hartes as this seruant of God had: suche
courage, suche manhoode, suche feruent loue to our Maister. Who
wolde lye one daye drowned in sinne? who wolde lyue one daye in
suche slauerie as we doe? who wolde eate huskes with the prodigall
sonne amonge swyne, seeynge he may returne home, and be soo
honorablye receyued, and entertaynede by his olde father, haue
so good cheere, and banquetinge, and heare soo greate melodie,
Luc. 15. ioye, and triumphe for his returne? I saye no more heerin (deare
brother) than thow arte assured of, by the woorde, and promise of
godes owne mouthe: from whiche can proceede nether falshode nor
deceyte. Returne then I beseeche thee: laye hande faste on his
promise, whoe will not fayle thee: runne to hym now he calleth,
whiles thow hast tyme: and esteeme not all this worlde woorthe a
strawe, in respect of this one acte. For so shalt thow be a most
happie, and thryse happie man, and shalt blesse hereafter the howre
and moment that euer thow madest this fortunate resolution. And I

for my parte (I trust) shall not be voyde of some portion of thy good happe and felicitie: At leastwise I doubt not, but thy holie cōuersion shall treate for me with our common father, whoe is the God of mercies, for remission of my many folde sinnes, and that I may [431] serue and honoure hym together with thee all the dayes of my lyfe: whiche ought to be bothe our petytyons: and therefore in bothe our names I beseeche his diuyne Maiestye to graunt it to vs. For euer and euer. Amen.

The ende of the fyrst booke:
touching resolution.

III.

The Contempte of
the World, and the Va-
nitie thereof, written by the reuerent
F. Diego de Stella, of the order of
S. Fr. deuided into three bookes,
And of late translated out of Italian into
Englishe, with conuenient tables
in the end of the booke.
[A very ornamental device of the letters IHS]
In nomme [*sic*] *Iesu omne genu flectatur. Philip.* 2
Anno domini. 1584.[1]
[trans. G(eorge) C(otton)[2]]

---

[1]n.p. Tr. G. C. [George Cotton.] Pr. [Rouen, Fr. Persons' press.] Allison and Rogers, I, Entry 294. *STC* 10541.

Diego de Estella (1524-1578) was born at Estella in Navarre. At the age of seventeen, he entered the Franciscan Order of the Observance; he later became one of the great preachers of his day. For awhile he was "preacher to the court" of Philip II, and St. Teresa of Avila asked him to preach at the foundation of the second reformed Carmelite convent at Salamanca. *The Contempte of the World* is a translation of his *Libro de la Vanidad del mundo* (Toledo, 1562). This work was extremely popular and was translated into several languages: Italian (Florence, 1573, 1581), French (Lyon, 1580; Paris, 1587), Latin (Cologne, 1585), and German (1586). For an account of Estella's life, influence, and bibliography, see the *Dictionnaire de Spiritualité ascétique et mystique,* ed. Marcel Villers *et al.* (Paris, 1932-   ), IV, 1366-1370.

In 1586, a Protestant, T. Rogers, translated the *Libro de la Vanidad del mundo* into English under the title *A Methode vnto mortification called heretofore the contempt of the world* (*STC* 10542).

[2]Little is known of George Cotton, the translator. It is possible that he is the George Cotton who for over twenty years paid two hundred pounds a year in fines for refusing to attend the Protestant church services. His house at Warblington served as a retreat for priests, especially those who came from Douay or Rheims by boat in the night. George Cotton of Warblington was arrested and confined to Winchester jail, where he died in chains (Bede Camm, *Forgotten Shrines* [London, 1910], pp. 88-89). The dedicatory epistle of this translation to the Briggitine nuns of Rouen was written in prison.

[This work begins with a woodcut of the Nativity and Latin verses, Sig. AI^v, followed by a dedicatory epistle to the Sisters of St. Bridget in Rouen, Sigs. A2^r-A4^v.]

[B]

Of the Despi-
singe the vanitie of the
worlde.
The first parte.

*How that we can neither tast of God,
nor enioye any spirituall delighte and
diuine comforte, yf first we despise
not the world, and the Pleasures therof.*

Chap. I.

No man can serue twoe maisters saith Christ our Sauiour. The comfort that is of God, is sweete and delectable, but this is not for all men, but for those onelie whiche despise the vanities of the worlde. It is impossible to tast of God, and to loue disordinatlie the thinges of this lyfe: All men woulde gladlie enioye the sweete con- uersation of our Lorde, but few there be that will forgoe their owne commodities, and willinglie despise the earthlye delightes. [B^v] They desyre greatlie to haue the inward comforte of the soule, but with all the desyre to satisfie their owne appetites. But yf thou wilt folowe Christ, thou must denye thy selfe.

Thou must withdrawe thy selfe from the world, yf thou thinkest to enioye God for God and the world be contrarie, they haue noth- inge common betwixte them neyther maye they inhabite together: cast of therfore the loue of the worlde, yf thou wilt that God shall haue accesse to thy soule: Neyther mayest thou fullie tast of the sweetenes of God, vntill thou doest fynde that the pleasures of the world be waxen bitter vnto the, and vnpleasant. And when thou shalt accompte of these wordlie³ thinges to be harde and harsh of tast, then shalt thou fynde thy soule disposed to receyue the inward comfort of Iesus Christ. For as it is vnpossible for the with one eie to

---

³*wordlie,* obs. worldly

looke vpward to heauen, and with the other to looke downe warde
to the earth: so is it against reason to haue thyne affections here on
these earthlie thinges, and enioye withall the spirituall cōfortes of
heauen. If thou wilt enioye God it is necessarie for the to depryue
thy selfe of all kynde of wordlie & sensuall comforte: That comforte which cometh from man, must needes be vile and of no ac-
cōpte, since it hyndreth the comforte whiche cometh from God.

Thou must not seeke for God in the plea-[B2]sant fieldes, nor in
delightsome gardeins, neyther in the pleasures of this worlde, Synce
Moyses one so deare vnto hym, founde hym out amongest the
thorney busshes of harde pennance and sharpenes of lyfe. Therefore
doe those worldlinges neuer deserue to fynde hym, that doe not
seeke hym any where, but amongest pleasures and delightes. But flie
from all worldie comforte asmuch as thou mayest and then shalt
thou be refresshed at gods owne hande. Dispatch all worldlie care
frō thy soule, to the intent that their maye be place for the loue of
God to rest therein where it maye be suerlie planted, and take fast
rootinge. *Exd. 3.*

God would not permitte that his holye Arke & the idole Dagon
should haue both one Aulter. And allthoughe the Philistines did
earnestlie labour to haue it so, yet could they neuer bring it to passe
that they might both abide together. God will not that the Idole of
vice, whiche thou doest adore, should haue any place there, where as
his diuine person remayneth: he cōsenteth not that the world and he
shoulde be adored together. *1. Reg. 5*

And therefore yf thou wilt loue God, as thou oughtest to doe,
thou must not sett by the glorie of this worlde. God neuer appeared
vnto Moyses whilest he remayned in Egipte, no more owghtest thou
to haue any hope of seeing hym, whilest thou liuest in darkenes of
the world. Refuse the [B2ᵛ] Pallace of Pharao, despising the
honours & vanities in whiche thou liuest, that thou mayest finde in
the desert of solitarie lyfe, (as Moyses did) the helpe of God and
his spirituall comfortes. *Exod. 2.*

Exod. 16.

Whilest the flesh pottes of Egipte doe sauour well in thy
mouth, thou shalt neuer tast of the heauenlie manna. Thy stomack
being full of nawghtie humours thou canst neuer receyue the precious foode of heauen. Despise from the bottome of thyne harte, all
that is delightfull here vnder heauen, And thou shalt easelie make
thy soule thereby, to mounte aboue the heauens, & to receyue the
ioyes thereof. Many be desirous to haue respect vnto both, And

geuing them selues vnto God, doe yet reserue their wordlie commodities still to them selues. Let it not be greuous vnto the, to
seperate thy selfe from thy frendes and kynnesfolke when they doe
gyue the any impediment toward the waye to heauen, For God
reuealeth not his hidden secrettes vnto thy sowle, in the presence of
other witnesses, neyther will he be conuersante with hym that is
vnquyet, and is occupied aboute wordlie busines.

There is none beloued of the worlde, but he that is dryuen
away frō Christ: And there is none that is beloued of Christ, but he
whome the worlde despiseth. Thou canst not perfectlie loue God but
yf thou doe first despise thy selfe, and the worlde for God: And by
this mayest thou knowe, [B3] whether thou louest God, yf thou
cōferre the loue that thou bearest hym, with the loue thou bearest to
the world: for so much the more as thou louest God, so much the
lesse, shalt thou esteeme the worlde.

Our Lorde will not haue our hart deuided, nor parted in peeces,
but will haue it whole to hym selfe.

And therfore that thou mayest not lose a thing of so great a
price, esteme but lightly these trāsitorie things. And this is the
readie way to get the perfect cōfort of spirit.

[Here follow one hundred nineteen chapters on the subject of
rejecting the world and its vanities, Sigs. B3ʳ-a5ʳ; the work concludes with a table of contents, Sigs. a5ᵛ-a8ʳ, and a woodcut of the
Virgin plus a Latin hymn, Sig. a8ᵛ.]

IV.

An Epistle in the Per-
son of Christ to the Faithfvll
soule, written first by that learned Lan-
spergivs, and after translated into
English by one of no small fame, whose
good example of sufferance & liuing,
hath and wilbe a memoriall vnto
his countrie and posteritie
for euer.

[Woodcut of Christ teaching the multitudes]

Imprinted at Anwerpe. 1595
Cum Priuilegio.[1]
[trans. Philip Howard, Earl of
Arundel[2] and John Gerard, S. J.[3]]

---

[1]Imprint false; pr. [secretly in England.] Allison and Rogers, I, Entry 438. *STC* 14627.

There is an earlier edition of this work which is not listed in the *STC* according to Allison and Rogers (I, Entry 437):

An epistle or exhortation of Iesus Christ to the soule, that is deuoutly affected towarde him. n.p.d. [1592-93]. Without title page. Tr. [Philip Howard, Earl of Arundel, probably in conjunction with John Gerard, S. J.]. Pr. [secretly in England.]

Lanspergius (1489-1539), whose real name was John Gerecht or Justus, was a Carthusian monk. He studied philosophy at Cologne before entering the Charterhouse of St. Barbara in 1509. From 1530 to 1534 he was prior at the Charterhouse at Cantave near Juliers; he was also during this time preacher at the Court of William, Duke of Juliers, and confessor to the duke's mother. He ended his life as subprior at the Charterhouse at Cologne. He is famous for having made the first Latin translation of St. Gertrude's *Revelations* (Cologne, 1536). The Carthusian press of Notre-Dame-des-Près (Tournai) issued a revised edition of all of Lanspergius's Latin works in 1890 (*Catholic Encyclopedia*, VIII, 739).

The present work is a translation of his *Alloquia Jesu Christi ad animam fidelem,* which was first published in the *Minorum Operum libri XIII posteriores* (Cologne, 1555-1556). The *Alloquia* was published singularly at Louvain in 1572 (*Dictionnaire de la théologie catholique,* ed. A. Vacant *et al.,* 15 vols. [Paris, 1925], VIII, 2607). The *Alloquia* has been translated into Spanish, French, Italian, and German. For an account of the author and an account of his works, see the *Dictionnaire de la théologie catholique* (VIII, 2606-2609).

[2]Philip Howard, Earl of Arundel (1557-1595), was the eldest son of Thomas Howard, Fourth Duke of Norfolk. He was tutored by the famous Gregory Martin before he entered Cambridge, where he received the M. A. degree in 1576. Although he had been married to Anne Dacres, the eldest daughter of Lord Dacres in 1571 when he was but a child, he forsook her generally and spent much of his early life as a courtier and flatterer of Queen Elizabeth. He was present at the renowned theological debates of Charke, Fulke, and Whitaker vs. the imprisoned Edmund Campion in 1581. For a vivid account of these debates, see Evelyn Waugh's *Edmund Campion* (pp. 181-192). Apparently moved by Campion's brilliance and sanctity, Philip Howard decided to reform his dissolute life and join the Catholic cause. In 1583, Elizabeth, suspecting a plot against her government, visited Arundel Castle and soon after had Philip arrested but very shortly released. In 1584, he was formally reconciled to the Catholic Church by Father William Weston, S. J. Because of the omnipresent danger of further arrests and fines, Philip decided to flee England, but he was again arrested—this time on board the departing ship. In 1585, he was committed to the Tower, where he remained for ten years. He died under strange circumstances, his friends attributing his death to food poisoning (Gillow, I, 65-66). He translated Lanspergius while he was in prison.

[3]John Gerard (1564-1637) was the second son of Sir Thomas Gerard, knight, of Bryn, Lancashire. He received part of his education at the English College at Douay and later at Rheims. In 1579, he was attending Exeter College, but because of religious tensions, he felt obliged to leave. In 1581, he went to Clermont College, a Jesuit institution, in Paris. In the same year he accompanied Fr. Thomas Derbyshire, S. J., to Rouen, where he met Fr. Robert Persons, who

[This work begins with an introduction to the reader, Sigs. A2ʳ-A3ʳ; a caveat to the reader in verse, Sig. A3ᵛ; a long poem in the form of a dialogue between Christ on the cross and a Christian, Sigs. A4ʳ-A6ᵛ and the table of contents, Sigs. A7ʳ-A8ᵛ.]

[1]

An Epistle or Ex-
hortation of Iesus Christ to the soule,
that is deuoutly affected toward
him, wherein are onely contained certaine diuine inspirations, which will teach a man
how to knowe himselfe,
and instruct him in the
perfection of true
Pietie.

Iesvs Christ the Sauiour of the worlde, and King of heauen and earth, being ready to embrace those that earnestly and truly desire his grace, with his mercifull & fatherly armes, wisheth to his Spouse, that is, to the soule which loueth him (for whose sake he willingly suffered death that he might vnite her to himselfe) all perfect and true felicity.

O my deerely beloued Daughter I haue spoken to thy heart by secrete inspirations, but thou wouldest [2] neuer giue eare vnto my

---

was at Rouen supervising the publication of his *The First Booke of the Christian Exercise*. Gerard returned to England and decided to join the Jesuits, but he was arrested for illegally attempting to leave the country and was committed to a Protestant uncle for indoctrination. Remaining resolute in his Catholic faith, Gerard was sent to the Bishop of London for further indoctrination and finally to Marshalsea prison. Through the influence of friends, he was released in 1585. In 1586, Gerard entered the Society of Jesus at Rome. Almost immediately he was sent to the English mission, and from that time his life became one of tense drama and adventure. In 1597, he was arrested and committed to the Tower; in 1606 he made a dramatic escape, but he remained in England for several years in disguise, working for the Catholic cause. We find him in 1609 as Master of Novices at the English Novitiate of the Society of Jesus at Louvain, and for eight years he was Rector and Master of Novices at Liège. In 1622, he returned to Rome, where he spent his remaining years as spiritual father to the young aspirants to the English mission at the English College (Gillow, II, 423-430). Gerard's autobiography has been translated from Latin by Fr. Philip Caraman, S. J., and entitled *The Autobiography of an Elizabethan* (London, 1951). The American edition is entitled *The Autobiography of a Hunted Priest* (New York, 1952), and it contains an interesting introduction by Graham Greene. For a bibliography of Gerard's works, see De Backer (Pt. 1, III, 1343-1345).

motions, wherefore since thou diddest care little to answere me, much lesse to obey me, I am enforced by the great loue I beare thee, to write vnto thee, that at the least thou mayest bee content to reade what thou diddest neglect to heare, & by reading both better beare away my exhortation, and more deeply imprint it in thy minde. For that charity which moued me to offer my selfe, not onely to all danger, but euen to death it selfe, for thy sake, will not suffer mee to leaue any thing vndone that may tende to the furtherance of thy saluation: And although thou dost not in any sort requite my loue, because thy hart is inclined to outwarde vaine, and transitory things, and so by that meanes too much affected and addicted to my creatures: Yet cannot I withdrawe that charity, wherewith I am alwaies ready to imbrace thee, which exceedeth the loue of any father or mother towardes their children, or of any earthly Parent whatsoeuer: For I am not onely wil-[3]ling to graunt thee my grace and fauour, but desirous to accept thee for my spowse, and will daily enrich thee with greater and better blessings, than any that this world can yeeld thee, if thou wilt follow my counsaile. But for that thou hast contemned me whē I came to visite thee, and hast not harkened to my inspirations, thou art become by this euill custome of thine so much distracted in thy soule, and so far beside thy selfe, as thou art neither able to conceiue what thou hast lost, nor yet the misery wherein thou art. And the lesse that thou dost bewaile and lament thine owne misery, the more doth thy case deserue to be pittied and lamented. What shall I say O my daughter? thou shouldest be an example to others, and thy life an instruction to those that goe astray: the sweete sauour of thy good conuersation, ought to bee a holsome medicine for the curing of such as are weakened with infection of sinne, and thy words as a consuming fire, to inflame the harts of those that heare them: But now [4] thou art thy selfe so corrupted with the desire of childish vanities, so busied with a multitude of vnprofitable matters, and so subiect to many hurtfull passions, as thou art distracted in thy soule, and hast it so much polluted with filthinesse, as it is possessed with wandring thoughts and vaine imaginations; Selfe loue doth as yet raigne in thee, and till thou mortefie that, thou canst neuer enter into my bed, or be partaker of my delights: So as thou which oughtest to teach others, standest now in neede of being taught thy selfe. I write not this to the end, that I meane to reiect thee, but because I would let thee know how far thou hast erred, & am desirous that thou shouldest vnderstand thy own losse and danger; & I do not only allure thee, but I do also prick thee forward to returne from thence, home againe vnto mee.

Wheresoeuer thou art, whatsoeuer thou dost, or whether so euer thou goest, my eye is neuer off on thee, looking and searching into all thy acts, all thy motions, and all the secrete inten-[5]tions of thy hart.

And if at any time I spie in any of these the least vnfaithfulnes to mee, who am most faithfull, I am iustly offended and angry; for I did suffer not onely with all patience, but euen with all willingnes, many despites, reproches, griefs, and torments for thy sake. O my most deare daughter, to passe ouer in silence all the paines and torments which I did endure, tell mee I pray thee, what man would haue suffered so many and so great disgraces for his friend, as I did for thee? And yet I indured them when thou wert mine enemy, when thou hadst* done no good at all, when thou didst neither loue nor know mee, yea before thou wert borne did I loue thee, and suffer these grieuous and innumerable torments for thee. Why then wilt thou turne away thy self from me? why dost thou seeke quietnes without mee? thou art sickly, and yet wilt wander abroad: If I forsake thee, who will receiue thee? who can cure thee? Alas my daughter how far art thou deceiued? whether so [6] euer thou turnest thine eyes, or vppon whatsoeuer thou dost fixe thy minde; yet shalt thou finde no peace, no ioy, nor any rest, but in me onely. Thy senses deceiue thee, & they which seeme to loue thee doo abuse thee, and thou also dost deceiue thy selfe, when thou refusest a soueraigne medecine that would helpe thee, and receiuest ranck poyson, which will kill thee. Alas my daughter, alas my spouse; I know how often, beautifull and goodly things in shew, but vaine things in deed, (which when they professe most loue & faith vnto thee, are most ready to beguile thee) doo allure thy senses, and drawe thy affection, and how often also they deceiue thee with their snares, & leade thee from mee with their guiles. O deare daughter, remember that thou art a spouse, and let not the loue of any other thing but onely thy husband enter into thy hart. Desire nothing but his fauor, that thou maiest be beautifull in his eyes, and please him, and be for euer beloued of him. I stande desiring thee, and waiting for thee, I [7] wish that thou wouldest returne vnto mee with all

---

*hadst] *ed.;* dadst

thy hart, and forsaking all these vanities, apply thy selfe wholy to deuotion, and giue thy selfe daily to humility, that I might then vouchsafe to talke with thee in more familiar sort and reioyce thy minde, with far better and purer delights, than those wherein thou hast lyen drowned.

I require no multitude of workes at thy hands, wherewith to trouble thee, but a chast, faithfull & pure hart, which may seeke to please me, & not delight it selfe. I desire a sincere loue, and a feruent deuotion, that is a ready and forward will to honour and obey mee, and a sincere & pure intention in performing of all those things that I commaund. I wish that thy hart should be cleare and free from any other loue whatsoeuer, and if thou wouldest presente it to mee in this sorte, I woulde indue thee with greater consolations and far more excellent blessings, than either thou darest presume to desire, or art able to conceiue. I am a husband that is bashful, and therefore will neuer [8] come vnto thee, when I see thee busied with other matters altogether vaine and vnprofitable. When I come I must finde thee alone, for I stand knocking at thy dore, being very weak, and quaking for cold, euen in the same forme that I carried when I was vnlosed frō the Piller, where being bound, I was whipped and wounded for thy sake, and this I doo, that I may make an impression of my selfe in thy minde, wounded as I was, & that thou imbracing me with the armes of thy loue, I may vnite thee vnto mee, and inflame thee with my woundes, that doo yet boyle with the feruent heate of that charity which I carry towards thee. Oh if thou wouldest acknowledge me for thy husband, & loue me as thou ought to doo, wouldest thou not both quickly drawe me into thy hart, and also before I came, with a most desirous will, attend and long for my comming, and wouldest thou not then cloath the naked, and giue fire to warme him that is a colde, that thou mightest bee made worthy to receiue againe the chast im-[9]brasings of my loue, and to inioye the sweet taste of my spirite?

How much would it please me that thou haddest a certaine & firme trust in me, and were as willing to bee with me, as I am desirous to bee with thee, seeing all my delight consisteth in being with the Children of men. So should the fortitude of thy minde, be dayly augmented, and the true sweetnes of thy soule continually increased. But this trust in me can neuer be without a distrust in thy selfe, & both these graces, are onely obtained by pouerty of spirit, which is a most precious Iewell. But I know well inough what

doth with-hold thee from attaining to this vertue, thy stomacke is
ouerlaide with the loue of this worlde, and by that meanes infected
with such an extreame coldnes, as it maketh thee to loath and
abhorre the worde of God, which is the food of thy soule. But if
thou desire to increase in vertue, & to strengthen thy mind with the
following of that course, thou must receaue the word of God
greedily, disgest it [10] perfectly, and still retaine the nourishment
of that within thee. The reason therfore that thou canst not thirst
after my iustice, is because thou art already filled with the cold meat
of worldly conuersation and vanitie, and that is the cause also why
these things do delight thee, which sauour neither of piety nor deuotion. Simplicitie of heart is loathsome vnto thee, and the exercise of
holy meditations, thou accoūtest as time lost. Thy minde beeing
loaden with the cares of this worlde, cannot ascend vp vnto mee.
For although thou raisest it by force for a while: yet it presently
falleth downe againe into her earthly cogitations: so as thy soule
being distracted, thy heart inconstant, thy minde wauering, and thy
desires insnared with the loue of worldlie pleasure: thou art
troubled when thou art awake, and not quiet when thou art a sleepe.

And when thou liest in this misery, O vnwise daughter, then
thou complainest that thou art drie and barren, without my consolation. If this did [11] happen vnto thee, by the meanes of my
prouidence (as it hath to manie other of my friends,) and not by
thyne owne negligence: there were no reason why the wanting of
this sensible grace of mine shuld molest thy soule. But seeing thy
owne slouth and negligence is the cause that thou liest languishing
in this barren drienes: If thou desire my consolation, if thou wish
for my comming, if thou doe long to bee vnited vnto me, thou must
forsake all those vanities, that doe please thee without me, & only
study to serue me, indeuouring continually to perfourme those
thinges, which agree best with my liking, and are most pleasing vnto
me, and making this thy cheefest care, thou must labour with all
thy force & might, to see my will as nere as thou canst, in all
creatures fulfilled. Moreouer in dooing hereof, let thy whole studie
be to content mee, and to relie onelie vppon me. So shalt thou finde
my presence more often with thee, & by it, thy spirit shall be as it
were made drūck with ioy, thy conscience shalbe [12] comforted,
thy heart quieted, & thou shalt then possesse the perfecte rest of
most sweet contemplation. Oh if thou hadst once come into that

wine Celler, out of doubt thou wouldest euen with a certaine thirst-inesse, more earnestly desire to be there, and more often. But no man can enter into it, sauing such as desire me aboue al things, loue me aboue all things, esteeme me aboue al things, & make acount of me as all in all. For hee that findeth no other consolation but in me, hee that thinketh himself vnworthie to receiue any consolation from me, may he that desireth affliction so much in this world, as he taketh himself to be wrōged, when I send him any consolation at all, and doth as willingly accept it at my hands, when I leaue his soule barren without any comfort, as when I replenish it with my conso-latiō, to whom all ioy without me is a torment, hauing his minde wholy fixed vpon me, & his desire only bent to serue me. Such mē as these be, I say are my special friends, at whose dore I doe freely knocke, & [13] willingly enter: these are the men to whome I gladly offer my selfe, & impart my secrets. These men am I wont to visite in sundrie sortes, as seemeth fittest in my iudgment,* by stirring thē vp in such sort as is meete & agreeable for the deuotion and loue which they beare me.

[Here follows, in essence, a resumé of the ascetical life with ex-hortations on such subjects as prayer, the sacraments, temptation, etc., pp. 13-252.]

[252]

The Conclusion.

I deliuer these exhortations vnto thee, as to my Daughter & spouse (O soule) and as a rule to instruct thee howe thou shouldest put off the olde man, and walke hereafter in newnes of spirit, and how thou shouldest daily bende and endeuour thy selfe with [253] all thy force to grow to more perfection. Therfore as often as by reading ouer these thinges, thou findest that thou haste not obserued all in suche sort as I haue commaunded thee, or that thou haste faulted in some little part thereof, so often still renewe thy good intention, by stirring vp a newe feruor of zeale in thee. And although I giue thee these to read: yet I desire notwithstanding that the eares of thy* hart should alwaies be open to my inspira-tions, whereby thou maiest not onely outwardly reade them, but inwardlie heare these lessons from me.

---

iudgment] *ed.;* indgment
eares of thy hart] *ed.;* eares of my my hart

And the reason why I would haue these inspirations laide before
thine eies, is because thou art for the moste parte delighted with
vaine letters and messages from thy friends, which doo procure in
thy heart nothng but distraction, an vnsauery kinde of disquiet, &
a perilous kinde of darkenesse. Therfore when thou hast contemned
these vanities & forsaken them quite, I haue giuen thee these
wholsome instructions, that thou mightest haue [254] occupie thy
minde withall. And that thou mightest by the consideration of thē, &
for the loue of me despise al other things which seeke to pollute
thy hart. And the more that I who am thy spouse, & gaue thee
these lessons (O soule) ought to be beloued, the more acceptable
ought this instructiō to be vnto thee, which proceeded from me, that
am not only worthie to bee beloued, but most worthie of all thinges
to be beloued, & deserue aboue all thinges most to be desired, yea
and ought before all things most to please & delight thee. I wold
haue thee also the more faithfully to obserue these precepts, seeing
all these things which I haue deliuered vnto thee, are not to delight
a carnall & worldly hart, but a spirituall, and such a one as is deuout
towardes mee, & seeing they doo not please the eares with picked
phrases, and trifling words, but they feede the louing soule with
truth and holsome counsaile: It remaineth onely nowe to warne
thee, that thou be watchfull & diligent.

[255] For I stand at the doore of thy hart & knocke.

Open thy hart therefore vnto mee (O my sister, O my spouse)
giue mee thy hart, and desire me onely, seeing I do so much desire
thee, but assure thy selfe of this one thing, thou canst neuer receiue
mee as long as thou louest any thing besides me: Thou canst neuer
haue mee, as long as thou hast any thing of thy selfe without mee,
thou canst neuer enioy me, as long as thou possessest thy selfe: Goe
therefore out of thy selfe, and forsake thy selfe, that I onely may
possesse thee, & that thou onely maiest possesse me. This is a short
time which is present, but that which followeth, is without all limita-
tion of time, and eternall without ende.

Be watchfull therfore (my Daughter) I do once againe exhort
thee, receiue me for thy husband, O soule, O daughter, O spouse,
and shewe thy selfe in all puritie without all hypocrisie, or dissimulation, a spouse worthie of me. Loue me which am thy Lord
[256] and redeemer, thinke of mee, take heede to thy selfe, haue
consideration of thine owne estate: Cleaue vnto me, and perseuer

with me to the ende. Liue happily henceforth in mee, and so I bid
thee hartely farewell.

[This work concludes with instructions for all men who wish to
attain spiritual perfection, pp. 256-283; verses for helping to remember the rules mentioned above, pp. 283-285; a short treatise on the
love of God, pp. 286-296; and a hymn on the life and passion of
Christ made after the manner of an alphabet, and other hymns, pp.
296-301.]

V.

[A2]

Nyne Rockes to
Be Avoyded of
Those Which
sayle Towardes the
Port of Perfection.[1]
[T.H.D.[2]]

Contrariorvm eadem est scientia saith the Philosopher,[3] one and
the same science is of contrarie thinges: Good we ought to know,
that wee may embrace it; euill, that wee may eschew it. The ship-
man must know as well the sandes and rockes of the Sea to auoyde
them, as the plaine & safe pathes thereof to sayle them. And in like
maner the deuout Christian tending to that perfection, which may be
had in this life, ought not onely to seeke after the practicall knowledge of vertue, and euerie good thing which may further him in [A2ᵛ]
his voyage: but likewise after the Theoricall, or speculatiue
knowledge of euerie impediment, hinderance, and let, which may
stay him therein. Of the former part hath bin written by diuers
Religious Authours matter almost infinite: and of the latter many
things, but in a prolixe and defused manner, which may not so well
be carried away, & imprinted in memorie as breifer rules, and
shorter admonitions: which consideration caused me, to set in a
briefe maner before thine eyes (good Christian) these nine Rockes,

Topic

---

[1]The title page is missing on the New College copy to which I had access.
Allison and Rogers (I, Entry 267) list this work as follows:
   D., T. H. *Nine rockes to be auoided, of those which sayle towardes the port
of perfection. Gathered, and compiled by T. H. D.,* Doway, Francis Fowler.
1600. Imprint false; pr. [secretly in England.]
   This work does not appear in the *STC.*
[2]T. H. D. is unidentified.
[3]Aristotle, *Topica,* I, xiv. 105ᵇ.

collected and translated out of Religious Authours, which thou knowing before hand, mayest auoyde and shun as perilous places, apt, not only to hinder thee in thy vertuous course, but also to worke thy aeternall perdition.

[Here follow the first six rocks to be avoided—self-love, inordinate love of creatures, sensuality, vainglory, bitterness of heart, and propriety of will, Sigs. A2^r-B2^r.]

[B2]

The Seventh
Rocke.

**Immode-
rate study.**

    The seuenth is an immoderate studie, about meere speculations, where deuotion is not sought for, but reading is frequented, either for it selfe, because it delighteth, or els for bare knowledge. These kinde of studentes become vaine, puffed vp with opinion of them-selues; presumptuous & voyde of deuotion; which indeede can prattle of spirituall things, but neuer were worthy to taste thereof. Studie not thou, to the end thou maiest be accounted learned, but that thou maiest become a de-[B2^v]uout Christiã. Neuer think thou knowest any thing, neyther desire to know any thing, but Iesvs Christ, and him crucified. Exercise thy selfe continually in the life and Passion of thy Sauiour, and haue an incessant desire in as much as thou canst to be like vnto thy Lord, in sustaining patiently what-soeuer he shall lay vpon thee. Seek only to know God and thy selfe: for in knowing of him thou wilt be mooued to reuerence him. The holy men of old time humbled them-selues wonderfully in the presence of Almighty God, because all their studie and indeuour was to know him, which they atteyned vnto in a more high manner, then those which busied them-selues with other speculations, & therefore became they so deuout & religious. Let all thy care, study, and endeuour be to know heauenly thinges and busie not thy selfe about other impertinent studies, which eyther hinder thee, or at the least profit thee little in the seruing of God.

Examples.

Deut. 14.

God would not haue any other beast offered to [B3] *him, but such as did chue their cud; which is meant, that none are fit for him, but such as meditate and studie spirituall matters.*

Salamon *sayeth, the eyes of a wise man stand in his head; that*   Eccle. 2.
is, the vnderstanding of them which be wise, is alwaies fixed in that
head, which is by the Apostle saide to be Iesvs Christ. Ephes. 4.
Make therefore thy studie that booke, wherein thou mayest euer
reape some profit for thy soule, & trouble not thy selfe much about
other knowledge, for in knowing this practically thou knowest all
thinges.

[Here follow the eighth and ninth rocks to be avoided—
wandering of the mind and tepidity, Sigs. B3ʳ-B5ᵛ.]

[B6]

The Lad-
der of Perfection,
having in it nine staves,
whereby a deuoute Christian may
clime, and ascend vp to such perfection*
as may be attained vnto in this life; the
greatest part whereof is taken, or
translated out of Hen-
rie Herpe⁴ *by*
T.H.D.

To the end that thou maiest know (deuout Christian) how much
thou haste forsaken thyselfe, and profited in the seruice of Almightie
God, by denying thyselfe (which is the foundation of profitting) wee
doe set here before thine eies a ladder of nine staues, for thee to
clime vp by to such perfection, as thou mayest atchieue vnto in this
[B6ᵛ] vale of miserie. The which staues or steps thou diligently
beholding, maiest see thyne owne wants, and in most profound
humility, mayest endeuour most feruently to clime vp higher, alwayes considering that the higher thou climest vp, the more is thy
good hap, and felicity, and that the fruite and profit thereof, none
shall reape but thou thy selfe.

---

*perfection] *ed.*; perfecti-
⁴Henry de Herp or Harp was a fifteenth century Franciscan priest of the
Strict Observance and a distinguished writer on mysticism and asceticism.
He was born near Louvain. Very little is known about him until 1450 when
he entered the Franciscan Order. He was provincial of the Province of Cologne
from 1470 to 1473. Later he became the guardian of the convent at Mechlin
in Belgium, where he died in 1478. His major work, *Theologia Mystica*, was
published posthumously by a Carthusian named Thomas Loher at Cologne in
1538 (*Catholic Encyclopedia*, VII, 293-294).

[Here follow the first four staves, a progression through the
purgative states of the soul, Sigs. B7ʳ-C1ʳ.]

[C1ᵛ]

The Fifth
Staffe.

Vpon the fifth Staffe stand such, as in all their workes, exercises,
and conuersations, resigne their own will to Gods pleasure, obeying
not only diuine inspirations, but also their superiours: yea, and
euerie man, whensoeuer, and wheresoeuer, it may be done according
to reason, for the honour of God, and mortification of themselues,
seeking after puritie of hart, with sparkeling desires, and feruent
prayers, as well externall, as internall, by which they desire to
please God, and to be vnited to him. These sort of Christians haue
found out the right way to heauen, and are more deare to Almighty
God, then all those which wee haue spoken of before: but yet, because
they haue not long beene trained vp in these exercises, they be
subiect to inconstancy sliding backe to their own wil, pleasure, &
liking: wherof they repenting turne againe to god, resigning vp
thēselues as they did before.

[Here follow the sixth, seventh, and eighth staves, Sigs. C2ʳ-
C3ᵛ.]

[C3ᵛ]

The Ninth
Staffe.

Vpon the Ninth, and last Staffe stand they, which by hard &
strōg exercises, and by heauenly desires, for the loue of God, haue
almost consumed their flesh and blood, and the marrowe of their
body, and doe seeme to haue no other forces then these, which the
liuelines of the spirit doth afford them: for their blood is boyled in
the feruour of Gods loue, which chalengeth in them [C4] dominion,
and causeth nature to doe & suffer aboue nature. These are the most
deare children of God, vpon whom hee bestoweth the fulnes of his
gifts, & graces. Neuerthelesse they rest not in such, as for themselues, because they haue vtterly extinguished all respect of theyr
owne profit, and delight, because they haue planted themselues only
in Faith, accompanied with nothing but Charitie, by which they
desire to sustaine all aduersitie, for the honour of God, and the

saluation of their soules, without any assistance of diuine comfort, because they thinke them-selues worthy of all abiection, & desolation, deeming them selues inferiour to euery creature without fiction, wishing nothing more then to be dispised and trodden vnder foote of all men, yea and to indure all paine & miserie, euen vnto most bitter death. As touching the outwarde man, they seeke after the most abiect thinges, and are destitute of all humane comfort, and concerning the inward man, they desire onely Charitie, voide of all sensible consolation, and loaded with all desola-[C4ᵛ]tion, and oppression of hart, in such sort, as they can neuer suffer so much, but still they desire to suffer more, to the end they may more perfectly be like to their Sauiour, who in his Passion by only loue did wrastle with sensualitie, being destitute of all comfort, that hee might redeeme vs and teach vs, this to be the way of denying our selues, by which wee ought to follow through the straite gate of saluation, him which is blessed for euer.

[Woodcut of Christ carrying the cross and a biblical passage]

VI.

A

Memoriall
of a Christian Life.

Wherein Are Treated All
such thinges, as apperteyne vnto a Christian to doe, from the beginninge of his conuersion, vntil the ende of his perfection.

Deuided into Seauen Treatises: the particulars whereof are noted in the page followinge.

Written first in the Spanishe tongue, by the famous Religious Father, *F. Lewis de Granada,* Prouinciall of the holie order of Preachers, in the Prouince of Portugal.

[Woodcut of the letters IHS surrounded
by scenes and objects from the Passion]

Imprinted at Rouen, by George L'oyselet.
Anno Domini.　M. D. LXXXVI.[1]
[trans. Richard Hopkins[2]]
[This work begins with a brief table of contents, p. 2.]

---

[1]Allison and Rogers, I, Entry 472. *STC* 16903.
[Anr. ed.] Imprinted at Rouen, by George Loyselet, 1599. Imprint false; pr. [secretly in England.] Allison and Rogers, I, Entry 473. *STC* 16904. This work is a translation of the first volume of Granada's *Memorial de la vida christiana* (Lisbon, 1565). Although Granada's works were immensely popular among English Protestants, no Protestant adaptation of this work was made; probably, as Maria Hagedorn points out, the distinct Catholic character of this book was unappealing to those outside the Catholic Church (p. 57). Luis de Granada (1504-1588) was a Dominican ascetical and mystical writer, whose works were written rather late in life and whose popularity was extensive both in Spain and abroad. St. Teresa of Avila in her Constitutions recommends Granada's work, and she herself thought very highly of them (E. A. Peers, *A Handbook to the Life and Times of St. Teresa and St. John of the Cross* [Westminster, Maryland, 1954], p. 163). Granada was born at Granada and entered the Dominican Order in 1524. He studied at Valladolid, served eight years as Prior of Escala Coeli Convent near Córdoba. spent some time at Badajoz, and finally went to Portugal, where he became the Provincial of his Order and confessor to Doña Catalina, the Queen of Portugal (E. A. Peers, *Spanish Mysticism* [London, 1924], p. 90). In 1572, he retired to the Convent of Santo Domingo at Lisbon, where he passed the remainder of his life in prayer, silence, and the writing of spiritual books. For an excellent modern study of Granada, see Raphaël-Louis Oechslin's *Louis de Grenade ou la Rencontre avec Dieu* (Paris, 1954). The standard biography of Granada is Luis Muñoz's *La vida y virtues del V. P. Luis de Granada* (Madrid, 1751). Maria Hagedorn's *Reformation und Spanische Andaschtsliteratur. Luis de Granada* in *Kölner Anglistische Arbeiten* (XXI [Leipzig, 1934], pp. 1-165) is a standard work on the influences of Granada in England.

[2]Richard Hopkins (d. 1590) entered St. Albans, Oxford, as a commoner at the age of seventeen and was in residence there in 1563. He was probably the nephew of Stephen Hopkins, who was confessor to the Bishop of Aquila, the Spanish Ambassador at London, and also was chaplain to Cardinal Pole (Gillow, III, 385). Hopkins left Oxford because of religious tensions there and studied law for some time at the Middle Temple, but he withdrew later because of religious disquietude. In 1566, he was in Louvain, where he was influenced by his friend, Dr. Harding, to go to Spain and to learn Spanish. Having become proficient in Spanish, he returned to Louvain to translate into English Spanish devotional works. He died at Paris around 1590 (Gillow, III, 385-388).

[3]

To the Right Hono-
rable, and Worshipfvll, of
the Fower Principall Howses
of Cowrte in London, professinge the studie
of the Common Lawes of our Realme.

Vnderstanding by good intelligence, of the general wel liking,
and gratefull acceptation, that your Honours and worshippes haue
had, of the *Boke of Meditations,* of the reuerend Religious father *F.
Lewis de Granada,* published of late by me in our English tongue,
and dedicated vnto you,[3] I haue bene thereby much the rather prouoked to dedicate also vnto you this boke of the same Godlie *A Commen-*
Awthor, intituled *a Memoriall of a Christian life:* which among all *dation of*
his bokes of deuotion is accompted most profitable for all sortes of *this boke.*
Persones. Because it conteyneth all such Godlie instructions, as are
necessarie for euerie Christian, from the time of his Conuersion
from his sinfull life, vntill he attayne vnto the perfection of a Christian life.

And trewlie, the Methode and order that the Awthor hath taken
therein is so excellent, and the doctrine, and instructions so singu-
larlie well treated, for direction both of the learned and vnlearned in
spirituall life, (wherein the Awthor hath verie discreetelie framed
his stile to serue both their capacities, and especiallie of the vnlearned,) that diuers Godlie learned Diuines intending to treat in
like maner of the same argumentes, haue plainlie, and with great
humilitie confessed, that he writeth with such a rare vertuous spirit,
and hath such a singular gift in explaining his instructions, and in
pearcing the hart of a Christian reader, with his zealous Godlie
aduises, and persuasions, that they haue therefore either [4]
abridged, or translated his bokes, & directed them vnto diuers noble
vertuous personages, that requested them to treat of those matters.[4]

And for mine owne opinion, hauing read a great number of spirituall bokes in diuers languages, (all worthie certainlie of great com-

---

[3]*Of Prayer, and Meditation* (1582). This work is entry XII in this anthology (pp. 175-211).

[4]Granada's popularity in England is unquestionable. For an interesting
discussion of Elizabethan translations (Catholic and Protestant), see Helen
White's *English Devotional Literature* (pp. 104-110). Such well-known persons
as Francis Meres and Thomas Lodge are numbered among the translators
of Granada.

mendation,) yet coulde I neuer finde anie, whose spirite, and wise order of writing hath so well liked my tast, and iudgement, as this Godlie Authors bokes, & especiallie this *Memoriall of a Christian life*.

In which boke he is greatlie to be commended, for that in treating therein of the dewe reformation of our liues, and consequentlie of the whole Christian State, he hath followed the Godlie order of proceedinge of S. Iohn Baptist, and of our Sauiour Christ, and of al his Apostles, Bisshoppes, and Priestes, in foundinge the Christian Religion, in all Countreis, that haue bene conuerted to the faith of Christ: I mean, by preaching to the people, to do Penaunce for their synnes, and to Confesse them, and to shewe frutes worthie of penaunce, by doinge austere paynfull workes of Satisfaction for them.

And woulde God, that the late Apostatas, *Luther, Zuinglius, Oecolampadius,*[5] *Caluin, Beza,* and other their schollers, pretending nowe to be reformers of Christes Catholike Churche in this our corrupt age, had followed the same Godlie order of proceeding in their maner of preaching Reformation.

For in my simple Iudgement, the right assured waye to reforme Christendome, beinge at this present so farre corrupted in euerie Countrey, is not by force of Armes, nor by terror, & constraint of greiuous penall lawes, forfeitures, confiscations, and executions with terrible deathes: because the Christian Commonwealth in such a general corruption of al estates cannot by anie other means be dewlie reformed, mainteyned, and preserued, but by such as it was at the first fownded, and increased. As by the Bisshoppes & Pastors preaching of Penaunce, contempt of the worlde, mortification of the flesh, & geuing themselues apparant good example thereof to the common people, and shewinge more Christian Charitable zeale in their deedes, than in their wordes, which was the godlie order of proceeding of the Apostles, and auncient holie Bishopes their Successors, in founding, and increa-[5]singe the Christian Religion in the Primitiue Churche.

And the like godlie order of proceeding for Reformation of the Christian State, hath in some ages afterwardes bene vsed by *S. Benedict, S. Barnarde, S. Dominicke, S. Frauncis,* and by al the

Matth. 3.
Vers. 2.6.8.
Marc. 1.5.15.
Marc. 6.12.
Luc. 13.1.5.
Luc. 24.47.
Act. 2.38.
Act. 19.18.
Act. 16.20.
Hebr. 6.1.

The right assured waie to reforme Christendome.

---

[5]John Oecolampadius (1482-1531), whose real name was Hussgen, was a German reformer. His leadership helped establish Protestantism at Basle and Berne. He was a champion of both Luther and Zwingli (*Oxford Dictionary of the Christian Church*, ed. F. L. Cross [London, 1957], p. 976).

Sainctes, which haue in their times by their wonderfull extraordinarie godlie example of leadinge holie penitencial liues, in vtter contempt of the world, & mortifienge their fleshe, by continuall fasting, watching, prayer, wearing of haircloth, disciplining, and whipping their bodies, & other austere vsage therof, conuerted manie thowsandes in euerie coūtrey of Christendome, some from Schisme, & Heresie, and some from their dissolute licētious careles liues, whereby the whole Christian State that seemed in their times in a maner incurable, and vnpossible to be reformed, did recouer a godlie Reformation. And therevpon deuotion hath in such wise generallie increased emonge all Christian people, that they haue builded such a great number of goodlie Churches, Chappels, Monasteries, Hospitalles, Colledges, and other holie fowndations, in euerie Christian Countrey, remayning euen yet for the most parte vntil this our tyme. So as our Sauiour Christ hath bene much glorified by the same & the Christian Religion held in wonderful admiration, euen emong the Iewes, Turkes, Sarasins, & other Infidelles, that were otherwise professed deadlie enemies vnto it.

Not one of the auncient Christians that builded our Churches Colledges, and other holie foundations, were of the Caluinistes Religion.

But we see, that the late Apostatas, *Luther, Zuinglius, Caluin, Beza,* & other newe pretended reformers of Christes Catholike Churche,[6] woulde in no wise followe the auncient holie Bishoppes, Pastors, and Religious persons, & other Sainctes, in their godlie order of proceedinge for Reformation of the Christian State, and therefore their frutes haue prooued accordinglie. For theise late Apostatas, hauing addicted themselues vtterlie to discredit all the auncient vertuous Bishoppes, Pastors, and Gouernors of Christes Catholike Churche, in al ages, and Countreis, since Christes time, yea, & most of the Christian doctrines beleeued and professed by our auncient holie forefathers, haue maliciouslie endeuored, by procuringe Schismaticall innouations in Religion in diuers Countreis of Christendome, and by infectinge the ignorant artificers, & other simple people, with their newe Heretical licentious doctrines, to abolishe awaye thereby the Catholike [6] Religion, and in place thereof to found a newe deuised politike licentious Religion, consisting of manifold different Sectes, that as professed enemies to al vnitie, & vniformitie in Religion amonge al Christians, are not ashamed openlie to protest, that their doctrine is to professe and vse diuers

Note, that in our age, the seuerall formes of Gouernment of the Common

---

[6]It is noteworthy that Hopkins does not mention by name the English reformers in his condemnation. His intention throughout the dedication is to stress the common tradition of the Catholic Church and the Church of England, as opposed to the "foreign influence" of Lutheranism and Calvinism.

wealthes of Florence, Siena, Pisa, Geneua, Holland, & Zealand, have chaunged, and altered, from one forme or kinde of gouernement, vnto an other forme or kinde of gouernement. And so by the Caluinistes newe doctrine, the like variable chaunginges should be of the formes of gouernement of the Churches there, which can not be, without manie horrible incōueniences.

In the printed englishe boke of disputation with F. Campion in the Tower, in the fourth dayes conference. folio. 102. Dd. iiij.

Genes. 15. Vers. 1.15. Exod. 33. vers. 17.19. 4. Reg. 1. Luc. 1.28.30. Luc. 10.20. Iohan. 14.3. Iob. 9.28. Rom. 8.17.

variable formes of Gouernment of their newe Churches, in euerie Countrey, and State, conformablie to the diuers, and seueral variable formes of Gouernement vsed in euerie Common wealthe in Christendome. And consequentlie, their *Lutheran, Caluinisticall, and Puritan Churches,* can neuer be firmelie, & peaceablie setled in anie one vniforme Religion, & order of ministration of Sacramentes, throughout al Coūtreis of Christendome: but shalbe euermore totteringe, and waueringe, in alteringe, & chaunginge diuerslie, & variably, the formes of gouernement of their Churches, in euerie Countrey, and State, as often as the forme of Gouernment of anie Commonwealth amonge them doth alter, and chaunge, from one different forme of Gouernement to an other.[7]

[This theme continues, pp. 6-11.]

[11] And therefore let no man maruaile, that theise newe Preachers doe neuer preache to the people, to doe penaunce for their synnes, and to fast and praye for them, seinge all their doctrines beinge wholie grounded vpon their newe Heretical licentious doctrine of iustification by onelie faith, (which newe doctrine they nowe terme to be the Soule of their newe Caluinisticall Churche,) are directlie contrarie to doinge of penaunce, and vnto all kinde of spirituall exercises of an austere vertuous life, and doe breede in all their followers onelie an arrogant presumption of securitie of their owne peculiar election, predestination, iustification, and saluation, whereby they are moued to singe psalmes in their Schismaticall Congregations, and at home, onelie to thanke God for the same. As though Almightie God had reueiled vnto euerie *Caluinist,* and *Puritan,* by such a speciall diuine reuelation that euerie one of them is of the number of the Elect, & predestinate vnto saluation, as he reueyled by a special diuine Reuelation vnto some fewe of the Sainctes, as vnto *Abraham, Moises, Elias,* and to the *most blessed Virgin* the mother of God, and to the *Apostles,* that they were Elect & predestinate to be saued: & as though all *Caluinistes,* and *Puritans* were alreadie raiginge and triumphinge in this mortal life with our Sauiour Christ in his glorious kingdome of Heauen, and nede not here in this vale of miserie, to mortifie their rebellious fleshe,

---

[7]Hopkins obviously wanted the Puritans to appear as politically dangerous to the established order, thereby possibly shifting at least some of the persecution from the Catholics onto the Puritans. He proposes such books as the present one as an effective antidote to the civil disorder which may arise from Puritan theology.

and to iudge them selues, and to carie dailie their Crosse, and to worke their saluation with feare, and tremblinge, as al Christians are commaunded in the holie Scriptures: & as though there were no daie of Iudgement for Christians to expect and feare in regarde of their sinnes.

2. Cor. 4.10.
Galat. 5.24.
1. Cor. 11.31.
Luc. 9.23.
1. Iohn. 2.6.
Phil. 2.12.
1. Cor. 9.27.
Psa. 118.120.
Iob. 31.14.23.
Ioel. 2.11.
Amos. 5.18.
Mat. 12.36.
Matt. 16.27.
Luc. 12.4.5.
2. Cor. 5.10.
Apoc. 14.
vers. 6.7.13.
Apoc. 22.12.

And it is wonderful, that the diuel hath so bewitched theise Apostatas of our time, that hauinge so arrogantlie presumed without anie lawful vocation, and awthoritie of the gouernors of Christes Church, & before they haue reformed their owne liues, to pretende to reforme all the [12] Ecclesiastical State of Christes Catholike Church, & hauinge proceeded therein with such a newe and straunge order of preaching of reformation, grounded vpon their newe Heretical licentious doctrine of iustification by onelie faith, contrarie to the order of preachinge of Penaunce, & of Confession, & of austeritie of life, vsed by S. Iohn Baptist, and by our Sauiour Christ, & his Apostles, & the auncient Christian Bisshoppes, and Pastors of the Primitiue Churche, & nowe perceauing them selues by their owne palpable experience, (as both the *Caluinistes* & *Puritans* in Englande do in their printed bokes plainlie confesse,[8]) that the people of our Realme are not more sanctified in their liues by their newe order of pretended reformation, than they were before their Schismaticall departure from the vnitie & obedience of Christes Catholike Church, but are & do daylie growe still worse, & worse, in pride, arrogancie, blasphemie, glotonie, dronkennes, adulterie, periurie, vsurie, detraction, lyenge, and in all kind of deceitfull & false dealing, yea, euen vnto a contempt of all the holie Mysteries of the Christian Religion, & to be vtterlie careles of their owne saluation, & to become Atheistes, yet will they still proceed in their newe disorderlie maner of reformation of Christes Church, and with an intollerable shameful

In D. Whitgiftes defence against the Puritans. pag. 176. See the Puritans epistle to the Church of England, in their second Reply against D. Whitgiftes defence. The frutes of the Caluinistes Religion.

---

[8]This is probably a reference to Thomas Cartwright's two attacks on John Whitgift entitled *A Replye to an answere made of M. Doctor Whitegifte. Againste the Admonition to the Parliament* (1573?) and *The rest of the second replie to Thomas Cartwright agaynst Master Doctor Whitgifts second answer* (1577) (Southern, p. 199n.). John Whitgift (c. 1530-1604) was the Archbishop of Canterbury, appointed by Elizabeth to that position in 1583 to succeed the Puritan Grindal. He was a vehement enemy of the Puritans and was especially zealous in repressing the Marprelate tracts. In 1584-85, he vigorously opposed the Puritan attempt to impose a Presbyterian form of government on the Church of England (*Oxford Dictionary of the Christian Church*, p. 1456). Whitgift, though opposed to Catholicism, favored episcopacy and ritual and thereby was more sympathetic, in attitude at least, toward Catholics than toward Puritans. By defending Whitgift against the Puritans, Hopkins obviously expected to win the favor of Anglicans and to lessen the antagonism against things Catholic.

impudencie, do so proudlie vaunt, & bragge, in vayne commendation
of them selues, & of their newe Caluinistical Religion, euen in a
printed Englishe boke published of late with Priuilege ageinst the
Puritans, that they affirme therein without blushing, that their newe
Caluinisticall Bisshoppes (notwithstanding they be notoriouslie
knowen to be exceding fleashlie, & couetous,) are for honestie of
life, not onelie to be compared vnto, but euen also to be preferred
before the auncient holie Bisshops of the Primitiue Churche: And
also that no Bisshoppes in anie age since the Apostles tyme haue
taught and helde so sounde, and perfect doctrine, as their newe
Bisshoppes in Englande doe at this tyme: and that their doctrine in
Englande at this daie is much more perfect, and sounde, by manie
degrees, than it was in anie age since the Apostles tyme: & that the
Sacramentes be nowe more sincerelie ministred in England, than
they were in *S. Iustine, Tertullian,* & *S. Cyprians* tyme, being so
neare the Apostles.

*See. D. Whit-
giftes defence
ageinst the
Puritans.
pag. 472.
473. 526.*

[Hopkins' attack on the Calvinists continues, pp. 13-23.]

[23] Nowe for Conclusion, I most humblie desier your honors,
and worshippes, not onelie diligentlie to reade ouer, but also
earnestlie to followe the Godlie instructions conteyned in this
notable vertuous boke. Wherein the Godlie Awthor hath excellentlie
well taught vs, howe to be sorowfull for our sinnes, & howe to
Confesse them, and make Satisfaction for the gilte of temporall
payne dewe vnto them, and with what dewe preparation and order
we must receaue the most blessed Sacrament of the Aultar. And he
hath also geuen vs verie notable good Christian Rules for the better
direction of our liues. And withall I haue annexed & dispersed in
some partes of this boke diuers additions, collected out of the best
learned Catholike bokes I coulde finde. The which additions, in
regarde of the present generall infection of our Countrey with manie
pestilent Heresies, are not onelie in my opinion, but in the graue
Iudgement also of other more wise, and learned men, thought verie
necessarie, for the better explaning, and vnderstanding of the
Churches doctrine, concerninge Confession, and Satis-[24]faction, &
diuers cases of Conscience. The additions are printed in a distinct
seuerall letter from the Awthors boke, sauinge that certayne deuout
prayers onelie of the Awthors be printed with the same distinct
letter. And whatsoeuer Commendation is to be geuen for the additions, is to be referred vnto diuers Godlie learned Diuines, that haue

assisted me therein, with their graue learned aduises, and corrections.

I beseeche Almightie God to blesse, direct, and confirme all your Honors, and worshippes with a principall Spirite, that yee maye so liue and die in the auncient Catholike faith and Religion of our holie Christian forefathers, that yee may raigne also with our Sauiour Christ and with them, in euerlastinge glorious felicitie in the kingdome of Heauen, where neuer yet came, nor can possiblie come, anie of the *Lutheran, Zuinglian, Caluinian, Puritan,* or other damnable Hereticall Sectes, that haue died vnrepentant therein, out of the vnitie, & obedience of Christes Catholike Churche. From Roan, vpon the holie Feast of the Conuersion of S. *Paule,* in the yeare of our Lorde. 1586.

By Him That Desiereth
aswell the saluation of all your honors, and
worshippes Soules, as of his owne Soule.

Richard Hopkins.

[1]

The Prologve to
the Christian
Reader.

Like as the tastes and iudgementes of writers haue bene diuerse (good christian reader,) euen so the matters and argumētes whereof they haue treated haue ben also diuerse. Some there haue bene, which beinge affectionated vnto the bewtie of eloquence haue emploied themselues to frame a perfit orator, takinge him from his childehode, and leadinge him through all the steppes and degrees of that facultie, vntil they haue brought him vnto the highest perfectiō of the same. Others haue endeuored after the like sorte to forme a perfecte prince, others a capitaine, others a courtier. And thus hath eche one trauailed to extolle and aduance that thinge with his penne which he most estiemed. Nowe of this are we right well assured, that emonge all the thinges [2] of this world, there is nothing of greater price and estimation, nothinge more excellente & diuine, thā

A Christiã
is ordeined
to a super-
naturall
ende.

a perfecte Christian. The which as he is ordeined vnto a supernaturall ende so the life which he liuethe is also supernaturall. For which cause he is called of the holie fathers a heauenlie man, or an earthlie angell. Wherefore sith that other faculties (which are so much inferior to this facultie, as their ende is inferiour to the ende of this) haue had writers which with so greate diligence haue sette forthe what soeuer seemed necessaire vnto the perfection of them, euen from the firste beginninge vntill the latter endinge, how much more conuenient were it that the like diligence shoulde not be wantinge in this heauenlie profession, the which as it is of higher dignitie than all other professions, so is it a harder matter to apprehend it exactelie, and therefore hath more nede to set forth and written of. Nowe this is the thinge (good Christian reader) which I haue so manie yeares desired: to wit, to see some booke that should treate particulerlie howe to forme a perfit Christian, and that might conteine a briefe somme of all such thinges as do appertaine vnto the professiõ of this heauenlie life. For like as good artificers do endeuor to haue all such tooles and instrumẽtes as belonge to their occupation, and as those that studie any arte or science do seeke to haue some booke wherein is conteined whatsoeuer [3] concerneth that science, that hauinge eche thinge sette in order together in one place their memorie might the lesse be distracted, euen so me thought it was verie requisite to do the like in this profession, which is the arte of artes, and science of sciences: to the ende that all such as desire to serue almightie God (hauinge this commoditie readie framed to their handes) might verie easelie finde out an instructiõ, and light, to directe their liues, and that the ghostlie fathers, and Catholique preachers, whiche are zealous of the Christian common weale, might also haue without any greate charge whether to referre their ghostelie children, and hearers, and such as come vnto thẽ for counsel, to vnderstãde whatsoeuer belongeth to their profession.

I know this right well that there want not for this purpose at this daie a number of bookes which do conteine verie sounde and Catholique doctrine: howbeit for the greater parte of thẽ they do attende to some one particuler matter, and will not binde them selues to treate in a smalle volume of all such matters as do concerne a perfecte christian life. And albeit that the Catholique Catechismes (which are sommes or abrigementes of the Christiã doctrine) do treate of euerie thinge that appertaineth to the same, yet for so much as these haue respecte to declare the substance of thinges, and such as belonge to the vnderstãdinge thereof, the doctrine of such Ca-[4]techismes apperteineth rather to speculation, than to practize: I meane hereby, that such doctrine tendeth rather to giue light to the vnderstandinge, than to moue the wil vnto the exercise and vse of vertue.

Now for this cause I haue determined with the grace of god, and helpe of the writinges of the holie fathers, who in diuerse partes of theire writinges haue handled all theise argumentes, to gather out of them all this booke, wherein is treated of all theise matters. In whiche booke I meane to forme a perfecte christian, trayninge him throughout the passages and exercises of this life, euen from the beginninge of his conuersion, vntill he come vnto the ende of perfection. And in doinge this, I make accompte that I take it in hande so rough, and vnwrought, as if one shoulde hewe it downe in the wood with his boughes and barke, and shoulde beginne to labour vpon it by litle and litle vntill he bringe it vnto his due perfection. For the performance whereof, in the firste treatise I set before him paradise, and hell, and the greate benefites which do accompanie vertue: and withall the bounden dutie he oweth to followe the same, that by this meane he may be induced to make a firme determination with him selfe to forsake sinne, and retourne vnto the seruice of his lorde, and creator. Afterwardes presupposinge this resolute determination in him, forsomuch as the entrie vnto this waie is by the [5] sacrament of penance, I teache him in the seconde treatise after what sorte he ought to do pēnaunce for his sinnes: where are set forthe manie considerations, and praiers, that serue to moue him to an earnest sorowe and abhorringe of the sinnes and offences of his former life. And there is also an instruction to teach him how to confesse him selfe of them, and how to satisfie almightie god with due satisfaction. After confession, there followeth the receuinge of the most blessed sacrament of the Aulter, and so ensueth immediatlie the therde treatise, wherein he is taught after what sorte he ought to prepare him selfe to communicate worthelie, and what thinges are requisite thereunto, with praiers also which are to be saide both before and after he hath receaued the most blessed sacramente. When he hath receiued theise sacramentes, it followeth forthwith that he doe amende his life: and therefore I haue adioyned the fourth treatise, whiche handleth the same matter: And for somuche as there be some Christians that content them-

What the intention of the Author is in this booke.

The first treatise.

The secōd treatise.

The third treatise.

The fourthe treatise.

selues with doinge only that which is of necessitie to be done for
their saluation: and some others also that will passe more forwarde,
and walke to perfection, (the which persons not beinge contented
with the charge of the commaundmētes, will laie moreouer vpon
them selues an other charge of such thinges as are taught in the
ghospell by waie of counsell onlie) therefore I haue sette [6] forthe
in that treatise two rules of good life, the one is cōmon for the first
sorte, the other is straiter and more spirituall for the other sorte.
And because no mā can either begynne or perseuere in good life
without the helpe of the grace of god, the which is obteined by
meanes of praier, therefore I haue immediatlie after the instructions
and rules of good life treated of praier. Now wheras there be two
kindes of praier, the one which is pronounced with the voice, cōmonlie called *vocall praier:* the other which is conceaued in the minde,
commonlie called *mentall praier:* of the first I haue treated in the
fiuethe treatise, where are sette out manie Vocall praiers seruinge
for diuerse purposes and vses of a Christian mans life: and there are
also declared the conditions requisite to a good praier: but of the
seconde kinde, which is *mentall praier,* I haue hādeled in the sixthe
treatise, where I treate onlie of the matter of this kinde of praier,
which is the consideration of the principall misteries of the life of
our Sauiour Christ, and of the benefites of almightie God. For as
touchinge the rest that apperteineth to this argument, we haue alredie treated in our *booke of praier, and meditation.* After all this
there remaineth nothinge else but to arriue vnto perfectiō, (the
which consisteth in the loue of god) and of this I haue treated in
the seauenthe and last treatise, wherein al such thinges are declared
as serue to obtein this supreame vertue, as [7] those also which doe
hinder it. And there be moreouer set forthe certaine considerations,
and praiers, wherein he ought to exercise him selfe for the obteininge
of the same vertue.

The Fi-
ueth trea-
tise.

The six-
the trea-
tise.

*The perfe-
ction of a
Christian
consisteth
in the loue
of god.*
The sea-
uenthe
treatise.

This is nowe Christian reader the course of all the Christian life,
deuided into theise seauen iourneis, whereunto may be reduced
whatsoeuer this heauenly philosophie teacheth vs.

And for somuche as the foure first treatises do conteine doctrine
cōcerninge thinges that ought to be donne, and the other three that
followe doe serue rather for the exercise of praier, and of the loue of
god, (the which be such thinges as a man ought alwaies to haue in
his handes) I thought it good therefore to deuide this whole booke

into two Volumes: to the ende that euerie man might alwaies carie
with him in his bosome the seconde volume without any great
burdē,[9] beinge so necessarie as it is for all times, and places. And
because all theise matters are treated here brieflie, it seemed to me
verie conuenient to call this booke a *memoriall,* as wherein a man
vseth to write such thinges as he hath to doe in a briefe sorte. And
yet the briefenes of this booke is not such, but that it conteyneth all
such thinges as seeme necessarie for the argument of the same.

    Trewe it is, that the matter of this booke is verie copious, and
plentifull, wherein there be manie thinges to be saide, and verie wor-
[8] thie to be committed to writinge, but theise may remaine for
other writers. And yet in case it shall please almightie god to pro-
longe a litle while the time of my life, (which so swiftlie runneth
awaie in post) I may then handle more at large some partes of this
booke, especiallie the exhortation to good life, and the rules of good
life, & the treatise of the loue of god, together with the treatise of
the life of our Sauiour Christ. And albeit the thinge we pretēde here
to doe, (which is to forme a perfecte Christian) be properlie the
worke of the holie ghoste, yet neuertheles like as grace excludeth
not our trauaile & industrie, but must rather of necessitie concurre
therewith, euen so the inwarde instruction of almightie god excludeth not the owtwarde teachinge of men, but doth of necessitie
require the same. The which office particulerlie apperteineth vnto
the Priestes, and pastors of the Catholique Church, vnto whom almightie God referreth vs, that they shoulde teache and informe vs in
his lawe. And therefore emonge the priestlie vestimentes of the
highe priestes, there was one that was called the *Rationall,* (the
which was put vpon his breast) wherein were written theise wordes,
doctrina, & veritas: Doctrine: and Trewthe: the which two thinges
shoulde be in the breast of *Aaron,* to the ende that from thence as
from a principall fountaine they might be deriued vnto all the
others. And this is so principall an [9] office, that *Moyses* reserued
it onlie for him selfe by the aduise of his father in lawe Iethro, who
counseled him to committe all other causes, and tēporall affaires
vnto other iudges, but for such thinges as apperteined vnto the religion and seruice of god, and teaching of the people the Ceremonies

Why this boke is called a memoriall.

Deut. 17. verse. 12.
Malac. 2. 7.
Luc. 10. 16.
Heb. 13. 17.

Rational.

Leuit. 8. 8.

Exod. 18. vers. 19. & 20.

---

    [9] Only the first volume was published by Hopkins. At the end of the
translation, however, he states: "The Second Volume of the Memoriall of
a Christian Life I haue alreadie translated, and am preparing it towardes
the Print. . . ." (sig. Pp7ᵛ) To my knowledge, the second volume was not
published.

of the lawe, and after what sorte they ought to serue and honor almightie God, that he shoulde reserue that to him selfe. And because certeine priestes were afterwardes negligent in doynge this office, almightie God sente vnto them one of his Prophetes to tell them theise wordes: because thou hast caste awaie the science and knowlege of my lawe, I will also cast the awaie, that thou shall serue me no more in the office of prieste hood. And for a most greuous punishement almightie God threatened them by his prophet Esaie theise kinde of scourges, sayinge: that by reason of theire great synnes *he wolde punish them with a strange and terrible punishment, which shoulde be, that the wisedome of the wise shoulde perishe and the vnderstandinge of the sagest emonge the people shoulde be obscured.* Now as the wante of knowlege in the superiors is here declared to be one of the greatest scourges & terriblest plagues of God: euen so also is the wāte of knowlege in the inferiors no lesse plague and punishment of God. For when the light of the vnderstandinge is taken awaie, which gwideth all our doinges, and is as it were the principall [10] wheele of this clocke, that ruleth and moueth all the Christian life, what may be looked for els, but blindenes, and ignorance, with other great incōueniences. And that this is the cause thereof, all the holie scriptures doe clearlie witnes vnto vs. Almightie God saith by the Prophete Esaie: *This people is not wise, and therefore he that created them shall not take pitie vpon them, neither shall he that formed them pardon them.* And in an other place. *Therefore* (saith he) *was my people made captiue, because they had no knowlege, and their nobles died for honger, and the multitude of them perished for thirste.* The verie same is confirmed by the Prophet Baruche, sayinge: that the cause of the captiuitie of the children of Israel, and of theire wanderinge through the landes of their enemies, was *for that they had forsaken the fountaine of wisedome.* And vnto this verie cause he attributeth the condemnation of the Giantes, sayinge: that *because they had no knowlege they perished through their ignorance.* For remedie whereof saint Paule writeth vnto the Collossians that the worde and doctrine of Christe should be plētifullie preached emong them, and that one shoulde teache an other, and admonish them of such thinges as they ought to doe. Wherfore sith there is no office (be it neuer so base) but that it needeth some rules and preceptes to haue it well and rightlie discharged, how much more neede hath this office, beinge

Osee. 4.
Iere. 30.

*The igno-
rance of
priestes &
pastors is a
great scourg
of god.*
*Esaye. 29.
verse. 14.*

*The light
of the vn-
derstãdinge
is the guide
of the Chri-
stian life.*

*Esaie 27.
11.*

Esaie 5. 13.

*Baruc. 3.
verse. 12.*

Baruc. 3. 28.

*Coloss. 3.
verse. 16.*

the greatest of all other offices, which is to knowe how to please and [11] serue almightie God, to obteine the kingdome of heauen, and to preuaile against the forces and wilie deceiptes of our enemie the deuel? How shall a simple vnlearned man vnderstande how much this matter importeth him, if there be not laide before him the promises and threatninges of almightie God, and the great benefites also for which he is bound to serue him? How shal he Knowe how to confesse his sinnes perfectlie, if he be not instructed in the partes of the sacramēte of pennaunce, and how he ought to behaue him selfe in euerie one of them? How shall he be sorowfull and re- pentant for his sinnes, if there be not declared vnto him the reasons and causes that shoulde moue him to be sorowfull for them? How shall he communicate and receaue the most blessed sacrament worthelie, to the cōforte and profite of his soule, if he be not taught those thinges that belonge thereunto? How shall he knowe which waie to order his life, to obteine vertues, and to eschewe vices, if he knowe not the meanes whereby he ought to seeke for the one, to resiste the other, and to vnderstand the temptations and snares of the enemie? How shall he make any praier that shalbe fruitefull vnto him, and accompanied with such conditions, & vertues, as be required thereunto, if he haue not some instruction to teache him howe to praie? How shall he obteine the loue of God, if he knowe not the meanes whereby it [12] is obtained, and the impedimentes and lettes that doe hinder him from it, and the exercises wherein he ought to exercise him selfe for the obteininge thereof? Of all this light we stande in greate neede for all theise thinges aforesaide, sithence we bringe them not with vs from our mothers wombe, but we are rather borne in such wise, that we may well be figured by that mā in the ghospel, who was blinde from his natiuitie.

How neces- sarie this booke is.

Ioan. 9.

And although it be the office of Catholique preachers to cure this blindnes with the light of godes worde: yet nothwithstandinge theise be not euerie where to be founde, neither do all preachers treat of theise so necessarie matters, nor yet can they well (speakinge gen- erallie) descēde to such particularities, as this moral doctrine re- quireth. The which as it is exercised in particuler workes, so it requireth particuler instructions: which manner of teaching is not vsed in pulpittes. And for all theise causes the readinge of deuout Catholique bookes is verie profitable: for somuch as they be vnto vs as it were domme preachers, which are neither tedious for lengthe, (because we may leaue them of when we list,) neither do they leaue

What is the office of a preacher.

Deuout ho- lie bookes are dome preachers.

vs with a greedie appetite by reasō of theire briefnes, for that it is in our owne power to continewe the reedinge of them so longe as we mynde to take profit thereby.

Now who is able to expresse the fruites that come of the worde of God beinge interpre-[13]ted and declared vnto vs by the Catholique Church: sithence it is the light that cleareth our vnderstandinge, the fier that inflameth our will, the hammer that mollifieth the hardnes of our harte, the knife that pareth awaie the superfluities of our passiōs, the candle that giueth vs light in all the passages of this life, the seede that yeldeth the fruites of life euerlastinge, finally, the foode and sustenance that susteineth, deliteth, fatteth, and strengtheneth our soules in God. The which fruites euerie one may enioy by readinge bookes conteininge holie Catholique doctrine.

To conclude so greate is the light and fruite that cōmeth by reading such bookes, that we haue seen by experiēce that many persōs haue changed their state of liues by readinge of bookes of deuotiō. The which persons being afterwardes demanded, what shoulde be the beginninge and chiefest cause of this their cōuersion and change of life, haue plainelie answered, that by readinge this or that booke of deuotion their mindes were moued so to doe. Consider that treasoror of the quene of Ethiopia, was he not reading of Esaie the Prophet in his chariot, at what time almightie God conuerted him by the meane of *Saint Philip,* by taking an occasiō of the same readinge? And those so notable and princelie workes which kinge Iosias did in all his kingdome, from whence did they proceede, but onlie of the readinge of a holie booke that was sente [14] vnto him from the priest Helchias? And that wonderfull cōuersion of Saint Augustine had it not his beginninge also by readinge of a holie booke? He him selfe writeth in the eight booke of his Confessions a thinge worthy to be recorded, the which for that it is so notable I haue thought good to rehearse it in this place.

[Here follows St. Augustine's account, pp. 14-18.]

[18] And albeit that this spirituall foode hath bene at all times verie necessarie (as the breade for our life,) yet is it much more needefull now in theise our corrupte daies. For in olde time in the primitiue churche the priestes and Curattes were so feruent and carefull in preachinge of the worde of God, that that might suffice to preserue and increase the faithfull people in vertue without any other readinge: but nowe alas, the priestes, and euen suche as [19]

The worde of God interpreted by the Catholique Churche is verie profitable. Ierem. 23. verse. 29. Psalm. 118. 130. 140. Luc. 24. 32. Psalm. 118. 105. Luc. 1. 79. Luc. 8. 15. 1. Mach. 12. 9. How great profite commeth by readinge of holie bookes.

Actes. 8. 30.

4. Reg. 22. verse. 13.

The conuersion of saint Augustine.

haue cure of soules, do beleue that they are bounde to nothinge els, but onlie to minister the sacramentes, and to saie a *masse* at their times appointed, and herewith they content themselues for the moste parte in villages, and townes, yea and in some populous cities also. Wherefore the greater the wante is that we haue at this daie in this behalfe, the greater neede* we haue to supplie the wante of good Catholike pastors, and Curattes, with good and deuout bookes.

Take therefore (good Christian reader) this smalle present, the which may in a litle volume, and with a smalle charge supplie in parte this defecte. For it may serue thee for a preacher, to exhorte thee vnto good life: for an instruction, to teache thee howe to leade a good life: for a confessionall, to instructe thee, how thou oughtest to confesse thy sinnes, and to make due preparation, when thou intendest to communicate, and receaue the most blessed sacrament of the Aulter: It may serue also for a booke of deuotion, wherein thou maist exercise thy selfe in praier, and it geueth thee moreouer abundance of matter for meditation: in which pointes are compre- hended the somme of all Christian Philosophie. And if this *memo- riall* be worthie of commendation, it is for that it conteineth matters so vniuersall, that it treateth of such thinges as doe apperteine to all Christians whatsoeuer they be, aswel to the beginners, as to those [20] that haue proceeded further in the spirituall life, and are come to some perfection. And if the fruite that shalbe reaped hereof, shalbe so greate as my diligence and trauaile hath bene in gathering all theise matters together, and in settinge them forthe in so plaine and easie a stile, to prouoke the appetites of such as are weake (vnto whom some times I direct my speeche) I shall accompte all my labor and paines to be verie well emploied. For so much as no bodilie labor can be so greate, that it may counteruaile with the least profit that ariseth in spirituall thinges.

Both townes and citties haue in this our corrupt age to ma- nie lewde bablinge he- reticall preachers: but the Aw- pleyneth of the great want of good Ca- tholike preachers.

thor com-

The Ende of the
Prologve.

[Here follow the first, second, and third treatises, which consider amendment of life, the three parts of confession (contrition, confes- sion, and satisfaction) and the Holy Eucharist, pp. 21-485.]

---

*neede] *ed.;* ueede

[486]

The Fovrthe Trea-
tise: Wherein Are Con-
teined Twoe Principall
Rules of the Christian life.

The Prologe.

When a man is now conuerted vnto Almightie God with all his hart, & hath procured the purifieng and cleansing of his sowle by meanes of theise twoe Sacramentes, [Penance and Holy Eucharist] of the which we haue treated here before, it remaineth, that he doe foorthwith applie all his care and diligence to the amendement, and well orderinge of his life: whereof we wil nowe treate in the Rules folowinge. And because grace foloweth commonlie the orderly pro-cedinge of nature, which procedeth alwaies in her workes from lesse to more: that is to saie, from lesse perfection to more perfection: therefore we will likewise procede in this doctrine, geuinge two Rules, and orders of life: the one for such, as beginne newly to serue God, and haue a desire to be saued: and the other for such, as doe besides this, desire to increase, and profit euerie daie more & more in the waie of vertue.

*Grace pro-
cedeth from
lesse perfec-
tion to
more per-
fection.
Two Rules
of a Chris-
tian life.*

[487] For the better vnderstanding whereof it is to be con-sidered, that all this doctrine of good life the prophet Dauid hath aptly diuided into two principal partes. The one is *in not doing euel:* and the other *in doing good:* that is to saie, the one in banishing from the sowle all kinde of vices: and the other in furnishinge & adorning it with all kinde of vertues. This is the clearest & most perfecte diuision, that might be geuen in this matter. For by obseru-inge of theise two pointes a man becommeth a newe man, and a newe creature, destroyeng with the first parte the image of the olde and earthlie Adam, and reforminge with the seconde, the image of the newe Adam, which is our Sauiour Iesus Christ. And withall, by this meane he commeth to be a man supernatural, & diuine. For as he was created for a diuine and supernatural ende: (which is, to see Almightie God in his owne glorie, and excellencie,) euen so the life, that disposeth him to this ende ought to be also supernatural, and diuine: sith that (accordinge vnto the Rules of philosophie,) the ende, and the meanes thereunto ought to be of one selfe same order, and proportion.

*Psalm. 33.
vers. 15.
Declina a
malo, &
fac bonum.*

*2. Phisic. 1.
23.*

And although in the exercise and practise both of life, and of doctrine, theise two thinges goe alwaies ioyntely together, (for vices can not be conquered without the helpe of vertues,) yet to geue more light vnto the matter, and for the plainer distinction of the doctrine, we wil seperate (so much as is possible) the one from the [488] other. In like maner it is meete to be aduertised here, that emong such thinges, as are conteined as well in this Rule, as in all other the like, some are of bounden dewtie, and some of will, or of perfection: that is to saie, some are *of Cōmaundement,* as the Commaundementes of God, and of his Churche: and some *of counsell,* as all other thinges, that are counselled vs in the Holie Scriptures: the which counsels doe helpe vs, for the better fulfillinge of such thinges, as are geuen vs in Commaundement, and also to atteine vnto greater perfection. This is verie necessarie to be aduertised, to the ende, that a man maie vnderstande, what he is bownde to doe of necessitie, and what dependeth of his will: & that he maie perceiue, in what degree eche of theise thinges is required of him, (that hauing this aduertisemente he maie vse greater diligence in such thinges, as he is bownde of dewtie to doe, than in others, which be but only voluntarie,) and that he maie also neuer leaue the one vndone for the other, (as we see some do:) which is a great abuse, and disorder. And for this cause it shalbe declared in the beginninge of this Rule, what we are bownd to doe of dewtie, (which is comprehēded in verie fewe wordes:) and afterwardes manie other thinges shalbe added, which do helpe to the fulfillinge of them, and to the obteininge of greater perfection. For although the keepinge of the Commaundementes doe suffice vnto saluation: yet, because in the waie of God, a man shoulde neuer take [489] contentation in his owne doinges, nor saie, I haue sufficiently perfourmed my dewtie: therefore manie other thinges shalbe here adioyned besides the essential thinges, for the behoofe of such as haue an earnest desire to profit and increase alwaies more and more in all kinde of vertue.

Vices can not be subdewed without the helpe of vertues.

Emonge the thinges that are proposed vnto Christians, some are of Commaundement, and some of counsell. Math. 19. vers. 12. Math. 19. vers. 21. Act. 4. vers. 34. 35. 1. Cor. 7. vers. 25. 1. Cor. 9. vers. 15. 16.

A mā maie not take a contentation in his owne doinges.

The ende of the Prologue.

[Here follow the rules for a good life, pp. 489-609. Hereafter follow an advertisement to Volume Two and a lengthy table of contents for the present volume, Sigs. Pp7ʳ-Qq4ʳ.]

VII.

The
Spiritval
Conflict.

Writen in Italian by a deuout
Seruant of God: and lately
translated into English
out of the same
language

*Militia est vita hominis super
terram Iob cap i. ver. i.*

[Woodcut of a crown of thorns surrounding the letters IHS]

Printed at Antwerp
1598[1]
[trans. John Gerard, S. J.[2]]

---

[1]Imprint false; pr. [secretly in England.] Allison and Rogers, II, Entry 759. This edition does not appear in the *STC*.
 [Anr. ed.] n.p.d. [1603-10.] Anon. Pr. [Douai, Charles Boscard.] Allison and Rogers, II, Entry 760. Not in *STC*.

 The authorship of this work has been disputed, but it is generally conceded that Lorenzo Scupoli (1530-1610), an Italian Theatine priest, is the author. Scupoli was born at Otranto and entered the then new order of clerks regular known as the Theatines at the age of forty. He made his novitiate at Naples under the direction of St. Andrew Avellino and pronounced his vows in 1572. In 1577, he was ordained a priest. Scupoli lived at various Theatine houses throughout Italy—in Naples, Genoa, Rome, and Venice. A victim of calumnious denunciations, he was laicized by the General Chapter of his Order in 1585. He submitted patiently to this severe disciplinary measure and passed the remainder of his life in retirement and prayer. In 1610, he died at Naples (*Dictionnaire de la théologie catholique*, XIV, 1745).

 Although the first edition of *The Spiritual Conflict* entitled *Combatimento spirituale* (Venice, 1589) appeared with the signature of Hierome, Count of Portia, Scupoli is generally accredited with having written it. A Spanish Benedictine, Dom Juan de Castagniza, and a Jesuit, Achille Gagliardi, have been at times suggested as possible authors of this work also. For a discussion of the problems of authorship, see the *Dictionnaire de la théologie catholique* (XVI, 1745). Vezzosi's *I Scrittori dei cherici regolari detti teatini* ([Rome, 1780], p. 276 seq.) contains a listing of the various editions of the *Combatimento*. Pierre Pourrat's discussion of the work in his *Christian Spirituality* (III, 239-246) is valuable, especially in showing the place of this book in the Catholic ascetical tradition.

 [2]Allison and Rogers, among others, agree that the translator of the *Combatimento* is John Gerard, S. J. For biographical details of Gerard, see pp. 99-100, n. 3.

[This work begins with a dedicatory epistle to the Abbess and Sisters of the monastery of St. Andrew in Venice and is signed by Hierome, the Count of Portia, Sigs. A3ʳ-A3ᵛ.]

[B]

The Spirituall
Conflict.

Non coronabitur nisi qui legiti-
mè certauerit. 2. Tim. 2.
He shall not be crowned that
doth not striue lawfully.

Wherein the perfection of a chri-
stian man consisteth: and of foure
things necessary to obtaine
the same.

Chap. I.

If thou hast a desire (most deare daughter in Christ) to attaine vnto the height & top of perfection, and by litle and little to draw neare vnto God, [Bᵛ] and to become one spirit with him, (which is the greatest & most excellent enterprise that possibly can be named or immagined.) First of all, thou must know wherein consistes the truth & perfection of spirituall life: for that many without anye farther cogitation of care, suppose it to be placed in the rigor, and austeritie of life, in maceration of the flesh in waring of haire-cloth, in watching, in fasting, and other like sharpenes and bodily labour.

Others, and especially women persuade themselues that they are neare vnto it when they say many vocall prayers, heare many Masses, and long seruice, frequent the church and Sacraments. [B2]

And many other also, (amongest the which you may finde some clad with religious habite liuing in cloisters) persuade themselues that this perfection whollye consisteth of the frequenting the Quire, in silence, in solitarinesse, and in well ordered discipline. And thus some in these, and some in other external exercises beleeue, that the perfect state of spirituall man is founded: but yet notwithstanding it is not so, for although the foresaide exercises are somtimes meanes to obtaine spirite, sometimes fruits of spirite, yet cannot it be saide, that in these onely consisteth christian perfection, and the true spirite: they are without dowt forcible means, [B2ᵛ] for obtaining the spirit to thos that do wel, and discreetly vse them, for the better getting of strength & force against their proper malice, and frailtie, to arme themselues against the assaults of our common enemies; & to prouide vs of those spirituall helpes, whiche are very necessarie to all the seruants of God, but specially to yong beginners. They are also fruits of the spirit in them that are indeede spirituall and illuminated; who chasten their body because it hath offended their Creator, and to subdue and keepe it vnder in his seruice: they keepe silence and liue solitarily, to eschewe euen the least thing that might offend God, and to haue spiri-[B3]tuall ioy and their conuersation in heauen.

They attend to the worship of God, and workes of pietie, they praye and frequent the most holy Sacraments, for the glorie of his diuine Maiestie, & to vnite themselues always more and more in loue with him.

But now vnto others,³ who place their whole foundation in these aforesayde externall exercises they may minister sometimes (not for anye desert in themselues (for they are almost holy) but through the default of them that vse them) more occasion of ruine, then doe apparant and manifest sinnes: whilst they being only addicted to thē, do leaue [B3ᵛ] the inward man forsaken, and in the hands of their naturall inclinations, and of the inuisible diuel; who seeing them out of the right waie, permitteth them not only to continue the aforesaide exercises with great delight, but also to walk according to their owne vaine fancie as it were amidst the delights of Paradise, where they perswade themselues to be eleuated amongst the quiers of Angells, and seeme in a maner to feele God within them: at which times they finde themselues altogether swallowed vp in certaine meditations, full of high curious and delightful points, and as yet were forgetting the worlde, and all creatures, they seeme to bee rapt to [B4] the third heauen, but in how great errors they finde themselues entangled; and how far they are from that perfection which we goe about to finde, may easily be perceiued, if we consider their life and manners: for these kind of people are

---

³This emphasis on interior, ascetical discipline was particularly strong among the Theatines; in fact, they have been accused of excess in this respect (*Dictionnaire de la théologie catholique*, XIV, 1745). The moderate approach to external discipline in the spiritual life found throughout this work immediately suggests the same spirit that is found in the most famous of all English medieval manuals of asceticism, *The Ancrene Riwle*.

wont to bee too much addicted to their owne iudgement, curious and diligent obseruers, and murmurers at other mens actions and words; but if they be touched in any one point of their vaine reputation, or debarred from those deuotions whiche they commonly vse, or restrained from their accustomed often receiuing, they are without measure offended, and disquieted.

And if God (to bring them [B4ʳ] to true knowledge) send them or permit them to suffer any trouble, infirmitie, and persecution, (which neuer happen but by his diuine will, and are the very touchstone of the loialtie of his seruants) then they discouer their false foundation and the inward rottennes and corruption of their pride; so that in euery accident, whether it be sorrowfull, or ioyfull, they will not resigne or humble themselues vnder his diuine hand, neither according to the example of his humbled and afflicted sonne, doe they abase themselues vnder euery creature accompting their persecutors for their dearest friendes, and imbracing them as the instruments of his diuine good-[B5]nesse, and workers of their spiritual health, true reformation and mortification.

Wherefore it is most certaine, that all such are in very great danger, for hauing their internall eie dimmed, and beholding onely their externall acts, (which are good) they attribute to themselues many degrees of perfection.

And thus puft vppe with pride, they become iudges of others, and there is left no means of their conuersion, but by the extraordinary goodnes and help of God; for it is more easie to reduce to well doing an open and publike sinner, then one that sinnes secretly, and is couered with the cloake of apparent vertue. [B5ʳ] Thou seest therefore good daughter most plainely, that the trueth of spirituall life, is not to be found in the aforesaid things, in that maner that we haue spoken of. And thou must vnderstand, that it consisteth in no other thing, but in a true knowlege of the bountie, and greatnes of God, and of our owne littlenesse, or nothing, and naturall inclination to all euill; in the hatred of our selues, and in the loue of God, in the full abnegation of our owne will, and in resigning it to the will of God, subiecting our selues not only to him, but for his loue to euery creature, and all this for no other end, but onely to please him, and bicause he deserues thus to be [B6] loued and serued.

This is the denying of our selues, which our Redeemer doth seeke in vs. This is the obedience whereunto he calleth his faithfull seruants, both by word and example. This is the crosse which by his sweetest law of loue is laide vppon their shoulders.

To this loue, and tru charity, so oft and particularly in his last Supper hee inuiteth his deare Disciples, with all his friends and children.

And because thou aspiring to the top of so great perfection, must vse force with thy selfe, and couragiously ouercome thy owne will, both in great and little things: it behooueth thee of necessity with [B6ᵛ] al redinesse of mind to prepare thy selfe to this combate, sith the crowne of so great a victorie is not giuen, but to them that fight valiantly. This battel, as of all other, it is the hardest: so the victorie gotten by the same, is of all other most glorious and most deare vnto God.

For if thou attend to tread downe and to kill all thy disordered appetites, and desires, euen the very least; thou shalt doo a thinge more pleasing, and a greater seruice to Almightie God, then if keeping any one of them voluntarilye aliue thou shouldest whip thy selfe till the bloud ran downe; or shouldest faste more then the old Hermits and Ancho-[B7]rites, or shouldest conuert to good life thousands of soules: for although the conuersion of soules be more deare to our Sauior in it selfe, then the mortification of one final passion of our will; yet notwithstanding thou oughtest not to wil or work any thing more principally, then that which the same Sauiour most stricktly wills and requires of thee: and hee without doubt is more pleased that thou shouldst labor with thy selfe to mortifie thy passions, then that leauing one vnmortified in thee, thou shouldst serue him in anye other thing, though greater and of more moment in it selfe.

Now then O daughter, [B7ᵛ] since thou seest wherein Christian Perfection consisteth: and that to obtaine the same, thou must take vppon thee a continuall and sharpe warre: it is necessary that thou like a valiant champion and enemie of thy selfe, do prouide thee of foure things, as necessarie armour, to the end thou mayst get the victorie and remaine a conqueresse in this spirituall battell, and these be, first, distrust of thy selfe, second, confidence in God, third, exercise, fourth, and prayer; of al which by the helpe of God I will intreat particularly and briefely.

[Here follow Chapters 2, 3, 4, and 5 on the distrust of self, on trust and confidence in God, on keeping the understanding free from curiosity, and on the will, Sigs. B8ʳ-C9ᵛ.]

[C10]

Of two Wills which are in man,
and of the Battell between
them.

Chap. 6.

Thou must vnderstand O daughter, that in vs therare two Wills the one of reason, and therefore called reasonable, and superior : the other of sence, which is called sensuall, and inferiour : the which is also vsually signified by these names of sence, appetite, flesh, and passion.

And although both these may be called Will, yet neuerthelesse, because reason it is which maketh vs men, when wee will any thing with the sense only, it is not vnderstood [C10ʳ] that it is truly willed by vs, vntill such time as we incline by our superior will, to will it.

Hereupon all our spirituall Battell[4] principally consisteth in this, that this superior Will being placed as in the midst between the diuine wil, which stands aboue, and the inferior, which is that of the sence, continually assaulted by the one and the other, whilst either of these assaieth to draw it and to make it subiect, and obedient vnto them.

To those that haue already got the habite of vertue, or vice, and intend alway to proceede in the same, this fight is not painfull, for the vertuous easely agree vnto the diuine will, the other follow that of [C11] the sence without any difficultie.

But they which are full of the euil habites of vice, (especially in the beginning) finde great paine and trauell, when they resolue to change their wicked life into a better, and taking them selues from the world, and from the flesh, do giue themselues to the loue and seruice of Iesus Christ.

For the strokes which the superior wil then sustaineth of the diuine wil, and of the inferior, (which alwaies are skermishing with it) are mightie and strong, and makes it well to feel them, not without great noyance of the combatants.

None may presume euer to ariue to any degree of vertue, [C11ʳ] nor to be able to serue God, if he will not labour in good

---

4The military imagery and vocabulary found in this work suggest the influence of the meditation on the Two Standards of St. Ignatius of Loyola in the *Spiritual Exercises* (pp. 45-47).

earnest, and support the paine which is to be felt in leauing those delights, whereunto at first his affection was fast tied.

Hence it commeth to passe that very fewe attaine to the state of perfection, because like cowardly souldiers they will not stand fast, and constantly fight, and suffer the dints, which the resistance of an infinite number of their self wills bringeth with it, which dooth alwayes fight against them: but retiring backe, leaue their weapons and themselues in the power of their enemies who tirannize ouer them.

Here is laide open a deceit by so much the more daunge- [C12] rous, as it is lesse perceiued, that many which attend to the spiritual life, being louers of themselues, more then is requisite (and yet in trueth they know not how to loue themselues) for the most part chuse those exercises, which most do please their taste, and they leaue the other which touch the quicke of their naturall inclinations and sensual appetite against the whiche all reason would they should turne al the force of their fight.

[Here follow Chapters 7 and 8 on the manner which one should fight against the motions of sensuality and on what one should do when his superior will seems overcome with his inferior will, Sigs. C12ᵛ-D9ʳ.]

[D9]

That we ought not to flie the occasions of Combate.

Chap. 9.

Besides all this that I haue saide vnto thee, whiche thou must doe, to cloath thy self with the habites of vertue: I put thee inmind, that it is not conuenient, that thou flye from the occasions of combat, which offer themselues vnto thee; and that if thou wilt get the habites of any vertue, (as for example of pacience) it is not good that thou shouldst withdraw thy selfe from those persons, actions, or thoughts, that moue thee to impatience: wherefore thou oughtest not to shunne, but rather, to hold [D9ᵛ] as deare, the conuersation of any person, that may be grieuous vnto thee, and conuersing with him, thou oughtest to keepe thy mind readie and prepared to suffer any troublesome, or displeasing thing whatsoeuer which may happen by him: for doing otherwise, thou shalt neuer accustome thy selfe to pacience.

So also in like maner if any worke be noysome, and irkesome to thee, either by it selfe, or for the person, that hath imposed it vpon thee, or because thou wouldst doe some other thing, that doth better content thee: leaue not for all that to take it in hand, and to continue the same troublesome actions although in doing of it [D10] thou shouldst finde thy selfe vnquiet, and leauing it, thou shouldst be in rest: for thus thou shouldst neuer learne to suffer, neither that should be any true quiet, thy mind not being purged from passion.

The same thing I saye vnto thee concerning thoughts, which sometimes* disturbe, and trouble thy mind, that they are not wholy to be driuen from thee, but rather to be esteemd, for with the trouble they bring thee, they accustome thee to suffer crosses & contrarieties.

And he that shal otherwise instruct thee, doth rather teach thee to flie the griefe which thou feelest, then to obtain the vertue which thou desirest.

Yet notwithstanding it is [D10ʳ] very true, that it behoueth a yong champion or a new beginner to behaue himselfe, and skirmishe in these aforesaide occasions, with warinesse and dexteritie, sometimes to encounter them, sometimes to giue grounde, according as more or lesse he hath obtained the habite of vertue.

But for all this he must neuer quite turne his backe from the fight, and flie in such sort that he seeke wholy to forsake all trouble and irkesomenesse, for hee which at that time should saue himselfe, being at another time assailed, should not haue then in his neede, wherewith to defend himselfe from the blowes of impatience, vnto the which he shuld [D11]be** open, with great daunger when they do fall vppon him, because he should not bee armed, and strengthened with the habits of the contrary vertue. These admonitions serue not in carnall vices, of the which (as I haue saide) I will intreate by themselues.

[Here follow Chapters 10 to 33 dealing with such matters as how to resist one's passions and senses, how to keep inner peace, how to combat the assaults of the Devil on one's soul, how to pray, how to receive the sacraments, how to oblate one's self to God, Sigs. D12ʳ-I6ᵛ.]

---

*sometimes] ed.; sometines
**be] *ed.;* he

[17]

The Conclusion.

There might be many other things said concerning this exercise
of so great importance; but let this suffice, forasmuch as now I am
able to discourse vnto thee, which for all that thou shalt finde
to be not alittle, if thou doost force thy selfe to effect the things
which I haue propounded. But respecting the capacitie of thy vnder-
stāding, and the breuitie which was needefull for me to vse, it
behoueth thee to ioyne therevnto an attentiue consideration; for
thereby (but much more by continuall exercise & practise) thou
mayest get alwaies greater strength and force by thy victory.

[17ᵛ] Resolue thy selfe couragiously in the name of God to take vp
thy weapons: for this is a battel that no man can flie, and he that
doth not fight, of necessitie remaineth vanquished and slaine: and
hope of peace there is none; since thou hast to deale with those
enemies that most cruelly kill them, who most seek to ioyne in
friendship with them. Be not dismayed because they are fierce and
mightie, seeing that all their might and force is in the hand of that
captaine, for whose honor thou dost fight: and in this battaile none
can loose but he that will for himself: and if thy Lorde [for] whome
thou doest wage this battell, should not to readily graunt* [18] thee
the victorie, yet faint not; for thou oughtest to be more then assured
(and this also shall help thee to fight confidently) that he by his
goodnes and power, turneth all things euen those that seeme most
contrary (be they of what sort soeuer) vnto the good of his faithful
warriors. Therefore if thy victory be prolonged, rest assured, that
it is either to deliuer thee from pride, and to keep thee vnder;
or to the end, thou mayst increase in vertue, and become a
more expert, and wel practised souldier, or for some other good of
thine, which** he then for thy profit [Three lines of the text are
mutilated.] [18ᵛ] be vngratefull to this Lorde which loueth thee so
much, and for thee hath suffered death, & ouercom the world; take
this battell in hand with a coragious hart, and attend according to
the good pleasure, and commaundement of thy captain, to the total
destructiō of al thy enemies, for if thou leaue but one aliue, it shalbe
as a chip in thy eie, or a launce in thy bowels, which shal hinder
thee in the course of so glorious a victory.

[Two Latin inscriptions]

---

*whome . . . graunt] *ed.*; whome thou doest wa < .. > this battell, should
not to r < ... > i < .. > g < .. > unt
**which] *ed.*; < . > hich

VIII.

A

Breefe Methode or
Way

Teachinge all sortes of Christian peo-
ple, how to serue God in a moste
perfect manner.

Written first in Spanishe, by a Religious man, named *Alphonso.*

And reduced owte of Latin into En-
glish in manner of a Dialogue
for the easier vnderstanding
and capacities of the
simpler sorte.[1]

By I. M.[2]

---

[1] n.p.d. [1602-05.] Pr. [secretly in England.] Allison and Rogers, I, Entry **18**. This work does not appear in the *STC*.

Alonso de Madrid (c. 1480-c. 1542) was a Franciscan priest of the Province of Castile or Carthagena (*Dictionnaire de Spiritualité ascétique et mystique,* I, 391). Very little else is known about him.

The Spanish title of this work is the *Arte para servir a Dios* (Seville, 1521). There were at least ten editions of this book before 1570 (Pierre Guillaume, "Un précurseur de la Réforme catholique," *Revue d'histoire ecclésiastique,* XXV [1929], 267-268). By 1785, there were nine more Spanish editions. As the numerous editions indicate, this work was immensely popular. It was translated into several European languages and into Latin (see footnote 4 below). Guillaume calls it "un des premiers ouvrages ascétique écrits dans une langue romane" (p. 260). Such well-known spiritual writers as St. Teresa of Avila (*Obras completas,* ed. M. Aguilar [Madrid, 1945], p. 74) and St. Francis de Sales (as quoted by Mother Mary Majella Rivet, O.S.U., "The Influence of the Spanish Mystics on the Works of Saint Francis de Sales," unpubl. diss. [Catholic Univ. of America, 1941], p. 22) have recommended the *Arte.*

[2] I. M. is probably John Mitchell or Michel, a Carthusian monk at Bruges in Flanders during the 1560's and 70's. Little is known about him, except that before the suppression of his Order in England by Henry VIII, he had been Prior at Witham (Lawrence Hendriks, *The London Charterhouse* [London, 1889], p. 282). Dom Maurice Chauncey in his account of the Carthusian Order in England during the Protestant persecutions, entitled *The Passion and Martyrdom of the Holy English Carthusian Fathers,* 1570 (ed. G. W. S. Curtis [London, 1935], pp. 141-142) indicates that John Mitchell did not flee England during the first wave of persecution but remained in England until, under Queen Mary, the monasteries could again be established. However, in July of 1559, he fled with his brother monks to Bruges (Chauncey, p. 157). For Mitchell's likely acquaintance with M. C., to whom this translation is dedicated, see note 3 below.

[A1ᵛ]

To the Right Woor-
shipfull, & vertuous Catholick*
Lady, the La. M. C.[3]

Albeit mankinde, by the stinge of originall sinne, be dead ye
wounded in body & soule,** as spoyled of immortalitie*** & all
diuine graces, broughte into a wofull state of all miseries, &
naturallye inclyned to doe euill, to the greater encrease of his owne
damnation: yet the grace & mercy of God, haith not altogether
abandoned nor forsaken vs, but (without any our good desert) haith
lefte vs in this exile & vale of woes, diuers helpes, remedies, &
meanes, whereby we may attayne to his graceous fauoure**** agayne,
& (after this transitorie lyfe) be aduaunced to high glorie and the
eternall ioyes in heauen. These meanes are his holy graces & vertues
by which we may be moued & made able to serue him, & to conforme our selues to his will in all thinges. Oure perfect sanctity &

---

[3]Margaret Clement or Clements, née Gigs (1508?-1570). Elsie V. Hitchcock
in her edition of William Roper's *The Life of Sir Thomas More, knighte*
(*EETS,* 197 [London, 1935], p. 104) suggests 1505 or 1506 as more likely
birth dates. Margaret Clement was the adopted daughter of Sir Thomas More.
In 1530, she married a physician named John Clement. During the persecution
of religious orders in 1537, Mrs. Clements administered to ten Carthusian monks
imprisoned at Newgate by disguising herself as a milkmaid and later by lowering
food through a hole in the roof of the prison (Hendriks, pp. 224-225). Margaret
Clement, remaining loyal to her Catholic faith in the face of great perils, fled
England during the reign of Elizabeth. Her husband and she stayed for awhile
at Bruges, the site of the exiled English Cathusian monastery (Hendriks, p. 289).
Later her husband and she moved to Mechlin, where she died in 1570.
    Since Margaret Clement had befriended the Carthusian monks so generously
and heroically in Newgate and since it was Bruges that she first fled to in exile,
it seems quite appropriate that I. M. should dedicate his work to her, a Recusant
like himself who had been "tossed too and froe daungerously by the enemies of
godds holy Churche" (sig. A4). It must be noted that Allison and Rogers assign
1602-05 as the possible date of publication for this work. It seems highly probable 1) that this date is incorrect, 2) that Mrs. Clements received the work in
manuscript before its publication later, or 3) that there was an earlier edition
of the work than the one surviving. Another possibility is that the book is
dedicated to Margaret Clement's daughter, Mother Margaret Clement, O.S.A.,
who was the Prioress of St. Ursula's Convent at Louvain for many years. She
was professed on October 11, 1557, and elected Prioress of the community in
1569. In 1606, when Mother Margaret celebrated her golden jubilee as a nun,
there were twenty-two English nuns in St. Ursula's along with the native
religious. She ended her life at St. Monica's Convent, an establishment founded
for English nuns living in exile (Gillow, I, 500).

   *Catholick] *ed.;* Cath $\langle\,\cdot\,\rangle$ 1 $\langle\,\cdot\,\rangle$ ck
  **soule] *ed.;* s $\langle\,\cdot\,\rangle$ ule
 ***immortalitie] *ed.;* immortali $\langle\,\cdot\cdot\,\rangle$ e
****fauoure] *ed.;* fanoure

frendshipp with god standeth in this pointe, that we be of the [A2] same spirit with him, in euery thing we doe. And though he be a most graceous & bountifull Lorde, & exceedingly desireous of our eternall happy estate: And haith moreouer abundantly prouyded whatsoeuer may be necessary or conuenient for our welfare: yea & through the excesse of his diuine loue, haith lefte nothing vndone that might helpe or doe vs good: yet haith he lefte it in our owne choyce, & free libertie, whether we will accept and vse his graces, endeuour to gett perfect holines, & serue him as he desyreth for our good, or noe. Great ruyne and destruction of all good, is made in oure soules by sinne, but it is in our owne power to repayre again this losse & calamitie, and to obtayne perfect holines, which we may doe, if (cooperating with goddes grace) we suffer our selues to be moued in all our actions onely by goddes holy spirit & will, as S. Paule saithe his children to be.

To instruct this, many deuout bokes & Treatises haue bene writen by learned [A2ˇ] & holy men in all ages, teaching what we ought to doe, discoursing at large of the natures of all vertues & vyces, & yelding sufficient matter for all sorts of holy Meditations touching the maiestie, goodnes, & other perfections of god: Touching heauen, hell, Iudgment, death, sinne, vertue, and the rest: Perswading to good lyfe & terrifyinge from euill: All commodious woorkes & commendable trauells of good men. But amonge them all I neuer founde hitherto any comparable to a litle booke, deuulged by a religious man named *Alphonso,* in the Spanish tonge. In which goulden Treatise, he geueth vs an exacte & perfect way, how we may repayre againe the ruine & wofull state of our soules, by sinn: & by rightly seruinge God, attaine to the perfection of true holines & loue of him. This Author leauethe the large & goodly discourses of vertues & vyces, their reasons, examples, perswasions, & all poynts of Meditations, (as all beinge sufficienntlye Taughte and handled, by others innumerable [A3] and to be founde euery where,) and breefely touchinge the ende for which God created and placed vs on earthe, what bounde & dutie we haue of seruinge him: what abiection & miserie our soules & bodies are brought vnto by sinne: He sheweth a breefe, yet a most exacte way and manner, how by the instrumentes and powers of oure soule, namely our vnderstandinge and free will, helped by godds grace, we may put in practise and execution, to his most holy honour, and our owne greatest profitt, whatsoeuer is taughte & conteyned in other bookes, how we may repayre our state againe, caste of all wicked customes, expell all vitious habitts, enryche & bewtify oure selues with all vertues, make all our woorks most preceous, acceptable, & meritorious, in goddes sight, becom holy chaunge our selues owt of poore, naked, & abiect persons: into most glorious & diuine creatures: And finally be vnited to God in most perfect manner of frendshipp & loue.

This preceous Iewell, I sende you [A3ᵛ] as a token of my good affection, towardes your spirituall welfare, which I haue translated owt of latin,[4] not yelding woord for woord, but (cullinge owt the principall poyntes & pithe of euery Chapter) haue reduced it into the forme of a Dyalogue,[5] thereby makinge it more easye & playne, for the capacities of the simpler sorte, whom also I wish, may take commodity therof, as I assure my selfe, your La. and euery one may doe, that reade & diligently practise, what is taught therein: without which practise, all knowledg is vnprofitable and vayne. It is not writen for vitious persons, suche as delight to lyue & wallow in sinne, without regarde of God or their own soules health, for these will take noe benefite hereof, but the Author haith prepared & directed this woorke, for the great good of vertuous soules who are resolued to serue God: & standing in battell against the worlde, the flesh & the deuill, haue a sincere desyre, to liue well & woorke their owne saluation. This good euery one that rea-[A4]dethe it, may reape: that knowinge thereby their owne poore & imperfect state, & behoulding how farr of they are from that degree of perfection they should & might arryue vnto; They may abase them selues in their owne conceyte, carry an humble mynde before heauen & earthe, of their owne imperfections & vn-worthines, which is a good stepp to further vertue: and be moued now & then, to work som particuler acts after the manner hereof which assuredly will be most pleasāt to God, & most meritorious to their own soules aboue all other woorkes they shall doe.

Now in your afflicted state wherein you are tossed too and froe daungerously, by the enemies of godds holy churche, for your

---

[4]The translator of the Latin edition is Jean Hentenius (1499-1566), a Flemish Dominican. He finished the Latin translation of the *Arte* in February, 1560 (Guillaume, p. 270). The oldest surviving edition is entitled the *Libellus aureas de vera Dei apte inserviendi methodo* . . . Lovanii, apud Petrum Zangrium Titelanum ad insigne Fontis, anno 1576 (Guillaume, p. 270). Note that I. M. called this work the "goulden Treatise" (sig. A2ᵛ).

[5]Neither the original Spanish nor the Latin is in the form of a dialogue, this being the invention of I. M.

constancy in the catholick Faith: Alphonso will teache you how to fraught your shipp, with all sortes of vertues, more preceous then the Indian Treasures, that you may come well loaden to the porte, when your Lord shall ende your voyage. How also to endure patiently, the ra-[A4ᵛ]ginge & furious stormes of Godds ennemies: And how finally to keepe alow sale, and an humble conceite of your selues in all the good you doe, & to referr all the honour & prayse therof vnto God the owner & geuer of all good giftes. For it is a most certaine way to losse & shipp-wracke of all, to impute any good to your selfe, or to carry a high conceit of your owne well doinge.

Many vertuously disposed soules, delight greatly in varietie & chaunge of their spirituall Exercises, & imbrace with greate affection euery noueltye, seking to know many wayes to serue God: & euer think that to be preferred as the best, which is straunge and vn-known to them, & that which they throughly know and haue vsed, they either loath or litle esteme, such is the inconstancye of our nature. But this new-fangled mutabilitye, exceedingly hindreth all spirituall good and the progresse in all vertue. And with out com-parison better it were diligently to kepe & practise one (thoughe it be a [A5] meaner) then to be either negligente in the best, or to be allwayes inconstantly flitting from one to an other: for so should a man neither goe forwarde, nor grow perfect in any.

Be familiar therefore & stay youre selfe with Alphonso (good Madam) for so shall you profitt greatly. And beware you be not content with the vertue you haue allready gotten: For our Lorde & God was made man, & vouchsaifed to dye, for to aduaunce vs to a higher & perfect state of holines in this lyfe: For this same ende also he would that Angells shoulde minister vnto vs: And finallye for the same ende he haith geuen vs the vse of heauen & earth with all his creatures in them. Remember me I beseche you in your deuotions. And thus I committ you to God.

Your seruant
in our Lord.
I. M.

[A5ᵛ]

The Preface of
The Author Alphonso.

Sainct *Ambrose* saith, that ignorance of the order & manner how to woorke, greatly troubleth the qualitie of our meritt. Neither is it to be thought (as the same Author affirmeth) that we haue full knowledge of a thinge which we know we ought to doe, vnlesse we know withall the order of proceedinge in the same.

Whereupon it is manifest, that it profiteth verie litle, if one know what is writen for seruing God, & be ignorāt in what manner and order it is to be done. And albeit arte & knowledge of euery good thinge, floweth from God the supremest artificer, & many be illuminated[6] by his goodnes, & preuented with benedictions of delighte & sweetenes: yet for all that we must not omitt to doe what is in vs, to seke (as we are bounde) his commaundementes & will, & other thinges which be necessary for doinge perfectly whatsoeuer is pleasing vnto him. For which [A6] purpose the breefe forme & Methode which here we sett downe, will be profitable, that we may know & woorke those greate thinges, which the holy scriptures teach vs. The which to doe it is noe lesse needefull that some arte be sought owte, then for doinge any other thinge which we couett rightly to know or woorke. To fynde owte this arte, the holye Doctoures haue spente much tyme, & haue lefte it writen at large in diuers volumes: of all which, we will gather a breefe conclusion or somme. But this short work being cheifly ordeyned for the Exercyses of the soule: it will seme somtymes verye obscure to them which haue not bene exercysed in the knowledge & operations of the powers of their soule. Yet we shall shewe after a while in the prosecution of the book this Methode to be so farre from obscuritie, that it bringeth greate lighte to all other bookes of lyke argument.

Neither lett any thinke it superfluous or vayne, that we geue Documentes whereby we may be helped to [A6ᵛ] serue God, when as all the Scripture witnessith such to be necessary. And S. *Paule* saith, that we are helpers or coadiutors of God: but he either helpeth not rightly, or not sufficientlye, that helpeth not as much as he can & oughte. Neither is it any other thing in vs that we helpe God, then that we moue our soule in all our workes, according to

1. Cor. 3.

---

[6]By stressing the will and the intellect in contrast to sensibility and sentimental mysticism, Alonso de Madrid was combating the Illuminists of his own day. The Illuminists were considered a significant threat to Spanish Catholicism, since their de-emphasis of free will and their emphasis on the direct action of God on the soul were feared to be fertile ground for Protestantism (Guillaume, pp. 265-266). I. M., we may assume, saw Alonso de Madrid's emphasis on free will and the necessity of order in the religious experience as a wholesome antidote to the prevailing Protestant thinking of England.

the prescripte rule of this present arte, as sacred diuinitie at large declareth.

The Philosopher in his Metaphisicks affirmeth, that mankinde liuethe by arte: in which place he semeth by this propertie to distinguish man from vnreasonable creatures, for that all these are moued onely by naturall instinct without* arte: but man is ruled by arte & reason: Wherefore he may be said to serue God as it weare onely by naturall instinct, lyke to creatures voyde of reason, that is moued to serue him that way, by which he feeleth greatest consolation & sweetenes without regardinge by his vnderstandinge & reason, whether there be a-[A7]ny other manner, wherby he may be able, to serue God more excellently.

Moreouer there is noe cause, why any should alledge the vnction of the holy Ghost, to teach vs in all things, & therfore any art or Methode where by we may learne to serue God, is needeles**: which sayinge is true, presupposinge that we our selues also be his coadiutors or helpers, endeuoringe to know & woorke, as we are taughte in the sacred scriptures, & in this arte which we are to geue. For the vnction of the holy ghost, teachethe not them that are vnwillinge to learne, nor them that are idle, or make resistance.

Furthermore leste the sweete yoke of our Lorde seme heauye to any, let vs consider that it is not a thing to be merueled at, if some dayes are to be spent, for getting so highe knowledg & wisdom, as is heare conteyned and taught in this arte. For if in learninge Grammer or Logick (artes farr inferiour to this) one comsume & spende 3 or 4 yeares, yea all his lyfe, if he [A7ᵛ] will be perfecte in any of them: how much better is our lyfe bestowed (yea if it be wholly spente therein) for the perfect learning of this arte most high & diuine of all other artes, which our supreame maister Iesus Christe, came to teach vs, with his so great toile & payne.

Moreouer, he that beginnethe to learne this arte, must consider, that it will happen to him, as it is wonte to happen to infantes, who hauinge perfect soules, yet want the vse of reason: and hauing in their bodyes handes & feete,*** yet can not goe or worke: but when they once begin to waxe and to moue their limmes, they goe, yet with great difficultie, & with fallinge now & then: but growing elder, & vsinge daily Exercyse, they goe so freelye, that they can runne at their pleasures.

---

*without] *ed.;* withont
**is needeles] *ed.;* is-/needeles
***feete] *ed.;* fecte

The same hapneth in these Exercises, whyles one desyrethe purelye to serue god after this Methode: For albeit our soules be perfect & intyere, yet so mightely are we bounde & oppressed & without strength to mooue* [A8] our selues in the perfecte way manifested in the holy gospell, & declared in this arte which we sett owte, that at the firste, we can not walke or goe at all, or if we be moued or attempt this, it is with such difficultie, that our goinge is well neare nothing. Yet notwithstanding let vs manfullye endeuour to doe what is here prescribed so well as we can: for whiles we shall scarse dare, to hope to gett the perfection taught vs, we shall by practyse yea so runne by these high pathes that it may be said truly, our motions to be rather the motions of an Angell flying, then of a man walking on earth.

None oughte to pretende any excuse why he serueth not God after the manner we haue here sett downe, cōtenting him self with the litterall obseruation of som religious rule, or the commaundements of God, as sufficiente to saluation. For as the Apostle saith, Goddes will is that we be holy and perfect. Seinge therefore riches allready gotten, do not suffyce nor cōtente the louers of the world, but all-[A8ᵛ]wayes they wishe & couet more, yea often contrary to Goddes commaundement. Neither in lyke māner ought we to be contente with these spirituall riches we haue allreadie: but labour to increase them dailye, & augmente the rewarde we expecte, seinge God doth vehemently desyre that we so do. But if our appetite couet not this, for the profitt we may gett thereby, at the least it shoulde extende it selfe to desyre it, because we know it to be gods will that we be magnifyed & enryched in all thinges, as the children of so eternall & glorious a Father in heauen, who admonisheth ve saying, *Be you holy, because I your Lorde god & Father am holy.*

This booke may be intitaled, *The Way, Arte or Methode, of fitly seruing God* : which may be deuyded into three partes. The first conteyneth certaine vniuersall documents, instructions, or rules, whereby we may be directed in all our actions. The seconde part cōteyneth certaine particuler Exercyses, in which the seruant of God muste be [B1] exercysed, that he may repaire the ruine and corruption which sinne haithe brought into his soule.

The Third part treateth of the loue of god, and those thinges which he commaundeth to be loued, in which loue consistethe the

---

*mooue] *ed.; mooue/mooue*

fulfillinge of the Law, and of all our good. And let him marke that shall reade this, how much labour & diligence he bestoweth, that desyreth to be conninge and furnished in some prophane arte, and how meete it is, that more diligence be vsed in this affayre.

These considerations therfore had & chefely relying vpon the assistance of our supreme maister Iesus Christ, our eternall God and Lorde, we will begin the foresaid arte & Method.

[B2]

The First Chapter.

How the Pilgrim

and the Ermit mett, & of
their conference.

In *Mantua,* there once dwelled a Knight called *Probus,* who for his valour, wisdom, and other vertues, was much renowmed in his countrye, & of all states very dearely beloued. He was of a most deuout & religious disposition, studying more to serue & please the omnipotent king of heauen, then the worlde or any earthly prince.

About the solemne feast of Easter, he woulde goe on pilgrimage, to visitt *Ierusalem* & other deuoute places of the holy lande. And as he traueled through a deserte in *Siria,* he missed his way & was benighted: And wandering too & froe, he espyed at the laste a candle shyninge from the syde of a rock: thither he wente with all hast, & called of them within. By and by there came forthe a fatherly [B2ᵛ] oulde man named *Alphonso,* & asked who he was that called so vntymelye at his Cell? I am a pilgrime for the holy lande said *Probus,* & goinge astray in this wildernes, I espyed by good happ your candle, & am come to craue harbour with you this night. All that come in godds name be welcome to me sayd *Alphonso.* I thanke you good Father said *Probus.*

When they were come within the Cell & sett downe, eche behelde other verie earnestly. And *Probus* said, I meruell good Father, how you can endure to liue this austere lyfe in your course attyre of sack cloath, with slender fayre in this vneasie hoale. I haue endured it said *Alphonso,* these many yeres I thanke God, and during this mortall lyfe, I desyre noe change. In what sorte I pray you saide *Probus,* haue you spent your lyfe in this solitary place, & what busines haue you had to kepe you here thus long? This māner of lyfe seemeth verye horrible to mannes nature. Mannes nature indeede my sonne said *Alphonso,* would [B3] not endure this, if it were not drawn on & fedd with greater comforthe an other way.

The onely busines wherein I bestow my self in this place, is continually to serue my Lord & God: which trade of lyfe, is to me so sweete, pleasant, & profitable, that it ouercometh all the horrour, payne, & other difficulties, which the frailtie of my nature fyndeth. What excedinge ioyes also I haue by the hope of myne eternall reward with God for seruing him as I doe (if by his grace I perseuer to the ende) my tonge can not expresse.

It semeth said *Probus,* your seruing of God is more then ordinary: For I serue him also as I thinke, yet haue I not any such ioy therein as you speake of. My dyett is daintie, myne apparell ryche, my howse sumptuous, and yet with all these, I fynde small pleasure or ease in seruing God.

These temporall commodities saide *Alphonso,* I want voluntarilye, because it best pleaseth my Lorde that I so doe, & that I be content with ne-[B3ᵛ]cessaries, without encombring my self with such superfluous thinges as you speake of, which if I had or desyred, woulde perhapps much hinder me in godds seruice, & are assuredly nedelesse, to my lyfe, health, or good estate: But the perfect seruice of God, which bringeth to man true comforth delight, & benefite* in this lyfe, and a ioyfull hope of inestimable rewarde in heauen, consisteth not in the wante or hauing of these temporall commodities: For you also in your welth and abundance (if you knew the way) mighte perhapps serue God with as much pleasure & benefite, as I doe in this pouertie wherein you see me liue. For our Sauiour said: *Blessed be the poore in spirit, because theirs is the kingdome of heauen.* Which happy blessing & pouertie not onely they may enioy that wante all earthly treasures & commodities: But also the greatest princes in the worlde, in the middest of their wealth & abundance.

If this be so said *Probus,* I beseche you teach me the way, for I confesse [B4] I know it not: & if I can learne this lesson, I think I haue greate aduantage of you, that liue thus austerely in this desert. Perhapps noe great aduauntage said *Alphonso,* for it is noe lesse gratefull & acceptable vnto god & noe lesse meritorious to our selues, to forsake all temporall commodities for his seruice, then to

---

*benefite] *ed.;* beneftte

possesse & vse them to the same ende: yea the frailtie of man and the corruption of our natures considered, it is muche lesse perill to want them then to haue thē. For the more we encomber & distract our small abilities abowt earthly thīgs the lesse able are we to attende and wholly yelde our selues to heauenly. But I shall willingly teach you the best way of seruinge God that hitherto I haue knowne. Sett asyde therefore all other thoughtes; & marke well what I shall say. When you conceaue me not, aske bouldly what my meaning is: For it is lost tyme to vs both, if I proceede, & teach more than you vnderstande. Good Father said *Probus,* seing you geue me leaue, I will [B4ᵛ] make bould to interrupt you when either I conceaue you not, or doubt in any poynte. So doe in godds name said *Alphonso.*

First then I must lay you downe a few considerations & instructions, of great importance, and which are the foundations & groundwork whereon we must stay & raise vpp all the frame we are to buylde. And you must often and verey carefullye call them to mynde, if you think to profitt in this way of seruing God. I shall doe my best endeuour* therein said *Probus.*

The First Instrvcti-
on, shewing to what ende God crea-
ted Man, & placed him vpon
earth.

Cap. 2

The first instruction said *Alphonso,* & the foundation of all often & seriously to be considered, is, that God (as the holy Scriptures** and Fathers teach) created and [B5] sent vs into this world, not to enioy & rest in the transitory commodities & pleasures thereof: but that (taking of godds creatures so muche as may suffyce our necessities) we occupy & bestow our selues and all the reste we haue, in seruing & honoring our lord, who haith prepared for our rewarde, the blisse of heauen, wherein we shall possesse for euer, God him self, that is, an infinite good, and in him, all good thinges more aboundantly then we can imagin. To honour & serue God therfore (my sonn) are we come into this world. All we doo besydes this is nothing els but loste laboure, vaine and hurtfull tryfl-

---

*endeuour] *ed.;* endeuonr
**Scriptures] *ed.;* Scrip-/ures

ing, dishonorable to the noble children of such a father as God is.
No doubt father said *Probus,* but we were created to serue God as
you say: But what kynde of seruice dothe God requyre of man, & is
by man of bounde & dutie to be performed.

[B5ᵛ]

The Second Instrvc-
*tion, of two manners how to serue
god, & how Man is bounde vnto them.*

Cap. 3.

There be two sortes of seruinge god said *Alphonso,* & two waies
in lyke manner are we bounde to serue him. The firste is in the
obseruing of godds commaundementes, which we are all bounde to
kepe vnder paine of eternall damnation to hell fyre. The second is
more perfect, & is this, that (forsakinge all earthlye thinges, and
withdrawinge our hartes from the loue thereof) we caste oure affection wholly vpon our heauenlye Father which is an infinite goodnes, & in all thinges laboure to be of the same spirit & will with
him, accordinge to the example which our Sauioure the naturall
Sonn of God left vs whiles he serued here on earth, not for any
nede of his owne, but to instruct vs how we [B6] ought to serue our
Lorde. This way Christ taught the yong man which had kept the
commaundementes when he said, *If thou wilt be perfect, geue all
thou hast to the poore, & com & folow me.* How are Christians
bounde to this manner of seruice said *Probus?*

Not vnder payne of eternall damnation said *Alphonso,* as in the
first way, but by a Law of frendshipp with god of equity & gratitude, wherein all the children of God that woulde not be reckned
base-minded, vngratefull, & foolish, should moste carefully keepe
them selues, that they may appere the worthy children of so
graceous a Father. For to all it is geuen in commaundement, that we
loue our Lord with all our soule, with all our hart, with all our
minde, and with all our strength.* And to all he said: *Be you perfect as your heauenly Father is.*

As he deserueth much blame that going to som place for dispatch of som weightie & necessary affaires, & neglecting & leauing

---

*strength] *ed.;* sttength

the thing he wente to doe, trifleth away his tyme in vyle [B6ᵛ] sportes & abiect thinges: so likewise is he much blame worthy, that being borne into this world to serue the high maiestie of God with all his powers & abilities, (which seruice is most due vnto God, & most profitable to the seruant) yet omittethe it because it is not commaunded him vnder paine of death, bestowing him self in the mean season, in a meaner and more abiecte kynde of seruice, mixed with muche worldly vanitie, that most swiftly passeth away, & bringthe with it much euill. And albeit God haith left it in our free choice and curtesye, yet the bound of frendshipp, equitie & gratitude, requireth that we endeuoure to serue him (to whom all honour and seruice is most due) in the best manner we are able. The first way to serue God said *Probus,* is plaine & manifest to all Christians, but the other apperteyneth onely to you Eremites, to religious persons, and Clargie men.

As the first said *Alphonso,* is common to all Christians, & taught euery where: so there is no Christian but [B7] he may be taught, learn, & performe the seconde. I can hardly think so said *Probus,* for we may not all forsake the world & cast all our hartes vpon this perfect seruinge of God you speake of. No person said *Alphonso,* is made a Christian, before he first solemnly renownce the worlde, with all the pompes & vanities thereof, & yelde him self to the obedience & seruice of God. And therefore the profession, not onely of Ermits, religious persons & Priestes: but of all true Christians also, is to forsake the world, & serue their Lord with all they are & haue. For as I said God created man for this ende, & for all temporall & earthly things, no man doth rightly vse them or can haue them, but to his exceedinge harme, vnlesse he turne them wholly to the seruice, & honoure of his Lorde, whose in truth they be & not mannes but for a litle tyme to vse as god haith ordeyned & commaunded, which seruice we ought to yeld to God, not onely in keping his generall commaundements, but in the [B7ᵛ] perfectest manner. as Christ our Lord by his owne example* haith taught vs all. And this seconde is that, which now I purpose to teach you,** that is, how ryche men, artificers, & all sorts of people, may serue their Lord and God most perfectlye. This will be most comfortable to vs of the world said *Probus,* but it semeth a most difficult thing to be done.

---

*example] *ed.;* exawple
**you] *ed.;* yon

[Here follow the third and fourth instructions on sin and man's need to repair for sin, the fifth instruction on pure intention in all man's actions, and the sixth instruction on good habits, Sigs. B7ʳ-E1ᵛ.]

[E2]

The Second Parte.

The Second Parte, Con-
teyning certayne spirituall Exercyses,
wherby the soule is adorned, bew-
tifyed, and rightlye disposed to
the perfect actes of louing
& seruinge God.

The *first Exercyse how the ser-*
uant of God shoulde purge his
soule from all sinne.

After they had refreshed them selues with breade and water, which was the Ermits vsuall fair: he begann & saide. My sonn, the firste thinge and Exercyse, wherein a man muste occupy him selfe, to gett a fitte disposition, to loue and serue God, is to extirpate* or roote owt of his soule, all euill, that is, the filthe of sinne: that when he would do any seruice to his lord, there be nothinge that may offend the eyes of so highe a Maiestie. This done, he muste a-[E2ᵛ] dorne and bewtify his soule with good habitts and vertues, whereby he may appeare gratefull & acceptable to him in his seruice. Of these two thinges, I will therefore now speake, and first how to roote owt and destroy sinn.

You must know then, that sinne is the most vyle and detestable euill that can be deuysed, & bringethe to any reasonable creature that committeth it, vnspeakable harmes and mischeues. For by sinn, we loose God, who is an infinite goodnes. By it we contemne, dis-honour, and iniury, our louinge Lorde, in the fowlest manner that may be. By it, we frustrate in oure selues, the effecte and frute, of Christs painfull lyfe, and moste bitter passion, and conculcate or treade vnder foote, his preceous blood. By it we defyle and make moste lothsom & abominable our owne soules, washed and sanctifyed

---

*extirpate] *ed.;* exirpate.

with the blood of oure Sauiour, and chosen to be the sacred temples of Godds Maiesty. By it we pollute our harts, the Altars & Tabernacles of the holy Ghoste, where he [E3] delightethe to dwell. By it we loose godds fauour, and all his graces, the eternall ioyes of his kingdom, with all our right and tytle thereunto. By it onely we are made the boundslaues of the deuill, the felowes and companions of all wicked men both aliue & deade, & of the damned spiritts in hell. By it, we are made the reprochfull enemies of God, the moste abiect, contemptible, and dishonorable of all his creatures. And finally by it we purchase assuredlye to our selues, endles damnation, eternall woes, and the horrible tormentes of hell fyre.

All which euills and miseries, are iustly dew to him, that by sinn committeth high treason againste his supreame Lorde, who vouchsaifed to dye for him.

Now the sorowes and teares of all goddes creatures are not sufficient to destroy or take away one sinne: much lesse the penance & teares of one man that haith committed the same.

But the mercy and clemency of oure Lord is so great, that he will not haue [E3ᵛ] vs to dispaire: And desireous of our weale, haith prouided vs a remedie, & is content to pardon & forgeue our sinns, assone as we for our parts, haue hartie sorow & contrition for the same: What besides is needefull or requisite, he supplieth it of his owne, & restoreth vs againe to his grace & fauour. It is meete therefore that we lamente & sorow for our* sinnes, consideringe we haue done so many euills by them both against God & our selues.

How shoulde we doe this as becometh vs said *Probus?*

The way is this said *Alphonso.*

With your vnderstandinge present to your selues, the euills which come of sinne as before: & then compell your will (principally for the offence & dishonour of God, and because it is his will that you sorowe for them) to lament, and to desyre that you had not committed them, nor iniuried godds maiesty: which acte of your will, you muste often labour to produce; now in generall for all your sinnes: now for one particular sinn, now for an o-[E4]ther, & this with the greateste endeuour you can, to haue hartie greif and contrition, notwithstanding you feele your self somtimes voyde of sensible sorowe or paine, for this is in godds hande and not in your owne, to haue at your pleasure, but doubtlesse he will bestow it also on you, if you endeuour to gett it as you may.

---

*our] *ed.;* out

I vnderstand all this said *Probus.*

Then will I passe said *Alphonso,* to the second thinge, which I tould you was requisite, for the expellinge of our corruption & euill habitts.

What is that said *Probus?*

[Here follow the second exercise on hatred of self, the third exercise on prayer, the fourth exercise on humility, the fifth on vainglory, the sixth on patience, and the seventh on the four natural passions, Sigs. E4ʳ-H6ʳ.]

[H6]

The Thirde Parte.
Conteyning *the way how to
loue God, our neighbours,
and our selues.*
Of the Love of God.

After they had slepte a whyle, & *Alphonso* finished his vsuall deuotions: they came together againe, & *Alphonso* said.

[H6ᵛ] Now my sonn, if you be satisfyed in all thinges we talked of yester night: Let vs goe forward as I promised you. I rest fully satisfyed said *Probus,* in all you haue said hitherto: Therefore I pray you procede to teach me how I may loue God.

The loue of God said *Alphonso,* is a fyre, which God would haue allwayes burninge, on the Altar of our soule, & if you throughlye knewe the worthines and excellency thereof, all woulde seeme litle, that hitherto we haue said, of the reparation & adorning of the soule, by which so high a woorke is to be performed. For the acte of louing God is of so greate excellency, that noe Sainct in heauen, nor any thinge that is or can be created, can doe any woork more high or perfecte. For which cause the sonn of God him self, calleth this the greatest and first commaundement. Yea if all the endeuours & strengthes of Angells & men, were heaped together in one Angell or man, he coulde do nothing more worthy, then is the acte of louing [H7] God. And nothing that is or can be made, by the omnipotente power of God: can be sufficient to loue God with that perfection which his infinite goodnes & worthines doth deserue.

This loue of God, incomparably excelleth all other supernaturall vertues or woorks, & without it, none other gift or qualitye that man haith, profitethe him anythinge at all, or is to be estemed, as S.

Mat. 22.

1. Cor. 13.

Paule saith larglye. This is the incessant & eternall woorke of God him self: For he being of infinite goodnes & excellency, is infinitely to be loued, and is continuallye occupyed with all his infinite power, in louinge* his owne infinite goodnes & ioying in the same. And nothing being more consonante to equitie, nothinge so profitable or glorious to our selues, then that we loue him, who is an infinite good, & infinitely to be beloued, & whom we cā not sufficiently loue as he deserueth, albeit our strength & abilityes were infinite: His moste holy and righteous will is, that we doe the same thinge, [H7ᵛ] with all our forces, which he dothe continually with his: that is, loue him & ioy in him with all our harts, power, & strength. Yea & so greatly he requyreth & desireth this most diuine woork of vs, that he would yeld him self to a most cruell death, that so he might procure & prouoke vs to loue him, & all this for our good, & not for any benefite of his owne.

All other thinges besides this loue of God which are commaunded vs, or in the holy scriptures requyred of vs, are but for that they be helpes to this loue, & to omitt them, would greatly hinder the same. Vyces & sinnes forbidden vs, are nothing els, but ā inordinate loue of vaine things, which occupye the place of our hartes, deputed onely for God. Neither doe vertues serue for other ende, then fitly to dispose the soule for this loue: Which vertues notwithstanding, are so necessarie for this loue of God, that it were great presumption, to thinke we coulde obtein it, without great exercyse in them.

[H8] To loue God said *Probus,* must of necessitie be a worke, of great excellencye and worthines: but I pray you tell me what this loue is, and how it may be done.

[Here continues the discussion of the love of God, followed by discussions of love of one's neighbor and love of one's self. Next follows a short discussion of thanksgiving, Sigs. H8ʳ-L2ᵛ.]

[L2ᵛ] Now is it tyme, you were traueling. I will bring you into your way againe.

I thank you Father said *Probus.* And beinge come to the way, they embraced eche other and departed, *Alphonso* to his solitary cell, & *Probus* towarde Ierusalem.

Deo gratias.

[A table of contents and errata follow, Sigs. L3ʳ-L4ʳ.]

----

*louinge] *ed.;* lou <.> nge

IX.

A Breefe Collection
Concerning the Love
of God towards Mankinde, & how
for diuers causes we are iustlie
bounde to loue & serue him.
With Preparation to
Prayer, and certaine necessarie prayers and
thankesgeuing to God for his bene-
fites, daylie to be vsed.
Also a deuote Meditation to procure
Contrition, and excite Deuotion
With other vertuous prayers.

Ecclesiast. 18.
Before Prayer prepare thy soule: & be not as
a man that tempteth God
[An ornament]
Printed at Doway, by Lavrence
Kellam at the signe of the
holie Lambe. 1603[1]
[Woodcut of Christ, p. 2]

[3] *Being desirerous (good Reader) to haue published some*
short Collection of most necessairie praiers, but hindred by diuers
vrgēt occatiōs: I thought good, in respect of my duty to God, and
necessity of the time presēt, rather with the poore widowe, to offer
vnto him this simple Mite, for the increase of his honour in helping
of the godly, then altogether to geue ouer my purpose. And wheras
true vertue, cōsisteth principallye in the loue of God: without which
our praiers are of no force. I haue here prepared a litle Treatise
concerning that matter, and in what respect wee are bounde to serue
him: in which, as in a glasse we may clerelie behold our ingra-[4]*ti-*
tude,* towards so louing a Lord. And because manie rather of cus-
tome then true deuotion, so rashlie goe about that holie woorke of
prayer: I haue set doūe a preparation therunto, with necessarie
prayers, Meditations, and thankesgeuing, to be vsed daylie. Farewell.
    [5] [The title is here repeated.]

---

[1]Allison and Rogers, I, Entry 142. *STC* 5554.
*ingratitude] *ed.*; ingra-/itude

The great and incomprehensible charitye of our Lorde towardes
Mankinde, maye be cōsidred fower sundrye wayes.

First in the dignitie of our Creation. Secondly in taking our
coruptible nature. Thirdly in susteining for vs his B. passion. And
fourthly in his great benefits and bountiful giftes, both spiritual &
corporal, which may iustly kindle & inflame the hartes of al true
Christians, to render to him again that which he requireth of vs,
which is nothing else but a loueing harte, a iuste & vpright life.

[6] In the dignitie of our Creation, hath he shewed, that he loued
vs more then any other creature in the world: & that in two things.
First in creating and making vs according to his owne Image &
likenes: secondly in constituting vs Lords and Gouerners ouer al his
other creatures.

In taking of our nature, he hath also shewed that he loued Mankind better than Angels, & that in three respectes. First in honour,
because he assumpted our nature, & not the nature of Angels: Secondly in loue, in that he repayred Mankinde with his precious bloud,
& not them. And thirdly in vision, because in heauen we shall possesse more ioye in Contemplation of Christes Humanitie then the
Angels, in that we shal see our nature, vnited to the deuine Nature.

But in suffring his B. Passion, he hath shewed [as we may say]*
that he loued vs better then him selfe, geuing for our [7] Saluation
freely his whole Body & life. And here marke, that in this B. Passion of our Sauiour, we may learne fiue notable thinges.

First it teacheth vs to geue him hartie thanks for the glorious
fruite which we haue receiued by the same, which gratfulnes is a
thing so acceptable vnto him,** as S. Aug. saith, that nothing
maybe more. This B. Lambe of God which was conceiued & borne
without sinne, wold thus suffer for vs, that by his painful Passion,
he might pul vs backe from the filthy pleasure of sinne. He suffred
in all his members, that with our mēbers, we might willingly serue
him. Hee offered for vs his precious blood the price of our Redemption, that we might offer our bodies with al the force of the same to
doe him seruice.

Secondly it teacheth vs to loue him, because aboue all things, he
loued vs.

Thirdly it teacheth vs how much we [8] ought to detest & hate
sinne, for which he susteined such a painful & dolorous Passion, yea

---

*author's brackets
**vnto him] *ed.;* vnto—/him.

he abhorreth it so much, that not withstanding his great desire of
our Saluation: he condemneth the sinner for one deadly offence to
perpetuall payne & tormente.

Fourthly it teacheth vs Fortitude, to withstand strongly any
aduersity, paine or tribulation, for the honour & loue of him, that
loued vs so much: & also for our owne Saluation, because tribulation in this world paciently sustained is the ready way to heauen.
This blessed Passion being called to remēbrāce there is nothing so
harde, as S. Isidore[2] saith, which is not with an equal minde toller-
ated. Let vs therfore as true Souldiers, diligently studye to suffer
with him: & thē no doubte we shall, as S. Paule saith, be pertakers
of his cōsolatiōs & Ioyes.

Fiftly it teacheth vs Humilitie, for if Christ, which was the
Sonne of God, [9] abased & humbled him selfe so much as to descēd
from his glorious Kingdome, into this vale of misery, to take vppon
him oure base Nature, & suffer such an ignominious death with
what face can man lifte vp him selfe in pride, & contemne so louing
a Redeemer? This Humility is the ground & foundation of all
Vertue, & without that no vertue can be acceptable in the sight of
God which caused our Sauior so carefully in his holye Gospell, to
admonish vs of the same, saying. Learne of me, for I am meke &
humble in hart. And S. Ambrose saith, that how much more abiect a
man is in this life: so much the more he shalbe exalted in the world
to come. Woulde thou haue al vices, saith one, destroied within
thee? Learne then to be truely humble. To which agreeth S. Augst.
saying. Humilitie is the Quene of vertues, the death of vyces, the
looking glasse of virgins, & the harboure of the [10] holy Trinitie. It
is only humilitye, saith S. Bernard, that exalteth: & she alone
leadeth to life, because saith he, this is the way, & ther is none
other. And therfore S. Gregory saith well, that whatsoeuer a man
doth is lost, if it be not kepte by humility. God graunt vs to imbrace
this Vertue, & to imitate that swete Lambe, which as S. Bernard
saith, was borne poore, liued poore, & dyed poore.

Now touching his bountiful Giftes, it driueth me into a mase, to
remember them. First how he hath made vs, as is before said, to his
owne B. Image and likenes, geueing vs the noble giftes of Memorye,
Reason, & Will: & hath made the Soule of man so noble, that noth-

---

[2]St. Isidore (c. 560-636) was a learned Spanish Archbishop and Doctor
of the Church. His most famous work, the *Etymologiae,* was a standard textbook throughout the Middle Ages (*Catholic Encyclopedia*, VIII, 187).

ing is able to fill or satisfie it, but him selfe alone. It may well be occupied, as S. Bernarde saith, with all other thinges: but filled or satisfied, can it not bee.

He doth inrich vs also with his grace & doth visite comforte & strength vs, [11] with his good inspirations, & motions to Vertue: And in the end, hath prepared such Ioyes for vs, as passeth all vnderstanding, either of man or Angels.

And for the giftes corporall, they be also such & so many, as are maruelus to cōsider. He hath created for our behoofe the Elements, with the Sunne to geue vs light by day, & the Moone to illuminate the night. The Fyre to keepe vs frō coulde: & the Ayre to mitigate his heate, and preserue our health. The Water to washe away our filthines. The Earth with his variable Fruites to susteine vs, & with his beautiful Flowers, to recreate vs: Besids the great diuersity of Beastes, Foules, and Fishes, for our norishment & delight.

He hath geuen vnto vs our Wittes, & right Limmes, with Beauty, Strēgth, & comlye shape. He hath kepte & deliuered vs from many daungers, both of fire & water, thunder & tempest, slanders, [12] shames, & many other euels, with the which, for our sinns, he might iustlye haue punished vs: & whē we offended in deadly sinne, haue cast vs headlong into hell: & yet of his tender loue hath forborne & spared vs.

O what shall we render againe vnto God for all his Benefits? how infinitly are wee bounde to loue & serue him, not only in respect of his goodnes in him selfe (which is the cheefest cause indede) & of his tender loue towards vs: But also in respecte of the greate delight he taketh in our seruice, yea muche more thē he doth in the seruice of his Angels, & the reason is this because man doth not only serue God of loue as the Angels doe: but also with laboure & paine, which they doe not: For he laboreth more in seruing him one day, then they haue donne since the beginning of the world: & therfore doth God singulerly delighte in our praiers, & other good [13] workes, & shal geue vs, if we continew to the ende, a double Crowne of glorye, that is both in Bodye & Soule.

And here vnderstand, that for diuers causes we are iustly bound to serue him.

First for our Creatiō, because we are created only to that ende: & therfore all our members & strengthe of bodye & Soule, are to be imploied & exercysed in his holye Seruice.

Also we are bounde to serue him in respect of his louing seruice done vnto vs, who saith by his Prophet Esay, *Seruire me fecisti in peccatis tuis,* that is, thou hast caused me to serue in thy sinns: As when he praied, fasted and preached, when he was whipped & crowned with thorne, whē he caried his Crosse, & theron suffered painfull death: & besides all this, in token of his great loue, he serueth vs still with his owne blessed Body & blood in the holy Sacramente, & therfore euery way are we bound [14] most louinglye to serue him againe.

Also we are bound to serue him, in respect of our Obligatiō & Vowe, made in Baptisme: hauing ther vowed & promised so to doe al the time of our life.

Likewise for his great Benefites, as is beforesaid, bestowed vpon vs.

And lastlye for that inestimable glory that he hath promised to al those that loue, and truly serue him to the ende.

But because no Seruice can be acceptable vnto him, which procedeth not from a cleane and pure harte: It shal not be here amisse to declare brefely, by what meanes the same may be obtained & gotten.

First he that would serue God truely in cleānes of harte & Conscience muste daily behould, and looke into his workes, and diligentlye consider his whole state and conuersation, & see if there be any thing in the same reprehensible, or contrary to the will of God: because [15] the knowledge of our selfe, is the beginning of our health & Saluation.

Secondly what-soeuer he findeth in him-selfe, in which he hath offended God: he must hartely repent, & humbly aske mercy for the same, firmely purposing therof to make a cleare and perfecte confession, so soone as he maye.

Thirdly he must with careful study, and deuoute prayer, continually desire of God, to kepe & defend him frō sinne: for as the holy Prophete saith, Except God kepe the city, he watcheth in vain that keepeth it. Therfore euery man ought to serue God in greate humilitie, & with cōtinual watche & warde ouer him selfe. The difficulty of Perseuerance in well doing appeareth in the fall of Lucifer from heauē, of Adam frō Paradice, and Iudas frō the nomber of the xij Apostles: what cause haue we therfore to pray, as our Sauioure counseleth vs continually, hauing experience of our [16] owne weaknes & debility in resisting temptations. In somuch that som-times through one only worde, we are prouoked to anger and im-pacience.

Therfore it behoueth vs euer to stand in feare for offending God, and to that ende saith the Scripture. Blessed is the man that is euer fearfull. And S. Bernard saith, that feare and Religion are knit to gether: & that the one can not remaine without the other. God geue vs grace, that we may dailye studie to obtaine this most noble vertue, that the blessinge which Christe speaketh of in the Gospel, may light on vs: where he saith Blessed be the cleane in hart, for they shal see God, To whom be all honoure for Euer-more. Amen.

[Here follow a prayer of thanksgiving to the Holy Trinity and a short introduction to prayer, pp. 16-18.]

[18] *What is to be Premeditated before praier.*

When you intēd to offer the Sacrifice of Prayer, & Praises, to almighty God, & prepare you to praier.

Recale your Senses, & gather to gether your wittes, & with an humble, attentiue, & deuoute mind lifte vp your harte to God: Reu-erently standing vpright, with your handes ioyned before your breste, & lifted vpp.

Pause then a litle while, & aduised—[19] lye* consider with your selfe wherefore you come, wheraboute you goe, and what busines, you now take in hande.

Also, before whom you are present, the Petitions you will aske, and the Offerring you meane to make.

Remember you are now, before a moste mighty & Deuine Maiesty: The Creator, and Redeemer, of your selfe & all Mankinde, whome Infinite Numbers of Angels, & all the Caelestiall multitude doe continually adore & worshipe, with feare & tremblinge.

And your selfe, a most wretched & vnworthey Creature, fraile vnstable, falling from him: dulle, & vn-apte to call vpon him. And yet, his mercy is so muche, & his goodnes so great, that he is euer, ready to heare, & graciously to graunte, your lawful requestes, and to receiue you when you come vnto him: & also to forgeue you al your offences, when you are hartely sorye, & aske mer-[20]cye for them.

Likewise, he is one that hath, and doth, most bountefully bestow vpon you, al thinges necessary for body and soule: & hath and doth, defend & kepe, feede & nourish, you, & al creatures.

---

*aduised-/lye] *ed.;* aduised/lye

And that before his diuine Presence, you nowe presume to enter, and to present your selfe: To Intreate, beseech, & Require mercye, and forgeuenes of sinnes, for your selfe & al others: & to offer the Sacrifise of Prayse, & Thankesgeuinge.

Therfore, with al humility, & reuerence, prostrate your selfe at the feete of his mercye: & Indeuore with deuotion, to accomplish that you come for.

But before you begin your praiers, that you maye the rather, offer them with cleannes of harte, & geue thankes to God, not only for his Benefits, but chefely for his goodnes in him selfe; Make it fully knowen to your harte (as [21] true it is vncertaine whether you shal liue to the ende of your Prayers or not: Indeuor therfore thay maye be such, as if it shold so happen before you had ended them, that so through the mercy of God, they may be acceptable vnto him, for the ful forgeuenes of your former offences & the receiuing you to his fauoure.

And that you may the more perfectly, beginne, continew, and ende, al your prayers, and other good actions In the Name, & to the honoure, and glorye of God, the moste holy and blessed Trinitye: & haue in minde his greate goodnes towardes you, & Benefits bestowed vpon you, & geue thankes for them, and also, that the Passion of our Lord, may take the more effecte, the benefit of it be Imparted, the fruite ther of Inioyed: and in al spiritual Practices remembred: You may, yf it please you, begin your Prayers, in manner as foloweth Meekly fal-[22]ling on your knees, your hart & ioyned hands, being Eleuated to God.

[Here follows a collection of prayers and meditations on sundry topics, pp. 22-81. Of particular note is one meditation on contrition ascribed to Richard Rolle of Hampole, pp. 47-58.]

X

Certayne deuout Me-
ditations very
necessary for Christian men
deuoutly to meditate vpon
Morninge and Eueninge,
euery day in the
weeke:

Concerning Christ his lyfe and
Passion, and the fruites
thereof.

Vigilate & orate, vt non intretis in
tentationeum. Math. 26.

Watch and pray, lest you fall
into temptation. Math. 26[1]

[compiler anonymous]

[Aii] ¶The preface of the Author to
certaine Meditaciõs which must
be dayly saide according to the
nombre of the seauen daies
in the weeke.

Among al our godlye and deuoute Meditaciõs (good christian
Reader) there can be none better, more acceptable to God and more
commodious and necessary to man, or more fyt for vs to the at-
tayninge of a good and happy lyfe, then at all tymes to occupie our

---

[1][Colophon:] Duaci apud Iohannem Bojardi [*sic*], 1576. Imprint false;
pr. [London, William Carter.] Allison and Rogers, I, Entry 227. *STC* 17775.
Later collections which include parts from this work are:
[*A Manual or Meditation.*] 9 pts. Printed at Doway by I. R. [1580-81.]
Imprint false; pr. [secretly in England at the Greenstreet House press.]
Tp. missing. Each entry of this collection is listed separately in the *STC*:
17776a, 14107, 25131, 20194, 14108, 5183, 11182, 20199, and 14568. Allison and
Rogers, II, Entry 520.
[Anr. ed.] *A Manual o* [*sic*] *Meditation, and most necessary prayers:*
with a memoriall of instructions right requisite. Also a summarie of Catholike
religion: and an absolute order of confession: with directions for receiving:
& other necessary thniges [*sic*]. 9 pts. n.p.d. [1580-81.] Pr. [secretly in Eng-
land at the Greenstreet House press.] This work does not appear in the *STC*.
Allison and Rogers, II, Entry 521.
[Anr. ed.] *A Manual, or Meditation, and most necessary Prayers . . .*
and other necessary things fit for all well disposed persons. n.p.d. [c. 1596.]
Pr. [secretly in England.] I. R., the compiler of this collection, attributes
the *Certayne deuout Meditations* to St. Peter Canisius, S. J. (sig. A4).
Not in *STC*. Allison and Rogers, II, Entry 522.
For a short criticism of *Certayne deuout Meditations,* see Southern (pp.
206-208).

selues in the continuall remembrance and meditacion, of the lyfe and passi-[Aiiᵛ]on of our Lorde Iesus Christ, the which thing is plainly shewed & declared not onely by the example and doctrine of diuerse holy and learned men, but also by experiēce it selfe, which is our chefe mistris in all things we doe. And if thou would flee from sinne & shun vice, then consider with thy selfe, what great things the onely sonne of God, both dyd and suffred the space of three and thirtie yeares, to thend thou might bee deliuered from vitiousnesse and sinne. If thou loue humilitie, gentlenesse, pacience, obedience, charitie and other vertues that were [Aiii] in Christ, & if thou desier to bewtifie thy soule with these: then cast thine eye on the perfect and liuely patern of all vertue, which is thy Lord Christ himselfe. If thou art desirous to cōtemne the world & all worldly vanities, & nothing to care for the same, then way earnestly with thy self what kynde of lyfe Christ our Lorde, lead when he was liuinge here, how poore it was, how lyttle it was accounted of and how contemptuous it was, how full it was of labour and sorow, what taunts and conspiracies, and how bytter a death he sustayned for thy loue [Aiiiᵛ] and saluaciō. And finally if thou would stir vp and inflame thy mynde to the loue of god, & giue him thanckes. What can in such a case be more effectuall then stil to call to remembraunce Christe his lyfe and passion, and how many and how great benefites wee haue receiued thereby. Wherevpon the Apostle sayd for good cause: Remember you him who sufferid such reproch against him selfe at the handes of sinners, that you should not quaile nor be dismayed in hart: And Sainct Peter sayth: for that Christ suffered in flesh see that you be also comfor-[Aiiii]ted with the remembraūce therof. But to thintent that thou good (Christian Reader) mayest vse these meditacions to thy greater profit, thou must obserue this order that foloweth: that at suche tyme as thou myndest to praye thou presētly reade ouer al those chefe poïts, that are to be thought vpon concerning that daye, then pause somewhat in contemplatiō of that wherein thou tooke most pleasure in thy meditacion. And directing thy contemplacion to some vertue, seriously consider with thy self how diligētly christ exercised himselfe therein, who [Aiiiiᵛ] gaue thee an example earnestly to folow his steppes. Then determyne with thy selfe to imitate that vertue which thy prayer entreateth of that day, & to increase dayely in the same: labour also eftsonnes in the day tyme, to call to mynde that which thou purposed with thy selfe &

that thou wilt omit no occasion, whereby thou mayst putte that vertue in practise in thy selfe. The chefe pointes thou haste to consider of are fiue. The first is fetched from Christ his infancy. The second is deduced out of his lyfe, the other three are taken from his passion.

[A^v]

Vpon Sunday thinke on Christ his humilitie.

First cōsider with what humilitie the sonne of God, he who was the chefe Monarche of all the world came from heauen, and shrowding him selfe in the pure wombe of the humble Virgin Mary, debased himselfe taking on him the shape of a seruaunt. Desier therefore the same Lord to giue thee perfect humilitie, and that he will endewe thee with such grace, that all pryde, vaineglory, and delighte in thy selfe may be vtterly rooted out of thy hart: and at sundry tymes [Av^v] consider with thy selfe, to how many and how great imperfections as yet thou art subiect vnto, into what vices, thou dost dayly and miserably fall, and how lyttle hetherto, thou hast increased in vertue.

Secondly consider with what lowlynesse of hart he suffred him selfe to be Baptised of S. Iohn Baptiste, as though he had bene a sinfull creature that had stode in neede to be washed & made clean: who notwithstanding being perfect god and man, was free from all spot of sinne, and gaue to saint Iohn all suche grace, as was in [Avi] him. Therfore thou that art as it were a poore worme after the example of thy creatour, submyt thy selfe to all such as teach and instruct thee, albeit they are inferiour and worse then thou.

Thirdly, call to mynde that merueylous humilitie of his, when at the tyme that his passiō drew neere, to shew man his infirmitie, he opened his sorow to his disciples and sayd: My soule is very sad vnto death. Whereas for all that, he it is that giueth perfect ioye, not to those onely that are in earth, but to such also that liue in heauen, learne therefore [Avi^v] not to put to much truste in thy selfe, nor to presume ouer much of thyne owne strength in temptacions, whether they chaūce by inward suggestiō or other ways, but beinge lowly in thyne owne sighte, be not ashamed bothe to aske, and to receiue counsell also of other men.

Fourthly remēber how hūbly Chryst the most mightie Lord of all other, as it wer a man vtterly destitute of all helpe, cast him selfe prostrate on his face, & with his teares prayed to his Father, that we might be ryd of our sin & his loue was so great towardes [Avii] vs, that he swet bloud aboundātly. For this cause in all thy miseries and heauinesse of hart humbly pray to Christ thy Sauiour, and for the loue thou bearest to him, haue no respect of thy selfe, but refer thy selfe wholly to his good pleasure.

Fyftly thincke with thy selfe with what humilitie and howe willingly he yelded himselfe to his heauenly Father (to whom as touching his godhead he was equall for all that) sayinge: Not my will but thine be fulfylled. And that he disdayned not to be comforted by an Angell, who [Avii^v] otherwyse is the comforter of all the world, & comforteth all men in their extremities. Se therfore that thou in most humble maner from the bottome of thy heart, submit thy selfe to god his will, in all thinges that may happen to thee, either by motion of mynd or outwardly looking for heauenly comforte with moste assured hope.

At the end of thy medita-
tion say this praier.

O Lord Iesu Christ sonne of the liuinge God, thou who [Aviii] art the true God, and the moste mightie maker and perseruer of all thinges, who to leaue vs an example of humilitie, came from the hye heauen down to the earth, here takinge on thee our frayle & weak nature, who as an vnpure & sinneful creature would needes be baptised of Sainct Iohn thy seruaūt, and at such tyme as thy passion drewe on shewed thy sorowfull hart to thy louing disciples, and lying groueling on the groūd after thou had swet bloud and water, dyddest put thy selfe wholly to thy Father his pleasure, and dyddest besides all this [Aviii^v] many other thinges, wherein were euident tokens of merueilous humilitie. I beseech thee graunt mee perfecte humilitie, willingly to submit my selfe to all men that I thinck not to wel of my selfe, but be vile and of no reputacion in myne owne sight, and desier so to be accounted of others. Who liuest and raignest with the father in the vnitie of the holy Ghost God world without ende. Amen.

[Here follow similar meditations and prayers for Monday (mildness), Sigs. Aviii^v-Biiii^r; Tuesday (patience), Sigs. Biiii^r-Bvii^v; Wednesday (obedience), Sigs. Bvii^v-Ciii^v; Thursday (kindness), Sigs. Ciiii^r-Cvii^v; Friday (charity), Sigs. Cviii^r-Diiii^v; and Saturday (the bounty of Christ), Sigs. Diiii^v-Dviii^v. Here follow directions on how to offer oneself to God in the morning, a collection of prayers for diverse occasions, directions on how to prepare oneself for retiring, and another collection of hymns and prayers for diverse occasions, Sigs. Ei^r-Hviii^r.]

XI.

The godly garden of
Gethsemani, furnished with
holsome fruites of Meditation
and prayer, vpon the blessed
passion of Christ our
Redeemer.
[Device of a shield with the word
SVRSVM flanked by two wings]

Cant. I.
Fasciculus Myrrhae dilectus meus mihi:
inter vbera mea commorabitur.
A nosegay of myrrh is my true loue to me:
Betwene my brestes his dwelling shalbe.[1]
[trans. anonymous]
[Woodcut of the Crucifixion, Sig. Ai^v]

[Aii]   ¶To the Reader.

By chaunce happeninge vppon this litle Treatise written in the Italian by a deuoute person, as it appeareth, and one specially professed by rules of Christian life, to the glorious name of Iesu: for my small vnderstanding in that tongue, and further exercise therein, I put on it an English habite of suche course weauing as skil serued me. And finding therein suche sweetenes as is always proper to so

---

[1] n.p.d. [c. 1576.] Pr. [London, William Carter.] Allison and Rogers, I, Entry 467. *STC* 11803a.
Other editions:
[Anr. ed.] n.p.d. [c. 1576.] Anon. Pr. [London, William Carter.] Allison and Rogers, I, Entry 466. This work does not appear in the *STC*.
[Anr. ed.] *Meditations, of the life and passion of our Lord and Sauiour Iesus Christ. With the arte how to meditate.* n.p.d. [1596-98.] Pr. [secretly in England.] Allison and Rogers, I, Entry 468. *STC* 16648.
This work is a translation of Gaspar Loarte's *Instruttione e avertimenti, per meditare la Passione di Christo Nostro Redentore; con alcune Meditationi intorno ad essa* (Rome, 1571). For biographical notes on Loarte, see p. 56, n. 1.

good matter, I thought good [Aii^v]to bestowe my simple trauayle though with more charges, in presenting onely the same to a speciall good friend or two: as a winter flowre to weare in their bosome, or red Rose nowe at Christmas, by my tenure or seruice due: whiche they might at their pleasure ioyne with other posies of their accustomed deuotions. If thou, good Reader, chaunce vpon any one booke thorough the liberalitie of the printer, or otherwise by more number printed then I purposed, I haue therefore to desire thee to accept it with good will, as I know they do to whom of pur-[Aiii] pose I vowed my trauels, & also that thou wilt excuse and beare with all the faultes committed by the Printer or me for this time, which are not so great to frustrate thee or me of the fruite of thy exercise or expectation herein, which is encrease of pietie and deuotion. Of which thou mayst assure thy self to reape as much fruit to thy comfort as is possible of so litle a treatise.

I haue called it by the name of the garden of Gethsemani, alluding in my fansie to the Garden where Christe prayed and shed both water and blood for mankinde: which name for neede [Aiii^v] may put thee sometime in mind oftner to resorte to this garden of exercise, and to haue Christes wordes to his Disciples there alwayes sounding in thy eares & slumbring minde: Can ye not watch with me a litle while? &c. Also our heauēly Salomon and Sauiour Christe inuiteth his spouse the Church in these words: Come into my garden my sister and wife: And she our mother founde no flowre or fruite in this paradise of god more to hir liking, than this tree of life, the blessed crosse of Christ: as may wel appeare by hir own words: A nosegay of myrrhe is my true [Aiiii] loue to me, and within my brest his habitation shal be. Meaning by the myrrhe, whiche for the bitternesse thereof was geuen Christ to drinke in his extreme thirst, and which for the sweete smell agayne, serued amongest other thinges to annoynt his body in the sepulchre: That she reioyced in nothing more then to gather hir selfe a posie of the bitter paynes and sorowes that Christe suffered for hir and hir faythfull children. Then according to hir example, as children rightly nurtured in hir lappe, let vs not thinke it tedious to followe hir course and steppes, [Aiiii^v] and say with her: In the sweete sent of thy oyntmentes (Gracious Lord) I do runne after thee. And let vs holde alwaies in our breast, and keepe in memory by continuall meditation, all the grieuous tormentes and troubles which our sauiour suffered for the redemption of the worlde, that therby we may learne and knowe the length & the breadth, the height & depth of that moste healthfull tree and Crosse of Christ, which of his great mercy I beseeche him graunt both thee & me good Reader.

[Av]

Of the fruite of suche deuout meditation, and of the
maner and order of this
litle Treatise.

Amongst all exercises of deuotiō that a Christian man can haue, one of the most fruitefull and most acceptable to God is, to be often and deuoutely occupied, in calling to remembrance and well to consider in minde (which otherwise we terme to meditate) the passion of Christ our redeemer. The which all the Doctours that write thereof af-[Avᵛ]firme, and also reason and experience do playnely declare the same. For by such holy meditation the soule is inflamed in the loue of Christ, considering howe tenderly he loued it, how muche he suffered to saue and beautifie it: and moreouer it feareth and is ashamed of his sinfulnesse, knowing & seeing how grieuously it was punished in the sonne of God, who as the Prophet Esay saith, was stroken of the father for the sinnes of his people. Yea the soule thereby receiueth in hir selfe and increaseth newe and freshe desires to amende the life: seeing the liuely and mar-[Avi] ueilous examples which particularly do shine in the holy passion of Christ. And likewise it is thereby styrred and pricked forwarde to geue thankes & prayse for his infinite goodnesse and mercy, that it hath pleased him with so tender loue to be made a sacrifice, and to suffer so bitter death, that he might geue vs miserable and wretched wretches, life and saluation. And thus finally the soule may seeme in some parte to pay the great debt it is bounde in, feeling in it selfe the great benefite it hath receiued, when it calleth to remembraunce and bethinketh [Aviᵛ] particularly the manyfolde sorrowes, iniuries, and tormentes which the sauiour of the world suffred in his death and passion: and doth know that this seruice is most acceptable to him, and also is sory for them who do not the like, but forget the great kindnes of their Redeemer.

So then, for this and many other fruits gathered of this blessed meditation, certayne Doctours affirme that those gayne more, which euery day do meditate with deuotion, some little part of the passion of Christ, than if they should exercise manye prayers, fastings, disciplins and [Avii] chastenings of the body otherwise. And therefore albeit many haue copiously at large written hereof, yet notwithstanding for the better commoditie and helpe of them that haue not such bookes, & specially for suche our Christian brothers and sisters sakes, that haue a desire to exercise them selues in the meditation of the passion of our Lorde, we are moued to finde out some meanes howe they maye with more facilitie and taste godlily occupie them selues therein. Whiche I doubt not, my good brother, but thou shalte well proue, if thou be willing with [Avii^v] attention diligently to marke what shall in this little Treatise be layde before thee, wherein thou shalt finde great sweetenesse in applying thy selfe to so heauenly an exercise, both necessary and highly commended. For here thou shalte see in figures set foorth the Images of those mysteries thou hast to call to thy remembrance and mind: in beholding wherof thou maist be holpen to be more setled and stayed in memorie and minde of that imagination which is so imprinted within thee.[2] Herein also are declared the poyntes to discourse on, and so to proceede [Aviii] with more deuotion in thy meditation. Or if thou knowe not howe of thy selfe to make these or the like talkes or speeches with God, then I say, this may teache thee the order and maner howe, because herein is shewed thee howe to geue thanks to thy Redeemer for that which thou shalt meditate or call to minde he hath suffred for thee: and also what thou oughtest to praye for, conformable to that poynt and parte of the passion thou hast to meditate vpon. Which doing (by Gods grace) with as great deuotion as thou canst, thou mayst then well hope thou [Aviii^v] shalt not at any time be occupied therein without fruite: the which shal be so much the more, as thou shalt more earnestlye perseuer in so godly an exercise.

¶Diuers profitable wayes how
to meditate vpon the blessed
passion of Christ our
Redeemer.

It is declared in the booke of the Prophet Daniell, that there was shewed in a vision to Nabuchodonosor, a tree planted in the middle

---

[2]The woodcuts in this book, which are quite elaborate and detailed, are intended by the author to be functional, not merely decorative.

of the earth, which tree was very hye, garnished with goodly leaues and abun-[Bi]dance of fruite. By this tree is figured Christ crucified in the middest of the earth, vnder the shadow of which tree whosoeuer is willing to rest him selfe, and recorde within his minde the most holy passion, he shall finde fruite both sweete and copious, and that so much the more, as his vnderstanding shall serue him in more diuers sort to meditate on the same. And therfore ye must note that ther be diuers wayes to meditate vpon the holy passion, & out of eche of them there may be gathered new varieties of fruites: for that you shall finde one fruite and taste [Bi*] when you do in your meditatiō take sorow & compassion within your selfe for the great torments & iniuries which Christ suffered: and an other kinde of fruite when thou shalt meditate thereon in minde to followe the great vertue that is taught thee therein, and so in diuers other sortes, as your meditation may runne for diuers other endes and purposes. And although the deuotion of euery man may deuise different wayes of exercise in this meditation: yet neuerthelesse I thought good in this litle treatise to set foorth certyne sortes, which I hope shall [Bii] not a little further and helpe such as be willing to serue their turne therewith.

The first maner or sort which is generall, and here set foorth before the rest we intende to speake of, may be called historicall or literall: whiche consisteth in knowing wel the letter and historie of that mysterie which thou purposest to haue in minde and contemplation: the which thou must as freshly remember and consider of, as it were presently set before thine eyes.

The second maner of this meditation is, by way of compas-[Bii*]sion: that is to say, for that intent that thou wouldest haue compassion, and as it were lament and be sory for the grieuous tormentes, reproches and sorowes which thou conceyuest in thy minde that Christe hath suffred for thee: considering wel the quantitie and qualitie therof, with other circumstances which do encrease the sorowes and passion, and therefore the more styrre thy heart to pitie and compassion.

The third maner is, to meditate by way of compunction or contrition, which is to that end that thou mayst be pricked with [Biii] remorse of cōscience and sorow for thy sinnes, which are with such rigour and crueltie punished in thy redeemer, for that he was offered vp as a raunsome and price for them, so to make satisfaction before the iustice of his eternall Father. And this shall cause thee to

hate them the more, and to keepe thy selfe the more warely hereafter frō committing the like offences agayne, when thou shalt consider how muche they offended God, that he would punishe the same
with so great seueritie.

The fourth maner and sort of meditation is, by way of imita-
[Biiiᵛ]tion or following, that is, to the ende to followe the marueilous
vertue and rare examples that Christe our redeemer showeth and
setteth foorth in his passion, as well in the wordes which he spake,
as in the workes which he did, and in the maner of his suffering. All
which to consider is a certayne liuely example and paterne of perfection, for thee to vse as a glasse to beholde what vertue wanteth in
thee, and so to vse thy selfe that thou mayest obtayne it.

The fifth maner and sorte of meditation is by way of thanks
giuing, that is, in rendring of [Biiii] thankes and prayses to God for
his bountifull goodnesse, calling to remembraunce the innumerable
giftes and great benefites which are giuen thee by meanes of this
holy passion: the whiche are so great that no vnderstanding of man
is able to comprise them. Yet notwithstanding, those whiche by this
discourse thou art able to vnderstande, may suffice to stirre thee to
giue thankes and prayse to thy Lord God, which hath done so
muche for thee.

The sixt maner is by way of admiration: for hauing well considered in thy minde the vn-[Biiiiᵛ]speakeable charitie and loue of
Christe, in that he hath offered him selfe to suffer so bitter and
shamefull death: and likewise the infinite wisedome and iustice of
God, declared in the bitter passion of his deare sonne: thou shalt
become as a man rauished out of him selfe, beeing amased of so high
and wonderfull things.

The seuenth maner is, by way of ioye and hope: For if thou
consider that all which Christe hath suffered, and that death which he
hath sustayned, was onely for thy remedie and behoue, and that by
such meanes [Bv] he would make satisfaction for thy sinnes, and
leaue to thee the treasures of his redemption and mercies, if thou be
willing to helpe thy selfe therwith: Calling I say, these and the
like thinges to thy remembraunce, they may cause thee to reioyce
and be glad in hope that by this helpe thou mayst agayne recouer
that infinite treasure which thou haddest lost, and he by this meanes
hath purchased for thee.

The eight and last maner of meditation vpō this blessed passion, is, by way of loue. For because the principal fruite which thou mayst seeme to gather of [Bvʳ] that thou hast meditate vpon, is a certayne exceeding tender loue of our Lorde him selfe, which so vouchsafed to suffer and dye for thee.

And nowe that thou mayst in all these maners and wayes of meditation knowe the better how to proceede, these instructions and declarations following may serue thy turne.

[Here follow an explication in greater detail of the preceding eight methods, Sigs. Bvᵛ-Iiʳ, and certain advices for meditation, Sigs. Iiᵛ-Liiᵛ; hereafter begin the meditations proper. As an example I choose the nailing of Christ to the cross. Sigs. Liiiʳ-Pviʳ are omitted.]

[Woodcut of the nailing of Christ to the cross with the Latin inscription *Crux recipit fessum, claui palmasque pedesque Traijciunt, sedant, fellea vina sitim,* Sig. Pviᵛ]

[Pvii]

Of the nayling of Christ vpon
the Crosse, ye may meditate
these poyntes.

1 Howe that being with great trouble and trauell nowe come to the mount of Caluarie which was the place where the malefactours shoulde put him to execution, in steade of good wyne which they vsed to geue others that went to their sorrowfull death to comfort their spirites, they gaue Christ wine that was myxte with gall, because there shoulde no member or part, nor yet anye sense remayne in him without torment.

[Pviiᵛ] 2 Remember the inhumanitie of them to spoyle him of his garmentes, which was a new cause of griefe and torment to that most meeke Lambe, and a renuing of the exceeding sorrowes which he suffered. And likewise call to minde howe that beeyng spoyled of his garmentes, hee stoode all naked, in most bytter sorrowes, griefe and shame.

3 Then further consider, with howe great crueltie they caused hym to bee stretched vppon that harde bedde of the Crosse, which they had prepared for him: In the which they perced throughe and nayled with bygge grosse [Pviii] nayles, the most holy hands and feete of him, that made bothe heauen and earth. And on the other

syde consyder wyth what exceedyng patience and charitie hee suffered so great tormentes as no tongue suffyceth to expresse.

¶The prayer.

No tongue most mercifull Iesu, sufficeth to giue thankes and prayse worthye to thee, for thy burning charity, which caused thee with so great patience to beare and suffer the incomparable tormentes thou diddest [Pviiiᵛ]feele, what tyme thou wast nayled vpon the Crosse.

For albeit the griefe & smart of thy paine and sorrowe were exceedyng great: yet without all comparison muche more passing great and vnspeakable was the greatnesse of thy loue that prycked thee forwarde to suffer it.

Thy verie works, O Lorde, prayse thee, and for my parte I thanke and praise thee, as much as I maye, confessing my selfe neuer to be able to thanke thee for the least parte of that I am bounde vnto thee.

And therefore I praye the [Ri] for those moste biteer sorowes and for the entier loue of thine, which caused thee for the saluation of the worlde to suffer so greeuous tormentes: that thou wilt graunt me grace that they maye be alwayes fixed in my harte and minde as the percing arrowes of thy tender loue, and that renouncing all vayne loue of this worlde, I maye be surely nayled and fastened to thee in perfect loue and obedience. And for so muche as thou art figured by that cluster of grapes whiche the two men broughte on a staffe vppon their shoulders from the lande of promise, [Riᵛ] and waste troden foorth in that wine presse of the Crosse, that out of thee should flowe moste sweete wine to sweeten and ouercome* our soules: sweeten and fil my soule with that wine which causeth men to become chast and pure.

And cause that I be fast nayled with thee, with the nayles of thy loue and charitie. Thoroughly nayle my fleshe with the feare of thee, that it be not rebellious agaynst the spirite: and let my hands and feete be so nayled with thine, that they neither moue nor stretche besides thy blessed will. And geue [Rii] me so abundant grace, that I may be desirous to suffer, and to be dispraysed of all men for thee, and to be pressed downe for thy diuine loue. Amen.

[Here follow the remaining meditations on the Passion of Christ, Sigs. Riiᵛ-Sviiiᵛ.]

---

*ouercome] *ed.;* o-/ouercome

XII.

Of
Prayer, and
Meditation.
Wherein Are Con-
teined Fowertien Devovte

Meditations for the seuen daies of the weeke,
bothe for the morninges, and eueninges. And in
them in treyted of the consideration of the principall holie Mysteries of our faithe.

Written Firste in the Spanishe
tongue by the famous Religious father. F. **Lewis**
de Granada, *Prouinciall of the holie*
order of preachers in the Pro-
uince of Portugall.

[Woodcut of Christ and followers carrying their crosses with the
following Latin inscriptions: *Si quis vult post me venire, abneget
semetipsum, et tollat crucem suam quotidie, et sequatur me. luc. 9.
vers. 23 Qui dicit se in ipso manere, debet, sicut ille ambulavit, et
ipse ambulare. 1. Johan. 2. verse. 6.*]

Imprinted at Paris by Thomas Brumeau, at the signe of the
Olyue. Anno Domini. M. D. LXXXII.[1]
[trans. Richard Hopkins[2]]

[aij]

To the Righte
Honorable, and
Worshipfvll, of the

---

[1]Allison and Rogers, I, Entry 476. *STC* 16907.
    [Anr. ed.] Rouen, George L'Oiselet, 1584. Allison and Rogers, I, Entry
477. *STC* 16908.
    There were at least three Protestant versions of this work published during
the reign of Elizabeth—1592, 1599, and 1601 (Southern, p. 206).
    Of Prayer, and Meditation is a translation of the first part of the three parts
of Granada's *Libro de la Oracion y Meditacion* (Salamanca, 1544). It is the
first translation into English of one of the great Spanish devotional writers of
the sixteenth century (Southern, p. 197). The translator, Richard Hopkins,
states that he used for his translation the Spanish edition printed at Antwerp
in 1572 by Christopher Plantine (sig. B3).
    For notes on Granada, see p. 112, n. 1.
[2]For notes on Richard Hopkins, see p. 112, n. 2.

fower principall howses of Cowerte in London, professinge the studie of the Common
Lawes of oure Realme, Richarde
Hopkins wishethe dewe cōsideration of
the holye mysteries of the Christian Religion.[3]

Dan. 9.11.
& 12.
Matt. 24.
Marc. 13.
Luc. 21.
2. Thess. 2.
1. Tim. 4.
2. Tim. 3.
2. Pet. 2.
Apoc. 11.12.
& 13.

The holy scriptures affirme in diuers places, that the nearer we
approche towardes the comminge of Antichriste, and the ende of the
worlde, the more perillous will the tymes be for all Christians. And
the perill hereof arisethe cheefelye of the greate enuye and malice of
Satan, who fearinge the ende of the worlde, knowinge that then his
tyrannous kingdome therein will haue an ende also therewith, ex-
tendeth the vttermoste of his rage againste all faithfull Christians,
and assaulteth them dailie more and more with diuers wilie tempta-
tiōs, and terrible persecutions, to procure them thereby to folowe his
*most wicked rebellious example: [aij*ᵛ*] that is, to breake gods holie*
commanundements, to contemne his diuine ordināces, to neglecte his
seruice and honoure, and by pryde and rebellion to lose the image of
god, and embrace the image of Satan, and so to be vtterlie vnapt to
attaine vnto those euerlastinge heauenlie māsions of felicitie, and
glorie, for which man was created.

Wherfore to the intent that all Christians might be more cir-
cumspecte, and strēgthened, to resiste faithfullye against all Satans
wylye deceytefull temptatiōs in this our daungerous age, approch-
inge so neare towardes the comminge of Antichriste, and the ende of
the worlde (as by manye coniecturall signes it seemeth) a holye

---

[3]Southern points out that there was a measure of audacity in Hopkins'
dedicating his translation to the gentlemen of the Inns of Court, considering
the law prohibiting the publication and distribution of Catholic books in England
(p. 198). Likewise, he notes that it was certainly a bold move to name the
author and announce him as a Spaniard in view of the fact that Spain was
England's arch-enemy and the seat of numerous real and supposed threats
against Elizabeth's power (p. 198). As a final shock, Hopkins sent a copy
of the translation to Francis Walsingham, the trusted lieutenant of Lord Cecil
and a well-known anti-Catholic. Hopkins' intention apparently was to disarm
his critics by being open and friendly, by pointing out the non-controversial
nature of the translation, and by expressing his desire to serve the good interests
of Elizabeth's government (Southern, p. 198). Throughout the dedication Hopkins attempts to win the favor of the Anglicans for Catholicism by stressing
their common traditions at the expense of the Puritans and their violent break
with tradition. It is interesting to note that Hopkins' second translation of
Granada, *A Memoriall of a Christian Life* (pp. 86-114) is also dedicated to the
gentlemen at the Inns of Court.

Angell hath forewarned vs hereof verye preciselye in the revelacions of S. Ihon, thunderinge out theise woordes with a great voice: woe be to the lande, and sea, because the Deuill is descended vnto you, hauinge a greate rage, for that he knoweth he hath but a shorte tyme. And this greate rage of his is the more to be feared in this our corrpute age, for that we reade also in Sainte Ihons revelations, that the Deuill shalbe let lose towards the ende of the worlde for a smalle tyme. In other ages and tymes of our holye christian fore-fathers the deuills exceedinge great malice and mightie power hath bene moche restrained and bownde throughe the great vertue of the Cross, and Passion of our Saviour Iesus Christe, communicated then verie plentifullie vnto the Christian people generallye by their de-voute frequentinge of the holie Sacramentes of the Catholike Churche (which be holie vessells of grace) whereby our Christian forefathers have bene [aiij] greatelye strengthened to resiste faith-fullye againste the moste horrible temptations of Schisme, Heresie, Infidelytie, and Atheisme, and to live generallie verie holie and aus-tere Christian liues in the feare and service of almightie god, and in dewe reuerente obediēce to the Catholike Churche. But nowe where-as in this our vngratious age suche a number of horrible sectes, and heresies, and suche a generall corruption with pride, dysobedience, lyenge, detraction, gluttonie, incontinencie, infidelitie, Atheisme, and all kinde of dissolute wickednes doe abounde and raigne more and more in all partes of Christēdome, woe bee therfore to the Lande, and sea, (as the holye Angell hath forewarned vs) because the Deuill is nowe discended, and let lose towardes the ende of the worlde for a smale time, hauinge a greate rage, for that he knoweth he hathe but a shorte tyme to continewe his tyrannous kingdome in this worlde.

And the verie cause of this so extraordinarie lettinge lose of the deuil nowe more and more towardes the comminge of Antichriste in the ende of the worlde, saincte Paule seemeth to explane in this sense: that for so muche as the wicked will not receiue the trew doctrine of the Catholike Churche with charitie, humilitie, obediēce, and thankfulnes, to the ende they maye be saued, therfore Almightie god letteth lose the devill nowe emonge them, by permittinge him to sowe in their prowde inconstante wilfull myndes manye erronious opynions, and heresies, that thei maye believe in lyenge.

[aiij^v]*And certainlie if we will aduisedlye consider the wylie pro-cedinges of the deuill in sowinge so manifolde sectes and heresies in*

Apoc. 12. vers. 12.

Apoc. 20. vers. 3. The deuill shalbe let lose more and more the nearer that Anti-criste ap-prochethe.

2. Thess. 2. vers. 10. & 11. The Catho-licke reli-gion daylie decreasin-ge, & here-sies daylie increasinge vnto worse and worse

sectes, is an
euident argu-
ment that
the diuell
is more let
lose towardes
the comminge
of Anti-
chirst.*

Note Satās
wylie pro-
ciedinges
in this cor-
rupte age.

*this vngratious age, and the finall ende whereunto he directeth them,
we maie euidentelie perceaue, that it is to cause all Christians nowe
towardes the comminge of Antichriste to be first dissolute in their
liues, and after dowtefull in their faithe, and then to contemne all
the holie Sacramentes, and other Mysteries of the Christian Religion, and afterwardes hauinge by degrees remoued awaie out of
their Churches all holie memories of our Saviour Christe, and of his
blessed Mother, Apostles, Martirs, & other of his glorious Saintes,
and also out of their myndes all feare of God, and of his dreadefull
iudgementes, then they be easelye induced by him shortelie after to
become harde harted, and vnsensible to conceiue anie spirituall
thinges, and also at the laste to become Atheistes, without anie conscience, Religion, or beliefe that there is a God. And so Antichriste
findinge his waie so open and readie prepared for him, maie then
come frielye when he will, and cause himselfe to be receiued as a
Messias, and adored as God, findinge the Christian people generallie
without anye deuotion and Zeale to the seruice and honour of our
Sauiour Iesus Christe, and without anye beliefe that there is a God.*

*Nowe emonge all the wylie deceitfull deuises of Satan for ouer-
throwinge of the Christian Religion, and so to prepare the waie for
Antichristes comminge, there is none (in my simple iudgemente) of
greater force, and consequence, than his so earnest endeuour to procure all Christians vtteryle to contemne and [aiiij] forgette all the
holie misteries of the Christian faithe. Which if he coulde possiblie
compasse (as he laboureth verie earnestlie therein by diuers craftie
meanes in this our corrupte age) then vndowtedlye all the whole
Christiā Religion, and euen our Sauiour Christe himself, and his
blessed Mother, and all his holie Apostles, and Martirs, and other of
his glorious saintes woulde consequentlie in a shorte time after be
generallie contemned, neglected, and forgotten througheout all
Christian countries.*

*And to write here freelie my minde as I thinke, it woulde seeme
verie meruailous vnto me (if I were not fullie perswaded that the
deuill is nowe more and more let lose (as Saint Ihon in his reuela-
tions hath forewarned vs he shoulde be for a shorte time towardes
the ende of the worlde) howe the deuill coulde preuaile so farfoor-
the, as to induce a whole newe late secte of heretikes that be called*

---

*Last nine lines of this gloss were written as two lines under the text in
the original.

Puritans (professinge in gaie wordes to be more pure, more sincere, and better professours of Christes gospell than anie other Christians either be or haue bene in anie age since the Apostles time) to write of late so vnchristianlie by common consent euen in an Englishe printed booke[4] *againste obseruinge in the Churche the most auncient yearelie solemne holie feastes of* Easter, *and* Pentecoste, *and against all speciall meditations at anie one solemne time of the year more then at others of Christs Resurrection, or of the Comminge of the Holie Ghoste, or of the hower of our deathe: because (saie theie) theise meditations shoulde be vsed continewallie euerie daie in the yeare, and owght not to be appoynted by the gouernors of the Churche to be* [aiiij ͮ] *vsed at anie one speciall time more than at others. Whereby euerie godlie christian reader maie easelie perceiue howe the deuill beinge nowe let lose laboureth verie buselie by theise counterfaite pure gospellers vnder a wylie deceitfull colour of ad-uauncinge continewal meditation and memorie of the holie Misteries of the Christian Religion euerie daie in the yeare, to haue no man-ner of meditation or memorie of them emonge Christians anie daie at all: that so by their suttle wicked doctrine a readie open waie maie be prepared in all Christiã mens Churches and mindes for* Antichristes *comminge.*

In the puri-
tans replie
against D.
Whitgifte,
pag. 120.
121. 122. &
163.

But ô the wonderfull prouidence and care of our Sauiour Christe to preserue a continewal knowledge and reuerence of his holie Misteries emonge all faithfull Christians in his Catholike Churche, as hath verie manifestelie appeared in all ages since Christes Ascen-sion vntill this our corrupte age. And surelie it is a matter worthie of greate and deuoute admiration for anie good christian to consider, howe the Apostles, and the aunciente holie Catholike Byshops their successours beinge by our Sauiour Christes owne promisse assured-lie inspired, assisted, and directed by the Holie Ghoste from time to time in gouernement of the Catholike Churche in all truthe, haue with suche diuine wisdome disposed the whole yeare into so manie seuerall holye festiuall daies, as that thereby haue bene represented, and preached vnto all Christian people in all Christian Churches throughout Christendome a continewal solemne instruction, memo-rie, and reuerence of the holie Mysteries of the Christian Religion. In so muche as the common Christian people by [av] *those holie festiuall daies alone (albeit they wanted not also diuers other holie instructions therein in confessions, and Sermons,) were in all ages*

How in all
ages hathe
bene pre-
serued e-
monge
Christians
a cõtinewal
knowled-
ge and re-
uerence of
the holie
misteries of
our faithe.
Matt. 28.
vers. 20.
Iohn. 14.
16.
Iohn. 16.13.
1. Tim. 3.15.

---

[4]See p. 117, n. 8.

sufficientlie instructed in the holie Mysteries of their Christian beliefe: I mean, they were thereby made to vnderstāde so muche of them, as (hauinge withall a dewe religious respecte to preserue a continewal reuerence in them to the dignitie of suche highe holie Misteries) was fullie conueniente for their weake capacities, and for the comfortinge and strengtheninge of their faithe, and as they were bounde of necessitie to knowe.

[Here follows a listing of the principal feasts of the Christian Church which our author recommends to the devout reader, Sigs. av^r-avi^r.]

[avi] *But alas theise golden times be paste, and ended,* [*i.e.* the days when these feasts were generally observed by all Christians] *and the deuill beinge let lose nowe more and more towardes the comminge of* Antichriste, *and the ende of the worlde, we finde by palpable experience, that since the time that suche a free licentious libertie hathe been permitted vnto euerie lewde bablinge Minister to raile againste all the holie aunciente diuine ordinaunces, vsed and allowed generallie so manie ages in all Christian Churches, and to terme them in blasphemous manner Antichristian inuentions, and to preache openlie in pulpittes, and publishe in printed bookes whatsoeuer newe hereticall opinions the ennemie of mankinde suggesteth into their fantasticall heades, the faithe of Christians is thereby generallie become so weake, and inconstante, and in verie manie or most persons so wholie vndermined, and vtterlie ouerthrowne, and their hope is so transformed into presumption, and their charitie is waxen so colde, and so litle pietie, loue, deuotion, reuerence, and Zeale remaine in them towardes the seruice of Almightie God, and so muche Pride, gluttonie, incontinencie, lyenge, detraction, disobedience, with moste horrible contention, schisme, heresie, infidelitie, Atheisme, and all kind of iniquitie doe generallie abounde throughout Christendome, that we haue good cause to feare, leaste that terrible time approcheth nowe verie neare at hande, which our Sauiour forewarned vs in the gospel, to wit: that at his comminge to iudge he shoulde hardelie finde faithe in the earthe.*

Luc. 18.
vers. 8.

Wherefore we haue nowe verie great neede of [avi^v] *extraordinairie spirituall helpes to strengthen our weake mindes, to withstand so manie deceitfull temptations of the enemie of mankinde in this so corrupte and daungerous age. And for this purpose I haue translated out of the Spanishe tongue diuers bookes of a verie holie* and famous learned religious father called Lewis de Granada, *whose deuoute manner of writinge hath (in my simple iudgement) a singulare rare grace to pearce the harde harte of a dissolute sinner, and to moue and dispose his minde to the abhorringe of synne, to the contempte of the worlde, and to the feare, loue,* and seruice of Almightie God. And I vnderstande that his bookes haue wroughte wonderfull muche good, not onelie in* Spaine, *and* Portugall, *but also in* Italie, Fraunce, *and* Germanie. *And I thinke there bee fewe countries in* Christendome *but haue his Spanishe woorkes trāslated into their tongues. And it is nowe about foureteene yeares agoe, since the time that* Master Doctor Hardinge[5] *(a man for his greate vertue, learninge, wisdome, Zeale, and sinceritie in writing againste heresies, of verie godlie and famous memorie) perswaded me earnestlie to translate some of those Spanishe bookes into our Englishe tounge, affirminge, that more spirituall profite wolde vndoutedlie ensewe thereby to the gayninge of Christian sowles in our countrie from* Schisme, *and* Heresie, *and from all sinne, and iniquitie, than by bookes that treate of controuersies in Religion: wich (as experience hath nowe plainelie tried) doe nothinge so well dispose the common peoples myndes to the feare, loue, and seruice of almightie God, as bookes treatinge of deuotion, and [avii] howe to leade a vertuous life doe. The dewe consideration whereof hath so prouoked or rather pricked me in conscience, that I haue resolued to publishe (godwillinge) in printe all my translations, in case I shall perceiue that suche as be godlie, wise, and learned, shall like of them. And first (as it were for an assaie) I haue here printed his deuoute Meditations of the principall holie Misteries of the Christian Religion, which booke I finde greatelie commended by diuers godlie learned men.*

It maie be that some readers of this booke beinge not greatelie acquainted with the holie exercises of a spirituall life, will imagin that the Authour dealeth to austerelie in some of theise meditations:

Obiection.

---

[5]Dr. Thomas Harding (1516-1572) was recognized both in England and abroad as a scholar of the first order. In 1542, he was appointed lecturer of Hebrew at New College, Oxford. In 1559, fearing possible imprisonment in England for his Catholic faith, he fled to Louvain, where he assisted Cardinal Allen in establishing the English College at Douay. In 1566, Pope Pius V appointed him apostolic delegate to England with the power to give faculties to priests in England for absolving heresy and schism. He was a friend and example to many exiled Catholics on the Continent. He was known to be an ardent and zealous controversialist. For more details of Harding's life, see Gillow (III, 124-128). For a bibliography of his English works, see Allison and Rogers (I, Entries 372-378).

*loue] *ed.;* lone

as namelie in his *Meditations of synnes: of the hower of death: of
our dreydfull accompte at the terrible daie of iudgemente: and of
the moste horrible paines of hell. And perhaps some politique wise
men will saie, that for so muche as the common people in our
countrie haue beene for the moste parte of our corrupte age altogether accustomed with hearinge and readinge of diuers other contrarie newe erronious* doctrines, tendinge directlie to a careles
dissolute life, thei be therfore nowe waxen so carnall and negligent
of the saluation of their sowles that theise Meditations be to full
of threateninge and terror, for suche nice and lose consciences. For*

Answere.

*answere to this obiection, it is to be noted, that the Author beinge
(as I am informed) not onelie a greate learned and religious deuout
olde father, but also of greate wisdome, grauitie, iudgemente, discretion, and of longe experience as well in preachinge, and hearinge of
Cōfessions, as in diuers gouer-*[avii^v] *nementes in his religious order,
and perceyuinge verie euidentlie that farre more Christian sowles be
loste in this our corrupte age with ouermuche presumptuous confidence and securetie of their saluation, than with ouermuche feare of
leesinge the same, hathe therfore framed his manner of writinge in
theise meditations chieflie againste the infinite nomber of presumptuous and careles dissolute Christiãs, that presume most certainlie, and
assuredlie to be saued, and yet doe liue verie dissolutelie all their
whole lyfe time, without all care of keepinge gods commaundementes,
and without all feare of their accompte at the dreadeful daie of iudgemente, notwithstandinge that our Sauiour Christ himselfe who shalbe
then our Iudge, hathe by plaine and expresse wordes forewarned vs in*

**Matt. 19.
vers. 17.**

the gospell of saint Mathewe, that if we will enter into the Kingdome
of heauen we muste Kepe his commaundementes, *which euerie Chris-
tain maie be able to kepe, beinge assisted, strengthened, and holpen
therein with the grace of God, which is neuer denied to anie that
praieth dulie for it: and also that we muste at the daie of iudge-*

**Matt. 12.
vers. 36.**

mente geue an accompte of euerye idle worde.

*And verelie if we peruse diligentlie the holie scriptures, we shall
finde that not onely Enoch in the lawe of Nature, and afterwardes*

**Epist. Iude.
vers. 14.**

*all the Phophets, but also sainte Ihon Baptiste, and our Sauiour
Christe himselfe vsed the same manner of preachinge that this religious godlie father dothe here. And they thought it to be the verie
best and rediest waie for conuersion of sinners from their sinfull*

---

*erronious] *ed.; erronions*

dissolute lifes, to shewe plainelie vnto them the damnable state [aviii]
they liue in, and to put them in mynde of the seuere iustice of
almightie God at the terrible daye of iudgemente against all suche as
endeuour not to kepe his commaundementes. [This theme is continued, especially by citing Scripture, Sig. aviii^r.] *And I am per-*
swaded [aviii^v] *that all godlie wise and graue men will easelie agree*
in this opinion with me, that this manner of preachinge of the terror
of the daie of iudgemente, and of the moste horrible paines of hell, is
muche more needefull nowe in this our corrupte age in Englande,
and Scotlande, than in Italie, Spaine, or other Catholike coun-
tries, sithe so great numbers of them are infected with so manie
hereticall licentious doctrines, that haue caused them to put quite
awaie out of their myndes all feare of God, and of his terrible iudge-
ments, and to presume most certainelie and assuredlye to be saued
by their onelie faithe, and so are generallie become vtterlie careles of
endeuoringe to woorke their saluation with feare, and tremblinge,
and doe lue as dissolutelie as anie barbarous Pagans, and Atheists:
In so muche as all godlie aunciente wise men doe greatelye lamente
to see by experience the terrible prophecie of Dauid to be generallie
verified at this daie throughout our Realme: which is, that the
iudgements of almightie God be taken quite awaye from the face of
the vngodlye. And if theise and suche like godlie Meditations and
considerations of the terrible threateninges and iudgements of al-
mightie God againste the wicked, be not a fitt remedie for their
conuersion from their careles dissolute lifes, what other remedie then
can possiblie be deuised for them?

Philip. 2.
vers. 12.

1. Cor. 4.4.
2. Pet. 1.10.

Psal. 9.
vers. 26.

Howbeit I haue verie greate hope, that with the grace of God
theise godlie Meditations will woorke muche good effecte for the con-
uersion of manie of them. For vndoubtedlie that man is verie wilfull
and obstinate in his wickednes, that readinge aduisedlie all theise
godlie Meditations is not moued inwardelie [b] *in his harte in some*
parte of them to the feare, loue, and seruice of almightie God, and to
the abhorringe of synne, and amendement of his life. And suche
readers as shalbe inwardelie moued and called thereunto by al-
mightie God, I coniure them in his holie name, and in regarde
of their owne saluation, not to make sad the Holie Ghoste, in
hardeninge their hartes, *and resistinge vngratefullie and wilfullie*
againste his diuine inspirations, when it shall please his infinite
goodnes, and mercie, with suche singuler loue to knocke and calle at
the dore of their hartes, but in anie wise to open it out of hande,

Ephes. 4.
vers. 30.
Psal. 94.8.

and receiue him most humblie into their hartes, with suche louinge hartie interteynement, submission, thankefulnes, seruice, and honor, as duetie requireth they shoulde doe vnto their most highe soueraigne lorde, and Creatour, that hath suche a speciall louinge care of their saluation.

Nowe this booke of Meditations, and whatsoeuer els I haue translated, and shall godwillinge hereafter publishe in printe, I doe most humblie offer vnto the seruice of almightie God for the benefite of our countrie. And for so muche as I am verie warie and assured that this boke conteineth not anie thinge whereby I maie iustlie incurre anie penaltie prescribed by anie Lawes of our Realme, I am the bolder humblie to recommende it by this my dedicatorie Epistle vnto your Honours and woorshipps: partelie for that I haue spente some parte of my time in the studie of our Common Lawes in the Middle Temple *emonge you, and am verie moche bounde vnto diuers of you: But chiefelie for that I knowe right well the greate* [b^v] *capacitie and dexteritie of your spirites, the grauitie of your iudgementes, and your wisdomes, experiences, authoritie, and example, to be of suche principall estimation, and worthie respecte in our Realme, that in case ye doe Zelouselye emploie your endeuours to the due reuerente consideration of the holie Mysteries of the Christian Religion, (as I doute not but verie manie emonge you doe,) your holie example will generallie allure a greate nomber throughout our whole Realme from all contentious disputinge, and iarringe aboute theise late newe controuersies in Religion, to embrace firmelie and Zealouselie the aunciente Catholike beliefe, and to imitate the vertuous liues of our holie Christian forefathers, who had muche more aboundance of the grace and lighte of the Gospell of our Sauiour Christe, than we haue in this our vngratious corrupte age, as verie manifestlie appeareth by their so manifolde good Christian fruites lefte by them vnto vs, to the glorie of our Sauiour Christ, and of his deare spowse the Catholike Churche, and to the continewall greate admiration, confusion, enuie, and dispite, of Lucifer, and of all his rebellious wicked spirites, and of all Iewes, Turkes, Heretiques, and other Infidells his adherentes.*

And (requestinge here humbly pardon, and licence, to treate in a familiar maner with the yonger sorte) I desire your Honors and woorshippes continewallie to remember what greate inclination ye haue vnto vertue more than others of obscure parentage, and base

An exhortation to yonge noble men and gentlemen.

estate, *in regarde of your noblenes, and magnanimitie, which euer inuiteth you to imitate the noble vertuous steppes of your noble Chri-*[bij]*stian auncesters, and to set vpon highe and noble vertuous enterprises, and to doe all your workes noblie, and excellentlie, that ye take in hande. As also to consider, that a vertuous life is the greatest and moste noble ornamente of nobilitie. And that for this ende cheefelie almightie God bestoweth vpon noble personages here in earthe principalitie, rule, gouernemente, and honor, that thei shoulde giue vertuous and godlie example vnto all others that be vnder their rule, and gouernemente. And by experience we finde that ordinarilie no bysshoppe or other preacher is able with such facilitie to plante vertue emonge the common people, and cause them sin-cerelie to loue, honor, and embrace it, as noblemen, gentlemen, Magistrates, and Gouernours are able to doe, in case thei them selues do giue good apparante example of vertue, religion, and deuo-tion, and be Zealous also in procuringe all others to doe the like. And therefore I beseeche you to determin with an honorable con-stant resolution to employe your time in the moste noble exercises of vertue, and to feare, loue, serue, and honor almightie God, who is your most noble, highe, soueraigne Lorde and Creator, and not to suffer either your studie or practise of the lawes, or other your worldye offices and affaires to be so greate an impedimente vnto your spirituall exercises, but that you maie haue euer one windowe open towardes the heauenlie* Ierusalem, *as Daniel had in his chāber in* Babylon, *prayinge there three times in the daie towardes the earthelye* Ierusalem. *And in case your worldlie impedimentes be ouer greate, then wisdome requireth that for saluation of your sowles you* [bij^v] *doe caste them awaie from you. And imitate here-in the worldlie foresighte of wise Marchauntes when they be in daunger of drowninge in a stormie tempeste vpon the sea, who vse at suche times for saluation of their liues to cast into the Sea their ryche merchaundise, and all their troublesome heauie encombrances, thereby to cause their shippe to saile more safelye. And I doe also humblie beseache all good Christian readers that shall like well of theise spirituall exercises to remember me in their deuoute praiers, that I proue not like unto those foolishe carpenters that made* Noes *arke, who made it to saue others from drowninge in the generall fludde, and yet were drowned them selues.*

Thus with all due humble submission of my self, and my tra-uailes herein to your honours, and woorships, I humblie craue pardon for passinge here somwhat the bowndes of my profession,

Dan. 6.
vers. 10.

and treatinge as a diuine of spirituall matters, accordinge as since my departure from the Middle Temple *by some studie and readinge of diuers spirituall bookes, and continewall conuersation theise fifteene yeares with manie vertuous and Learned Catholike Priestes in these partes I haue bene instructed. And I most humblie beseache almightie God that theise Godlie Meditations maie woorke so good effecte in all your myndes, as I haue often times verie earnestlie requested of his diuine Maiestie. From* Paris, *vpon the holie festiuall daie of* Pentecoste. *In the yeare of our Lorde. 1582.*

[Here follows a note on the edition which the translator used, *i.e.,* the Spanish edition printed at Antwerpe by Christopher Plantine in 1572, Sig. biijʳ. Hereafter follows an exhortation to the Christian reader on the value of prayer by Bernard de Fresneda, Bishop of Cuenca, Sigs. biijᵛ-bviiʳ. The last part deserves attention.]

[bvii] From receauinge which fruites [of prayer] no man is here excluded: for so much as the Awthor [Luis de Granada] hath with a rare wisdome in such wise tempered the doctrine, and accommodated him selfe vnto all states, and conditions of persons, that neither the verie highe and learned haue anie cause to leaue it, as ouer base for them: not the verie lowe and vnlearned to refuse it, as ouer highe for their capacities. For here is made a conuenient prouision of competent meates both for the one sort, and for the other. And because the [bviiᵛ] Awthor vnderstode right well how farre the mouthes of men now adayes are owt of tast, and how much they are more affectionate vnto the fleshe pottes of Egypt, than to the breade of Angels, I meane hereby, rather to the readinge of prophane bookes, by reason of the pleasant stile wherewith they thinke they are written, than to the bookes of spirituall doctrine, which are commonly written with more simplicitie, he hath therefore dressed this meate in suche wise, and hath written this doctrine in suche a sweete and pleasant stile, that it maie prouoke an appetite vnto this boke, euen in such persons as doe otherwise lothe good and holesome foode:[6] besides, that the verie matters them selues are exceedingly

---

[6]Granada is frequently compared to Lyly. J. G. Underhill in *Spanish Literature in the England of the Tudors* (New York, 1899) points out that "Granada's reputation rose with that of Lyly, and was based on the same fundamental grounds. . . . Lyly became the leader of a fashion, and Granada the most popular author translated during the closing years of Elizabeth's reign. One was animated in his work by a strong moral sense, the other by a religious ecstasy; but the pre-eminent vogue of both was due to the cultivation of an exaggerated style" (p. 207).

well chosen, and of great profite. And because it were the parte of rude and rusticall persons to geue thankes to the bees that make the honie combes, and not vnto almightie God who created the flowers from whence the bees gather the honie, which they worke in their hiues: I exhort all persons to geue thankes to the deuoute and Learned Author of these workes, for these so sweete and sauorie honie combes which he hath here geuen vs, in such sorte that they omit not to procede further, and to geue thankes to almightie God also, who hath sent the flowers wherewith this honie is made. And withall I make humble request vnto all men [bviii] that I may be partaker of the prayers they shall make by meanes of the good disposition which (I truste) with the grace of God the readinge of theise holie and excellent deuoute workes shall cause in all godly and deuoute Christian Readers.

Bernard de Fresneda
Bishoppe of Cuenca.

[Here follows a dedicatory epistle to the Reverend Fathers Don Antonio de Cordova and Lorenço de Figveroa, two noblemen who recently entered religion, Sigs. Aiʳ-Aiijʳ.]

[Aiij]

The Prologue and Argvment of This Booke.

Praier, (to define it properlie) is a petitiõ we make vnto almightie God, for such thinges as are apperteining to our saluation. Howbeit praier is also taken in an other more large sence; to wit: for euerie lifting vp of our hart vnto god. And according to this definition, both meditation and contemplation, and euerie other good thowght maie be also called a praier. And in this sence we do now vse this worde** becaus the principal matter of this booke, is of meditation, and consideration of thinges apperteyning to almightie God, and of the principall misteries of the Catholike faith. {*What prayer* is. An other definition of prayer.}

The verie thinge that moued me to treat of this matter was, for that I vnderstode, that one of the principall cawses of all the euilles, that be in the world, is the want of consideration: According as the Prophett Ieremie signified when he said. *All the earth is destroied with desolation, becawse there is none that thinketh with attention* {The want of consideratiõ is one of the principall cawses of all the euilles in the world. *Ieremie 12.*}

---

*prayer] *ed.;* payer
**worde] *corrected in errata from* vorde

vpon the thinges apperteyning vnto God. Whereby it appeareth, that
the verie cawse of [Aiij^v] our euills is not so much the want of
faith, as the want of due consideration of the misteries of our faith.
For trewlie if there were no want in this behalfe the misteries
of our faithe be of so great vertue, and efficacie, that if the
verie least misterie of them, were considered with attention, and
deuotion, euen the same would be a great brydle and redresse of our
liffe. For who would euer goe about to committ anie sinne, if he
considered that almightie God died for sinne? and that he punyshethe
sinne, with perpetuall bannishement out of the kingdome of heauen,
and with euerlasting paines and tormentes in the horrible fyer of hell?

Whereby ye maie see, that although the misteries of our faith, be
of verie great force, to encline our hartes vnto goodnes: yet because
there be verie manie Christians that haue no due consideration of
the thinges they beleue, therefore they worke not such effecte in
there hartes, as such misteries being well weied and considered were
able to worke. For like as the phisitions affirme that if we will haue
a medecine to helpe a sicke man, it is necessarie, it be first wrowght
and digested in the stomak with naturall heat, (because otherwise it
shall not be anie profitt to him at all:) euen so also, if we will haue
the misteries of our faith to be profitable and healthfull vnto our
soules, it is requisite they be first wrought, and digested in our
hartes with the heate of deuotion and meditation: because otherwise
they shall profit vs [Aiiij] verie littell. And for want hereof, we see
that manie Christians, which are verie whole and sownd in matters
of faith, be yet in there liues verie licentious and dissolute. And the
reason is, because they do not consider, and weigh the holie
misteries which they beleue: and so they keepe their faith, as it were
fast locked in a corner of a chest, or as a sword in the scabarde, or
as a medecine in the potticaries shoppe, and vse not the benefitt
thereof, for such purposes, as it serueth. They beleue generallie, and
as it were in a fardel or grosse sōme, all such thinges as the Catholike Church beleueth. They beleue that there shalbe a iudgment, that
there shalbe paines for the wicked, and glorie for the good: but how
manie Christians shall ye finde, that do consider after what sort this
iudgment, these paines, and this glorie shalbe, with other the like
circumstances?

Now this is the cawse, why the holie scripture so earnestlie
commendeth vnto vs, the continuall consideration, and meditation of

The consi-
deratiō of
the miste-
ries of our
fayth is a
greate bri-
dle to with-
hold us
from syn-
ne.

The cawse
whie ma-
nie Chri-
stianes,
that are
sounde in
matters of
faythe, be
yet verie
dissolute
in theire li-
ues.

Verye few
Christians
doe set thē
selues to
cōsider the
misteries
of our
faithe.

the lawe of God, and of the misteries thereof: Which is indeede the studie of true wisedome. Consider I pray you, how instantlie Moses that great prophett and frynde of God commendeth this vnto vs: saying: *Prynte these my wordes in your hartes and carie them*   *Deuteron. 5.* *bound as it were for a signe in your handes, and teach them to your children, that they may thinke vpon them. When thou shalt be sitting in thy howse, or trauaylinge in the waie, when thou shalt lie doune to slepe, or rise vp in the* [Aiiij*ᵛ*] *morning, thinke and medi- tate vpon them, and write them on the thresholdes and gates of thy howse, that thou maist alwaies haue them before thine eies.* With what more effectuall wordes could he commend vnto vs, the con- tinuall meditation, and consideration of heauenlie thinges, then with these? And no lesse doth Salomon commend the same holie exercise   *Prouerb. 1.3.* vnto vs in his Prouerbs: where he exhorteth vs, to carie the lawe of God alwaies, as it were a chayne of gold about our neckes, and at night to goe to bed with it, and in the morninge so sone as we awake, to beginne immediatlie to exercise our selues in the same: Blessed is that man, that is so occupied. And so doth Ecclesiasticus tearme him, when he saieth: *Blessed is the man, that dwelleth in the*   *Ecclesiast. 14.* *house of wisedome, and meditateth vpon the lawe and commande- ments of God, and exerciseth him selfe in iustice, and reasoneth of holie thinges by his vnderstanding. Blessed is he that considereth her waies in his hart, and vnderstandeth her secretes. He shall looke in at her windowes, and hearkē at her doores. He shall abide beside her howse, and fasten a stake in her walles. He shall pytch his tent besides her.*

Now what other thinge maie we inferre of all this, but that the holie Ghost intended, by all these metaphors, to expresse vnto vs the cōtinuall exercise, and cōsideration, wherewith the iust man is al- waies occupied, in searchinge the worckes and wonders of almightie God. And for this verie cause, emonge the praises of the iust mā,   *Psalm. 1.* this is put for one of the most prin-[Av]cipall: that his exercise is to   *Eccles. 31.* meditate vpon the lawe of our lord, daie and night; and that he is alwaies cōuersāt in the secrecie of parables: geuing vs hereby to vnderstand, that all his trade and cōuersatiō must be, in searching, and meditating vpō the secretes and wōderfull worckes of almightie God. And euen for this verie cawse also, were those misticall beastes of Ezechiel represented vnto vs with so manie eies; to signifie   *Ezech. 1.* vnto vs, that the iust man stādeth in greater neede of the continuall consideration, and sight of spiritual thinges, then of a number of other exercises.

By this therefore we see plainlie, what great neede we haue of this holie exercise, and consequentlie how blyndelie and fowlie they are deceaued, that either despise or make little accompt of the holie exercise of praier, and meditation: not considering that this is openlie to gaynesaie and contemne that thing, which the holie Ghost hath with so great instancie commended vnto vs. I wishe that such persons would reade those fiue bookes of cōsideration, which S. Barnard wrote vnto EVGENIVS the Pope.[7] And there shall they perceaue, of how great importance this holie exercise is, towardes the obteyning of all vertues.

Now for this cause manie Catholike and religeous persons, vnderstanding what great and inestimable fruit ensueth of this godlie meditation, haue gone abowt to exercise them selues ordinarilie therein, and haue appointed [Av^v] euerie daie certein speciall times and howeres for the same. Howbeit oftentymes they waxe colde, and geue ouer this holie exercise, by reason of two difficulties they finde in it. The one is the want of matter, and of consideratiōs wherein they maie occupie there cogitation at that time. And th'other is the want of feruencie and deuotion, which is verie requisite to accompanie this holie exercise, in case we mind to haue anie fruit and commoditie thereby. In steed whereof, they find manie times great drynes of hart, and withall a great combate of diuers and sondrie thowghtes. For remedie of which two inconueniences, I haue ordeined this present booke, which is deuided into two principall partes.

The first part, for remedie of the first inconuenience, treateth of the matter of praier, or meditation: wherein are contened fowertiene meditations, seruing for all the seuen daies of the weike, both in the morninge and euening. And these meditations do conteine the principall places and misteries of our faith, and expecially the consideration of those misteries, that are of most force, and power, to brydle our hartes, and to incline them to the loue, and feare of God, and to the abhorring of sinne. In like maner there are sett out, the fiue partes of this exercise, which be Preparation: readinge: meditation: thankes geuing: and petition: which is done to this end, that a man maie haue great varietie of matters, wherein to occupie his

Marginalia:

Two difficulties in the exercise of praier and meditation.

The ordre and diuisiō of the contentes of this booke.

The firste parte of this booke.

---

[7]At the request of Pope Eugenius III, who reigned from 1145-1153, St. Bernard of Clairvaux, wrote his *De consideratione* (c. 1149-1152 or 53), an ascetical treatise stressing the necessity of the hierarchy to lead lives of sanctity.

hart: [Avi] wherewith to procure and stirre vp the tast of deuotion, and withall wherewith to illuminat and instruct his vnderstanding, with diuers cōsiderations, and instructions. Besides this, there is also treated therein, of six kindes of thinges that are to be considered in euerie one of the pointes of the Passiō of our Sauiour: that both they, and all the rest, maie minister vnto vs more plentifull matter for meditation. These three thinges are sett forthe in the first part of this worcke, for remedie of the first inconuenience.

The second part, for remedie of the seconde inconuenience, treateth of those thinges, that do helpe vs vnto deuotion, and likewise of those, that doe hinder vs from the same. It treateth also of the most common temptations, that are wont to molest deuout persons. Moreouer there are geuen certein aduices to be a direction vnto vs that we erre not in this waie. These fowre articles are sett out in the seconde part of this booke. _{The seconde parte of this booke.}

After these I haue added the third parte, in which is treated of the vertue of praier, and of her two companions, fasting, and almes deedes: to the intent, that when a man seeth, that in all the booke there is treated of praier, and of the paines he owght to take for the same: he maie vnderstand, how well his labour is employed, which is bestowed in obteining of a thinge, of so great and wonderfull profitt. _{The thirde parte of this booke.}

Peraduenture the Christian reader wilbe offended with the length of the meditations, [Avi^v] which we haue here sett fourth for the seuen daies of the weike. Howbeit for this I haue manie answeres. The first is, considering that in these meditations, is treated of the principall places, and misteries of our faith, (the consideration whereof is of so great importance, for the due orderinge and reforming of our liffe) it behoueth me therefore to enlarge my style (in these matters espetiallie) by reason of the great fruit, and commodetie that maie ensue vnto vs by the same. For in this booke our meaning is, not onelie to geue matter of meditation, but much more to showe the ende of meditation, which is the feare of God, and amendment of our liffe. For the procuring whereof, one of the thinges that most helpeth vs, is the profound and long consideration of the misteries, that are treated in these meditations. For certeinlie these fourtene meditatiōs, be as it were so manie sermons, in which is laide, as it were a certein batterie to mans hart, to cawse it to yeald, (so much as is possible) and to surrender it selfe vp into the handes of his rightefull and true souereine Lorde. _{The ende of meditation is the feare of God, and amendemente of our life.}

This was the cheifest cause that moued me to make the meditations so longe. Besides this, I see not, why the ghest that is inuited, should complaine that the table is to full furnished with manie dishes, sith we bynd him not (as by waie of constraint) to make an ende of them all, but onely emonge so manie sundrie thinges to make his choice of that, which serueth [Avii] best for his purpose. Moreouer (that there might be the lesse occasion of complaint) I haue putt the somme of each meditation at the beginninge thereof, to the intent that such as minde not to passe anie further, might there haue such thinges breiflie abridges, as be necessarie for the time, they intend to bestowe in this holie exercise.

The Ende of the
Prologe.

[Here follow ten short treatises on consideration, meditation, and prayer, Sigs. Avii^v-D^r.]

[D^v]   How the Exercises of
prayer, consideration, and meditation, &c. ap-
perteyne not onelie to religious personnes,
and priestes, (thowghe principal-
lie vnto them) but vnto the
laitie also.

S. x.

Bvt peraduenture thou wilt saye, that these exercises of praier, consideration, and meditation, do appertein, onelie vnto religious persons, and preistes, and not vnto the laitie. True it is I graunt, that these exercises do principally appertein vnto religious persons, and priestes, by reason of their state and profession of life: but yet neuertheles, the laietie are not vtterlie excused of vsinge some kinde of exercise of praier (thowgh not in so high a degree, and perfection) if they minde continually to preserue them selues, and to liue in the feare of God, without committinge any deadly sinne. For euen the laitie also, are bownde to haue Faith, Hope, Charitie, Humilitie, the feare of God, contrition, deuotion, and an hatred against sinne. Now seinge all these vertues be for the most parte vertues affectiue, (as we haue alreadie declared) which affections must necessarily procede of some consideration of the vnderstandinge: if this consideration be not exercised, how shall the-[Dij]se vertues be preserued?

Marginal note: Laie men are bound to haue faith, hope, charitie, humilitie, and other vertues : as well as religious persons and priestes.

How shall a man helpe him selfe by faith, if he do not sometymes consider such thinges, as his faith telleth him? How shall he be enkendeled in charitie, and strengthened in hope; how shall he brydel him selfe with the feare of God? How shall he be moued to deuotion, to sorrowe for his sinnes, and to the contempt of him selfe (wherein consisteth the vertue of humilitie, which apperteineth vnto all kinde of persons) if he do not consider those thinges, wherewith these affections are wont to be inkendeled, according as we haue before declared? Neither owght a man to passe ouer these thinges, in the exercise of consideration, with to much speid, and in post hast. For emonge the miseries of mans hart, one of the greatest is, that it is so sensible to vnderstand the thinges of the worlde, and so vnsensible to vnderstand the thinges, apperteinyng vnto almightie God. In so much that vnto the one, it is, as it were, a verie drie reede, and to th'other, as it were, grene wood, that can not be set on fier, and enkendled, but with verie great labour, and trauell. And therefore we must not in our exercise of consideration, passe ouer these thinges in such hast, but staie, and pawse for a tyme in them, more or lesse, according as the holie Ghost shall instruct vs, and according also, as the busines and occupations of euerie man in his state, and vocation of life, shall geue him leaue. And it is not a matter [Dij^v] of mere necessitie to haue certein times appointed euerie daie for prayer.*

Vnto these thinges ye maie adde furthermore, the danger of the world, with all the great difficulties, men haue to preserue them selues without sinne, in a bodie so euill disposed, and in a world so dangerous, and emonge so manie ennemies, as we haue continuallie assaulting vs on euerie side. And therefore (if for that thow art not a religious person) thy state of life do not bynde the vnto so much exercise of praier and meditation, yet the greatnes of the danger and perrill, wherein thow liuest in the worlde, must needes bynde the to vse some exercise therein. The state of a religious person (I confesse) is greater then thyne, but thy danger of falling into synne, is also greater then his. For the religious person is protected, and garded, by his superior, by inclosure within his monasterie, by obseruance of his rules, by obedience, by praiers, by fastinges, by sainge daylie diuine seruice, by the awsteritie of his order, by good companie, and religious conuersation, and by all other spirituall exercises, and vertuous labours of the holie monasticall life; in so

Note why the laietie live in more danger of fallinge into deadlie synne, then religious persons.

---

*for prayer] *corrected in errata from* for consideration

much that euen the verie walles of their monasteries be a great defence, and sauegard vnto them, to keepe them from the occasions
and dangers of synne: but the laie person liuinge, practisinge and
dealinge daylie and howerlie in the thronge, and presse of the
worlde, (besi- [Diij] des that he is destitute, and vnprouided, of all
these greate helpes, and sauegardes) he is compassed about also on all
sides, with dragons, and scorpions, and treadeth alwaies vpon ser-
pentes, and baseliskes: I mean, the dangerous conuersation with
wicked persons, and the continewall occasions, and temptations, of
fallinge into deadlie synne, both at home, and abrode, within him
selfe, and without him selfe, both at doores, and at wyndowes, and
hath a thowsand seuerall diuelishe engins, and snares, laid to en-
trappe him at all times, both daie and night. Emonge all which
dangers and temptations, for him to kepe his hart pure, and his eies
chast, and his bodie cleane, in the middes of the raginge fiers of
youth, of nawghtie companie, of lewd conuersation, and emonge so
manie euill examples of this wicked world, (where there is scarselie
harde one worde of God, but rather iestinge and scoffinge at all
such, as be geuen to vertu, and godlines) it is one of the greatest
wonders, that almightie God worketh in the world. Wherefore if the
religious person owght to be alwaies armed, because he is by his
profession a man of warre, euen so must the laie man be armed also
in his maner, (althowgh not in so highe a degree) not because the
perfection of his state of life, doth bynde him so much thereunto, but
by reason of the great perill and danger he lyueth in. For as well
doe they goe armed, that haue ennemies, as those that be [Diijⱽ]
souldiers, and men of warre. The souldiers goe armed, by reason of
the bonde, and dutie of their professiō, and the others goe armed by
reason of their necessitie. Emonge which spirituall weppons, we doe
not onely put praier, cōsideration, and meditation: but also fastinge,
sylence, hearing of sermons, reading of deuout bookes, frequentinge
the sacramentes, and auoidinge the occasions of sinnes, with all
other awstere vsage of the bodie. All which thinges be, as it were, a
certeine bryne, and pickle, to kepe and preserue this corruptible, and
euill inclined fleshe of ours, that it breede not wormes, and stenche
in it. For vndowtedlie, since the corruption of original sinne, it is
the greatest and hardest matter of the worlde, for men to kepe them
selues anie longe tyme, without deadly sinne, lyuing in such a
corrupt and dissolute wicked world as this is. For if those verie

persons, that do vse all these spirituall helpes, and exercises, are all
that not withstanding muche molested with the feare, and danger of
fallinge into deadlie synne: what shall becomme of those, that do
neuer vse anie of all these spirituall exercises, scarselie in all their
life! And if the holie king Dauid, and manie other sainctes (that
liued with so great warines, and vertuous discipline, and went armed
with so manie kindes of spirituall weppons) did notwithstanding
take such great falles, at what time the occasions of synne, we-[Diiij]
re ministred vnto them, what shall become of them (trowlye) that
make none accompt at all, of anie of these spirituall exercises.

[Here follows a short treatise entitled "An Answere to an Ob-
iection, that some slouthefull Christians doe make . . .," Sigs. Diiij^r-
Dvi^v; hereafter follow short pieces on consideration and the five
parts of prayer, Sigs. Dvi^v-E^r. Next begin the meditations themselves beginning with the meditation assigned for Monday morning,
Sig. E^r. I have chosen to illustrate these meditations by reproducing
in its entirety the meditation for Friday morning beginning with
Sig. Mv.]

[Mv]   Fridaie
                         Morninge.

This daie (when thou hast made the signe of the crosse, and
prepared thy selfe hereunto) thou hast to meditate vpon the
misterie of the crosse: And vpon these seuen wordes, which our
Sauior spake beinge crucified on the same.

[Mv^v]   [Woodcut of the Crucifixion and
                 Biblical passages in Latin][8]

The text of the holie Euangelistes.

They came (saieth the holie Euangelist) to the place called   *Math. 27.*
Golgotha, that is to saie: the place of dead mens skulles. And they
gaue him vinegar to drinke mingled with gaule. And when he [Mvi]
had tasted thereof, he woulde not drincke. It was then three a
clocke. And they crucified him, and with him two theues, one at the
right hande, and the other at the lefte. And so was the scripture
fulfilled, that saieth. And he was reckoned emōge the wicked. And
Pilate wrote also a title, and put it vpon the Crosse. And it was
written: Iesus of Nazareth kinge of the Iewes. This title manie of

the Iewes did reade. For the place where Iesus was crucified, was neare to the citie: and it was written in Hebrewe, Greeke, and Lattin. Then said the high preistes of the Iewes to Pilate: write not: the kinge of the Iewes, but that he saied, I am kinge of the Iewes. Pilate answered: what I haue written, I haue written.

[Mvi^v] Then the souldiars when they had crucified Iesus, tooke his garmentes, and made fowre partes, to enerie souldiar a parte. And they tooke his coate also, which was without anie seame, wouen frō the toppe throughout. Therefore they saied one to an other. Let vs not deuide it, but cast lottes for it, whose it shalbe. This was done, *Psalm. 21.* that the scripture might be fulfilled, that saieth. They parted my garmentes emonge them, and vpon my coate they cast lottes. So the souldiars did these thinges indeede.

Math. 27. And they that passed by, reuyled him, wagginge theire heades, and sayeinge: Fye on thee, thou that destroiest the tēple, and buildest it in three daies, saue thy selfe. If thou be the sonne of God, [Mvii] come downe from the crosse. Likewise also the high preistes, mockinge him with the Scribes, and elders, and Pharisies, saied. He saued others, but he cannot saue him selfe. If he be the kinge of Israell, let him now come downe from the Crosse, and we will beleue him. He trusteth in God. Let him deliuer him now, if he will haue him. For he saied: I am the sonne of God. The verie same wordes also, did the theeues, who were crucified with him, cast in his teethe. But Iesus saide. Father pardon them, for they knowe not what they doe.

Luc. 23. And one of the malefactors, that was crucified with him, blasphemed, sayeinge: If thou be Christe, saue thy selfe, and vs. But the other answered, and rebu-[Mvii^v]ked him, sayenge: Neither doest thou feare God, bringe in the selfe same cōdemnation? We are iustlye punnished: for we receaue accordinge to our doinges. But this man hath done nothinge amisse. And he saied vnto Iesus. Lord remember me, when thou commest into thy kingdome. Then Iesus saied vnto him. Verelie I saie vnto thee, This daie shalt thou be with me in paradise.

Ioan. 19. There stoode by the Crosse of Iesus, his mother, and his mothers sister, Marie the wife of Cleophas, and Marie Magdalene. And when Iesus sawe his mother, and the disciple whom he loued standinge by: he saied vnto his mother: Woman, beholde thy sonne. Then he saied to the disciple: beholde thy mother. And from that [Mviii] howre, the disciple tooke her for his mother.

Abowte the ninthe howre, Iesus cried with a lowde voice: sayenge: Eli, Eli, Lamasabacthani: that is: My God, my God, why hast thou forsaken me? And some of them that stoode there, when they harde it, saied. This man called Elias. Some other saied: let vs see, if Elias will come and saue him. *Math. 27.*

Afterwardes Iesus knowinge that all thinges were fulfilled, that the scripture might be accomplished, saied: I am a thirst. And there was set a vessell full of vinegar, and they filled a sponge with vinegar, and put it abowt an hisope stalke, and put it to his mouthe. Now when Iesus had receaued of the vinegar, he saied: It is [Mviiiᵛ] finished. *Ioan. 19.*

And he cried againe with a lowde voice, and saied: Father into thine handes I commende my spirite. And from the sixte hower, there was darkenes ouer all the earthe vntill the ninthe hower. And the veile of the temple was rent in two partes, from the toppe to the bothom. And the earthe quaked, and the stones were clouen. And the graues opened them selues, and manie bodies of the Sainctes, which slepte, arose. And there were manie of his fryendes and acquaintance, and women beholdinge him a farre of. Emonge whom, was Marie Magdalene, and Marie the mother of Iames the yonger, and of Iosephe, and Salome, who had folowed him out of Galilee, ministringe vnto him: [N] with manie other women, that came in his companie to Ierusalem. *Luc. 23.* *Matth. 27.*

Meditations vpon
These Poyntes
of the Text.

We are now come (o my soule) to the holie mounte Caluarie, and we be nowe arriued at the toppe of the misterie of our redemption. O how wonderfull is this place? Verelie this is the howse of God, the gate of heauen, the lande of promise, and the place of saluation. Here is planted the tree of life. Here is placed that misticall ladder that Iacob sawe, which ioyneth heauen with the earthe, whereby the angells doe descende vnto men, and men doe ascende vnto almightie God. This is (o my soule) the place of praier. Here oughtest thou to adore, and blesse our Lorde, and geue him most humble, and hartie thanckes for this his most highe and excellent benefit: sayenge thus vnto him. *Genes. 28.*

We worshippe and adore thee ò Lord Iesus Christ, and we blesse thy holie name, [Nᵛ] forsomuch as thou hast by meanes of this holie Crosse redeemed the worlde. Thankes be geuen vnto thee O most mercifull Sauiour, for that thou hast thus loued vs, and wasshed awaie our sinnes with thy most pretious bloude, and hast offered thy selfe for vs vpon the same Crosse: to the ende, that with the most sweete fauour of this noble sacrifice, enkendeled with the fier of thy most feruent loue, thou mightest satisfie and appease the wrathe of almightie God. Blessed be thou therefore for euermore, which art the Sauiour of the worlde: the reconciler of mankinde: the reparer of Angelles: the restorer of the heauens: the triumphant conqueror of hell: the vanquisher of the diuell: the awthor of life: the destroier of deathe: and the redeemer of them, that were in darckenes, and in the shadowe of deathe.

Luc. 1.
Esaj. 55.

All yee therefore that be a thirst, come vnto the waters, and yee that haue neither golde, nor siluer: come, and receaue all these pretious treasures freely, without payinge anie thinge. Yee that desier the water of life, this is that misticall rocke, that Moyses strooke with his rodde in the wildernes, out of which there sprange water in great abondance, to satisfie the thirst of his afflicted people. Yee

Exod. 17.

that desiere peace, and amitie with almightie God, knowe yee that this is also that rocke, that the patriarke Iacob annointed with oyle, and erected vp for a title of peace, and amitie, betwene almightie [Nij] God, and men. Yee that are desirous of wyne, to cure your

Genes. 35.

woundes, this is that cluster of grapes, that was browght out of the lande of promise into this vale of teares, which is now crusshed, and pressed vpon the presse of the Crosse, for the remedie and redresse of our offences. Yee that desire the oyle of the grace of

Num. 13.

God: knowe yee likewise, that this is that pretious vessell of the widowe of Elizeus, full of oyle, wherewith we must all paie our dettes. And albeit the vessell seeme verie little to serue so manie, yet looke not to the quantitie, but to the vertue thereof: which is certeinlie so great, that so longe as there be vessels to fille, so longe will the vayne of this sacred licour ronne, and neuer ceasse.

4. Reg. 4.

A Contemplation vpon
the misterie of the Crosse.

S. I.

Awake, I praie thee now (o my soule,) and beginne to contemplate vpon the misterie of this holie Crosse, by the fruite whereof the hurte of that poisoned fruite is repared, which the forbidden tree caused vnto vs, throwgh the offence of the first man Adam. As the bridegrome [Nij^v] hath signified to his spouse in the canticles. When he saied: *I haue raised thee vp my spouse, from vnder the* *tree, because vnder an other tree thy mother was corrupted, when* *she was deceaued by the auncient serpente.*   *Cantic. 8.*

Consider then, how when our Sauiour came to this place, his cruell ennemies to make his deathe the more reprochefull, stripped him of all his apparell, euen to his innermost garment, which was wholie wouen throwghout without anie seame. Beholde now here, with what meekenes this most innocent lambe suffereth himselfe to be thus stripped of all his garmentes, without openinge his mowthe, or speakinge so much as one worde against them, that handeled him with such villanie: But shewed himselfe rather verie willinge, and readie, to be spoiled of his garmentes, and to remaine naked to the shame of the worlde: to the intent that the nakednes of such, as had throwgh sinne lost the garmente of innocencie, and grace receaued, might be* couered after a better sorte, than with the leaues of the figtree. Some holie fathers reporte, that the tormentors in pluckinge of our Sauiours garmentes, toke of his crowne of thorne, which then stucke fast on his head, and that afterwardes when they had stripped him starcke naked, they set it on agayne, and fastened the sharpe thornes to the brayne panne afresh, and so made newe holes, and woūdes therein, which was an exciedinge great [Niij] griefe, and payne vnto him. And vndowtedlie it is to be thought, that they woulde vse this kinde of crueltie against him, forsomuch as we are well assured, that they vsed manie others, and those verie strange in all the proces of his passion: especially consideringe, that the holie Euangelist sayeth, that they did vnto him, whatsoeuer they woulde.   *Genes. 3.*

Luca. 23.

Agayne, by reason of his garment, that stucke fast to the woundes of his scourginges, and bloude, which was now congealed vnto the same: at what tyme they pluckt it of from his bodie, (as those caitiffes were farre from all pietie, and mercie) they haled it of with such furious haste, and force, that they loosed, and renewed, all the soores of his whippinges in such ruefull wise, that his blessed bodie was in all partes open, and as it were slaine, and became all one greate wounde, out of which distilled bloude on all partes.

Consider now here (o my soule,) the excellencie of the goodnes, and mercie of almightie God, which sheweth it selfe so euidentlye in   The na-kedness of our Saui-our vpon the crosse.

---

*might be] *ed.,* might be be

this misterie. Consider, how he that clotheth the heauens with cloudes, and adorneth the feildes with flowers, and bewtie, is here spoiled of all his garmentes. Consider how the bewtie of the Angells is here defiled: how the height of the heauēs is here browght lowe: how the maiestie and omnipotencie of almightie God is here abased and put euen to [Niijᵛ] open shame, and reproche. Beholde, how that roiall bloude distillinge out from his brayne, trickeleth downe all alonge by the heare of his head, and by his sacred bearde, insomoche as it watereth, and dyeth the verie grownde vnder him. Consider what extreme colde that holie tender bodie of his suffered, standinge as he stode, all rente, and spoyled, not onelie of his garmentes, but also euen of his verie skynne, hauinge withall so manie gappes and wyde holes of open soores, and deepe woundes, throughout all his blessed bodie. For if S. Peter, notwithstandinge he was both clothed, and shodde, felt colde the night before: how farre greater smarte and colde did that most tender bodie of our sauiour abyde, beinge so naked, and full of soore bruses, and woundes as it was?

Ioan. 18.

Whereby it appeareth, that albeit our Sauiour in all the whole cowerce of his life gaue vnto vs so wounderfull examples of nakednes, and pouertie: yet at his deathe he gaue himselfe vnto vs, as a most perfit patterne and spectacle of this vertue. Forsomuch as at that tyme he was in such a poore case, that he had no place, wherevpon to rest his head. And to geue vs to vnderstand, that he had taken nothinge of the worlde, he died naked vpon the crosse, and had nothinge of the worlde to cleaue vnto him.

Our Sa-
uiour
Christ was
a most per-
fit patterne
of pouer-
tie vnto us
vpon the
crosse.

Accordinge to this example, we reade of the blessed holie father S. Francis, who was [Niiij] such a perfit and trewe folower of this pouertie of our Sauiour Christe, that at what time he shoulde geue vp the ghost, he stripped him selfe starcke naked of all he had vpō him, and threwe himselfe from his bed vpon the bare grounde, and beinge thus naked, he embraced the earthe, to imitate herein (as a faithfull seruante) the nakednes, and pouertie, of his Lorde, and Sauiour. Awake therefore (o my soule) awake now I praye thee, and learne thou also hereby, to imitate our Sauiour Christ, poore and naked. Learne to despise all such thinges as this transitorie worlde maye geue vnto thee, that thou maist be worthie to embrace our Lorde naked, with naked armes, and be vnited vnto him by loue, which ought also to be naked, without mixture of anie other strange loue.

S. Francis
was a perfit
folower of
the pouer-
tie of our
Sauiour
Christ.

How Ovr Saviovr Was
Nailed vpon the Crosse.

S. II.

Consider after this, how our Sauiour was nailed vpō the Crosse, and how passinge great griefe, and tormente, he suffered at that time, when those great, and square nailes were driuen in, and pearced through the most sensible, and tender partes of his most [Niiijᵛ] blessed bodie, which was of all bodies most tēder, and delicate. And consider also, what an extreme grieffe it was to the blessed virgin, when she sawe with her eies, and hearde with her eares, the mightie, and cruell harde strokes, which were so often, and so thicke laied on, and iterated one after an other vpon his diuine members. For certainlie those hammers, and nailes, as they passed throwghe the handes of the sonne: so did they also pearce the verie harte of his most tender, and louinge mother.

Consider moreouer, how they lifted vp the Crosse on highe, and how when they went about to ramme it in the hole, which they had made for that purpose (such was the crueltie of those tormentinge raginge ministers) that at the verie time of rearinge it vp, and placinge it therein, they let it falle furiouslie from them, with a iumpe into the hoole, with all the weight thereof: and so all his blessed bodie was sore shaken, and iogged vp and downe in the aier, and thereby his woundes were wydened and enlarged, and his paines, and grieffes more encreased.

Now therefore (o my sweete Sauiour, and redeemer) what harte is so stonie harde, that will not ryue in sunder for verie sorrowe, and griefe, sith the verie stones them selues were ryuen the same daie, consideringe the extreme paine, that thou sufferedest on the Crosse.

[Nv] *The sorrowes of deathe ô Lorde, haue compassed thee about,* *and the waues of the Sea haue ouerwhelmed thee:* Thou art myred in the depthe of the bothomles goulfes, and fyndest nothinge wherevpon to staie thy selfe. Thy father (ô Lorde) hath forsaken thee: what hope maist thou haue of men? Thy ennemies make outcries against thee: thy fryendes breake thy harte: thy soule is afflicted: and for the loue thou bearest to me, thou wilt not admit any maner of comforte. Vndowtedlie (ô Lorde) my sinnes were verie greate, and haynous, and that doth thy penance well declare. I see thee ô my kinge fastened to a tree, and there is nothinge to susteine thy bodie, but onelie three iron nailes, wherevpon thy sacred fleashe hangeth,

Psalm. 68.
Psalm. 17.

without anie other staie or comforte. When the weight, and swaie of thy bodie staieth vpon thy feete, then are the woundes of thy feete the more torne, and enlarged, with the nailes wherewith they are pearced. Againe, when the weight of thy bodie staieth vpon thy handes, then are the woundes of thy handes the more rente, and enlarged also, with the poyce of thy bodie. One of thy members cannot succour an other, but with equall preiudice, either of the one, or of the other. Now as touchinge thy holie head, beinge thus tormented, and weakened with the sharpe crowne of thornes, what pillowe hath it to rest vpon? O how well might thy armes (ô most excellent virgin) be here employed to supplie this office? [Nvᵛ] But alas thine armes maye not serue at this present, but onely the armes of the Crosse. Vpon them must our Sauiour staie his sacred head, when he will rest: and yet so, that the ease he taketh thereof is nothinge els, but a further driuinge in of the thornes, and fasteninge of the same deeper into the braine. Besides all this I see those foure principall woundes, as it were foure fountaines, alwaies distillinge out bloude. I see the grownde all besprinckled and bedewed rounde about with bloude. I see that most pretious licour all betrampled, and shed vpon the earthe, which *Genesis. 4.* crieth much better, then did the bloude of Abell. For his bloude *Heb. 12.* cryed for vengeance ageinst the murderer; but this most pretious bloude of thine O sweete Iesus, craueth pardon for synners.

Of the Compassion,
the Sonne Had vpon His
mother: and the mother vpon her sonne,
hanginge vpon the Crosse.

S. III.

The sorowes of the sonne were much increased, by reason of the presence of his most blessed mother, wherewith his dolefull harte was no lesse crucified within, than his holie bodie [Nvi]without. Two crosses be here perpared for thee (ō good Iesus) this daie. The one for thy bodie, and the other for thy soule. The one is of passion, and the other of compassion: The one pearcethe thy most blessed bodie with nailes of iron: th'other pearceth thy most holie soule, with nailes of sorowe. Who is able to declare (ô sweete Iesus,) what an vnspekeable greife it was vnto thee, when thou diddest cōsider the great anguishes of the blessed soule of thy holie mother, which thou knewest so certeinlie was crucified with thee on the crosse? When thou sawest her pittiefull harte pearced, and thrust throughe with the knife of heauines, and sorrowe? When thou diddest open thy blouddie eies, and beheldest her diuine face, whollie ouercome with palenes, and wannes of death. When thou sawest those most grieuous paynes, and anguishes of her minde, which was not resolued with deathe, and yet abode greater paines, then the verie paines of deathe it selfe. When thou beheldest those riuers of teares, which gusshed out from her most pure eies, and hardest those so lamentable deepe sighes, and sobbes, which burst out of her sacred brest, beinge enforced with the vehemencie of her most grieuous heauines, and sorowe. Certeinlie, ô Lorde, it can not be expressed with wordes, how muche this inuisible crosse tormented thy most pittiefull harte.

Luc. 2.

And who is able to declare also (o most [Nvi^v]blessed mother,) the greatnes of the sorrowes, and anguishes of thy dolefull harte. When thou sawest him dye with such grieuous tormentes, whom thou sawest borne with so great ioye? When thou sawest him scorned, and blasphemed of men, whom thous sawest praised of the angells? When thou sawest that holie bodie, which thou haddest handeled with so great reuerence, and browght vp with such motherlie tendernes, and chereshinges, so euill entreated and tormented by most wicked persons? When thou beheldest that diuine mouthe of his, (which thou haddest nourished with the milke of heauen) distempered with the bitter tast of gaulle, and vynegar? When thou diddest also beholde that diuine head, (which thou haddest so often times laied and rested on thy virgines brest,) all to begored now with bloude, and crowned with thornes? O how often diddest thou lift vp thyne eies on highe, to beholde that diuine shape, that had so often times reioysed thy soule in beholdinge the same? And how often agayne, did thyne eyes turne aside from him, because the tendernes of thy harte coulde not abide to see that dolefull sighte.

What tonge is able to expresse the greatnes of this sorrowe? If the soules that loue our Sauiour Christe truelie, and vnfaynedly, when they meditate vpon these sorowes beinge now past, haue such a tender compassion vpon him, what diddest thou then o [Nvii]most blessed virgin, beinge his mother, yea and more than a mother, when thou sawest presentlie with thine eies, such a sonne, suffer such a most cruell, and painfull passion? If those women that ac-

companied our sauiour when he went with his Crosse towardes his
death, beinge neither of kinne, nor of acquaintance vnto him, did
weape, and lamente, to see him goe after such a pittiefull sorte:
How great then was the abondance of teares that fell from thine
eies O blessed mother, when thou sawest him, who was so deerelie
beloued vnto thee, not onelie carryenge the Crosse on his shoulders,
but nailed also fast vnto it, and hoysed vp alofte vpon the same?

And albeit these thy griefes, and sorrowes were so great, yet
diddest not thou (ô blessed virgin) refuse the companie of the
Crosse, neither wouldest thou turne thy backe, but stoodest there
euen harde, and fast by the same; and not fallinge downe in sowndes,
nor yet ouerthrowen to the grounde, but like a stronge pillar stand-
Genes. 3.   inge vpright vpon thy feete, beholdinge with inestimable sorrowe,
and heauines of minde thy deere sonne crucified on the crosse: to the
ende, that like as Eue by beholdinge with delite that fruite, and tree of
deathe, was the occasion of the perdition of the worlde: euen so thou
(ô blessed Ladie) by beholdinge with greate griefe, and sorrowe, the
fruite of life, which then was hanginge [Nviiᵛ] vpon that tree of the
Crosse, mightest with thy presence, and eies, there see the remedie,
and redemption of the worlde.

An Other Meditation
of the Doctrine, That Maie
be learned at the foote of the Crosse.

S. IIII.

Ioan. 19.   The holie Euangelist saieth, that there stoode hard by the
Crosse, Marie the mother of Iesus: and his mothers sister, Marie
the wife of Cleophas: and Marie Magdalene. O that I were so
happie, that I mighte stande in the companie of these three blessed
Maries alwaies at the foote of the Crosse? O yee blessed Maries,
who hath caused you to stande so constantly at the foote of the
crosse? What cheyne is this, that thus holdethe you so fast lincked
vnto this holie tree? O sweete Christe which beinge deade, doest
mortifie the liuinge, and geuest life to the dead? O yee Angells of
paradise, be not offended with me, thowghe I a sinner, and a very
wicked person, be so bolde to come, and ioyne with this holie companie: because the loue I beare to my sweete sauiour draweth me
vnto them, and the verie same loue enforceth me, to embrace this

crosse. If theise [Nviii] three Maries, will not departe from the crosse? How can I departe from thence, knowinge that all my wealle, and saluation, consisteth in the same?

Assuredly the fyer shall first waxe colde, and the water shall naturally become hoate, before my harte shall departe from this crosse: sythence I vnderstande, what a lesson the loue of God teacheth me: to wit: How happie a thinge it is, to stande alwaies at the foote of the crosse. O holie crosse, thou drawest the hartes of men vnto thee more stronglie, than the Adamante stone draweth iron. Thou geauest a more cleare lighte to our vnderstandinge, thā the sonne doth to our eies. Thou enkēdelest a more feruent heate in our soules, than fyer doth in the verie cooles. Drawe me therefore (O holie crosse) vnto thee, with great force and might. Illuminate me continuallie, and enflame me with thy mightie power, that my thoughte and mynde maie thinke vpon none other thinge, but onely vpon thee, and maye neuer departe from thee. And thou ô good Iesus, illuminate the eies of my soule, that I maye vnderstande how to looke and fixe mine eies, and thoughtes, vpon the crosse: to the ende, that I maye not onelie beholde the cruell paynes, and tormentes, thou hast suffered for me, and so by beholdinge them, take compassion of them: But also consider the examples of so manie wonderfull vertues, as thereby thou hast discouered vnto [Nviii*] me, and inuited me to imitate, and followe the same.

Wherefore O most wise maister, and instructor of the worlde. O phisition of soules. Here I come to the foote of thy crosse to present vnto thee my soores, and woundes. Heale me ô my most mercifull, and omnipotent Lorde, and teache me what I ought to doe. I doe confesse, and acknowledge playnelie vnto thee (ô Lorde) that I am verie sensuall, and geuen ouermuche to the loue of my selfe, and I see well that this greatlie hinderethe my profitinge, and proceadinge in vertue, and godlines. Manie tymes for my recreation, and pastimes sake, or for feare of the paine of fastinge, and risinge vp early in the morninge, I passe ouer, and doe leese the godly and diuout exercises of praier, and meditation, with other holie spirituall exercises: by the losse whereof, I leese my selfe also. This sensualitie of mine is verie importune vpon me. It woulde faine eat and drinke verie finelie, and delicately, at such howers, and times, as it liketh: and after dinner, and supper, it woulde gladlie haue some idle talke, or els some pastyme, and recreation. It delighteth at such tymes to be walkinge in a faire greene garden, or orcharde, and

We may learne to overcome our sensualitie and selfe love by beholdinge our Sauiour Christ vpon the crosse.

there to take some sollace, and pleasure. Teache me now (ô most louinge Sauiour, and redeemer,) what I ought to doe, whereby to followe thy example; and helpe me with thy [O] grace, that I maie performe my dewtie in this pointe. O what a greate shame is it vnto me, to see after what sorte thou diddest handel thy blessed bodie, which was more tender, and delicate, than all other bodies. In the middest of the most bitter angwishes, and grieuous tormentes of thy death, thou diddest not geue vnto thy bodie anie other foode, or electuarie, but such as those cruell apoticaries had compounded of bitter gaule, and sower vineger for thee. Who then will from hence-forthe haue anie tongue to complaine, that the meate set before him, is either to colde, or to salte, or to freashe, or not well dressed, or that it was ouer late, or to tymelie made readie: consideringe what a table was here prepared for thee, ô my almightie God: and that in the tyme of so great necessitie? In steede of the mirthe, and pleasante talke, and entertaynmente, which I seeke to haue at my suppers, and feastes, thou haddest none other, but onely outcries and clamorous noices of them, which shakinge theire heades at thee, scorned, and blasphemed thee: sayenge: *Fye on thee, that destroiest*
Math. 27. *the temple of God, and in three daies buildest it vp againe.* This was the musicke, and mynstrelie of thy bankette: and thy walkinge in a garden, was to be fast nailed handes, and feete, to the crosse. And albeit there was an other garden, into which thou wentest after thou haddest ended thy supper, yet was it not to walke in for pleasure, [Oᵛ] but to praie: not to take the aier, but to sheide bloude: not to recreat thy selfe, but to be pensiue, and sad, and in a great agonie of deathe. Now what shall I saye of the other ease, and refresshinges, which thy blessed fleshe had? My fleashe would gladlie haue a softe bedde, curious and costly apparell, and a large and wyde howse. Tell me how (ô my sweete Sauiour,) what maner of bedde hast thou? What manner of howse hast thou? And what is thy apparell? Thy apparell is nakednes, and a purple coate of mockerie, and reproche. Thy howse is none other, but to stande openly abrode in the sonne, and aier. And if I seeke for anie other, I fynde it to be nothinge els, but onely a stable for beastes. The foxes haue theire holes, and the
Math. 8. birdes of the aier theire neistes, and thou that art the creator of all thinges, hast no place where to rest thy head. O curiositie, and superfluitie? How are ye two crepte in, and so vsuallie, and vni-uersallie receaued in this our corrupte age, throughout all the coun-

treys, and nations, of Christendome? O what maner of Christians be
we, that doe not vtterlie abandon from vs, all maner of fyne
deyntienes, curiositie, and superfluities, knowinge that our Lorde,
and maister, vtterlie abandoned from him, not onelie all maner of
deyntienes, and superfluities, but also euen such thinges, as were of
necessitie.

A notable
admonitiõ
against the
vyces of
deyntie-
nes, and
superflui-
tie.

    I desire now O Lorde to see also what [Oij] maner of thinge thy
bedde is. Tell me (ô sweete Sauiour) where doest thou lodge?
Where sleepest thou at noone daie? Here I sette my selfe at thy
feete: Teache me I most humblie beseeche thee, what I ought to
doe. For this my sensualitie will not suffer me to vnderstande well
this language of thy crosse. I desire a softe bedde, and if I awake
early in the mornynge at the hower of praier, and diuine seruice, I
suffer my selfe to be ouercome with slouthe, and drowsienes, and I
expect duelie for the morninge sleepe, that my head maie take an
other nappe, and so haue his full ease, and rest. Tell me ô my most
gratious, and louinge Lorde, what rest haddest thou on that harde
bedde of the crosse? When thou wast wearie in lienge on the one
side, how diddest thou turne thee on the other, to take the better
rest? What harte is not ouercome and broken in sonder herewith?
What? Is not this enoughe to kill all sensualitie in vs? O what a
comfort is this to the poore? What a confusion to the riche? What
an encouragement to the penitentes? And what a condemnation to
nice, delicate, and sensuall persons? Certeinly the bedde of our
Sauiour Christe is not for such fyne delicate wantons, neither is his
glorie in heauen prepared for them. Geue me grace (ô Lord) that I
maye by thy example mortifie this my sensualitie. And if it be not
thy blessed will to graunte me this request, I beseache thee then
euen now out of [Oijᵛ] hande to ende my life. For it is not meete,
nor seemelie, that thou, (ô my omnipotent Lorde, and redeemer)
beinge vpon the crosse, and hauinge none other comforte, nor re-
fresshinge, but onely bitter gaulle, and sower vinegar, I shoude seike
for sweete sauoures, delicate fare, sugered sawces, with other curious
deynties, pleasures, and ease, in this miserable life. It is not meete
that thou beinge thus poore and naked, I shoulde goe wanderinge
and leesinge my selfe after the transitorye goodes and riches of this
worlde? It is not reason that thou hauinge none other bedde, but
onely the harde and painfull crosse, I shoulde seeke to haue a softe
bedde, and other delicacie, and ease, for my wretched bodie.

Cant. 1.

we desire
to lye on
softe fe-
ther bed-
des and
our saui-
our Christe
laye on the
harde bed-
de of the
crosse.

**How our
Sauiour
Christe re-
bukethe
from the
crosse, our
pompe, de-
licacie cu-
riositie and
superflui-
tie.**

Be thou therefore greatelie ashamed, ô my soule, beholdinge our Lorde, and Sauiour, on the harde paynefull tree of the crosse: and make accompte, that from the same crosse he preacheth vnto thee, and rebuketh thee: sayenge: O man I haue for thy sake worne a crowne of thornes: and doest thou in contempte of me, weare a garlande of flowers, with golden chaynes, aglettes, bruches, and gaye oystreche fethers? I for thy sake haue stretched forthe my armes to be nayled, and tormented vpon the crosse: and doest thou stretche forthe thyne to pleasante games, and pastimes? I beinge a thirst at my verie death, had not so much as a litle colde water, and seekest thou after pretious wynes, delicate meates, and [Oiij] deyntie sugered sawces? I was on the crosse, and in all my whole life tyme, full of dishonors, reproches, and grieuous labours and paines, and doest thou spende all the daies of thy life seekinge after digni- ties, offices, promotions, estimations, pleasures, and delites? I was verie willinglie contented, that my syde shoulde be opened to geue thee my verie harte, and hast thou thyne open to vaine and danger- ous loues of the worlde?

What Patience We Ovght
To Have in All Trovbles,
and aduersities, followinge the example
of our Sauiour Christ.
S. V.

Thov hast taught me now ô Lorde from the chaire of the Crosse the lawes of temperance: teache me also at this present the lawes of patience, whereof I haue suerlie verie great neide. Thou hast cured that parte of my soule, which is called concupiscible: Cure also I beseeche thee, that parte, which is called irascible. Forsomuch as thy crosse is a medicine for all the whole man, and the leaues of that holie tree, are the healthe of all nations.

[Oiijᵛ] Sometimes I haue sayd, and purposed with in my selfe: I will neuer from henceforthe falle out, or be angrie agayne with anie man: I will surelie* keepe peace with all persones: and therefore I thinke it good for me, to auoyde all companie, and thereby to eschewe all occasions of trouble, contention, and anger.

---

*surelie] *corrected in errata from* furelie

But now, ô Lorde, I vnderstande my weakenes in this poynte. For to flee from companie, is not a meane to subdue anger: but rather to couer, and hide myne owne imperfection. And therefore I will from henceforthe carie euer with me, a mynde readie prepared, to liue not onelie with the good, but euen with the wicked also, and to keepe peace with such colericke, waywarde, and frowarde contentious persons, as doe abhorre peace. Thus I purpose from henceforthe to doe: grawnt me thy grace therefore ô almightie God, that I maie dewlie accomplishe this my good intent. If others shall take my landes, or goodes ayaye from me, graunte me thy grace ô Lorde, that I be not angrie not grieued therewith: seinge I see thee thus spoyled, and naked, vpon the Crosse. If they shall take my credite, honor, and estimation frō me, let not that cause me to breake peace with them: seinge I see thee here, ô Lorde, so despised, dishonored, and contemned. If my fryendes and acquaintāce shall forsake me; let me not therefore be confounded, seinge I see thee thus left alone, and forsaken not onely [Oiiij] of thy disciples, and fryendes, but also of thyne owne heauenly father. And if it shall seeme to me at anie tyme, that I am forsaken of thee, yet let me not for all that lose my confidence, and trust in thee: seinge thou diddest not loose thine, but after thou haddest made an ende of saienge those wordes. *My God, my God, why hast thou forsaken me?* Diddest forthewith recommende thy spirite into the handes of him, who had forsaken thee: sayenge: *O father into thy handes, I commend my spirite.* And therefore euen now at this instant I request, that from henceforthe all troubles, and persecutions maie come and falle vpon me, and not to spare me, forsomuch as all such thinges con doe nothinge els vnto me, but geue me occasion to be a folower of thee my sweete Lorde and Sauiour Iesus Christ.

Math. 27.

Marc. 15.
Psalm. 21.

But now (ô my Lorde) what if the troubles and persecutions shalbe verie great and longe, wherewithall shall I then comforte my selfe? For thy passions, althoughe they were verie greate, yet it seemed that they continued not anie longe tyme, forsomuch as all the martirdome of thy passion, did not continewe altogether twentie howers. Now he that hath bene tenne yeares bedridden, or lyen in fetters in harde prison, or in continuall necessitie, trouble, and dissension, within his owne howse, and famylie, what comfort shall he finde in thee, for so longe a combatte and tribulation? Answer (ô Lorde) I beseache [Oiiijᵛ] thee, vnto this demande, forsomuch as thou arte the worde, and the wisedome of the father. Tell me whether thou be the vniuersall comforter in all miseries, be they neuer so longe? Or else whether we neede to seeke anie other comforter for them? Verelie ô Lorde, we haue no neede of any other comfortor, but onely thee. For vndowtedlie, the crosse whereon thou diddest suffer, was not a martirdome of one daie onely, but it continued all thy whole life. For euen from the verie first hower, and instant of thy most holie conception, there was represented vnto thee, both the crosse, and withall, all the cruel bitter paines, and tormentes, that thou shouldest suffer vpon the same: and so thou haddest them all continuallie verie liuelie set before thyne eyes all the daies thou diddest liue here on earth. For like as all thinges both past, and to come, were present before the eies of thy diuine vnderstandinge: euen so also were all the martirdomes, and instrumentes of thy passion. There were the crosse, the nailles, the scourges, the thornes, the cruell speare, will all other thy most bitter paines, and tormentes, at all tymes as liuely present before thy sight, as when thou sawest them with thy eies the verie same frydaie, that thou wast crucified on the Crosse. We, though we suffer neuer so greate, and extreme paines, yet we haue alwaies some tyme of ease, either by meanes of phisicke, or other comforte: but thy pain [Oᵛ] was alwaies in a maner continuall, or at the least it did verie often times torment thee in thy sowle, duringe the tyme thou diddest liue here in this worlde. And albeit this consideration of thy bitter tormentes, and passion, had not tormented thee, yet was the verie zeale of thy fathers honor, and desire of the saluation of our soules, a continual torment vnto thee, which vndowtedlie did eate, and rente thy pittiefull louinge harte, and was a more cruell martirdome vnto thee, than the verie death it selfe. Wherevnto was also added the obstinate malice, which thou sawest in that rebellious people, (the Iewes:) and with all the stubbornnes and ingratitude of all other sinners, (for whose remedie and redemption thou wast sent) which woulde not helpe themselues with the benefite thereof, nor yet acknowledge the tyme of theire visitation. This was the cause of those pittiefull teares, thou diddest sheide vpon Ierusalem: and hereof rose the complainte thou madest by thy Prophet Esaie, sayenge: *In vaine haue I traueyled, and in vaine haue I consumed my strengthe.*

Wherefore O my soule, thou hast here with whom thou maist keepe cōpanie, and take comforte in thy longe paines, and troubles.

Marginal notes:

Our sauiour had his crosse and passion verie liuelie represented daylye before his eyes, from the verie first hower of his conception, vntill his deathe.

Luc. 19.

Esa. 49.

For althoughe the last paines, and tormentes, of the holie bodie of our Sauiour were shorte, yet were the greifes, and paines, of his pittiefull harte and soule verie longe, and continuall.

[Here follow the meditations for Saturday and Sunday morning and seven meditations for each evening of the week, Sigs. Ov^v-Mmiiij^v. Hereafter follow three treatises: the first on the way to meditate, the second on difficulties of mental prayer with advice how to overcome these, and the third on how to meditate on the Passion, Sigs. Mmv^r-Ssvi^v. The book concludes with a listing of errata and a table of contents, Sigs. Ssvii^r-Tiii^v.]

XIII.

A Spiritval
Doctrine,
Conteining a Rvle
To liue wel, with diuers Prai-
ers and Meditations.
Abridged by the Reverend Fa-
ther Lewis de Granada *of the holie order*
of Preachers.
And Devided into Sixe Trea-
tises, as is to be seene after the prefaces.
Newlie translated out of Spanish into English.
Psalm. 118. v. 35.
Deduc me in semita mandatorum tuorum.
Leade me (O Lord) in the path of thy com-
maundements.
[An ornament]
At Lovan,
Imprinted by Laurence Kellam
1599.[1]
[trans. Richard Gibbons[2]]

[This work begins with a dedication to Sir William Stanley,[3]
Sigs. +2ʳ—+3ᵛ.]

---

[1]Allison and Rogers, I, Entry 479. *STC* 16922. This work is a translation
of Luis de Granada's *Doctrina espiritual repartida en seis Tradatos* (Lisbon,
1587).

For notes on Luis de Granada, see p. 112, n. 1.

[2]Richard Gibbons (1549-1632) was a Jesuit priest and a renowned scholar.
He studied at Louvain and at the German College in Rome. In 1572, he entered
the Society of Jesus. For more than thirteen years he was a professor of
philosophy and mathematics, dividing his time between Rome and France.
Then as a professor of canon law and Hebrew, Gibbons taught in Spain,
Portugal, France, and Italy. Later he became the Prefect of Studies at Louvain.
He died at Douay in 1632 (Gillow, II,439-442). For a bibliography of his
works, see De Backer (pt. 1, III, 1404-1407).

[3]Sir William Stanley (1548-1630) was an adventurer and soldier of rather
dubious reputation. He served brilliantly in Ireland with Elizabeth's forces for
over fifteen years, and in 1585 he accompanied Leicester in the expedition sent
by Elizabeth to aid the United Province against Spain. At Deventer in 1587,
however, he surrendered his garrison to the Spanish, an action which the
Jesuits applauded and Cardinal Allen defended. He proceeded to the Spanish
court to advise on an invasion of England; Stanley suggested that Ireland be
used as the base of operations in such a venture. His reception in Spain was
not as warm as he expected, although the government was moved to allot him a
pension. By 1590, he was considered a declared enemy of England and of
Elizabeth. His later life was spent in obscurity and in small military skirmishes
(*D. N. B.,* XVIII, 969-971).

[+4]

The Translatovr
to the gentle Reader.

It hath seemed good to me, Gentle Reader, to let thee vnderstand in the beginning of this little booke, that som yeeres past, a
worthie and vertuous Gentleman of our nation,[4] had begon to translate out of Spanish into English, the Memoriall, and other spirituall
bookes, of that famous and Religious father *Lewis de Granada,* of S.
Dominicks order. Of all which, som haue ben put in print, som
others, I know not vppon what occasion, ar not yet com forth. But
whatsoeuer the cause maie be, certeine it is that in the meanetime,
the same Religious father being verie desirous, that all sort of men
should take the profit of such spirituall woorkes, as he with so
greate paines had vttered to the woorld, for theire soules good, and
auancement in the seruice of [+4ˇ] God, did, not long before his
death, drawe out an Abridgment of his forsaid bookes, moued
therunto for the reasons, which he him self hath set downe in his
preface to the Reader, as it goeth heere in the beginning of this little
volume. Which woork, when I had read and perused the same, liked
me so much, that I resolued with mie self to put it in English,
esteeming that as all the other spirituall woorks of this deuout
father, ar of greate comfort and consolation, to all the seruants of
Almightie God, so this would be of no lesse furtherance in spirite, to
such as would endeuour to vse the same. Especiallie considering, that
all that is conteined in this little booke, is matter apperteining rather
to practise of deuotion, and to kendle our affection in the loue of our
sweete Sauiour, then to frame greate discourses, and illuminate our
vnderstanding; albeit this part be also to be found heere, as much as
it maketh to the benifit of the other, and standeth with the briefenes,
which the Author now pretended.

This being so, it remaineth Gentel Reader, whosouer, and of
whatsoeuer Religion thou be, that thou endeuour to peruse this
booke, to the end, for which [+5] it was first writen, and is now
translated into English, that is to thine owne good and saluation.
Which thing thou shalt easilie perfourme, if thou procure, as neere
as God shall aforde thee grace, to reade and weigh that which is
heere conteined, with a reposed and quiet spirite, with a meeke and
humble spirite, with a spirite of patience and longanimitie, with a

---

[4]A reference to Richard Hopkins, p. 112, n. 2.

spirite altogether determined and resolued, to seeke sincerelie and purelie, not so much thine owne interest & contentment, as the honour and glorie of God, and to know his good will and pleasure, and with all thy power to put the same in execution. Neither must thou be ouercurious, or hastie to passe on in reading the contents thereof, but rather endeuour to staie thie self som space of time, in considering with much attention that, which thou hast read, and by this consideration to stirre vp, and prouoke thy will and affection, to practise & execute* that, which thou shalt vnderstand to be the best

---

*execute] *ed.;* excute

pleasure of almightie God, and most profitable to thine owne saluation. This is that which thou must doe, if thou pretend to take anie comfort or commoditie, by reading of spirituall and deuout bookes.

[+5ᵛ] Now then, deare Reader, hauing nothing els whereof to admonish thee, I wil end this mie preface, and remitte thee to the Author him self of this little woorke, desiring thee, for mie small paines bestowed in the translation, to be mindfull of me in thie praiers. Christ Iesvs direct thee. At Louan the *25.* of March, *1599.*

Thy hartie wellwiller and seruant in Christ Iesvs. *Rich. Gibbons.*

[+6]

The Avthor to
the Christian
Reader.

It is a thing notorious, good Christian reader, that the bread, which we dailie eate, is not so necessarie for the maintenance of our natural life, as is the doctrine of the woord of God, for the conseruation of oure spiritual life. This doctrine teacheth vs two principal things, to praie, and to woorke; vnto which two, be reduced al others what-soeuer. Of these two things infinite bookes haue ben writen. But for as much as this doctrine is so necessarie* at euerie foote-steppe that we make (by reason of the continual dangers, and temptations of our life) I haue determined to resume heere in few woords (gathered out of al mie bookes) that which hath seemed to me most fit for this purpose; to the end thou maist easilie beare about with the in thie bosom, that which ought to be alwais writen

---

*necessarie] *ed.;* neceessarie

in thie heart. And therfore I haue heere gathered and put together Sixe briefe treatises; *one of* Mental praier, *taken owt of mie booke of Praier and Meditation, with al the fourteene meditations abbreuiated, which were there set doune. And this trea-*[+6ʳ]*tise I haue put in the first place, because these meditations, besides that they giue vs abundant matter whereof to meditate, be also the best persuasions and motiues that can be found, to bring men to liue wel and vertuouslie. So that yf they serue not in the beginning for the exercise of meditation, yet they wil serue for perswasion to induce men to the feare of God, and changement of life. But because al men dooe not so much giue them selues to th' exercise of meditation, ether for their diuers affairs, or for other reasons which they may haue; therfore that these also want not the succour and help of praier, I haue added an other treatise of* vocal praier, *conteining manie praiers, which serue to obteine such vertues, as be most necessarie for th' edification of our sowles.*

Trulie al holie scripture doth euerie where declare vnto vs, the neede which we haue of these two exercises, because they be the weapons, which we haue most readie and at hand against our enimies, by whome we be alwais enuironed; & therfore we must goe wel armed with them, as long as our life lasteth. Heerehence it is that our Sauiour the night of his passion armed his disciples with praier, saying vnto them; watch ye and praie that ye enter not into tentation: *and Dauid armed him self with meditation when he said;* were it not (*o lord*) that thy law is my meditation. I had then peraduenture [+7] perished in my humilitie: *that is, I was then verie likelie to haue fallen when tribulation came vppon me. Seeing therfore that these two weapons be so assured and prooued for our warfare, it seemed to me conuenient to put them in this brife manual, that by such meanes they might be alwais at hand.*

*Now for so much as in the beginning we diuided the whole summe of Christian doctrine into these two things, praier, & woorke; hauing spoken alreadie of praier as wel Mental as Vocal, it ensueth that we treat hence forward of woorke, that is of the instruc-*tion and order of our life, hauing cheefelie regard of such as newlie begin to serue our Lord. And because of those som there be, that begin this life remainning still in the woorld, som others entering into Religion; for these last also I haue laid downe an other treatise, in which the thornes and brambles of our euil inclinations and passions he rooted out, and in their place ar set the plantes of

Sixe treatises of this booke.
1

2

Matth. 26. 41.

Psal. 118. 29.

3

4

Psal. 33.
8

vertues, *which doe order and perfectionate our sowles. And albeit these two last treatises maie seeme to be different in the titles, neuertheles the documents conteined in them both (especiallie those which concerne vertues) serue no lesse for the one treatise, then for the other: because such as desire to be saued, haue no other way for the same, but to goe* from vertue to vertue, vntil they see the God of Gods in Sion, *that is in* [+7ᵛ] *the glorie which is to com.*

Besides this, to th' end there want nothing for the dailie instruction of our life. I haue put heere also twoe other little treatises, whereof the one is of Penance and Confession: *the other is* of preparation for receiuing the blessed Sacrament of the altare. *And this may suffice for the preface of this little booke.*

[+8]   A Spiritval Doctrine Devi-
ded into sixe treatises.

The First Treatise is, of *Mental Praier.*
The Second Treatise is, of *Vocal Praier.*
The Third Treatise is, *A Rule of good life*
  for all sorts of men.
The Fourth Treatise is, *A Rule of good*
  life for Religious men.
The Fift Treatise is, of *The Sacrament of*
  Penance.
The Sixt Treatise is, of *receauing the bles-*
  sed Sacrament, with *a profession of the Ca-*
  tholique faith, according to the holly Councel
  of Trent.

[Here begins the first treatise on mental prayer, which contains a short introduction to the subject and meditations for each night and morning of the week, pp. 1-109.]

[109]
         Of Sixe Thinges That Maie
concurre in the exercise of praier.

———————

Chap. IV.

———————

These be, good Christian reader, the meditations in which thou maist exercise thy selfe, in all the daies of the weeke, that so thou want not matter, whereof to thinke. But* here it is to be noted, that some things maie goe before this meditation, and som others follow after it, which be annexed vnto the former, and as it were neighbours vnto them.

[110] For first, before we enter into meditation, it is requisite that we prepare our hart vnto this holie exercise, which is as to tune a viall, before we plaie vppon it.

After preparation foloweth the reading of that matter, which we be to meditate vppon that daie, according to the distribution of the daies of the weeke, as hath ben said before. Which reading is vndowtedlie necessarie for such, as ar beginners, vntill a man dooe know, what he owght to meditate vppon. After he maie proceede vnto meditation.

Next to meditation there maie folow out of hand a deuoute giuing of thankes for the benifits which we haue receaued, with an offering vp of al our life, and of the life of our Sauiour Christ. The last part is the Petition which is properlie called praier, in which we demaund all that, which is behoueful as wel for the saluation of our selus, as of our neighbours, and of al the whole Catholike churche.

These six things maie be exercised in praier, which things, emong other commodities and profits,** bring this also, that they yeeld vnto a man more plentie of matter, where vppon to meditate, setting before him all these diuersities of meats, that in [111] case he can not eate of one, he maie eate of an other, and that when he hath made an end of meditation in one matter, he maie enter into an other; and there find other matter, wherein to continew his meditation.

I know right wel, that nether all these partes, nor this order is alwaies necessarie, yet this manner will serue for nouices, and young beginners; that so they may haue som order, & direction wherby to gouerne them selues at the beginning. And therefore of anie thing that shalbe here treated, I would not that anie man should make a perpetual, or general rule: because my intent is not to make anie law, but to shew an introduction, thereby to direct nouices and beginners, and to put them in this waye: in which course after that they shalbe once entred, then the very vse and experience, and much more the holy ghost wil teach them the rest, that they haue to dooe herein.

---

*But] *ed.;* Bud
**profits] *ed.;* porfits

[112]

Of Preparation Which Is
requisite before praier.

Chap. V.

It shal now be requisite for vs, to treate particularlie of euerie one of these parts aforesaide, & first of the Preparation, which goeth before the others.

Being in the place of praier, kneeling or standing, thy armes stretched out in manner of a crucifixe, or prostrate vppon the grownd, or sitting (yf thou canst not settel thie self in anie other sort) after thou hast made the signe of the Crosse, thou must recollect thie imagination, & withdrawe the same from all things of this life, and lift vp thy mind to heauen, considering that our Lord beholdeth, and looketh vppon thee. Thou must also stand there with such attention and reuerence, as yf thou hadst God there reallie present before thine eys, and with a general repentance of thy sinnes (yf thie praier be in the morning) thou maist saie the general confession *Confiteor Deo, &c.* or (yf thy meditation be in the euening) thou maist examine thy conscience, touching all [113] that which, thou hast thought, spoken, or donne, or heard in that daie, as also, how forgetful thou hast ben of our lord; and repenting thy self of all the defects cōmitted that daie, and of al those of thy life past, and humbling thy self before the maiestie of almightie God, in whose sight thou standest, thou maist vtter these woords of the holie Patriarch.

Genes. 18. 27.

I wil speake to my lord, although I be but dust & ashes: and with the substance and matter of these few woords, thou maist, for som little time, entertaine thy self, considering wel what thou art, and what God is, that so thou maist with more reuerence, humble thy self before so great a maiestie, as is that of almightie God. For thou art a bottomlesse depth of infinite sinnes and miseries: and God is an infinite deepenes of al riches and greatnes: and being in this consideration, thou must dooe him al due reuerence, and humble thy self before his supreme maiestie.

With this also, thou must humblie beseeche this lord to giue thee grace, that thou maist stand there with such attention and deuotion, with such inward recollection, and with such feare and reuerence, as it behoueth thee to haue before so soueraine a [114] maiestie, and that thou maist so passe ouer this time of praier, that thou maist com from the same with new desires and force, to doe al such things as appertaine to his seruice. For the praier, which yeeldeth not this fruite, is to be esteemed verie vnperfect and of small valew.

Of Reading.

Chap. VI.

After the preparation is ended, there foloweth Reading of that thing, where vppon thow art to meditate in time of praier. Which Reading ought not be donne lightlie & hastilie, but with deliberation and attention, applying thereunto not onlie thy vnderstanding, to conceiue such things as thou readest, but much more thy wil, to tast those things that thou vnderstandest. And when thou findest anie deuout passage, staie somwhat longer vppon it, thereby to haue som greater feeling of that, which thou hast read.

Let not the Reading be ouer-long, that so thou maist haue more time for medita-[115]tion, which is of so much more profit, by how much more it waigheth, and entreth into the cõsideration of things, with more leasure and affection. Neuertheles, when thou findest thy hart so distracted, that it cannot enter into praier, then thou maist staie somwhat the longer in Reading, or ioine Reading and medita-tion together, by reading first one point, & meditating vppon it, and then an other, and an other in like sort. For in so dooing, when the vnderstanding is once bound to the woords of the reading, it hath not occasion to wander abrode so easilie, into diuers thoughts and imaginations, as when it goeth free and at libertie. And yet better it were to striue in casting of such thoughtes, and to perseuer and wrastle against them (as the Patriarche Iacob did all the night long) continuing in the work of praier: that in the end, when the wrastling is donne, we maie obtaine the victorie, our lord giuing vs deuotion, or som other greater grace, which is neuer denied to those, that labour and fight faithfullie.

[116]   Of Meditation.

Chap. VII.

Straite after reading foloweth meditation vppon the point which wee haue read. And this meditatiõ is somtimes vppon things, which

may be figured with the Imagination; as ar all the passages of the
life and passion of our Sauiour Christ; of the last iudgement; of
hel; or of Paradise. Som other times it is of things, which doe
apperteine rather to the vnderstanding, then to the imagination; as
is the consideration of the benifits of almightie God: of his goodnes
and mercie, or of anie other his perfections. This kind of meditation
is called *Intellectual,* and the other *Imaginarie.* And we ar woont to
vse both the one, & the other manner in these exercises, according
as the matter of the things doth require.

Now when the meditation is *Imaginarie,* we must then figure,
and represent euerie one of these things, in such wise as it is, or in
such wise as it might perhaps passe, and [117] make accounte, that
in the verie same place where we be, al the same passeth in our
presence, that by meanes of such a representation of these things,
the consideration and feeling of them maie be more liuelie in vs. But
to goe and meditate such things, as passed, eache in his oune place,
is a thing which doth cōmonlie weaken, and hurt the head.

And for this verie cause likewise, a man must not fixe his
imagination ouer much vppon the things, of which he meditateth,
that so he wearie not his* head.

But for as much as the principall matter of meditation, is the
holie passion of our Sauiour Iesus Christ, it is to be vnderstoode,
that in this misterie maie be considered fiue principal points, or circumstances, which concurre in the same: to wit, whoe he is that
suffereth: what he suffreth: for whome he suffereth; in what
manner he suffereth: And for what end he suffereth.

Touching the first point, which was, whoe hee is that suffereth:
I aunswere that he which suffereth is; the Creator of heauen and
earth; the onlie sonne of God; the highest goodnes, and wisdom that
can be imagined; the most innocent and most holie sonne of the
blessed virgin Marie.

Concerning the second point, to wit [118] what he suffereth: I
aunswere that he suffereth most grieuous pains, as wel in his
soule as in his bodie. For in his soule he suffered so great angwish
& affliction, as no hart is able to comprehend it; cōsidering the ingratitude of men, towards this so singular and high a benifit: The
compassion of his most innocent and blessed mother: The sinnes of
the world that were present, past, and to com, for all which he

---

*his] *ed.;* is

suffered. And in his bodie he endured cold, heat, hunger, wearines, watchings, iniuries, betraying, he was sould of his disciple, he did sweate drops of blood, he was spitte vppon, buffeted, so oftentimes bound, forsaken, euil spoken of, falslie accused, whipped, scorned, appareled as yf he had bene a foole, crowned with thornes, lesse esteemed then Barabbas, vniustlie condemned, he caried his owne crosse vppon his shoulders, he was crucified betwene twoe theeues, he did drink easell[5] & gall, and finallie he died a most opprobrious, & reprocheful death vppon the mount Caluarie, in time of greatest solemnitie.

The third point to be considered, is for whome he suffered: & euident it is, that he suffred for mankind disobedient & vngrateful, created of nothing, who of him self can dooe nothing, knoweth nothing, nor is anie [119] thing worth: for a creature of whome he neuer had, nor neuer was to haue anie neede. For a creature which had offended, & was to offend and disobey him so manie times.

The fourth point to be considered, is in what manner he suffered: where we shall see, that he suffred with such great patience and meekenes, that he was neuer offended nor angrie with anie bodie: with so great humilitie, that he made choice of the most contemptible death that was vsed in those daies: with so great readines and alacritie, that he went foorth to meete his enimies; with so great charitie, that he called his frind him, that betraied and sould him; healed his eare that tooke him; regarded with eyes of mercie him, that had denied him; and praied for those that crucified him.

The fift point to be considered, is wherefore and to what end he suffereth; where it is manifest that he suffered to satisfie the iustice of almightie God, and to appease the wrath of his father; to accomplish the predictions and prophecies* of the Patriarches and Prophetes: to deliuer vs from the thraldom of hell, and to make vs capable of heauen; to shew vs the waie to heauen with his perfect Obedience: and to confound the diules, whoe by reason of theire [120] pride haue lost that, which men dooe gaine through theire humilitie.

---

[5]*easell* (commonly spelled *eisell* or *eysell*), vinegar.
*prophecies] *ed.;* propheties

Of Thankesgiving.

Chap. VIII.

After meditation foloweth thankesgeuing, of which a man must take occasion of the meditation past, and giue thankes vnto our lord, for the benifit He hath donne vnto him in the same; as for example, yf the meditation was of the passion, he must thanke our lord that he hath redeemed vs with so great paines. And if it were of our sinnes; for that he hath expected vs so long time to dooe penance; yf it were of the miseries of this life, for that he hath deliuered vs from so manie of them; yf of the departing out of this woorld, and of the hower of our death; for that he hath deliuered vs from the daungers of it, and expected vs, and giuen vs life to dooe penance; and yf it were of the glorie of paradise, for that he hath created vs to be partakers of so great a felicitie: and so likewise we maie dooe in the rest.

And with these benifits thou must ioine [121] all the other benifits, of which we haue spoken before, which be the benifit of Creation, Conseruation, Redemption, Vocation, and Glorification: and so thou shalt giue thankes to our lord, for that he hath made thee to his likenes and image, and hath giuen the memorie, to remember him; vnderstanding, to knowe him; and wil to loue him; and for that he hath giuen thee an angel, to keepe thee from so manie daungers and perils, and from so manie mortal sinnes, and also from death, thou being in sinne, which was no lesse benefit, then to deliure thee frome erlasting death: and for that* he made thee to be borne of Christian parents, and gaue thee holie baptisme, and therein his grace, and promised thee his glorie, and receaued thee for his child.

Also with these benifits, thou must ioine other general and particular benifits, which thou knowest to haue receaued of our lord; and for these and al others, as wel publique as priuate, thou must yeeld him as hartie thankes as possiblie thou maist, and inuite al creatures, as wel in heauen as in earth, that they assist and help thee, to dooe thy dutie in this, and with this spirite and desire thou maist saie somtimes that Canticle: *Benedicite omnia opera Domini*

---

*for that] ; *ed.;* forthat

Domino, or els [122] the psalme: *Benedic anima mea Domino, &*   *Psal.102.*
omnia quae intra me sunt nomini sancto eius. Benedic anima mea
Domino, & noli ohliuisci omnes retributiones eius. Qui propitiatur
omnibus iniquitatibus tuis, qui sanat omnes infirnitates tuas. Qui
redimit de interitu vitam tuam, qui coronat te in misericordia &
miserationibus.

Of Offering.

Chap. IX.

This being donne, that is, when a man hath geuen thankes to our
lord with al his hart for al these benifits, then foorthwith the hart
naturallie breaketh out into that affect of the Prophet Dauid saying;
What shall I yeeld vnto our Lord for all those things which he hath   *Psal. 515.*
bestowed vppon me? And this desire a man in som sort satisfieth,   *12.*
when he geueth, and offereth vp to almightie God that, which of his
part he hath, and is able to giue him.

And for this end, he ought first to offer vp him self to God, for
his perpetual slaue,* resigning and laying him self wholie in his
hands, that his diuine maiestie dooe with him, as it shal best please
him: and iointlie [123] he must offer vp to him all his woords, his
woorks, his thoughts, and his paines, that is, whatsoeuer he doeth
and suffereth, that so al maie be to the glorie and honour of his
holie name.

Secondlie, he must offer vp to God the father, the merites &
woorkes of his sonne, and all the paines, which in this woorld he
suffered for obedience of him, euen from the manger vntil the
crosse; for so much as they al be our substance, & heritage which
he left vs in the new testament, by which he made vs his heires of al
these so greate treasures. And in like manner as that which is giuen
me, is no lesse mine, then that which I haue goten by mine owne
paines and labour; so the merites of Christ, & the right which he
hath geuen me, ar no lesse mine, then yf I had sweate and laboured for
them my self. And therefore a man maie with as much right, offer
this second present as the first, laying downe by order al our Sauiours woorks and paines, and al the vertues of his most holie life, his
Obedience, his Patience, his Humilitie, his Charitie, with al the rest;
because this is the most riche, and most pretious offer that maie be
offered.

slaue] *ed.*; sklaue

[124]

Of Petition.

Chap. X.

Immediatlie after that we haue offered vp vnto almightie **God**, this so riche a present, we maie then with great securitie, in vertue of the same, demaund of him whatsoeuer fauours & grace. And first let vs demaunde with great affection of Charitie, and with desire of the glorie of God, that al nations and people of the world maie know, praise and adore him, as theire onlie true God, and lord, saying, euen from the bottom of our hart, these words of the Prophet. *Let all people confesse thee, o God, let all people confesse thee.*

Psal. 66. 4.

Let vs praie also for the Catholike Church, and for al the Prelates of the same, such as be the Pope, Cardinals, Bisshops, and other inferior ministres and Prelates; that our lord wil gouerne them, and giue them light, in such sort, that they maie bring all men to the knowledge, and obedience of theire Creator. We must likewise praie (as S. Paul counseleth vs) *for kings, and for al those that be in dignitie, that* [125] *(thorough theire prouidence) we maie liue a quiet and peaceable life, in al puritie and chastitie, because this is acceptable before God our Sauiour, whoe desireth that all men be saued, and com to the knowledge of the truth.*

1. Timoth. 2.2.

Let vs also praie our lord for al the members of his mistical bodie; for the iust, that he wil conserue them in theire goodnes; for sinners, that it maie please him to conuert them; for the dead, that he wil mercifullie deliuer them, out of the great paines of purgatorie, and bring them to the rest of euerlasting life. Let vs praie also for **al** such as bee poore, sicke, in prison, in captiuitie &c. that God, through the merites of his sonne, wil help and deliuer them.

After that wee haue thus demaunded for our neighbours, let **vs** forthwith aske for oure selues. Now what we ought to desire for our selues, the particular neede of eche one wil teach him, if yet he know him self. Let vs also with this demaund pardon, and amendment of our sinnes, by the merites and paines of our Sauiour; and especiallie let vs request his ayde, and assistance against al those passions and vices, to which we feele our selues most inclined, and of which **we** be most tempted; and let vs discouer al these our wounds to this hea-[126]uenlie phisition, that by this meanes he will vouchsafe to heale, and cure them with the ointment of his grace.

After this make an end, with demaunding the loue of God; and in this demaund staie, and occupie thy self for the most part of the time, desiring our lord with most hartie affection and desire, to graunt thee this vertue, for so much as in it consisteth al our good, and so thou maist saie as foloweth.

An Especial Petition of the loue of God.

Above all this giue me, O lord thy grace, that I may loue thee with all my hart, with all my sowle, with all my forces, and with all my entrailes, euen in such sort, as thou desirest. O all mie hope, all mie glorie, al mie refuge, and al mie ioie! O the most beloued of beloueds, O florishing spowse, O sweete spowse, O honisweete spowse! O comfort of my hart, O life of my sowle, and the pleasant repose of my spirite!

Prepare, o my God, prepare, o mie lord, in me an acceptable dwelling place for thie self, that according to the promise of thie [127] holie woord, thou com to me, and repose in me; mortifie in me, what soeuer displeaseth thy sight, and make me a man according to thie hart; wound, o lord, the most inward part of my sowle, with the dartes of thie loue, and make me drunke with the wine of thy perfect charitie.

O when shall this be? when shall I please thee in al things? when shall al that die in me, which is contrarie to thee? when shall I be altogeather thine? when shall I leaue to be mine owne? when shall nothing els liue in me, but thou? when shall I loue thee most feruentlie? when shal the flame of thie loue wholie burne me? when shall I be altogeather melted, and pearced through with the woonderful efficacie of thy sweetenes? when wilt thou take me hence by force, and drowne me, transport me and hide me in thy self, where I maie neuer more be seene? when wilt thou free me from all these impediments and distractions, and make me one spirite with thee, that I maie not anie more depart from thee?

O deerebeloued, deerebeloued, deerebeloued of my sowle, o sweetenes of my harte; heare me, o lord, not for my merites and deserts, but for thy infinite [128] goodnes and mercie. Teache me, lighten me, direct me, and assist me in al things; that I maie dooe nothing, nor saie nothing, but that which is agreeable to thie sight. O mie God, mie welbeloued, mie deerest hart, and the verie good of mie sowle! O mie sweete loue, o my great delite, o mie strength! help me, o mie light, and guide mee towards thee.

O God of mie bowels, wherefore giuest not thou thie self to thie poore creature? Thou filleth the heauens and the earth, and leauest thou mie hart emptie and void? Seeing thou clothest the lilies of the field, giuest meate to the little birds, and feedest the woormes of the earth, wherefore doest thou forget me, whoe haue forgotten all others for thie sake? To late haue I knowen thee, o infinite goodnes! To late haue I loued thee, o bewtie so auncient, and so new. Wooe to the time, that I loued thee not: wooe to mee, since I knew thee not. Blinde was I, that I sawe thee not. Thou wast within me, and I went seeking thee abrode. But now, although I haue found thee late, suffer not, o lord, for thie diuine mercie, that I euer leaue thee.

And because one of the things, which most pleaseth thee, and most woundeth thy [129] hart, is that a man haue eys wherewith to behold thee, giue me, o lord, those eys, with which I maie see thee; to wit, eyes simple of a doue; eyes chast and shamefast; eyes humble and louing; eyes deuout, and geuen to teares; eyes attentiue, & discreete to know thy will, and fulfil the same; that when I looke vppon thee with these eyes, I may be seene of thee with those eyes, with which thou diddest view S. Peeter, when thou madest him to bewaile his sinne; with which thou didest behold that prodigal child, when thou receauedst him, & gauest him a kisse, of peace; with which thou didest behould the publicane, when he durst not lift vp his eyes to heauen; with which thou diddest behold Marie Magdalen, when she washed thy feete with the teares of her eyes; finallie with those eyes, with which thou didest behold the spouse in the Canticles, when thou saidest vnto her. *How bewtiful art thou, o mie dearling, how bewtiful art thou? Thie eyes ar as the eyes of doues;* that pleasing theee with the eyes and beutie of mie sowle, thou giue them those pledges of vertues and graces, with which they maie appeare alwaies faire, and bewtiful in thie presence.

Cantic. 4. 1.

O most high, most merciful, most gracious [130] Trinitie the father, the sonne and the holy Ghost, one onlie true God, teach me, direct me, and help me, O lord, in al things. O almightie father, for the greatnes of thy infinite power fasten, & establish my memorie

vppon thee, and fill the same with holie and deuout desires. O most
holie Sonne, for thy euerlasting wisdom clarifie, and illuminate my
vnderstanding, and bewtifie the same with knowledge of the highest
veritie, and of mine owne extreme basenes. O holie Ghost, the loue
of the father and the sonne, for thy incōprehensible goodnes ground
in me thy will, and kindle the same with so great fiar of loue, that
no waters maie be able to quenche it. O most blessed Trinitie, my
onlie God, and al my good! o that I were able to praise thee, and
loue thee, as all the angels doe praise and loue thee! O that I had in
me the loue of all the creatures* in the woorld, with how good a wil
would I aford it thee, and powre it out into thee? albeit neither this
were sufficient to loue thee in such wise, as thou deseruest. Thou
onlie canst loue thy self woorthilie, and woorthilie praise thy self;
because thou alone doest comprehende thy incomprehensible goodnes, and so thou onlie canst loue the same as it deserueth: so [131]
that onlie in that diuine brest of thy most gracious maiestie, the
iustice and lawe of true loue is entirelie obserued.

O virgin Marie! virgin Marie! virgin Marie! most holie virgin,
mother of God, Queene of heauen, ladie of the whole woorld, vestrie
of the holie Ghost, lilie of puritie, rose of patience, paradise of
delites, mirrour of chastitie, patterne of innocencie, praie for me
poore banished creature and pilgrime, and make me partaker of thy
most aboundant charitie. O al ye happie Saincts, and ye other
blessed spirites, that dooe so burne in the loue of youre Creator, and
in particular ye Seraphines, whoe enflame the heauens, and the
earthe with your loue, abandon not this my poore and miserable
hart, but rather purge the same, as the lippes of Esaie, from al sort
of sinne, and burne it with the flame of your most feruent loue, that
it maie loue this onlie lord, seeke him onlie, make his abode and
repose in him onlie, and this for euer and euer. Amen.

[132]

Of Certaine Advises, Which
ar to be obserued in this holie exercise.

Chap. XI.

Al that which hitherto hath ben said, serueth to yeeld vs matter
of consideration, which is one of the principall partes of this spiritual

---

*creatures] *ed.;* creatutes

affaire, considering that such, as haue sufficient matter of consideration, be but the lest number of so manie people; & so for want of
matter, whereupon to meditate, manie there be, that abandon this
kinde of exercise. Now we wil set downe breefelie somwhat touching
the manner, and forme which in it maie be obserued. And albeit the
cheefe maister of this woork, be the holie Ghost, yet experience hath
tawght vs, that som aduises be requisite and necessarie in this part:
because the waie to goe towards God is hard, & hath neede of a
guide, without which very manie goe long time lost and a stray.

[133]

The first aduise.

Let then the first aduise be this, that when we* set our selues to
consider anie of the a foresaide things, in theire times and exercises
appointed, we must not so binde our selues vnto it, that we esteeme
it ill donne, to goe from that to som other thing, when we finde
therein more deuotion, more tast, and more profit. For as in conclusion al this serueth for deuotion, so that which maketh most to this
purpose, is to be taken for the best. Howbeit a man ought not to
dooe this vppon verie light occasions, but when he perceiueth euident commoditie to com thereby.

The second aduise.

The second aduise is, that a man labour to eschew, in this exercise, superfluous speculation of the vnderstanding, and procure to
handle this affaire rather with affections, and feelings of the wil,
then with discourses and speculations of the witte. Wherefore they
vndowtedlie take not the right course, whoe in time of praier, giue
them selues to meditate vppon diuine mi-[134]steries, in such wise,
as yf they studied to preache them: which manner is rather to make
oure spirite to wander more abrode, then to recollect it; and to goe
more out of it self, then to be in it self. Therefore whoe mindeth to
dooe wel in this matter, let him com with the hart as it were of an

---

*we] *ed.;* ve

old woman ignorant, and humble, and rather with a wil disposed and prepared to feele, and to be affected towards the thinges of God, then with an vnderstanding purified, and attentiue to search and examine them; because this is a thing proper to those, that studie to get knowledge, and not to those, that praie and thinke vppon God, thereby to lament and moorne.

The third aduise.

The former aduise teacheth vs how we ought to quiet our vnderstanding, and commit al this busines to oure wil; but this present aduise prescribeth boundes, and limites to the same wil, that it be not to excessiue, not to vehement in her exercise. Wherefore it is to be vnderstoode, that the deuotiō which we seeke to obteine, is not a thing that may be goten by force of armes (as som parsons think, whoe by eccessiue [135] sighings, and enforced sobbings, procure to wring out teares and compassion, when they think vppon the passion of our Sauiour) for such force drieth vp the hart, and maketh the same more vnable to receaue our lords visitation, as Cassianus[6] affirmeth. Moreouer, those things ar wont to preiudice, and hurt the health of the bodie, yea somtimes they leaue the sowle so astonied, and agast by reason of the litell tast she hath there receaued, that she is loth to returne againe to this exercise, as to a thing, which she hath tryed by experience to haue ben verie paineful, and ircksome vnto her.

Let a man therefore content him selfe, with doing sincerelie what lieth in him, that is, that he esteeme him self to be present at that, which our Sauiour hath suffered, beholding (with a sincere and quiet eye, with a tender and compassionate hart, & prepared for what soeuer feeling it shall please our lord to giue him) that which he suffered for him, and so dispose him self rather to receiue such affections, as the mercie of God shall aford him, then to wring them out with teares. And when he hath donne this, let him not vexe him self anie more for anie other thing, though [136] it be not graunted him as he desireth.

---

[6]St. John Cassian (c.360-c.433) was a monk and ascetical writer of Southern Gaul and the first to introduce the Rules of Eastern monasticism into the West (*Catholic Encyclopedia*, III, 404-405).

The fourthe aduise.

Of all these aduises a foresaid, we maie gather what manner of attention we ought to haue in praier, for that in this exercise, it is cheefelie expedient, to haue our hart not heauie, nor dul, but liuelie, attent, and lifted vp on high. But as it is heere necessarie on the one side, to haue attention and recollection of hart, so it behoueth on the other side, that this attention be tempered and moderated, that it neither hurt our health, nor hinder oure deuotion. For som there be, that doe wearie theire head with ouer much violence, which they vse to be attentiue vnto those things, wherevppon they meditate, as we haue said before. And againe there be others, whoe to auoide this inconuenience, ar in theire meditation verie slack and negligent, and verie easie to be caried away with euerie winde. Now to eschew these two extremities, it is expedient that we vse such a meane, that we dooe neither with ouermuch attention wearie our head, nor with to much carelesnes and negligence suffer our thoughts to goe wandering whither soeuer they wil. [137] So that like as we are wont to saie to him that rideth vppon a froward kicking horse, that he hold the reines of his bridle as he ought, that is neither to hard, neither to slacke, that the horse neither turne backward, nor runne to headlong forward; euen so must we endeuoure that out attention in our praier be moderate, not forced with carefulnes, nor with violent labour and traueil.

But now especially we must be wel warie, that in the beginning of meditation wee dooe not trouble, and wearie our head with to much attention: for when wee doe so, our forces commonlie want vs to goe forwards therein, as it happeneth to a traueller, when he maketh to great hast in going, at the beginning of his iourneye.

The fifte aduise.

Bvt among al these aduises the principallest is, that he that praieth be not dismaied, nor geure ouer his exercise, when he feeleth not foorth with that sweetenes of deuotion, which he desireth. It is requisite to expect the cōming of our lord, with longanimitie and perseuerance; for that it greatlie appertaineth to the glorie of his [138] maiestie, to the basenes of our condition, and to the impor-

tance of the affaire which we haue in hand, that oftentimes we attend, and watche at the gates of his sacred palaice.

Now, when thou hast after this sort expected for a certaine time,
in case our lord shal then com vnto thee, giue him most hartie
thankes for his comming; and yf it seeme vnto thee that he com not,
humble thy self then before him and acknowledge, that thou art not
woorthie to receaue that thing, which is not giuen thee; and be
content that thou hast there made a sacrifice of thy self, denied
thine owne wil, crucified thy appetite, striued with thy self, &
donne at the least what thou couldest of thine owne part.

And in case thou haue not adored our lord with sensible adoration, according to thy desire, it is sufficient that thou hast adored
him in spirite and in truth, according as his wil is to be adored. And
trust me assuredlie, that this is the most daungerous passage of al
this nauigation, and the place where trew deuoute persons ar
prooued & tried, and that yf thou escape wel out of this daunger,
thou shalt haue prosperous successe in al the rest.

[139]

The sixte aduise.

This aduise is not much differing from the a foresaid, nor of
lesse necessitie then it; and it is, that the seruante of God dooe not
content him self, with what soeuer little tast he findeth in his praier,
as some vse to dooe, whoe when they shedd a feawe teares, or feele
a little tendernes of hart, perswade them selues, that then they haue
accomplished and performed theire exercise. But this is not enough
for the obteining of that thing, which heere we seeke for. For like as
a little dew or sprinkling of water, is not sufficient to cause the earth
to bring forth fruite (which doth no more but onlie alay the dust,
and wet the vppermost parte of the grownd) but it is needeful to
haue so much water, that it maie enter into the innermost part of
the earth, & there soke, and water through the same: euen so is it
requisite to haue here abūdance of this dew, and water of heauen, to
bring foorth the fruite of good woorkes.

And therefore we ar counseled, not without great reason, that we
take as long time for this holie exercise, as we maie. And better
it is to haue one long time for the same, then two short times: for

yf the time be short, al is spent almost in set-[140]ling the imagination, and in quieting the minde: and then when we haue quieted the same, we rise from our exercise, euen when we should begin it. And descending more in particular to limite this time, I am of opinion, that what soeuer is lesse than one howre and a halfe, or two howres, is to short a time for praier: because that oftentimes there is spent more than halfe an hower, in tempering our instrument, that is, as I said before, in quieting our imagination: and so al the rest of the time is requisite for the enioying of the fruite of praier. True it is, that when we goe to this exercise of praier, after som other holie exercises, our hart is then better disposed for this affaire; and so, like drie woode, is verie apte to conceiue more quicklie in it self this heauenlie fiar.

Likewise earlie in the morning our meditation may be the longer, because then our hart is much better disposed for this exercise, then at anie other time. Howbeit in case that a man haue little time, by reason of his manifolde busines, yet let him not omit to offer vp his mite with the poore widowe in the temple: for yf he faile not of his dewtie herein, throwghe his owne negligence, he that prouideth [141] for al creatures according to their necessitie, wil not want to prouide likewise for him.

The seuenth aduise.

Acording vnto this foresaide aduise, we wil giue an other verie like, wich is; that when oure sowle is visited either in praier, or out of praier, with anie speciall visitation of our Lord, we suffer it not to passe awaie in vaine, but take the commoditie and benifite of that occasion, that is offered vnto vs. For certaine it is, that with this winde, a man shall saile more in one hower, than without it in manie daies.

And so we read that the holie father S. Francis did, of whome S. Bonauenture writeth, that he had such a speciall care in this point, that in case our lord did visite him with anie speciall visitation, while he was traueiling by the waie, he caused his companions to goe before, and he staied alone behinde, vntil he had made an end of chewing, and digesting that sweete morsel, which was there sent vnto him from heauen. Whosoeuer they be that dooe not soe, ar wont cōmonlie to be chastised with this punishmēt, that theye find not almightie God, when they seeke him; because he found not them, when he sought for them.

[Here follows the second part of the first treatise on devotion, pp. 142-163; next come the second, third, fourth, and fifth treatises, pp. 164-392, followed by a profession of faith, pp. 393-397, as indicated on Sig. +8ʳ. This work concludes with a table of contents, Sigs. Aa5ᵛ-Aa8ᵛ.]

XIV.

The First Part
of the Medi-
tations of the Passion, &
Resurrection of Christ
our Sauiour.

———

With the Figvres
& *Prophecies of the olde Testamēt, & certaine Docu-
ments gathered out of
euery point of the
Gospell.*

———

Collected ovt of
diuers Holy Fathers, and other
deuout Authours, by the Reu.
Fa. Vincent Brv-
no of the Societie
of Iesvs.[1]

(* * *)

[trans. Anonymous]

[❤2]

———

The Printer to
the Reader.

———

[1]n.p.d. [1599?] Tr. Anon. Pr. [secretly in England.] Allison and Rogers, I, Entry 172. This work does not appear in the *STC*.

This volume is a translation of the first part of Vincenzo Bruno's *Meditationi sopra i Misterii della Passione di Christo N. S. Con le figure, et Profetie*

*The Authour of this deuout worke, hath set forth in 4. volumes
Meditations of the principall Misteries of the whole Life & Passion
of our Sauiour:*[2] *The two first containe the life of our Sauiour. The
third intreateth of the Passiō: The fourth of the seuen Principall
festiuities of our B.* Lady: *and of the Comū[ion] of the Saintes: that
is of the Apostles, Martyrs, Confessours, & Virgins in generall.*

But as in the Passiō of Christ *our Sauiour doth chiefly appeare
the excesse of his loue to mankind: so hath also this authour in
handling the same Passion exceeded his owne deuoute spirite which
abundanly hee sheweth in all the rest. For which cause, & for that
also this part was first of all others set forth by the authour himselfe: I presēt vnto thee (deuout Reader) first this his volume of
the Passion, which thou maiest vse as an assay or tast vntill thou
haue the rest.*

*But to the end thou maist not be ouer long delaied, but haue
speedely somewhat* [❧2ʳ] *wherwith to delight thy spirit: and for the
preuēting also of many dangers, to which so long a worke might be
subiect vnto in thes difficulties: I haue deuided this third volume
into .4. partes.*[3] *The First beginneth at the* Iewes *conspiracy against
our Sauiour: and reacheth vnto our Lordes deliuery vp to the*
Gentiles, *that is to* Pilate. *The second goeth forward vntill hee come
to* Mount Caluary. *The third containeth that which passed on*
Mount Caluary. *The last shall set forth the things which suc-*

---

*del Vecchio Testamento, e con i Documenti, Che da ciascun passo dell' Evangelio
si cavanno. Raccolte da diversi Santi Padri, e da altri devoti autori per il
Padre Vincenzo Bruno, Sacerdote della Compagnia de Giesu* (Venice. 1588).
For this entry and other bibliographical listings, see De Backer (Pt. 1, I,
266-271).

Vincenzo Bruno (1532-1594) was born at Rimini. After having practiced
medicine for some time, Bruno entered the Society of Jesus in 1558. Much
of the remainder of his life was spent at the Roman College, of which he was
twice rector. It was there that he died in 1594 (*Dictionnaire de Spiritualité
ascétique et mystique,* I, 1971).

The *Meditationi* were very popular and highly esteemed by spiritual
directors in Bruno's own day and for at least a century thereafter. St. Francis
de Sales, in particular, recommended their use (*Dictionnaire de Spiritualité
ascétique et mystique,* I, 1971).

[2]The whole work, of which the section on the Passion and Resurrection is
but one of four volumes, is entitled *Meditationi sopra i Principali Misteri della
vita, passione, e risurrenzione di Cristo Nostro Signore* . . . (1585). The third
volume concerning the Passion and Resurrection was printed separately in 1588
(See note 1 above).

[3]Each part was printed separately; Allison and Rogers suggest that each
was printed secretly in England in 1599(?) (I, Entries 173, 174, and 175).
These parts do not appear in the *STC*.

ceeded vntill the coming of the holy Ghost. Neglect not gentle Reader to benefit thy selfe by so great a treasure: & pray **vnto** *God that we may be long able to prouide the like for thy comfort.*

[❦3]

The Preface of the
Authour.

Almightie God hauing determined that *Moises* should builde him a Tabernacle: appearinge on the Mountaine, shewed him a sampler and paterne, according to which, he would haue him frame it, saying: *Inspice et fac secundum exemplar quod tibi in Monte monstratum est,* that is: Behoulde and doe according to the paterne shewed thee in the Mountaine. Exod. 25.

Which words were not spoken vnto *Moises* alone: but also to euery one of vs, whom God will haue to build a spirituall Tabernacle in which him selfe desireth to dwell by grace.

This Tabernacle shall then be more perfect & pleasing to his Maiestie, whē it shall come neearest to the Sampler which hee hath propounded vs which is his onely begotten Sonne Christ crucified, on whome as vpon a firme & sure foundation we must grounde and settle the ruinous building of our soule, as the Apostle S. Peter exhorteth vs, [❦3ᵛ] saying: *Ad quem accedentes, lapidem viuum, & ipsi tanquam lapides viui superedificamini, domos spirituales:* Vnto whome approching, as vnto a liuing stone, be ye also your selues superedified, as it were liuing stones, spirituall houses. Vnto Christ in like maner, as our onely sampler we ought to conforme all our actions, euen as hee himselfe saide to his Disciples: I haue giuē you an example, that as I haue done to you, so you doe also: in which thing is to be considered that which God said vnto *Moises:* that it sufficeth not only to behould: that is to say, to consider with our mindes, the life and actions of Christ our patern: but also it behoueth vs to doe, that is to imitate him with our workes: As also the bridegroome in the Canticles doth insinuat, speaking vnto his Spouse these effectuall wordes. *Pone me vt signaculum super cor tuum, vt signaculū super brachum tuum:* Place me as a seale vpon thy hart, & as a seale vpon thy arme, where Christ, after he had put the Church his Spouse in minde of that excesse of [❦4] charite which in his 1. Pet. 2. Ioh. 13. Can. 8.

Death and Passion he had so manifestly expressed, for gratitude and recompence of so great loue demaundeth & requesteth her, to haue in continuall remembrance this so singuler a benefitte, according vnto the counsaile of the wise man: *Gratiam fideiussoris tui ne obliuiscaris, dedit enim pro te animam suam.* Forgett not the frendship of thy suertie, for he hath giuen his life for thy sake. And this is that litle bundle of Mirhe which the Spouse desired to harbor between her breasts: instructing euery faithfull soule espoused to Christ by faith, to haue him continually in remembrance by often considering with deuout affection, and by frequent meditating the anguishe and affliction of our most benigne Sauiour: the necessities of his infancie: the wearines of his Trauailes, the labours of his Preaching, his often Watching & continuall Praier, the tentations of his Fastings, the teares of his compassion, the Persecutions and deceites of his enemies, and the daungers of his false brethren, in like manner, the Accusations, [❧4ᵛ] the Infamies, the Iniuries, the Disgraces, the Spittings, the Buffets, the Derisions, the Whippings, the Thornes, and the Nailes: adioining also vnto so many branches of this odoriferous bundle, the mirhe which was giuen him to drinke on the Mountaine: and the Gall wherwith he was fedd on the Crosse.

From this remembrance and consideration of the workes which our Sauiour wrought for our profite and commoditie, will arise a flame of most feruent loue which will kindle in our harts that heauenly fire wherof speaketh the Propete, saying: *In Meditatione mea exardescet ignis.* In my Meditation fire shall be kindled.

By meanes wherof we shall remaine wholly enflamed with loue of our Redeemer and Benefactour. And this is it which he chiefly desireth, that wee, considering how he loued vs and gaue him selfe for vs, shoulde loue him and carry him as a seale alwaies engrauen in our hart.

But because as *S. Gregory* sayeth the loue of God is not idle but worketh [❧5] great matters where it is: but if it refuseth to worke, than is it not loue at all: which our Sauiour him selfe had saide before when as he spake vnto his Disciples these words: *Si diligitis me mandata mea seruate.* If you loue me keepe my commaundementes: For this cause this spouse of ours is not cōtented with the onely remembraunce and consideration of his benefittes to moue vs to loue him, but farther desireth that we carry him as a marke

Eccle. 29.

Psal. 38.

Ioh. 14.

vppon our arme, and as a seale imprinted in our handes: which then we do performe, when we conforme all our actions, maners, and conuersation to the life and doctrine of Christ: when in euery thing we endeuour to imitate the examples which he hath proposed vnto vs, his Humility his Charitie, his Obedience, his Patience, his Meeknes, with the rest of his vertues: Seeing for this cause he came into the world and became man, that for as much as wee coulde not imitate him as God in his diuine operations, at least wise we might follow him as man doing humane works vpon earth: whē [❧ 5ᵛ] finallye with leading a life worthye of Christ we reuest our selues with the same Christ, as the Apostle willeth vs, writing to the Romanes. *Induimini Dominum Iesum Christum.* Put you on our Lord Iesvs Christ. Rom. 13.

Now to attaine to these two endes, that is to say, the loue of Christ & his imitation, wherin the whole perfection of a christian man consisteth: albeit all the misteries of his holie life do greatly auaile vs, not-withstanding these of his Passion and Death are of much more efficacie, to enflame our hartes with his loue, to moue our wills, and stirre vp our mindes to the desire and obtaining of those vertues which particularly do shine in the same.

For how-beit our Saviovr in the course of his life, shewed great variety of vertuous examples, yet neuertheless his last actions, were euery one of them excesses, and meruailous examples of all vertue: in manner as the fire then forceth it selfe to shine brightest, when it is neerest to be extinguished. Seing therfore that this part of our Sauiours [❧ 6] life is of so great efficacie and spirituall profite, albeit that other authors haue written of this selfe same subiect, with much pietie and learning, & with great fruit of souls, neuerthelesse finding my selfe by the speciall grace of our Sauiour in this vineyard of his, and forcing my selfe (seing that by means of weaknes of witte I am not able to keepe equall footing with most strong workemen) to followe at least their footsteps gathering some little handfulls which they leaue behind thē: haue collected together for my owne comfort and for other deuout souls, these small labours handling as particulerly as I can euery point of the Sacred Passion of our Sauiour. And to conforme my selfe the better vnto the wordes aboue rehearsed, which Almighty God spake vnto *Moises* at the building of the Tabernacle: Behold and do according vnto the paterne shewed thee in the Mountaine: I haue deuided euery one of these misteries into three parts: In the first wher of is set downe the sampler which

wee ought to behould and imitate, which [❧6ᵛ] is some action of our
Sauiour: that is, some one point of the Euangelicall historie, confirmed and auctorised with the Figures and Prophesies of the olde
Testament. In the second parte is sett downe after what manner we
ought to behould this sampler, which are some certaine considerations which may be deduced out of that point of the Gospel, in which
I haue procured with all possibilitie to set downe aboundance of con-
ceites, not so much of doctrine as of affection, the which rather may
serue to moue the will, and to enflame the hart with the loue of
Christ, then to feed the vnderstanding. In the third & last part
is handled, how we ought to imitate him with good workes, laying
downe some of the more principal documentes which may be collected out of that parcell of the Gospel. And this for our better
instructiõ: that conformablie to the example which Christ our Sauiour gaue vs, we may procure to frame our whole life, to cõforme
our maners, and direct all our actions: seeing that he that walketh
not as Christ [❧7] walked, abideth not truely in Christ neither is he
his member, for as S. Iohn witnesseth: he that saith he abideth in
him, ought euen as he walked, him selfe also to walke.

1.Ioh. 2.

   [Here follow a table of contents, Sigs. ❧7ᵛ-❧8ᵛ, and the first
sixteen meditations on the Passion of Christ, pp. 1-171.]

[171]

The XVII. Meditation.
How Peter *denied Christ thrice*
The Gospel.

Mat. 26.
Mar. 14.
Luc. 22.
Ioan. 18.

   Whilst Peter was without in the court, there cometh one of the
woman seruants which was [172] the dorekeeper or portresse who
seeing him warming him self, beholding him she saith, art thou also
of the Disciples of this man? but he denied it before thē all saying,
woman I am not, I knowe him not, neither wot I what thou saiest.
And he went forth before the court, and the Cocke crew. And after
a while an other seing him saide, and thou art of thē? But Peter
againe denieth with an othe saying, O man I am not, neither doe I
knowe any such man. And after the space as it were of one hower a
certaine other man affirmed saying, verely this fellow also was with
him, for he is also a Galilean, and they that stoode by said to Peter,
verely thou art of them for thou art also a Galilean, for euen thy
speach doth bewraye thee. And one of the seruantes of the high

Priest saieth to him (his cosen whose eare Peter did cut off,) did not I see thee in the Garden with him? Againe therfore Peter denied & said, O man I know not what thou saiest, and beganne to curse and to sweare that he knew not this man whō he spoke of: And immediatly the Cocke [173] crew againe, and our Lord turning looked on Peter, and he remembred the word of our Lord as he had said, that before the Cocke crow twise thou shalt thrise denie me, and going forth a dores wept bitterly.

Prophesies.

Abominati sunt me quondā Consiliary mei, & quem maxime diligebam auersatus*est me. My Councellors haue had me in abomination, & he whom I chiefly loued, turned him selfe from me.

Iob. 19.

2. *Inquilim domus meae sicut alienum habuerunt me, & quasi peregrinus fui in oculis eorum.* They which dwelled in my house accounted me for an alien, & I was as a stranger in their sight.

Idbem.

Considerations.

Consider how *Peter* his first feruour begining to decay, and the heate of charitie wexinge coole in his hart, he stood altogether a colde in the middest of that wicked troupe warmeing him selfe at the fire: Good *Peter* stoode warmeing him selfe at the fire, but he could not be warme, for that albeit he was present with his bodie at [174] that materiall fire, yet neuerthelesse he was farre distant frō the true fire which onely was able to shake off the colde which freezed his soule. See how *Peter* for that he was farre of from Christ, & adioined him selfe with those ministers of the Deuill, tentation did assault him, and beat him downe in such sort, that being strooken with the voice of a vile handmaid, it brought him for feare of death, to denie the Author of life. And most iustly did our Lord permit that he shoulde be first ouercome of a weake woman, both to represse his owne presumption, and likewise to geue vs an example, to learne to be humble, and not to trust ouermuch in our selues.

The. 1.
Point.

2. Consider what greate hurt one sinne bringeth vnto the soule, if presently with penance and repentance it be not amended, for that

---

*diligebam auersatus] *ed.;* diligebam a-/auersatus

one sinne with the weight of it selfe draweth vnto an other and all waies goeth from ill to worse, as is seene in *Peter,* who at the first simplie denied his master, the second time he added periurie, the third time to periurie he adioined cursinges [175] and detestations: But what doest thou, O *Peter,* is Christ so wicked a man that thou art a shamed to be his Disciple, & euen for to know him? Where are now those wordes which a litle before thou pronouncedst, *Lord I will yeeld my soule for thee?* doest thou not remember that the chiefe Priests seekinge false testimonie for to cōdemne thy master, thou with these wordes art the first which geuest sentence against him, and condemnest him for a reprobate and a contemptible person.

3. Consider how vnto blessed Iesus, not only his enemies but also his frēdes aggrauated his paines & heaped griefe vpon griefe, for that first he was much sorowfull to see him selfe betraied of one of his Disciples, afterward his sorrowe increased by seing him selfe forsaken of all the rest: finally this surpassed all other his sorrowes, to see him whom he had exalted aboue any other and had honored with so many prerogatiues, now as if he made smalle account & reckoning of him, remaining in the companie of his enemies, and as [176] if he esteemed it a shame that he shold haue bene his master to denie him in the presence of them all with so greate obstinacie and despite.

4. Consider with what sadnes the most pitifull harte of our Sauiour was oppressed, when he sawe the head of his Apostles, that most sound Pillar to be so miserablie vanquished and ouerthrowen: O how were all his bowels moued with compassiō and mercie for the infirmitie and fall of his Disciple? Wherfore howbeit he was in the middest of so many which on all sides did hale and pull him, notwithstanding hauing his eies more firmelie fixed on his Disciple for to succour him, then on him selfe for to defend him selfe, when he perceiued that good *Peter* now nere vnto vtter ruine, had thrice denied him he turned his benigne Face toward him and beholding him, with the eies of his grace, he made the bright beames of his diuine light, to shine most cleerely in that darke & obscure hart, by means wherof *Peter* presently returning vnto him selfe, knew his fault, and lamented it most bitterly.

[177]5. O most benigne Iesus how happie are they, which are in such sort beheld with your most merciful eies, since that they beeing

illustrated with the beames of your diuine light, beholding into the very depth of them selues, they may know their owne wickednes, and the brutishnes of theire soule, O how suddainly are they conuerted vnto you and how quickly are those cold & hard hartes mollified, kindled and moulten with loue and sending forth from their eies wholle streames of teares, doe say, Lord what will you haue me do? And certes it was no meruaile, that *Peter* wept bitterly, but more maruailous it is that his hart rented not a sunder with sorow and griefe when our Lord made him see his fall, and knowe the iniurie which he had done vnto his most sweet & louing Master. Might it please you O good Iesus, that your louing eies wold behold a litle my soule, which so many times at the voice of the handmaide of this my wicked fleshe, hath with such ingratitude denied and offended your diuine Maiestie.

[178]

The Praier.

Pray vnto Christ our Lorde, since that he permitted for our instruction, to be thrice denied of his most faithfull Apostle, whom afterward he beholding with the eies of his mercie he conuerted vnto penance, to voutsafe to behold thee in like maner, and to illuminate thy hart, that knowing the offences which thou hast done to his Maiestie thou maiest worthelie bewaile and lament the same, and not to suffer thee any more hereafter either in deede or word to denie him, or to be ashamed to serue him, but all waies to set forth his praises, and constantlye to confesse vntill death his most holy name.

Documents.

Wee ought not ouermuch to vaunt our selues, or presume of our force & vertue, but rather to stand in continuall feare & humilitie, to the end we fal not as Peter did, although he was the head of the Apostles & so feruēt.

2. We must flie and auoide such places and conuersation as minister vnto [179] vs occasion of sinning, for hard it is with those

which are euell to bee good, as Peter who whilst he conuersed with the Apostles, had mind to die for Christ, but afterward being in company of the Iewes he denied him so shamefully.

3. We ought to resist at the begining of tentation, and not suffer any imperfection how small so euer it seeme, to take any deepe roote in vs, least therby we fall into greater, as happened to Peter, who first contrarie to the councel which our Sauior gaue him fel a sleep. Secondly he fled: Thirdlye he denied him: and Fourthly he proceeded to periurie and cursing.

4. When by frailtie we fall into any imperfection, we must not therfore dispaire, neither remaine therin, but presently go forth out of it, and with sorow and teares amend it, as S. Peter did.

5. As long as we remaine in any occasion of sin, we must not thinke euer to be able to amend our selues or to profit in spirit, as Peter who whilst he remained in the house of Caiphas he could in deed often fall, but he could neither a-[180]mend him selfe or bewaile his fault vntill he went forth of the place.

6. They with Peter deny Christ who for worldly feare, or for some other interest or humane respecte, leaue to speake of such thinges as are conuenient, or els to make profession of vertue as euery Christian is bound to do, and much more a religious person: Let thē therfore remember how our Sauiour saieth: He that is ashamed of me in the presence of men, I will be ashamed of him in the presence of my Father and of the Angels.

7. Let vs procure to haue all waies before our eies our frailtie, and let vs rely only vpon a good will, for that is it vnstable, and changeth with euery light tentation, vnles God fortifie and conserue the same.

8. Albeit when we are in sinne, we can not by our owne force, rise againe without the helpe of Almightie God, notwithstanding the seruants of Christ, which serue him with good will, if they chance by frailtie to fall into some defect, they are perticulerly beheld and [181] raised vp againe by internall inspirations of our Lord, as he did with S. Peter.

[Here follow the remaining meditations on the Passion of Christ, pp. 181-200.]

XV.

The

Disposition or Gar-
nishmente of the
Sovle
To receiue worthily the blessed
Sacrament, deuyded into
Three discourses,
1 Preparation.
2 Presentation
before Christ.
3 Enterteinment.

Qui timent Dominum, praeparabunt
corda sua: & in conspectu illius, sancti-
ficabunt animas suas.

Those that feare God, will prepare
their hartes : and in his sight, sanctify
their soules Eccl. 2.

At Antwerpe.
Imprinted by Ioachim Trognesius.
1596.[1]
[Thomas Wright[2]]

---

[1]Init. T. N. Imprint false; pr. [secretly in England.] With an additional quire, y[8], comprising "A Conclusion, Conteining an Admonition to al the reuerend and religious Priests of England." *STC* 18335. Allison and Rogers, II, Entry 924.

[Anr. issue.] *The Disposition or garnishment* . . . [Without the additional quire.] Antwerpe, 1596. Init. T. N. Imprint false; pr. [secretly in England.] Not in the *STC*. Allison and Rogers, II, Entry 923.

[2]Thomas Wright (1561-1623) was the son of a prominent Catholic family in York. In 1577, he left England to matriculate at the English College at Douay. One year later he left Douay for Rome, where he became a student at the newly created English College there. In 1580, however, Wright left college to enter the Society of Jesus. Ordained to the priesthood in 1586, he began his priestly life as a public professor of Hebrew in Milan, and for the next nine years he taught in various schools throughout Europe. His continual discontent, caused by his not engaging in the English mission, grew, and at last he left the Society of Jesus, joined the English mission, and served as an informer against King Philip II of Spain. In 1597, Wright was imprisoned and was finally banished from England in 1603. He returned

[This book begins with Latin verses from the Bible and English translations, Sig. A1ʳ.]

[A2]

To the vertuous & zealous Matrone
Mistris S. H. and her Religious & feruent Sonne M. R. H.[3] perfect
deuotion in this lyfe to the
Eucharist, & full possession thereof in the
lyfe to come.

*In the depth of winter, when lighte lacketh, heate faylethe, Riuers
are congealed, a hoarie froste couereth the face of the earth; then
the vitall spring, vent forth of their hidden vaines, mor abundance
of water, a warmer liquor more feruent streames, a better digested
substance. In like sort (my deare frendes, whom I loue moste
effectually, because I knowe that you loue God effectually) it fareth
with youe while the light of true Faith and Religion, is banished
oute of Englande, the heate of Charitie exiled, the fluds of
almes and hospitalitie (which in former ages ranne amaine) are
frosen with imputatiue Iustice, and a solifidian erroure: while all the
churches are hoary white without Image, Taper, Alter, priest, sacri-
fyce, piety or de-*[A2ᵛ]*uotion**: *your faith shyneth more bright,
youre hope appeareth more firme, your charitie castethe a greater
flame, youre bowles of mercy issue forth fuller streames of liberalitie
& christian commiseration. When others lye either wallowing in***
wickedness, or buried in slepe, or drowned in sensualitie, many***
*houres before the sonne shewethe his beames aboue our horison:
youre prayers, youre sighes, your teares, appeare before the face of*

---

once again to Douay for a brief visit, but within two months he returned to
England accompanied by eight other priests. In 1610, he once again fled
England, probably spending some time at the College d'Arras. In 1623,
James I allowed the presence of a Catholic bishop once again in England.
Bishop William Bishop chose Wright as one of his eight canons, thus allowing
Wright to die in the England which he had worked so long and so zealously
to save (Theodore S. Stroud, "Father Thomas Wright: A Test Case for
Toleration," *Biographical Studies,* I [1952], 189-219).

[3]Mistress S. H. and her son M. R. H. are unidentified.

*deuotion] *ed.;* or/uotion
**wallowing in] *ed.; wallowing-/in*
***many] *ed.;* mauy

God. They spreade theire rayes in the Lande of the euerlastinge, as
acceptable to god, as delightfull to Angells. Your prayers ended in
voice and external shew but not in hart & internall deuotion, im-
mediatly foloweth some other godly exercyse of pietie and Reli-
gion: After some charitable worke of mercy and compassion, con-
sequently to this some good conference or study of spirituall bookes,
so that from morninge till night, you seme to me to doe nothing els,
but weaue such a spirituall Cortayne, as couered the tabernacle,*
more various for vertues, then That was with silkes: Or lyke those
chaynes of goulde the Spowse of Christe [A3] *besett with studs of*
siluer. Murenulas aureas faciemus tibi, vermiculatas argento. We
will make thee bracelets of goulde, studded with siluer. Cant. 1. But
aboue all youre singuler vertues, none stroke so deepe a maze into
me, as your feruoure & deuotion in receyuing the blessed Sacra-
ment. I know parte, but he onlye knowethe all, whom there you
participate, What hazard you put your selues into, to come by it,
with what Iubily of harte you communicate, and what notable effects
therupon enssue. Therfore to you I present these my simple
Meditations the which I am assured you practyse better, then I can
pen them. Therfore accepte them as a forme rather of that you doe,
then of what you should do. And in recompence of my paynes, I will
craue nothing els but one effectuall sighe to my sweete Sauiour
when you communicate, & enioy the heate of your deuotion, for that
I weigh aboue all treasures. From my cell in the Charter house at
Maclin.

Youres in Christ T. N.[4]

[A3ᵛ]

To the Reader.

In the firste ingresse of this discourse before I descended to any
particuler Treatise, I preconceiued, that these my sclender Meditations, shoulde come to the vew and censure of three sortes of persons; Catholicks, protestantes, & demi-catholickes, or catholique-like
prostestantes, or externall protestantes, & internall catholikes: some
call them Churche-papistes, others Scismatiques, whose mindes I
thoughte good to prepare in particuler before I went any further.
[A4]

---

[4]T. N. is a pseudonym for Thomas Wright (Allison and Rogers, I, Entry
923).

*tabernacle] *ed.;* ta-/nacle

To the Catholique Reader.

After I had finished my Former Booke, of the possibility and conuenience of the Reall presence of oure blessed Sauiour in the Eucharist,[5] my especiall frende (whō for loue I loue, & for vertue I reuerence) who was the cause of penning therof, insisted vehemently with me, to proceede to an other woorke, by declaringe the worthie disposition wherewith they ought to come who attend to reape the manifould fruites & treasures of this Sacrifice & Sacrament. His request for many respects, I could not nor woulde not resist, not onely for the reasons he brought, because the other serued for speculation, this for practtise: the other for deeper Iudgmentes, this for meaner capacities, the other tended to informe the vnderstandinge, this to moue affections: but also in regard of my owne proper exercyse & deuotion to the blessed Sacrament: that whyle I endeuored to teach others, I might instruct my self, [A4ᵛ] & lyke the water man, who by mouing his boate forward, makethe his owne iournay: so I by stirring others to feruour, mighte enjoy some heate therof my selfe. Yet I neuer minded, to let thē come to sight of the world but only to some particuler frendes, till he assured me of the great good he expected therof to many soules most pretious in gods sight, whose authoritie I permitted to weigh down mine owne Iudgment, & preuaile against myne owne reason, thinkinge that as god did refresh & reuiue Sampson by sending forth a spring of cleare water from an asses iawe, as he made a crow the cater and cooke of Elias, as with the rurall meates & rustick cates prouided for Abacuckes reapers, he fed his deare Prophet Daniell, & as verie often with vnfitt instrumentes, he wrought wonderous effectes: so perhaps he might doe by me, whom as vnworthy, he admitted to breake the substance of his Sacrament to his children, so he would directe to shewe them the maner of eating, to whose ho-[A5]nour & glory, I referr them both.

I am also to aduertyse thee, howe theese meditations, passe in prolixity mine accustomed maner of writinge, yet because I Iudged, they woulde not only helpe a man to receiue deuoutly, but also further him in many other spirituall exercyses: I was contented to

Iudic. 15.

3. Reg. 17. Da. 14.

---

[5]*A treatise, shewing the possibilitie, and conuenience of the reall presence of our Sauiour in the blessed sacrament* (Antwerp, 1596) Anon. Imprint false; pr. [secretly in England.] Allison and Rogers, II, Entry 925. *STC* 14574 and 24249.

folowe my frendes aduyse, who demed the treatise better, when the discourse was fuller.

Some I know woulde desyre an other parte hereunto adioyned, as an accomplishment of the whole, that is a Discourse of the frequent vse of this Sacrament, but I thought it superfluous, because he that readethe these 2 bokes, & weigheth as he oughte the inestimable & superexcellente riches communicated to them that deuoutly communicate, & besides his own frailtie, the temptations of the deuill, the euill examples and occasions of the world, if he may frequent this Sacrament often & will not, I hould him either verie vnwise, or very vitious. For who is he that feelethe him selfe [A5ᵛ] ded to the harte, and will not seeke a phisition, at whose handes he were sure to receiue a present remedy?

Were it not a follie to perswade this man with many reasons to looke for such a phisition to procure such a medicine, when Naaman Syrus came so far a iournay with vncertenty to be cured of his leprosie? Were it not madnes to perswade a man that were not madde, feelinge him selfe starue for hunger, to eate meate set before him? Were it* not doultishnes to exhorte a prisoner cheaned & fettered, to accept his libertie? Wer it not a want of sense, to perswade the blynde to desyre to see, the deafe to heare, the ignorante to be wyse, if they mighte come by those giftes of nature so easelie as we may by lyke giftes of grace communicatinge as we oughte, with due preparation & deuotion?

He therfore that will peruse the second treatise, if, as he readeth, he weigh the matter maturely, pondering it with the balance of catholicke iudgmente, he shall not neede much [A6] more to induce him, to eate of this foode, as necessary for the soule, as meate for the body.

Lastly when I cyte my booke of the possibilitie & conueniency of the reall presence, for breuitie sake I call it the booke of causes of the institution, for that the most part therof is Spente, in declaringe* 42. causes of the institution. Moreouer for that myne intention in settinge forth this discourse, was to helpe good catholickes to communicate deuoutly and religiously, therfore lest the lengthe of the book should terrifye them and bringe a loathsomnes (as though euery tyme they communicate, it weare necessary to transcourse the

4. Reg.
5.

---

*it] *ed.;* is
*declaringe] *ed.,* declariuge

whole tretise I haue at the end drawne a table where in one prospect, who haith red it once ouer, may call to Memory those heades and pointes that are requisite. I haue also in two woordes, Feare, and Faithe, comprehended almoste, the substance of the first and last treatise. The seconde is reduced to diuers Chapters, euery one seruing [A6ᵛ] for a particuler receiuing of the blessed Sacrament, so that perceiuinge what the woords represent & reading one Chapter, a man may sufficiently though not condingly, prepare him selfe to the Bl. Saccrament.

[A7]

To *the protestant reader, wherin is declared how we haue free will to doo good woorkes.*

1   Many erroures I fynd in the forged fancy of Protestants religion which roote owt of mennes hartes all christian deuotion & pietie. For graũt me once an imputatiue iustice, that Christes good woorkes & merittes alone, iustify vs before God, by only apprehension* of faithe; to what purpose then requyre they good woorks of vs? They answeare, as fruites of faith, but these fruites auaile me nothing to iustification the which wente before them, & iustifyed me without them, therfore imputatiue faith, cutteth vpp all good woorks by the rootes, that prepare the way to iustification.

2   After one is iustifyed, they haue prouyded dyuers other poysens to corrupt the plant of grace & iustice, lest by the indeuoure and cooperation of mannes good will, with the grace of God, it blossom deuotion,** & fructi-[A7]fy by good woorkes: as that all oure iustice, vertues, & operations, done either by the good inclination of nature, or helpe of godds fauoure and grace, are sinnes, a steaned clothe, abominable in Godds sight, deserue death & hell.

3   That we are not able (susteyned by Godds grace) to kepe his commãdements, to walke in his iustificatiõs withoute deadly sinnes & such offences as deserue damnation. That he which once inioyeth a lyuely faith, is iustifyed before God, & admitted into his fauour, seeth most euidently by his *Plerophoria,* that is a certayne internall

---

*apprehension] *ed.;* apprehensiou
**deuotion] *ed.;* deuotiou

& full perswasion, that god haithe accepted him into the nomber of his elect, and that as assuredly he shal neuer descēd to hel as Lucifer shal neuer ascend to heauen. What folowethe of this? *Edamus, bibamus, cras moriemur.* Let vs eate & drinke, to morow we shall dye. Let vs inioy All pleasures and voluptuousnes in earth, because we can not loose life euerlasting, & so we shall be perta-[A8]kers of Paradyse in this world, and in the world to come. But the protestant presently will reply, that such a man had neuer faith, because faith necessarily bringeth with it good workes. Ah poore wretches, then a protestant can not make such a resolution what hīdreth him? Haith he not liberty to sinn, although he lacke liberty to do well? Do we not see daily those that boasted somtimes of this security, to chang their religion & becom catholicks or puritans? This answeare declareth well what the protestants defende, but taketh not away the argument, as if a man should say, Dauid in killing Vrias had no charity. It is true, but this yeldethe not the cause why he had no Charity accordinge to the protestantes religion, no more then he that seeth a tree withered, rendereth a reason why the tree lacketh lyfe, by saying it lacketh leaues, because this is an effect: the reason is lack of norishment, or som fault in the roote. Nowe these men will sweare vnto death that they see [A8ᵛ] their faith as well as the best protestants in the world, which is, as they say, the life of all good woorks, and therfore they will lowse their senses to all lustes & ryotousnes.

1 Cor. 15. Is. 22.

2 Reg. 11.

[This attack on the Protestant concept of free will continues, Sigs. A8ᵛ-C7ᵛ.]

[C7ᵛ] I haue bene longer in this preface, then perhappes the proportion of the gate with the howse requyred by iuste Ceintrie, yet the opportunitie and necessitie, causeth builders often times to breake their square, as it befalleth me at this presente. And therfore I leaue of purpose an other discourse of the meritt of good woorks, the which I could proue as manifestly as this, & perhapps it weare as necessary: but an other occasion will not wante.

[C8] In the meane tyme, I request all protestants in the woundes of Christe Iesus as they tender their owne saluation, to ponder these reasons with the balance of indifferent iudgment, and dailye to goe forwardes in good workes for which they shall receiue theire Iudgment.

[C8ʳ]

To the Catholique-lyke
Protestantes.

Your case, as it is most miserable, so it is most compassionable, for it seemethe, you in harte desire to serue god, & yet this desyre is ouerweyed, with the desyre to enioy the worlde. Your case I said was moste miserable, because exiling oute of the Churche, you are like the straying shepe erringe in the desert mountaines, exposed to the pray of all rauening wolfes. You haue no weapons to defend your selues, depryued of the sacraments, spoyled of the communion of Sainctes, the incessant prayers & Sacrifice of Christs faithfull flock. Alas what will befall you? either the wylde & sauage beasts wil de-uoure you, or for lack of spirituall foode, you shall dye in those vnfrutefull soyles. What can the protestantes Churches afforde you? Ah infected sermons, corrupted with heresies. What prayers? Alas, howe will god heare them who will not here him? The Communion, o poysoned [D] cupp, better it weare for you to eate so much ratsbane, then that polluted breade, & to drinke so much dragons gall, or vypers blood, then that sacrilegious wyne. Noe doubte, but after that breade, entreth in Sathan, & after that cuppe, some of the infernall crew. This you know & in youre hartes confesse, & therfore your sinne is questionles the greater. You fauoure Catholicks and in what you can, doe them good. *Ah, quid prodest homini, si vniu-ersum mundum lucretur, animae vero suae, detrimentum patiatur?*

Mat. 16.

For what dothe it profitt a man if he gaine the whole worlde, and susteine the damage of his soule? What will it auayle you at the day of Iudgment, to haue fauored Catholicks, when you shall be condemned youre selues for half heritikes? What good Catholick is theare in england, that woulde not loose with all his harte, your temporall fauours, for your spirituall good, & wishethe not rather that you wear fauored of God, then gracious before men? If all the fauoures, riches, and trea-[Dᵛ] sures of the worlde, weare summed in one mannes dominion, yet who doubteth but that it weare better to receiue once deuoutly the blessed Sacrament, then to possesse them all. Therfore you may see what detriment your soule suffer-ethe, for the smale fauoures you minister vnto Catholickes. Ah feare not that they shall be destitute either of spirituall graces or tēporall fauours.

Cast your eyes vpon Goddes prouidence, & you shall see him tendering them, as the christall humoure of his eye. Abandon for Christe Iesus sake their externall conuersation in religion, whose company internally you deteste. For in very deede moste of the protestants hate you, the catholickes mislyke you, the deuils laugh at you, & god doth vomit you owt of his mouth. Woe be to that man that goeth with two hartes, that walkethe two wayes, that intendeth to serue bothe God & the deuill, to be Christes disciple, & a fauoryte of the worlde.

Apoc. 3.
Eccle. 4.

Mat. 6.

I wonder howe the verye hell you feele in your soules, the horrible tor-[D2]ture of youre consciences, enforcethe you not to leaue that hellish Sinagog?

In good sooth if euer you enter into your selues, & consider your presente state in what perills & laborinthes you haue caste your selues into: I meruel you either congeale not with feare, or pyne not away with melancholy, or your hartes burst not with desperation.

For in your owne conscience, you lyue in continuall, horrible, & sclanderous sinne. The houre of your death is euer imminent, the seuere Iudgmēt of God, you are assured you shall not escape, the eternall paines of hell you are certaine expecte you: & yet can you lyue merily, laugh, & passe youre tyme careleslye? This sinne of youres I take to be a sinne against the holy Ghost, and a fynall impenitency, because in youre hartes you haue determined, so longe as this rigour of lawes & punishment of Catholickes indureth you will perseuer in your accustomed irreligious profession of protestancy, from which, I say no more, but Christ Iesus deliuer you, for whose reclaime [D2ᵛ] I will not cease to pray.

[Here follows the first part, which deals with the remote and immediate preparation for receiving the Eucharist, pp. 1-80.]

[81]

The Second Part.
Of Preparation Whē
we Communicate.

The tyme when we communicate, I vnderstand, not the reall momente when we receaue the hoast, but a good little space going before, some halfe an houre or a quarter, at what tyme I approch near the place, wheare my Lord & Sauiour remaineth: or if I communicate at Masse, all the tyme of the masse.

At that present (accordinge to his precept) I will firste call to memory, his bitter passion: I will Imagine, I did see him distilling his sacred blood in the mount Caluarye, to washe my sinnes, to cure my soares, to deliuer me from deathe, to conducte me to a perpetuall lyfe. I will sitt vnder the shade of this tree, & see if he will let fall into the lapp of my hart, some of those frutes, which he brought from heauen, whose vertue causeth immortality.

[82] Heare I will sett my soule fully in order, to receiue my Lord. But because I know, that as one sorte of coloure, loathethe the eye, one sorte of meate cloyeth the stomake, therefore I will put on the habites of dyuers persons, who come all to this fountayn of life, to this tree of paradise, to this gate of heauen, to quench theire thirst, to restore their forces, to demaunde some spirituall refection.

1   First I will come as a begger poore & naked, to be appareled with this sacrament.

2 As wounded to deathe, to fynde heare the medicyne of lyfe.

3 As a sonne, to his father.

4 As a frende, to his frende.

5 As a souldier, to his Captaine.

6 As a scholer, to his maister.

7 As a creature, to glorify his Creator.

8 As one chayned by enemies, sekīg for his redemer.

9 As a gardin after winter withered, & dryed, to demaunde the dewe of heauen.

[83] 10 As an infant, to the breaste of his mother.

11 As lackinge some particuler vertue, lyke a Lazarus, to craue the crūmes of goddes grace.

12 As the three kinges came to adore Christ.

13 As a shipp in a tempest, to desire some prosperous goale.

14 As the prodigall sonne.

15 To honoure godds Sainctes.

16 As a hart, thirsting the fountaine of lyfe.

17 As a pilgrim.

18 As a faithlesse spowse, to her husbande.

19 As propitiation for the deade.

20 As a gratefull obsequy to God, for all his Sainctes.

21 As mouing to prayer.

[84]

Naked.
Cap. 1.

After the first & great fall of Adam, we know he lost his gar- *Gen. 3.*
mentes of immortalitie, and in lieu of them, was cast owt of paradise
not onely naked, but also disgraced with miserie, & shame: And
God to declare the base attyre & beggerie of his soule, appareled him
with the skinnes of beastes, that he mighte vnderstand, his Angel-
icall robes, were chāged into the verie scūme of brute creatures.
These beastly raggs he bequethed to all his posteritie, & left them as
a part of their inheritance. Yet this attyre by baptism we cast away,
Christ clotheth vs anew, *Quotquot baptizati estis, Christum in-* *Gal. 3.*
duistis. Howe many of you are baptysed, ye haue put on Christ. But
alas by actuall sinnes, we are turned owt of these garmentes, &
fallen into as beggerly an estate as before, in such sorte that oure
Sauioure [85] recounted to one, his internall misery, and spirituall
pouertie, who thoughte him selfe well appareled. *Dicis* (saith *Apoc. 3.*
Christ) *quod dives sum & locupletatus, & nullius egeo: & nescis*
quia tu es miser, & miserabilis, & pauper, & caecus, & nudus. Thou
saiest, that, I am rich, & welthie, & I neede nothinge: and thou
knowes not, that thou art a myser, & miserable, & poore, & blinde,
& naked. Lest I perhappes be fallen into this miserie, & be ignorant
thereof: I will request my sauiour, to cloth me with this Sacrament,
the which I know not onely to be meate to feede my body, but also
a garmente for my back. For me thinke I heare him from the crosse
(vnder which I sitt) exhorting me to buy this apparell of him to
clothe me againe. *Suadeo tibi emere a me aurum ignitum, probatum,* *Ibidem.*
vt locuples fias, & vestimentis albis induaris, vt non appareat con-
fusio nuditatis tua. I exhort thee to buy of me glowing gould,
proued, that thou maist be riche, & be appareled with whyte gar-

mentes, that the shame of thy naked-[86]nes doe not appeare. What goulde is this so glowing, so fyned, but oure Sauioure in the Euchariste, burninge with loue, not defyled with any impurity? For he is new goulde, neuer stayned with sinne, proued with temptations & tormentes. What can more enrich vs then this treasure? And what garment is more fitte & sutable to our soule then he that made it & redemed it, the first peece from whence it was cutt? For let vs gather all the good & profitt we receaue of our garments, & we shall most euidently see, how the Eucharist better appareleth our soules, then any garmentes our bodies.

Foure commodities our attire affordeth. Firste it keepethe the heate and warmnes of oure bodies. Secondly it defendeth vs from externall iniuries of weather, as rayne, wynde, coulde, &c. Thirdly garmentes adorne and deck the body. Fourthly manye garmentes yeld a most gratefull smell.

Let vs runn ouer them all and contemplate then in the Euchariste, the which concernethe the heate of oure [87] soules, the internall deuotion & Charitie, for those woordes, *ad literam* to the letter, must be thus vnderstoode, If you eate not the fleshe of the sonne of man & drinke his blood, you shall haue noe lyfe in you. That is, you shall loose your spirituall lyfe the heate of Charity, for without this garment it vaporeth forth. Therefore we must procure the Eucharist, to kepe in the vapoures & exhalations, that the soule may be warme with piety & deuotion.

Besydes, the Eucharist is meate, it norisheth, & what more preserueth & manteyneth oure naturall heate, then meate? Therefore the Euchariste in this surpasseth all sortes of garmentes: for if doth not onely cōserue the heate of oure soules that we haue, but also addeth an internall heate, which noe garment affordeth.

The Euchariste secondarily, protecteth vs from iniuries of spirituall enemies, who with tempestes of temptations, with congealed frostes of wicked examples, with boysterous windes [88] of persecutions, contende to extinguish the spirituall heate of grace and Charitie: But that table which Christ haith prepared for Dauid, againste thē that afflicted him: supplyeth the want of a winters robe, no could can pearce it, no winde passe through it.

The Eucharist thirdly, adorneth the receauers, by making one body with them: by cōmunicating to the soule, the richest treasures of heauen: by enduinge it with vertues: by refyninge the Image of

Io. 6.

Psal. 22.

God: by deifying all deuout Communicants with his presence. No scarlet, no purple, no stones, no pearles, no dyamondes, no clothe of tissue: may be compared to this attire. For as the soule surpassethe by thowsandes the body in perfection: so the garmentes of the soule, the garments of the bodie, by millions, in degree of excellency.

Lastly the Eucharist was represented by those garmentes which Iacob appeared withall before his oulde father Isaack, who feeling the fragrante smell thereof, *tanquam agri pleni, cui* [89] *dixit dominus,* As of a full feelde, the which God haithe blessed: gaue him that solemne benediction of the dew of heauen, & the fatt of the earth, aboundance of corne & wyne. Heare the soule appearinge before God with the spirituall garmentes of the Eucharist: the eternall Father, our true Father by creation, our Father which is in heauen, perceauing the supernaturall sente of this perfumed attyre: by the handes of the holy Ghost, raineth vpon vs his celestiall benediction, the dew of grace, and internall vertues, the fatt of the earthe, the frutes of all good woorkes, aboundance of corne & wyne, that is, the meanes how to receaue his blessed body & blood, vnder the formes of breade & wyne, as often as we desyre, for this questionlesse, is an exceding & excellente benediction. *Gen. 27.*

Therefore I besech thee o swete sauiour, since this Sacrament will couer so well myne ignominye and shame, conserue the naturall heate of my soule defende me from externall iniuries, [90] adorne me more decently, then any corporall attyre, render such a gratefull smell vnto the holy Trinitye, that thou wilte not permitt me to be ashamed vnder thy Crosse, that I dye not for could, where such warme apparell may be had, that I may appeare before the face of my God, & not hyde me from him, as my firste shamefull naked father did. Let me not be clothed with the skinnes of beastes, that is the garmentes of sensualitie, but with the robes of Angelles, the purple of Charitie.

But what is this contradiction swete Iesu I here in thy speach? Thou saiest that I am miserable, poore, blynde, & naked. Howe can a begger buy so riche a treasure? How can he that haith not cloathes to serue his necessity, bargaine for such marchandize, as will cause superfluitie? Did not thou say once, Come to me, & *emite sine pretio,* and buy without price? If I be a begger, I can not buy it; If I pay nothing for it, I buy it not, but thou giuest it to me. By these meanes, I must [91] buy it, & not buy it, which is a manifest contradiction. *Isa. 55. Apoc. 22.*

Apoc. 3.

Ibidem.
Mat. 13.
Psal. 94.

Mat. 6.

O blessed Sauioure, glory for euer be to thy name. Ah, no man appearethe so beggerly before him, but he may, (if he will) buy the moste pretious treasure of heauen, the sacramēt of the Eucharist, this obryzed gould,[6] this new goulde, this glowing gould, this approued gould, this goulde that will enryche him for euer. For God assistethe all men with his Grace, to saue them if they will vse it: He knocketh to enter, if they will open the doore of theire hartes: He soweth the seede of his woorde, in the feeldes of theire soules, if they will manure it; He cryethe vpon them, if they will heare his voice: He commaundethe them to come, if they will obey his precepts: yet because he will not draw any man but with free will, the nature whereof is suche, that it can not stande with necessitye or violence: it will haue libertie to doe & not doe.

This free will, this to doe that we might haue omitted, this libertie, is [92] all the pryce that god demaundethe, euen of the poorest beggers that lyue, for the greatest treasure that hart can conceaue: the which in verie deede, is not comparable with the rewarde, with the marchandise, that we buy: yet such is the goodnes of God, so much he pryseth our libertie, so greatly he estemethe this free loue, that he will geue him selfe wholly for it.

We buy then the Eucharist, because we geue God our free loue for it. We buy it not, because we pay an equall price for it: we bargayne nothinge for it, because the excesse of Christ, surpasseth so farr, all we can say or doe, that in comparison, all is nothing, yet this little (because it is oures) god accepteth for a meritt & desert.

Although the blessed Sacrament, adornethe our soules more gloriously, then euer Salomon was adorned in all his glory, & bewtifyeth it better, then euer the lillies of the feelde weare decked in their cheefest pryde: yet these garmentes wherewith Christ apparelethe our soules, differ in many pointes* [93] from the most pretious robes that euer clothed mannes body.

Firste because there was neuer garmente how stronge soeuer, but tyme woulde weare it, age consume it, vse make it vnapte for vse: But the garmentes of God are durable for euer: The more you vse them, the newer they appear: yea if of malice or wickednes, they be not cutt or torne, they will continew in all eternitie.

---

[6]*obryzed gould,* tried or standard gold
*pointes] *ed.;* pointes/poyntes

So long as the children of Israell wandred in the desert, so long *Deut. 29.*
as they were fedd with Manna from heauen, *vestes non sunt attritae,*
their garmentes weare not torne with wearing: so long as we feede
of this heauenly Manna in this lyfe, veyled with a clowde, & in the
other, face to face, our graceous garmentes shall neuer be consumed.

Secondlie there is no garment, but wynde and weather, water or *2*
rayne, mistes or snowe, in tyme will pearce it, let a man defend him
selfe as much, & so diligently as he can, either they Will fynde
hoales to passe, or soake [94] through the substance: but these garmentes of Christe are so well wouen, so well sowed, & so cloase:
that no temptation, noe persecution, noe distresse or tribulatiõ, can
passe through them to annoy the soule, if we doe our endeuoure. So
said she who had proued, *Aquae multae non potuerunt extinguere* *Cant. 8.*
Charitatem. Many waters could not extinguish his Charitie. Why
so? Because the heate thereof was garded and kepte in, with the
Garmentes of Christ, the sacred Eucharist.

Thirdlye all other garmentes, are basser then oure bodies, for *3*
comonly we begg them of beastes, and spoyle them of their skinnes,
to defende our skinnes, & consequently they eleuate not a man to a
higher degree then he was before, for an asse will be an asse although you trapp him with siluer & goulde. But these garments en-
haūce a soule to a more noble degree, to a higher dignitye, then it
had before, from the low estate of a miserable mã, to a certayne
confraternitie & societie of Angels, *Suscitans a terra inopem, et* [95]
de stercore erigens pauperem, vt collocet eum cum principibus, cum *Ps. 112.*
pr. populi sui. Raysinge from earthe the needy, and from the dunge
erectinge the poore, that he might place him with princes, with the
princes of his people. For as we declared in the booke of causes, by
this Sacrament, the receauers are deifyed by the reall vnion of oure
Sauiour with them: they are exalted to a supernaturall resemblance
of god, *Facti diuinae naturae participes,* Beinge made partakers of *2 Pet. 1.*
his diuyne nature. For in verie deede grace & Charitie, which our
Sauiour distilleth from this Sacrament, eleuate the soule, to a supernaturall & diuyne perfection, and consequently carrieth it beyonde
the boundes of nature: which neither the artificiall attyre of Salomon, nor the naturall garments of the lillies or roses, euer coulde
effect. Therefore if my blessed Sauioure would vouchsayfe to couer
my nakednes with these glorious garments, I woulde accounte my
selfe happy. I would not caste lottes with couetous souldiers to haue
all, or [96] loose all, for so perhapps I might go withoute them: but *Mat. 72.*

I craue them for loue, as the Liuerye of my Lorde. I would be known in the Court of heauen to carry his armes, his cognizanse, because I will glorye more therein, then all base worldinges in theire gaiest attyre.

[Here follow the remaining twenty chapters as indicated on pp. 82-83 of this work, pp. 96-238; Part Three considers what one should do after receiving the Holy Eucharist, pp. 239-293. Sigs. X6ᵛ-X8ʳ, which follow, contain a short table of contents. Hereafter follows an insert entitled "A Conclusion, Conteining an Admonition to al the reuerend and religious Priests in England," Sigs. yʳ-y8ᵛ. This work concludes with a complete table of contents (excluding "A Conclusion . . . Priests in England"), Sigs. Y1ʳ-Y2ʳ.]

XVI.

Breife

Meditations

of the Most Holy

Sacrament

And of Preparation, for

Receuing the same.

And of some other thinges

apertaining to the greatnes

and deuotion of so worthy a

Misterie.

Composed in Italian

by the Rev. Father

Lvca Pinelli of the

Societie of Iesvs.[1]

---

[1] n.p.d. [1595-1600.] Pr. [secretly in England.] Allison and Rogers, II, Entry 648. *STC* 19937.

Luca Pinelli (1542-1607) was born at Melfi in the Kingdom of Naples. In 1562, he entered the Society of Jesus. After having taught theology and philosophy for some time, he was sent to Germany to combat Protestantism. Pinelli taught theology with remarkable success at Ingolstadt (1575-1577?) and at Pont-a-Mousson (1577-1580). It was through his influence that in these two universities the *Summa* of St. Thomas was adopted as a textbook. After returning to Italy, Pinelli was Rector at Florence and at Perugia and later superior at Palermo, where he resided while he composed most of his ascetical works. The complete edition of his works was published in Italian (*Opere Spirituali*, 4 vols. [Venice, 1604-1609]) and in Latin (*Opera Spiritualia*, 3 vols. [Cologne, 1608-1614]) (*Dictionnaire de la théologie catholique*, XII, 2117-2118.)

The original Italian title of this work is *Libretto di brevi Meditazioni del santissimo Sacramento, e della preparazione alla sacra communione, con le sue imagini ed alla divozione di tanto Misterio* (Naples, 1597). (See De Backer,

[Device of letters IHS]
[trans. Anonymous[2]]

[Sig. A1ᵛ is a blank page; Sigs. A2ʳ-A5ʳ contain a brief table of contents and a general introduction on the Eucharist.]

[1]

The First
Meditation

Of the institution of the most ho-
ly Sacrament.

Chap. I.

Pointes to meditate.

1 Consider how our Saviour instituting for vs this most maruailous Sacrament declared the cordiall charitie which he had towardes vs, for that he coulde not giue vs any thinge more greate or
more pretious; as S. *John* most plainly signifieth saying. *Cum dil-*   *Ioan. 13.*
exisset suos, qui erant in mundo in finem dilexit eos.

[2] 2 Consider how that Christ instituted this most louing Sacramēt
whā he was to passe frō this world vnto his eternall father, hereby
to leaue vs a lively memory of his passion, suffered for vs, which
should inflame our hartes with loue towardes him.

3 Consider that which S. *Chrisostome*[3] affirmeth, saying, that
our Sauiour in the institution of this diuine Sacrament shewed his

---

Pt. 1, VI, 802-817). If De Backer's entry is correct in giving the date of
publication for the Italian as 1597, then Allison and Rogers have suggested a
date that is too early for the translation.

[2]The translator of this work is unknown. A. F. Allison in an article entitled
"The Writings of Fr. Henry Garnet, S. J. (*Biographical Studies,* I [Bognor
Regis, 1951], 16 & 20) argues that Garnet may be the translator of this work.
For note on Garnet, see p. 301, n. 2.

[3]St. Chrisostom, i.e., St. John Chysostom (c. 347-407) was the most prolific
preacher of the four great Greek doctors of the Church. His great gift of
eloquence won him the name Chrysostom (golden mouth). In 398, he became
archbishop of Constantinople (*A Dictionary of Saints,* ed. Donald Attwater
[London, 1958], p. 139).

desire to make vs one thinge with him selfe, for that is such a kinde of meate, that it conuerteth into it selfe all those which worthely eate the same.

*Luc. 22.
Mar. 26.*

4 Cōsider finally how that whē as the Iewes prepared cordes & the Crosse to binde and torment our redeemer, and Iudas went about this treason to deliuer our Sauiour into the hands of his eni-[3]mies then did he institute this most gratious Sacramēt to bind vs with the chaines of loue.

The Fruit.

The fruit* which ought to be gathered by this meditation is that the person which meditateth, shoulde vse actes of loue: rendering vnto Christ, who hath preuented us with such loue, as to feede vs with him selfe in this heauenly Sacrament.

A discourse in maner of a
spirituall speach

Is it possible my sweete Iesus, that loue towardes vs hath brought you to this, that being Kinge of eternall glorie & creator of the uniuersall worlde you would vouchsafe to becom meat for your vile and base creature. O love; exceeding greate is thy force: I thought that the wise [4] man had spoken sufficientlye enough of thy force and power when as hee saide *Fortis est vt mors dilectio.*

Cont. 8.

Love is as stronge as death. But now I see ful well that of thy force may be spoken much more; for that thy sharpe and swift arrows passed through the high heauens and arrived vnto the very breast of Almightie God, whither the persing darts of death coulde neuer come nor approche any thing neare. And not contenting thy selfe herewith thou woundest the hart of the louer in such sorte, that thou makest him to do what thou list and by transforming him into the thing which he loueth, thou dost not only seperate him from all created things as death doth: but also from him selfe. It would haue bene sufficient enough my [5] creator that thou*

*fruit] *ed.*; friut
**thou] *ed.,* thon

shouldest haue ben giuen vnto vs, for our Lord and our God, which thing your holy Prophet accompted for a greate blessednes when he saide *Beatus populus cuius Dominus deus eius.* Blessed is the people whose Lord is God. But loue hath farther inforced thee to doe those thinges which humaine wisdome cannot comprehend. It is verily most trew that thou being the God of maiestie, Infinite and Immortall, wast made man, not only to suffer and die for vs, but farther to feede our soules with thy most pure & sacred flesh. Thanked bee love which coulde so prudently finde out this maruailous meanes. Let therfore worldly wismē go & masure with their [6] small vnderstanding the infinitnes of this deuine loue. Wherfore (my Lord) with verie great reason *Abscondisti haec a sapientibus, & prudentibus, & reuelasti ea paruulis:* Thou hast hidden these thinges from wise and prudent men, and hast revealed thē vnto litle ons. But yet I cannot o my Sauiour but remaine al togither amased with the mightie boldenes of this your loue, since that, at the verie time whē as the torrents of your tribulatiō were so maruilously increased, that the onely thinking thereof in the garden made you to swet bloud: it made you so forgetfull of your selfe and of the torments which were prepared for you that you thought onely how to prouide for vs this most diuine meate. O most louing Iesus, full [7] well is it written of this your charitie. *Aquae multae non potuerunt extinguere charitatem, nec flumina obruent illam.* The great waters of your passion, & the fludes of your greiues coulde not hinder your charitie from bestoing vpon vs, this so pretious and so singuler a gift. O my soule, thy Prophet *Elizeus* made great account of the cloake which *Elias* his maister at his departure leaft him, with the which he deuided the waters of Iordaine and passed through them drie shodd: The Lord and God of *Elias,* being to pass from this world vnto his Father, hath left thee not a garmēt, but his most sacred body: to thentent he might be thy companion in this painfull pilgrimage, thy comfort in tribulation, & a most holsome meate [8] in spirituall life. Judge now therfore what accounte thou oughtest to make, & with how great deuotion thou oughtest to receaue him: Pray therefore vnto this thy most liberall benefactor that the same may not happen vnto thee, which happened vnto the people of Israell to whom Iesus our Sauiour was giuen for a maister and a guide, but they making noe account of so worthy a guide nor yet of his heauenly doctrine, remained still with the veale of ignorāce ouer their eies, and that which is worse, adioyned vnto their blindnes the vice of ingratitude.

Psal. 143.

Luc. 10.

Luc. 22.

Cant. 8.

4. Reg. <.>[4]

---

[4]Glosses in this text are sometimes illegible.

[Here follow the second, third, fourth, fifth, sixth, and seventh meditations on the Holy Sacrament, pp. 9-66.]

[67]

The Eight Medi-
tation.

---

*A spiritual exercise to prepare our
selves for receauing, when wee
goe to the Church.*

Chap. VIII.

Pointes to meditate.

---

1 That day wherein thou determinest to communicate in the morning assone as thou wakest, thinke that our Sauiour with greate desire expecteth thee in the Church, that for to come and repose him selfe in thy soule, wherfore thou like vnto a spouse for to please him, oughtest to vse more diligence in the inward adorning of thy soule, wherewith he is well pleased: then aboute the externall trimming of the bodie.

[68] 2 By the way as thou goest vnto the Church, consider what mirth and cheerfulnes thy good Angel keeper feeleth seing thee go to receaue his and thy Lord, and thou shalt pray that he will helpe thee to receaue him worthely.

3 Being entred in to the Church praie vnto the Blessed Virgine, or to some other thy deuoted Saint, to accompanie thee in receauing of Iesus thy Sauiour, who will be thy guest.

4 Assone as thou beginnest to see the Altar, where the Blessed Sacrament remaineth make humble reuerence there vnto, with thy harte, and esteeming thy selfe farre vnworthy of soe greate a maiestie, say with the Publican, *Deus propitius esto mihi peccatori.* God be mercifull [69] vnto me a sinner.

Luc. 18.

The Fruit.

The fruit of this eight meditation shalbe to procure a spirituall reioicing in thy soule, bycause thou art to receaue thy heavenly spouse, for this kinde of reioycing greatly pleaseth our Lord.

A Colloquium.
Kneeling downe before the Altar
make this, or some such like
speach vnto our Sauiour,
before thou doest com-
municate.

How greate fauour is this my beninge Iesus, which you now yeald me? Am not I that miserable creature which so often and by so many meanes haue most impudently offended you? What goodness is there in me that with particuler inspi-[70]rations you should drawe mee vnto your sacred table, If *Dauid* O Lord, made lame *Miphiboseth* to come vnto him, & would haue him to eate at his Regall and kingely table, and to be vsed as a Kinges sonne: because he was the sonne of *Ionathas* his speciall frend, of whom *Dauid* had receaued many benefites; But if you my Lord beholde me you shall finde me lame, both hand and foote, hauinge neuer done any thing well and worthie of praise and if farther you consider my first father *Adam* you shall finde disobedience & rebellion; Now that you my soueraigne Lord, infinitely more wise and more mightie then euer kinge *Dauid* was, make me an vngratefull worme of the earth to come vnto you, that I [71] might be fedde with the most pretious meate of your heauēly table, is a thinge of such exceeding greatenes, that it confoundeth me ouermuch; for that I am not onely vnworthie to approch nere vnto your sacred Altar, but also worthely deserue to be repelled farre of from you, as one that is colde, and vngratfull beholde O Lord I am come to receaue you in to the house of my soule. But O Alas, *Salomon* the wise, hauinge spent many yeares, & bestowed greate charges in building vp of a most rich & sumptuous *Temple,* Maruelled much with him selfe, that the God of maiestie would vouchsafe to come and dwell therein, wherefore being amased, and as it were besides himselfe said *Si enim caelum, & caeli caelorū te ca-*[72]*pere non possunt, quanto magis domus haec, quam aedificaui?* If heauen and the heauen of heauens can not cōprehend you, how wil this house which I have builded for you vpon earth, now, what shall I say who haue scarcely spent two howers to prepare my

2. *Reg.* 9.

3. *Reg.* 9.

soule for you? O my Lord, since that it pleaseth you to come and repose your selfe in the house of my soule, I humbly beseech you to make my soule a house of praier and consecrated to your heauenly father, to thentēt you may repose therein, and I remaine comforted: & singe with the Prophet: *Virga tua, & baculus tuus ipsa me consolata sunt.* your rod and your staffe haue comforted me.

Psa. 22.

[Here follow the ninth through the twentieth meditations, pp. 73-170.]

[171]

A Dialogve Be-
twixt a worldly and a spiritu-
all man, concerninge the
most blessed Sacrament
of the Altar.
In the which is disputed whether
it be better to Communicate of-
ten or seldome, supposing that
both the one, and the other be
dewlie done; that for loue and
deuotion; and this, for humili-
tie and reuerence.

Chap. XXI.

Worldling. I knowe not for what end & profit thou shouldest so often communicate because that I alwaies see thee with the same defectes, often disdainefull, and alwaies full of threatnings.

[172] Spirituall. I konw that others by often receauing are much amended of their defects, and if I should not often cōmunicate, without all doubt I should bee much worse, and peraduenture* euen at this instant I should haue bene burning in hell fire.

W.   How knowest thou, that thou shouldest be worse?

S.   Because experience teacheth me, that when I am shortly to communicate, I am more aduised in my actions, and I keepe my selfe more diligently from committing of sinnes, be they neuer soe small. Contrariewise when as I am not of a long time to communicate, I am not soe watchfull ouer my doings, and I finde my selfe sloe in

---

*peraduenture] *ed.;* peradueuture

my deuotions, and easely readie to fall in to imperfections, wherefore if [173] my soule reaped no other commoditie, this alone were sufficient enough, to make me to frequent this diuine Sacrament.

W. I doubt, that by receauing of our Lord so often, I shoulde loose both loue and feare of him which commonly proceedeth from ouer greate abundance, of familiaritie.

S. Nay rather it happeneth cleane contrarie, for if so be that by familier conuersation, and by often receauinge of our Lorde, should be laide open and discouered some imperfection of his, you had good reason to thinke that thereby would be diminished our loue & feare of him, as it often happeneth in humaine things; but here is no such matter, for that he being the infinite sea of all perfection, by how [174] much more a man conuerseth with him so much the more he perceueth his goodnes and his perfection, & therfore so much the more is increased in vs our deuotion, loue and reuerence towards, his diuine maiestie.

W. Be it as you would; yet experience teacheth that the often frequenting of any thing, albeit neuer so good, yet in the end it breedeth loathsomnes.

S. This is trew in temporall thinges, and in sensuall delights but as *S Gregorie* verie well noteth: *In spiritualibus delitijs saturitas appetitum parit.* In spirituall delightes plentifulnes causeth appetite, for that thē their goodnes is better knowne, & for this cause the more they are possessed, the more they are desired, for this respect also the diuine [175] wisdome saieth *Qui edunt me adhuc esurient, & qui bibunt me adhuc sitient.* They which eate me shall still hunger after me, and they which drinke me, shall still thirst after me.

Eccle. 24.

W. Saint *Paule* saith that hee which receaueth vnworthely receaueth the same to his eternall damnation, but if thou receaue euerie Sonday, it is a signe that thou accomptest thy selfe worthie, but is not this manifest pride? And therefore thou receauest vnworthely?

1. Cor. 1.

S. As though seldome receauing did make vs worthy, it is not so, but if by being worthie you vnderstand that one should be equall in perfection with this Sacrament, then it is certaine that no creature albeit most holie, no nor yet all creatures to-[176]gither are worthy of this Sacrament. Yea if such worthines were necessarie; no body could communicate; for that no creature can come vnto that perfection which should be equall with this Sacrament. In like sort that a man should receaue worthely is not necessarily required that he should be of excellent perfection and of rare and singuler vertue; for this is obtained by frequenting* this diuine Sacrament, therefore for to bee worthy, it is sufficient according vnto *S. Paule* that the partie which receaueth haue that disposition where-with God is contented; that is beforehande to examin his cōscience, to haue contrition and to confesse his sinnes; and so to receaue the B. Sacrament is not pride.

[This dialogue continues, pp. 177-197. It is followed by three treatises on receiving the Holy Euchraist, pp. 197-240; a listing of various miracles attributed to the Eucharist, pp. 240-285; and an admonition to the Christian reader, pp. 285-290. Hereafter begins an insert, the first part of which is composed of hymns and prayers in both Latin and English, pp. 1-17.]

[18]

Rembrances of
Mother Teresa di Iesu:[5] *whoe*
was foundres of the barefooted
Carmelitā Nunnes for her mo-
nasteries translated first out of
Spanish into Italian, and now in
to English for the profit of euery
deuout Soule.

1   The earth vntilled being neuer so fertil bringeth forth but brambles and thornes: euen so is the vnderstanding of man.

2   To speake well of all spiritual thinges: as of Religious persons and Preists.

---

[5]St. Teresa of Avila (1515-1582) was the foundress of the reformed Discalced Carmelite nuns. She is the only woman to whom the title, Doctor of the Church, is popularly, though not officially, given. In 1562, she initiated her reform among the nuns, and through the aid of St. John of the Cross, the reform spread to the friars as well. She was canonized in 1622 (*A Dictionary of Saints,* pp. 250-251). Her mystical writings, which include among others *The Interior Castle* and *The Way of Perfection,* are considered essential in the study of Catholic mystical theology.

This work is a translation of St. Teresa's *Avisos de la Madre Teresa de Jesús para sus monjas* (*Obras completas,* ed. M. Aguilar [Madrid, 1945] pp. 629-631). According to A. F. Allison, this is the first work of St. Teresa to be translated into English ("The Writings of Fr. Henry Garnet, S. J.," p. 21). It was first published in Spanish in 1583.

*frequenting] *ed.;* ferquenting

3 Emongst a multitud to speke alwaies litle.

4 To be modest in euery thing [19] which thou shalt doe, or manage.

5 Neuer to be ernest in things of small importance.

6 To reason with euerie one with moderate cheerfulnes.

7 To scoffe or iest at nothing.

8 Not to reprehend any, without discretion humilitie, and thy owne confusion.

9 To accommodate thy selfe to the Complexion of the partie with whom thou hast to deale, for the seruice of God, with the cheerefull to be merrie, with the melancholie, sad; finally to be all, vnto all, to gaine all.

10 Neuer to speke vnles thou hast first well thought of it, and cōmended vnto God our Lord what thou mindest to say, to the entent that thou speakest nothing that may offend him.

[20] 11 Neuer to excuse thy selfe without very probable cause.

12 Neuer to speake any thing of thy selfe that maye deserue praise, as of thine owne knowledge, vertue, linage, vnles thou hast some probable hope to reap therby some commoditie; and then doe it with humilitie, and consideration, because they are gifts which come frō the handes of God.

13 Neuer to amplifie any matter, but moderatelye to speake what thou thinkest.

14 In all thy conferences and cōuersations, to mingle alwaies some spirituall thing, & so thou shalt auoide many idle wordes, and murmurations.

15 Neuer to affirme any thing before thou knowest well.

16 Neuer to intermedle to giue [21] thy opinion in any thing, vnles thou art desired: or els charitie requireth it.

17 When as any one speketh of spirituall thinges, to harken vnto it with humilitie, and like a scholler to learn that for thy self which he shall speake well and maketh for thy purpose.

[These short spiritual exhortations continue, pp. 21-32, followed by a short collection of ejaculatory prayers, pp. 33-36.]

XVII.

The

Litle Me-

morial, concer-

ning the Good and

Frvitfvll Vse of

the Sacraments.

Wherein

Be handled such defects as some

persons commit in the vse

of them, and the remedies

therein to be practised.

Composed in Spanish, by the R. Father

Francis Arias of the Society

of Iesus, and newlie translated in

to our English tongue,

[An ornament]

Printed at Roan, 1602.[1]

[trans. Anonymous[2]]

[¶ 2]   The Preface to

the Reader.

Exod.

Lewis *of* Granada,[3] *that excellent and diuine* Beseleel[4] *of our*
time for the building and polishing of the spirituall tabernacle of

---

[1]Imprint false; pr. [secretly in England.] Allison and Rogers, I, Entry 38.
STC 742.

Francis Arias (1953-1605) was born at Seville, and before his entering
the Society of Jesus in 1561, he had been a secular priest. He was professor
of scholastic theology at Cordova, professor of moral theology at Trigueros,
and rector of the college at the latter place and also at Cadiz. He was held
in esteem by the great master of the spiritual life, St. John of the Cross,
and also is mentioned frequently and very favorably by St. Francis de Sales.
During his life time, Arias' personal sanctity resulted in his being esteemed
a saint. Much of his time was spent doing works of charity among the
Negroes, the Moors, and the inmates of prisons and hospitals (*Catholic
Encyclopedia*, I, 711). In 1588, Arias published at Valencia a volume entitled
the *Aprovechimiento espiritual,* which contained a series of treatises, one of
which was *Del buon uso de los Sacramentos* (*Dictionnaire de Spiritualité
ascétique et mystique,* I, 844-845).

[2]Most of the other English translations of Arias were done by the famous
Sir Tobie Matthew, but it is not certain that he is the translator of this
particular work.

[3]For notes on Luis de Granada, see p. p. 112, n. 1.

[4]Beseleel was the son of Uri, grandson of Hur of the tribe of Juda. He
was a skillful artificer and together with Ooliab was divinely called to
construct the tabernacle with its furnishings (*Dictionary of the Bible,* ed. John
Davis. 4th ed. [Grand Rapids, 1958], p. 94).

Christes church, amonge many other his notable monuments, intiteled one: The Memorial of a christian life.[5] *The first parte whereof intreating principallye of the Sacraments of Penance, and the Sacred Communion, was to the singular benefitte of our countrey, translated into the English tongue. God whose* hand is not abbreuiated, *hath in the same nation, raysed him vp a companion, like an other* Ooliab, *for the prosecuting of the same worke: one of whose small treatises I haue likewise translated, as desirous to inriche our country with so singular a treasure and because it is an* Addition *to a* [¶2ᵛ] *former worke, and so by the Author called: a name nothing fitting it now, when it commeth forthe alone, therefore haue I thoughte good after the imitation of that learned man, especiallye because as his, so this also contayneth a briefe note, of that which euery good christian oughte often to practise, concerning the Sacramentes of Pennance, and the holy Communion, to put it forth with the title of a* Memorial: *and the name* (litle) *I have added, both for distinction from the former, and also for that it is comprised in a farre lesse quantitie. And althoughe denied it can not be, that not onelie* Grannada, *but many others, haue learnedly entreated of the same subiecte, yet who knoweth not, that as mens vaines bee diuers in writing, so likewise their affections in readinge not all one, and therefore both with profitte and pleasure, many good workes may bee published* [¶3] *of the same matter, the latter either for methode, perspicuitie, or some other notable thinge, adding somewhat which in the former was wanting, and as it were with* Ruth *gathering vp such eares of corne, as slipped from the reapers handes: and that such labours may fruitfullie bee enterprised: beside reason, and common practise, wee haue also the example of the fower Euangelistes, who by direction of the holy Ghost, as with singular vnitie, so with profitable varietie, wrote the same life and death of our Sauiour Christe. This booke therefore, though it intreateth of Confession and Communion, the subiect of diuers excellent discourses, yet is it worthy to be imbraced, seeing the manner and scope thereof, is of that quality, as I thinke few can reade it, that will repent their small paines employed, and some haply be of opinion, that albeit others with* S. Iohn *came first to the* [¶3ᵛ] *monument, yet that this author with* Saint Peter *entred first in: and all such, whose harts God shal so effectually touch, as that they will not*

Esai.
Exod.

Ruth.

Iohn
v. 4.

---

[5]For selections from *A Memoriall of a Christian Life,* see Entry VI in this anthology.

g. 15.⁶

onely reade, but also carefully practise, may with much more reason
blesse the time, that they met with so heauenly a maister, for the
sauing of their owne soules, then euer did Dauid *blesse* Abigail *&*
her wise speech, hindring him from the killing of an other mãs body.
The principal intent of this Memorial *is, to inflame all with the loue*
of the Sacraments, and to stir vp our dull spirits, often to repaire
vnto those diuine fountaines of grace, from which so many and rare
benefittes doe flowe: to discouer also the vsuall disorders, into which
not only those that be carelesse, but euen the deuoute servants of
God doe sometimes fall, when they goe to confession, and to receaue
the blessed Sacrament, togither with singular remedies, how we may
auoid al such [¶ 4] inconueniences, and so free our selues, more &
more from sin, purchase greater abundance of grace in this world,
and eternall felicitie in the worlde to come: all which pointes he
doth so excellently performe, and like a diuine phisition search out
the secret and lurking diseases of our soule, and prescribe such
sweet and heauenly receits, that there is almost none so voide of
spirituall sence, but by reading, shal finde theire conscience* touched:
nor any proceeded so far in piety, but that they may make great
benefit of this small treatise, and generallye all that sincerely desire
the amendment of their life, and increase of vertue, shall feele their

Luc.
v. 32.

hartes burning in them, as the two Disciples did when our Sauior
walked in their company, and opened them the Scriptures.

One thing there is which the author in discoursing of such sins,
as many confesse not through culpable ignorãce, hath [¶ 4ᵛ] omit-
ted, to witte the dangerous error of many yonge persons, that with-
out the knoweledge or consent of theire parents, bestowe them selues
in marriage: and an other no lesse dangerous then the former, if not
more, and that is to make priuie contractes, whereof not only such
as liue vnder the charge of theire parents, but others also of all
estates & callinges bee some time foundᵉ guiltye. Of these pointes
though passing necessary, he maketh no mention, because the

4. c. 1.

councell of Trent *making all priuie contractes of no force, hath freed*
them frõ such inconueniences, which is not so here in our countrey
for lacke of publication, a thing required by the councell before that
decree can take anye place: and therefore I haue thought good to
say somwhat, both concerning the one & the other, (because they be

---

**Conscience] ed.; couscience*
⁶The copy of *The Litle Memorial* which was available to me had been
trimmed, thereby destroying in part many of the marginal glosses. I have
reproduced only what is legible in my copy.

sins very rife, and be accompanied with many and greate mischifes,
especially the second, as discord [¶5] *betwixt houses, ruines of*
families, the perpetuall state of adultery, and not seldome a con-
tinuall torment of conscience, as daily experience teacheth) to the
end that such as feare God, & be desirous to saue their soules, may
know what herein they haue to followe and practise.

[The translator here enlarges on this subject, Sigs. ¶ 5ʳ-¶10ʳ.]

[[¶]10ᵛ]

A Table of the
Chapters.

IX   Of other sinnes more secret, as pride of our owne proper iudgement, and selfe will, which many doe not know nor confesse through culpable ignorance.

X   Of a very profitable remedy againste the harme which commeth by secret sinnes & that is euery day to examine our conscience: and the manner howe this is to be done.

XI   Of an other singular meanes for a man to deliuer him selfe from secret sinnes, and that his confessions may be more fruitfull, and that is to haue one certaine ghostly father, vnto whom he ought ordinarily to confes his sins.

XII   Of an other excellent remedy, to deliuer our selues from the harme of secret sinnes, and to supplie the defects [¶ 11ᵛ] of our former confessions, and that is with care and diligence, to make a generall confession.

XIII   Of such defectes as be an impediment to many which doe often communicate, that they receaue not the plentifull fruite of the B. Sacrament.

XIIII   How for the receauing of more abundant fruite of the holy communion, conuenient it is to purifie the soule from veniall sinnes.

XV   How to receaue much fruite of the blessed communion, necessary it is for a man to prepare himselfe with recollection, and meditation: & what manner of meditations are good to be vsed for that purpose.

XVI   Of that outwarde reuerence, humilitie, and modestie, with which we ought to come vnto the B. Sacrament.

XVII   Of that quiet and repose, with which we ought to come vnto the holy communion: and what thankes are to be giuen vnto God after the receauing thereof.

XVIII   How to abstaine from the B. Sacrament without iust cause, is an impediment to spirituall profit: and how [¶ 12] that neither for negligence, or lacke of sensible deuotion, a man should giue ouer the holy communion.

XIX   How for scruples and vaine feares, we ought not to abstaine from the sacrament of the Altar.

XX With what moderation we ought to frequent the holy communion, that we doe not therein exceede, nor doe any thing contrary to due reuerence: and how we ought to leaue this to the iudgement of a discreet ghostly father.

XXI Of such rules as holy men prescribe, concerning the often receauing of the B. Sacrament.

XXII Of that discretion which ghostly fathers ought herein to obserue, according to the doctrine of holy men.

XXIII Whether the holy communion ought daily to be giuen to some persons of our time.

[Sig. ¶ 12ʳ is a blank page.]

[1]

The Litle Memoriall of a Christian Life.

Chap. I.

Wherein is briefely declared, the great
necessitie, which all Christians haue,
often to frequent the Sacrament of
Confession, and the holy Communion.

For as much as this booke, is published for the commodity of such persons, as be resolued to serue God, by setting downe before their eyes, such meanes as they haue to vse, both for the preserving them selues, and also proceeding forward in his divine service: and [2] further to exhort them, to put those meanes in practise: and seing one of them, and that of great force & efficacy, is to frequent the Sacraments, that is, often to be confessed, and to receaue the holy communion: two things are here for this purpose, especially to be handled.

The first is, to exhort al faithfull Christians, often to repaire to these holy sacraments, by declaring the great & wonderfull commodities, which by meanes of them be obtayned. The second is, to teach and instruct them, concerning the true and laudable vse of the sacrament of Confession, and the holy sacrament of the Aultar: and because to entreate copiously of these poynts, were too much for this small booke, therefore touching [3] this matter, I intend onelie to speake of that, which to me shall seeme most necessary, and worthy to be noted, of such as be resolued to serue God. The first poynt therefore which I meane to handle, shall be briefly to set downe before our eyes, how necessary it is, for al Christians, often to frequent the divine sacraments of Confession, and the sacred Communion: the second shall be to prosecute in particular, such abuses and disorders, as be more secret, and into which, even those that be determined to serue God, doe not seldome fall.

Concerning the first. Many & very effectuall be the reasons, which ought to moue and invite all faithful christians to frequent the Sacraments, that is, to con-[4]fesse themselues, and communicate once in eight, or fifteene daies, or at least once a moneth. For if they be such persons, as God hath voutchsafed so to favour, that since their last confession, they haue not fallen into any mortall sinne, very necessary it is for them so to doe, both to preserue themselues in Gods grace, & to increase in the same, and also in all other vertuous & heavenly gifts: to make themselues daiely more acceptable in the sight of God: to be more fit instruments to set forth his glory, & to advance the good of his Church: to make their salvation more certaine: to lay vp the treasure of greater merits in eternall felicity: to procure more light, and strength, both to know, and overcome all the temptations & [5]deceipts of the enemies of our soule: to doe the workes of vertue, with greater facilitie and sweetnes: to passe over this life, with more peace, and spirituall comfort: to be at our death more assisted and holpen, of God with plenty of heavenly succor: and so finally to depart this life, with more hope of salvation, greater quiet, and comfort of soule. For these, and such other like effects, and singular commodities, very necessary it is, I say, that the servant of God should often repaire to the sacraments. For albeit since his last confession hee hath not fallen into any mortall sinne, yet certaine it is, that hee hath committed many veniall, wherof some he doth know, and others, he doth not, and yet for all that not to be excused, be-[6]cause he might well haue known them: and these veniall or small sinnes, although they doe not spoile the soul of gods grace, yet doe they great harme, and put a man in such a case, that he doth thereby fal the sooner into those that be mortall, as else where hath beene handled: Certaine likewise it is, that a man is continually assaulted with daiely and divers tentations by the devill, the world, the flesh, & our corrupt nature, which doe put him

tract. 4.
p. 24.

in great danger, to fall into mortall sinne: and many of them be secret, and very perilous, and therefore passing necessary it is, that he should alwaies haue a remedy to deliver his soule from veniall sinnes, and great neede he hath of daiely strength, to resist all tentations: great neede [7] of the continuall dew of Gods grace from heaven, to mitigate his wicked inclinations: and all this doth he find in the holy Sacraments of confession, & communion, if he do often frequent them. And although it cannot be denied, but that there bee other remedies, for the purging of veniall sinnes, so most certain it is, that this of frequenting the Sacraments, if it bee done as it ought, is the best, and most effectuall of all other. Of the wonderfull effects, which the blessed sacrament of the Altar worketh in them that doe frequent it. *S. Bernard* giveth an excellent testimony: these be his words. *The most pretious sacrament of the body of our Lord, doth* Ber. in
de ce. do. *worke in vs two effects:The one is, that it doth diminish the sence of veniall sinnes: and the other is,* [8] *that it doth wholy take away all consent, to mortall sinnes.* And the holy man, doth proue this to bee true, by that experience, which the servants of God doe find & feele in their owne heartes, to whome he doth there speake in this manner. *If any of you, doe not now so often feele, neither yet so greate motions as before time you did, of anger, of envie, of carnality, and other vices, let him giue thankes to the body and bloud of Christ, which hee receaveth in the holy sacrament, because this is the effect thereof, and let him take comfort therein, for as much as God by this meanes doth cure and make sound the corruption of our nature.* Thus writeth *S. Bernard.* And the selfe same thing is confest by all holy men: and the generall councell of Trent, doth confirm the same declaring, that the blessed Sa-[9]crament doth worke this in all such, as receaue it with due preparation, to wit that it doth deliver them from consenting to tentations, pacifie their passions, giue them victory over their enemies, preserue and encrease thē in good life, by giving force and strength for al these foresaid ends. And from hence it commeth that in al cities & townes, where there be many, that often repaire to the sacraments, many there be also, which all their life long continue in Gods grace, without ever falling into any mortall sinne: And all ordinary ghostly fathers, be witnesses of this trueth, who find by experience, that christian people doe receaue this great commoditye by frequenting the Blessed sacrament of the Aultar with de-[10]votion and a vertuous disposition.

.13. c. 8.

These reasons aleadged, are sufficient to perswade all good Catholicks though not guilty in their conscience, of any mortall sin, often to confes themselues, and to communicat: but if since their last being at cōfession they haue committed any deadly sin, then besides the former reasons, greater necessitye haue they streight waies, and without delay, to goe vnto the sacrament of Confession: to witt, that by meanes thereof, they may come out of that damnable state, and deliver themselus, from all those mischiefes and harmes, which from that kind of sin do growe: as to be hated of God, & to liue in disgrace of the Blessed Trinity: to bee abhorred of heavenly [11] Maiesty, and to be captiues and slaues to Sathan the prince of darkenesse: to be subiect, and obedient to his will, and to lose the great value and merits of all the good works of their life past: to be in apparant danger of falling into greater sins, into greater blindnes, and hardenesse of hart, and finally into everlasting damnation. From al these evils, and mischiefs, and many more, annexed to these, that man is delivered, who after due preparation, purgeth his soul streight waies by confession. And although true it be, that onely by contritiō, with a purpose to confesse in time convenient, a man may deliver himselfe, from the state of mortall sin: yet to haue contrition without helpe of the sacrament, is an hard thing, vnto [12]which few doe attaine: for as much, as true contrition, conteineth in it selfe, a great hatred of sinne, by reason wherof, the soul doth in will abhorre and detest, all mortall sinne, more then all other evils in the world, & with all a firme purpose of amendmēt of life: and so resolutely determineth, never more to consent to any deadly sinne whatsoever, neither for interest or commodity, nor to avoide any paine or misery of this life: and togither with this, necessary it is, that the principall thing, which moveth a man to this hatred of sin, and amendment of his life, bee the loue of God aboue all thinges. And because men commonlye vpon their forsaking of mortall sinne, doe it not at the first, for this supernaturall loue of God, [13] but principally for feare of Hell and damnation: for this cause a very hard and rare thing it is, to haue contrition without the helpe of the sacraments: wherof it commeth to passe, that such as haue sinned mortally, and go not to the sacrament of confession, commonly they continue stil in the same bad estate, and so be subiect to al those mischiefes and dangers, which accompany mortall sinne, as before hath beene said: And the reason heereof is, because ordinarily without help of the sacraments, men ariue not to haue contrition, which yet is necessary to come out of mortal sin: but when they go to confession with that preparatiō which is requisite, if their soul be infected, streight waies are they delivered from mortall sin, & from [14] all those mischiefes before mentioned: for when a man confesseth him self having a perfect hatred of sinne, & a firme purpose of amendment, although the principall reason which moveth him, to forsake sin, be the feare of his owne damnation, yet with the helpe of the sacrament, shall he obtaine Gods grace: and this is that which Divines teach, and the holy councell of Trent doth declare, to witt that of attrite he becommeth contrite. For such was the infinite mercy of God, now in the lawe of grace, as to bestowe such efficacy vpon his sacramēts, that to him that wanteth grace, and doth not of his part, put any stoppe, or impediment, grace by meanes of them is given him, and to him that is already in grace, the same is en-[15] creased and augmented.

14. c. 4.

These be in summe, the most excellent commodities which faithfull people doe gaine by often repayring to the Sacramēts of Confession, and communion: and these bee the pittifull and most grievous evils, from which they be delivered. He therfore that is desirous of salvation, and resolved to serve God, and pondereth well this point, how can he let so great commodities slip out of his handes? how dareth he advēture the losse of so great gaine? how can he excuse himselfe from frequenting confession, the spring of life, and salvation, by meanes whereof hee is delivered from such notable evils of death, sinne, and everlasting damnation? and such purity of soul obtained, such divine [16] and spirituall beawty, and such treasures of grace and glorie? And how can he containe himselfe and not go often to the holy Sacrament of the Aultar? the bread of life, the death of sinne, the wel-spring of vertues, the medecine of our passions, the staffe and stay of our weakenes, the treasure of graces, the most pleasant repast of all heavenlye comfort, the roote of immortalitye, and the fountaine of all goodnes. And thus much may suffice, cōcerning the first point. Now will I come to the second, which is the principal thing that I intēded to intreat of, & wherof in very deede, we stand most in neede and ought carefully to be instructed in the same.

[Here follow the remaining twenty-one chapters, pp. 17-253, as indicated on Sigs. ¶ 10ʳ-¶ 12ʳ of this work.]

XVIII.

A Brief

Fourme of

Confession, In-

structing all Christian folke

how to confesse their sinnes, & so

to dispose themselues, that they

may enioy the benefite of true

Penāce, dooing the woorthy

frutes therof, according

to th'vse of Christes

Catholique

Church.

Newly translated into English, and set

foorth together with certaine other

godly brief Treatises and Pra-

iers, as is to be seene in

the side folo-

wing.

[An ornament]

Antverpiae,

Apud Iohannem Foulerum.

M. D. LXXVI.

Cvm Privilegio.[1]

---

[1]Allison and Rogers, I, Entry 143. *STC* 11181 and 24625. This work has at times been ascribed to Laurence Vaux since it was subsequently re-printed with later editions of Vaux's *A Catechisme of Christian Doctrine* (1567, 1568, 1574, 1581[?], 1583, 1590, and 1605). Both T. G. Law and Southern argue that the evidence clearly favors John Fowler as the translator and compiler (Southern, p. 412). The dedicatory epistle to the Duchess of Feria (see note 2 below) states that Fowler translated the treatise on confession from a Spanish original; I was unable, however, to trace the Spanish original.

John Fowler (1537-1579) was a printer and scholar of considerable repute. Born at Bristol, he attended Oxford, received the B. A. degree in 1556-57 and the M. A. degree in 1560 and was a fellow at New College from 1553-1559. His skill in Latin and Greek was generally applauded. Apparently at one time he renounced his Catholic faith by taking the Oath of Supremacy, but soon after Elizabeth's accession, he retired to Louvain and was re-instated in his old faith. In Louvain, Fowler set up a press for the publication of Catholic books. This press was later moved to Antwerp and finally to Douay. Fowler married Alice Harris, the daughter of John Harris, the personal secretary of Thomas More. Fowler died at Mechlin in 1578 or 1579 (*D. N. B.,* VII, 526-527). Also see Gillow (II, 327-328).

[Here follows a table of contents, Sig. a1ᵛ, and a dedication to the Duchesse of Feria,[2] Sigs. a2ʳ-a5ʳ.]

[a5ᵛ]

To the Reader.

Whereas in this great corruption of Faith and good life, there is also great want of good instruction for the amendmēt of both the same: & wheras yet the blindnes or malice of some mē is so great, that the very same meanes leaft by Christe and his Apostles in the Church for that end, they make so smal account of, that they both contemne, and condemne the same, & without al reason raile therat with full vncomely termes: it hath semed to many good and vertuous men right necessary, to set forth some such Treatise, wherein briefly is conteined bothe the right vse and ende of Shrift or Confession and also the due order that eche Christian man ought to kepe and obserue [a6] in the same. Whiche whoso shal duly peruse and examine, shall soone see, how litle reason or cause ther is, to make Confessiō a cloke or colour of any vice and lewednes, sith it is purposely ordeined for a meane and present Remedie against all vice and sinne.

There is no time nor place now, to entre into farther dispicions[3] with suche kind of persons, namely the same Argument being already

---

[2]Jane Dormer, Duchess of Feria (1538-1612), was during her early life a member of the household of Princess Mary and a play-fellow of Edward VI, whose tutor was Jane's maternal grandfather. A strong friendship grew up between Jane and Princess Mary and remained intact until the death of the latter. At the advice of Mary, Jane married Don Gomez Suarez de Figueroa of Cordova, Count of Feria, in 1558. In May of 1559, at Jane's insistence, the Count asked Queen Elizabeth if he might retire to the Continent and take with him the Carthusian monks of Sheen, the nuns of St. Bridget of Sion, and the Dominican nuns of Dartford, among others, thereby saving many religious from the persecution that was to follow very soon. Elizabeth agreed and the Count and his party left England. In July of 1559, Jane followed her husband to the Continent after paying her farewell to the Queen. Her reception on the Continent was warm and cordial. At Mechlin, she was delivered of her first son, Lorenzo, in September of 1559. The next spring the Countess proceeded to Spain to join her husband. They were in constant correspondence with their persecuted Catholic friends in England, but never did they openly break with Elizabeth. In 1571, Jane's husband died, after having been appointed Governor of the Low Countries. At least four Popes corresponded with the Countess: Gregory XIII, Sixtus V, Clement VIII, and Paul V. Catholics who fled England for Spain were received warmly by her and frequently provided for. Her generosity to convents and monasteries was well-known. When she died at Madrid in 1612, her piety and religious zeal were recognized by her contemporaries as exceptional (*D. N. B.*, V, 1150-1152).

[3]*dispicion,* examination or discussion

handled by diuers excellent great Clerkes, bothe in Latin, and in English also.

Only this I had further to warne the Reader, that hauing trãs-lated this Treatise into our owne Language, and being exhorted to set foorth the same for the better information of all sortes in this point: it seemed also very expediente, to adde therevnto certaine other godly [a6ᵛ] Instructions, Meditations, & Praiers seruing all to the same purpose: that is, for the auoyding of sinne, and purchasing of vertue, in the exercise whereof doth consist the whole life of the true beleeuer and folower of Christ. And this to be, and euer to haue bene the Doctrine and practise of the knowen Catholique Churche, not onely these present times, but al times and ages euen from Christe and his Apostles all along, haue & do most manifestly testifie & shew.

[Here follows an explanation of confession, the necessary pre-requisites, the manner of confessing, etc., Sigs. a7ʳ-b12ᵛ.]

[b12ᵛ]

The second Point.
Of the examining of our conscience
thriugh the ten cōmaundements
of God, and of the vnderstanding
of them.

Al be it that the ten Commaũdements of our Lord be such, that some do forbid vs the euil, & some do commaund vs the good: yet for al that, eche Christian mã ought [c] to know, that eche one of the Commaundementes doth both these two al at once: that is to saie, forbid vice, and commaund the vertue that is contrary to the same vice. As for example: in the first Cōmaundement writen in Exodus, we are forbid to make any Idolles, or to worship them: and so it semeth, that the abhominable* vice of Idolatrie is there for-bidden: how be it, it is withal no lesse charged vnto vs, to honour, woorship, and loue one only God aboue al things: the which are vertues contrary vnto Idolatrie. Likewise in the seuenth Com-maundement, God forbiddeth theft, and consequently he commaund-eth the contrary vertue, which is liberalitie and free giuing vnto them that are in necessitie. In the fourth, he commaundeth ex-pressely, that we honour our Parentes and Su-[cᵛ]periours: where it

---

*abhominable] *ed.;* abhomiuable

is cōsequently to be vnderstood, that the contrarie vice is forbidden vs, which is, to dishonor & disobey them. And so in al the other cōmaūdementes the like is found: for that there is not one emong them al that commaundeth, but that the same forbiddeth also, nor any one that forbiddeth, but it also commaundeth.

And therfor the penitēt person shal do wel, to kepe this order in running them ouer & in examining of his cōscience, that he haue regarde in eche Commaundement both to the one and to the other. For so is the perfection of the Law of God to be vnderstood, that we know how eche precept & cōmaundement is fulfilled, and how it is broken, & what is therein commaunded, and what forbidden: forasmuch as the office & duety of the seruant of God doth con-[c2]sist, not in the onely auoiding to do yl, but (as the Prophet Dauid saith) in doing good also to our neighbours when occasion requireth.   **Psal. 36.**

[Here follows a review of the first five commandments, Sigs. c2^r-c8^v.]

[c8^v]

The sixth and ninth Com-
maundement.

[c9] Thou shalt not committe adulterie, nor any fornicatiō, nor desire any other mans wife, nor haue any carnal accesse or behauiour vnto her.

What is commaunded in this
Precept.

To be chaste, to be moderate and sober in eating and drinking, honest in wordes and al outward gestures, to weare our clothes and apparel in al decent, sad & graue wise, without wanton deuises, and honestie, according to our degree and calling. We are also here commaunded, to procure and seeke al the meanes & remedies that we can, whereby to driue away and auoid the foule sinne of leacherie, & of al vncleane & beastly vice, the which remedies are these that folow.

[c9^v]

The remedies against leacherie and
vncleannes, and for the better
keping of the sixth Com-
maundement.

The first meane & remedie is to refraine & put out of our mindes al foule and vncleane thoughtes & imaginations: to chasten & exercise the bodie with labours & painful things, as fastings, watchings, visiting of holy places, praying, disciplines that is to wit, afflicting & putting the bodie to some sensible paine, reading of good bokes, & with exāples & liues of Saintes & holy men & wemen: to flee idlenes, & al yl occasions, & lewd wanton cōpanies & conuersations: and specially to vse cōtinual meditation & thinking on four things: to wit, death, domes-daie & last iudgement, hel & heauen: and last of al, with the mortifiyng of our owne desires and wil.

[c10]

What is forbidden in this Commaundement, and how it is broken.

This Commaundement is broken, in hauing any carnal accesse and copulation, how so euer it be, saue with a mans owne wife. And here the partie penitent in his confession must expresse, in what wise he hath offended in this sinne of leacherie, in al that he shal find himself guiltie and faultie against this Commaundement. And though he may not name any person particulerly with whom he hath sinned, yet he must particularly declare, with what maner of persons he hath offended our Lord. For the qualitie of the persons doth alter the nature of the sinne: as if it be with one that is a cōmon woman, or otherwise a harlot who is not assured by cōtract to any other mā [c10ᵛ]it is called Simplex fornicatio, single fornication: if with a Virgin or maiden, it is deflouring: if with a maried wife, or an espoused woman, it is adulterie: if it be done with force & violence, it is rape: if with any of our kinne within the fourth degree of consanguinitie or alliance, it is called Incest: if with any that is religious, or in a halowed place, it is sacrilege: if it be with a beast in any maner of wise, it is called the sinne of bestialitie or beastlines.

Also a man sinneth against this Commaundement in any accessories that go before, or go together with it, or ensue vpon suche actes: as, in beholding and casting of wanton lookes, in touching and wanton handling in any maner of wise, in sending messages and messengers to & fro, or letters, giftes, presentes, tokens, and suche [c11] like inticementes, as apparel, or any thing longing thereto, or in the wearing and vsing of his owne clothes and garmentes to procure wanton affection, in minstrelsie, songs, swete fauours and odours, or any like inuentions of amorours deuises, that are but allurementes tending al to suche carnal delights and pleasures.

Againe, this Commaundement is broken in misse-vsing a mannes owne wife by vnhonest conuersation with her, or committing any thing against the due order of nature, or by vsing her any waie perilousely while shee is with childe, or within the time of her natural and monthly course, or on high Feastes and Fasting daies.

Againe, in making any contract of Matrimonie, or in making and celebrating Mariage against the Orders and Lawes [c11ᵛ] of the Churche, or against the Decrees and Preceptes of our Bishops and Pastours. Item by ouermuch eating and drinking for such fleshly purpose, or by eating of meates or taking of things that prouoke and stirre vp the bodie to such fleshly motions. Finally in leading or keping companie with any person to any such act, or giuing counsell, or dissembling & holding our peace, or not letting & staying the same by any meane we cā, or helping toward any of al that aforesaid by dede, worde, or by any signes: by holding suche persons knowen in house to that ende, as brokers or baudes: by holding our selues & our minds long with delectation in any like thoughtes, or consenting with our wil to the same, & (to conclude) in al maner of dishonestie, and vncleannes of fleshly lust and appetite, [c12] or any thing longing thervnto, this Commaundement is violated and broken.

[Here follows an examination of conscience on the seventh and tenth commandments, Sigs. c12ʳ-d4ʳ; on the commandments of the Church, Sigs. d4ʳ-d8ᵛ; on the seven deadly sins, Sigs. d8ᵛ-e9ʳ. Next is a treatise on receiving the Holy Eucharist, Sigs. e9ᵛ [woodcut]-f12ᵛ. Hereafter follow prayers of St. Thomas More in English and Latin, Sigs. g1ʳ-k2ʳ, and "The Golden Litany" in English, Sigs. k2ᵛ-k12ᵛ.]

XIX.

⸿ A breefe Di-
rectory, and playne way
howe to say the Rosary
of our blessed Lady:
With Meditations for
such as are not exer-
cised therein.
Wherevnto are adioy-
ned the prayers of S.
Bryget, with
others.
Bruges Flandrorum
Excudebat Hu. Holost,
1576.[1]
[I. M.[2]]

[❡ ii]

⸿ To his deare and
weldisposed Sister, A. M.[3] encrease of grace, with perseuerance in the fayth
of Christe.

The talke which we had together (moste deare and welbeloued Sister) the day before I tooke my iourney to come into these countreis, haue not bin, neither are of me forgotten, and amōng al other your request concerning the Rosary of our Lady. Which re-[❡ ii[v]] quest want both of yeres and knowledge woulde not permit me to fulfill: but after I had bene here a whyle, I gat acquaintance of one, who for vertue and good life is accounted among the cheefe, to him vpon a time I declared what I had promised you, and likewise my vnability in performing it, beseching him for Gods cause to take a litle paynes in the matter, whom I founde as ready to satisfie my

---

[1]Init. I. M. Imprint false; pr. [London, William Carter and John Lion.] See Allison and Rogers, "Review of *Elizabethan Recusant Prose, 1559-1582,* by A. C. Southern," *Library,* VI (1951), 49-50 for further bibliographical information. *STC* 17136. Allison and Rogers, II, Entry 488. For an interesting criticism of the work, see Southern (pp. 214-216).

[2]I. M. is probably John Mitchell. For bibliographical notes on John Mitchell, see p. 139, n. 2.

[3]A. M., the sister of I. M., is unidentified.

request, as I was to de-[❧ iii] maunde him. When it was by him
finished, and I somewhat busied in copying the same to be sent vnto
you, by chance came into my chamber my cosen and freende I. Noil,[4]
who perswaded me to leaue off writing, and promised to procure
it to be Printed, for I haue (sayd he) a fit thing to be ioyned
thervnto, which was deliuered me by a good Gentlewoman, with
earnest request to haue it printed. Wherto I willingly cō-[❧ iiiᵛ]
sented, for in my selfe I perceiue the great discommoditie of ignorance, which causeth me to labour all that I may, to pleasure suche
as are like vnto my self (I meane in ignorance) And seeing my
Cosen hath caused it to be printed, although it be not so exactly
done, I confesse, as you would desire, yet accept it, I pray you, for
the Auctor within three or foure dayes after he had deliuered mee
the copie thereof, tooke his [❧ iiii] iourney into Italie, not thinking
that I would publish it.

I consented to haue it printed, for that I knowe there be many
good women in Englande that honour our Lady, but good bookes to
stirre vp deuotion in them are scarse: also I desire and hope to haue
prayers of them, into whose hands it shal happē to come: Desiring
God to geue you of his grace, that you may goe forward in his
seruice as you haue begun. I craue of you, [❧ iiiiᵛ] and al other into
whose handes this shal happen to come, that you wil in your prayers
remember mee. From the Englishe Charter house in Bridges,[5] the
vigil of the Assumption of our Lady. 1576.

Your brother
I. M.

[Here follow brief meditations on the first two joyful mysteries
of the Rosary, Sigs. Aiʳ-Aiiiᵛ.]

[Aiiiᵛ] Next you haue to consider, that our Lady dwelling in
Nazareth, and hauing prouided all thinges necessary in her owne
house according to her habilitie, to lay her great bealy in, she was
enforced vpon a soden to take her iorney to Bethlehem, by reason of

---

[4]Allison and Rogers suggest that I. Noil is a thin disguise for John Lion,
an English bookseller and printer, about whom very little is known, except
that he was very militant in the Catholic cause. In 1578, Lion fled England,
probably because of his association with William Carter, who in that year
printed Gregory Martin's *A Treatise of Schisme* (*STC* 17508) and was subsequently imprisoned. Lion was at Cambrai, and Southern notes that on
February 15, 1578, Lion was in Douay (p. 344). Little information is available
about his life after this time (*Library*, IV, 49-50).
[5]Bridges is Bruges.

a commaundemente that came from the Emperour, that euery one should pay their [Aiiii] tribute by a certayne day in the Towne where they were borne. Ioseph therefore and our Lady, hasting them selues to Bethlehem, when they came there, our Ladies time beeing come for her deliuery, beholde ther was no place in the towne for her & her sweete Sonne in anye Inne, the Towne was so full of people, the lodginges were all taken vp. And therefore was the Mother of God [Aiiii^v] enforced to turne into an Oxe stall that stoode by the high way, no better then an houel or cotage, and there brought foorth that blessed babe her deare Sonne, betweene an Oxe & an Asse, lapping him in suche poore cloutes as she had, & layde him in the maunger. Where ye may beholde our Lady borowing a little hay from the sely Asse, to lay her child vppon. And here ye maye consider with your selfe the [Av] great goodnes of God, that for his onely sonne prouided nothing that the world accompted needful, not housrome, not chāber, not chimney, not fyre, not bolster nor pillowe to lye vpon: and yet hath sent vs al these things with many moe, not onely to serue our necessities, but also to satisfie our vanities, As fine chābers right costly hanged, fayre bedstedes curiously carued, soft beds, not onely of fethers, but of [Av^v] downe also: Couerlets and counterpoyntes ful of silke, and testers with curtens richely wroughte and imbrodred, ful of al vanity and superfluitie. And yet scant cōtent our selues therwith: or if we be content, we be neuer the more thankefull vnto God, neither can we easily abyde to beholde or thinke vppon poore Christe lying in the maunger. Who in this poore estate not regarded of men, with great [Avi] ioy is proclaymed of the angels vnto the Shepheards singing with marueylous melodie, Glory be to God on high, & in earth peace to men of good wyl. Then walk againe with the shepheardes, and beholde poore Christ in the Crib, fal down with the Shepheardes and worshippe him that was borne that day thy sauiour Christ our Lorde. And considering how ioyful his mother was of al these, say the [Avi^v] thirde *Pater noster* and ten *Aues*.

[Here follow meditations on the remaining two joyful mysteries, the five sorrowful mysteries, and the five glorious mysteries, Sigs. Avi^v-Dvii^v, which are followed by a brief treatise on the Passion taken from St. Bonaventure and an exhortation to penance, Sigs. Dviii^r-Eiiii^v. Hereafter follows an insert, consisting of the "Fifteen Oos" of St. Bridget and other prayers, Sigs. Ai^r-Ciiii^v.]

XX.

Instrvctions and
Advertisements,
How to Meditate the
Misteries of the Rosarie of the most
holy Virgin Mary.
Written in Italian by the Reuerend Father
Gaspar Loarte D. of Diuinitie of the So-
cietie of Iesvs. And newly trans-
lated into English.

[Woodcut of Angels and the letters IHS, below which is the Latin inscription *Non nobis Domine, non nobis, sed Nomini tuo da gloriam.*][1]

[trans. John Fen[2]]

[Preceding the titlepage, Sig. i⸀ contains a woodcut of the Christ Child emerging from a heart. Sig. ii⸀ is blank.]

[iij]

The Avthovr
to the deuout
Reader.

Albeit the profite and importance of holye prayer, and meditation of heauenly thinges, hath not bene so wel vnderstoode heretofore,

---

[1] n.p.d. [1579.] Pr. [London, William Carter.] Allison and Rogers, I, Entry 469. *STC* 16646.

This work is a translation of Gaspar Loarte's *Instrutione e avvertimenti per meditar i misterii del Rosario, della Santissima Vergine Madre* (Rome, 1573) (De Backer, II, 770).

For a bibliographical note on Loarte, see p. 56, n. 1.

[2] John Fen or Fenn (d. 1615) is generally recognized as the translator of this work. Fen was a native of Montacute, near Wells, in Somersetshire. In 1550, he entered New College, Oxford, as a probationer, and 1552 he was appointed a fellow and began studying civil law. At the ascendency of Queen Mary, Fen was appointed Headmaster at Bury St. Edmunds, Suffolk, where his reputation as a teacher was acclaimed. During the early years of Elizabeth's reign, however, he lost both his teaching position and his perpetual fellowship. Shortly after this personal tragedy, Fen passed over to Flanders and later proceeded to Rome, where, after studying theology, he was ordained a priest. For sometime he was the confessor to the English Augustinian nuns at Louvain, employing his leisure time for writing and translating. Fen's younger brother James was a martyr for the Catholic cause, and his brother Robert, also a priest, was very active in the English mission (Gillow, II, 244-246).

For a criticism of Fen's work, see Southern (pp. 216-219).

yet is it nowe through Gods good grace so much the better knowen, as it is more vsed. And amongst other thinges which they are wont and may meditate that geue them-selues to this holye exercise, the deuotion of the holy Rosarie is one that is very commendable, very easie, and almost exercised of eche one; wherein the most highe and diuine misteries are conteined: especially being instituted by the glorious Patriarch S. Dominike, who receaued it by reuelation of our Lady, as his Religion doth witnes and ob-[iijᵛ]serue. And hauing in like maner bene confirmed by many Popes, and enriched with many graces, prerogatiues, and indulgences; namely, by Pius Quintus³ of holy memorie, as appereth by the authentical priuiledges which the Fathers of the saide Religiō haue in Rome, Bononia, Naples, and other places. Howbeit, because al knowe not how to meditate these Misteries (as it bohoueth) and by this lacke they loose a great part of the fruit which might wel be gathered thereby, for their helpe this present Treatıse hath bene composed; wherin is shewed, in what maner they ought to meditate with greatest profite and consolatiō of their soules. And that thou, welbeloued Reader, maiest the better vnderstande, howe fruitful this holy deuotion is to euery sort of people, and howe it behoueth thee to exercise thy selfe therin, thou maiest reade the Chapter folowing [iiij] wherein this matter is so amply intreated of, as I hope thou wilt not grudge to read the rest of the booke, meaning to embrace this so holy an exercise, which thou maiest assuredly beleeue, shal-be more profitable and pleasaunt, then painful and yrksome to thee.

[A woodcut of the Blessed Virgin and Child with Latin inscription appears on Sig. iiijᵛ.]

---

³Pius V (1504-1572) was a Dominican priest before being elected Pope in 1566. He is particularly known for his zeal in effecting a spiritual rejuvenation in the Church. It was he who excommunicated Elizabeth in the famous Papal Bull *Regnans in Excelsis* (1570). His pontificate was marked by continual struggles with the Protestants and Turks. In honor of the Battle of Lepanto (Oct. 7, 1571) in which the Turks were given a blow from which they never recovered, Pius V instituted the Feast of the Rosary, which was to be observed on the first Sunday of October. He was canonized in 1712 (*Catholic Encyclopedia*, XII, 130-131).

The most complete listing of indulgences attached to the Rosary, especially those granted by Pope Pius V, can be found in Henry Garnet's *The Societie of the Rosary* (pp. 30-34).

The Avthovrs
Preface touching the great profite and vtilitie
that may be gathered by meditating vpon the
life of our Sauiour Iesus Christe; and in what
maner we ought to meditate the misteries of the
Rosarie (which are intreated of in this
Treatise) and conteine in them the
principal part of this most
holye life.

Like as the Sonn of God vouchsafed to come downe from heauen
to earth, and to make himselfe man for the wel-fare and life of man,
according to that the selfe same word incarnate *a* saith; *I am come*
*that men may haue life, and that they may haue it plentifully:** euen
so, for the conseruation of this life of grace, and spiritual consolation of man, one of the thinges that maie moste chieflie helpe him
herein, is the often meditating of the life of the saide worde incarnate *Iesus Christe* our Sauiour, and the imitation of his most
meruailous [Ajᵛ] examples; sith, the celestial Father hauing
geuen him to the world for a *a* light, for a guide, and for a
Schoolemaster and teacher of men; and the Sonne him-selfe assuring
vs, that *b* al, whatsoeuer he did, was done to geue vs an example,
that we should do the same; what should such doo, as could not
enioy his visible presence here in earth? how should they be illuminated, guided, and instructed of him, if they had not this remedie of
the meditation of his moste holye life? by means wherof, he euen at
this day illuminateth, guideth, and teacheth vs, as though he were
present, with that he earst did (wandring corporally in this world)
speake, worke, endure, and teache.

It behoveth therfore, that this meditatiõ serue vs as a mirror,
wherin, by eftsons looking & taking view, we may with the eies of our
soule see that, which with the eyes of our bo-[Aij]die we neither
could nor can see; and according to it direct and frame our life, sith
a al Iesus Christe his actions were done for our institution and instruction; yea, as S. Iohn the Apostle *b* saith: *Who so saith that he*
dwelleth in Iesus Christe, that is to say, that he is a member and
seruant of Iesus Christe, *ought to walke as he hath walked.* As if he
had saide: Who-soeuer saith, that he is a member of Iesus Christ,
must be lowlye *c* and meeke, as Iesus Christ was; must contemne al

a. Ioh. 10. b.
Gal. 4. a.
1. Petr. 2.d.

a. Luc. 2. e.
Ioh. 1. a. 3. e.
8. b. 12. f.
Act. 13. g.
b. 1. Ioh. 1. a.
2. b.
Ioh. 13. b.
1. Petr. 2. d.

a. Rom. 15[4]
<·>

b. 1. Ioh. 2.
<·>

C. Mat. 11. d.

---

[4]The marginal glosses in this work are frequently illegible.
**plentifully*] ed.; *plentilully*

delightes, honours, and woorshipp of this worlde, as he did, seeking
in al things the only glorie of God, *d* & not regarding in any thing
his owne peculier estimation; he must loue frendes and *e* foes, doo
iniurie to none, and if any be done to him, *f* bear it patiently; desire
rather to serue others, thē to be *g* serued him self. To be short, he
must so loue his neighbour, *h* as if need require at any time, he be
ready to lose his life for his welfare and saluation.

[Aij*v*] Howe is it then possible for a true Christian to doo these
and so manie mo things as be necessarie to be done, to imitate Iesus
Christ a-right, but if he knowe that Iesus Christ him-selfe did first
practise and doo them moste exactly? and howe shal he wot them,
but by eftsons meditating his life, & the liuely & perfect examples,
which of such like workes he left vs? and howe may a man learne
the lessons of charitie, patience, pouertie, obedience, and of al other
vertues, but if he knowe the life of the Lorde of al vertues? and
therfore, as saith glorious S. Bernard: *a* In vaine trauaileth he to
attain vertues, that hopeth by anie other meanes then by the Lord
of al *b* vertues to attain them; whose doctrine is a nurcerie of
prudence; his mercie a worke of Iustice; his life a mirrour of temperance; his death a liuely paterne of prowes. Thou seest, Reader,
by this holye Doctour his [Aiij]wordes, confirmed by the testimonie
of so manie other famous men, howe necessary the continual meditation of Christes most holie life is, to the obteining of such vertues
as be needful for al those that couet to participate of the true and
euerlasting life.

[This theme, the value of meditation, continues, Sigs. Aiij*r*-Av*v*.]

[Avi] Howbeit, forasmuch as it is not long agone, that being commaunded by my superiors, I made a smal Treatise that was published abroade, touching the matter of the Passiō,[5] wherin were
certaine instructions and aduertisementes geuen, both of the principal pointes therof, and in what maner they were to be meditated;
mine intent was in this Treatise (being in like maner commaunded
me) to haue principally intreated of such other misteries of this
most holy life, as had not beene spoken of in the other Treatise.
Notwithstanding, whē I afterwardes had perceaued, how to write al
that might be gathered out of the holy Gospels touching the life,
preaching, and miracles of our Lord, would be a veri long thing,
and require a iust volume, I determined with my selfe to write onely

d. Ioh. 7. e.
8. g.
e. Mat. 5. g.
f. Luc. 6. d.
1. Pet. 2. d.
g. Mat. 20. d.
h. Mar. 10. g.

a. Ber. sub.
finē serm.
22. in Can.
b. Ps. 23. b.
79. 83. 88.

---

[5]*The godly garden of Gethsemani* (c. 1576) Entry XI in this anthology.

vpō the misteries of the Rosarie of the moste blessed virgin Mary;
sithens, besides that it [Avi^v] is so godly, renowned, and approued,
a deuotiō as is aboue-said in the Prologue; therein, in my fancie, are
the chief points of the life of Christ cōteined, frō the time of his
incarnatiō, vntil the sending downe of the holy Ghost; in-somuch as,
who-soeuer he be that shal meditate these wel, may assure him-selfe
to haue meditated the greater and the more principal part of his
most sacred life.

This is the thing therefore, my derelye beloued brother, which I
here present vnto thee; to wit, the meditations of the misteries of
the aforesaide Rosarie, whereof eche one, (as was done in the other
meditations of the Passion) is distinguished into three pointes, as-
wel for the perfectiō *a* and deuotion of this number, as also, that eche
one may meditate them more amply, and with lesse confusiō.

*Aug. ca. 16.
lib. 2. de
doct. Chris.
to. 3. & li.
2. q. euan.
cap. 6. to 4.
& in psal.
6. tom. 8*

But because the pointes which I noted in the other meditations
of the [Avii] sacred Passion were no whitt amplified and dilated, but
onely a bare text set downe of the matters that were to be meditated
vpon (the which was done, supposing that eche one would themselues, according to their deuotion haue dilated and amplified the
same) vnderstanding since, that if some doo make this discourse and
dilatatiō, yet, al for lack of capacitie doo it not; for this cause haue I
done mine indeuour in this booke, to content both th'one and
th'other; acknowledging my selfe, as S. Paule *a* saith, to be indebted
both to the learned and the ignorāt. For the lerned therfore, I haue
thought good, after a text wise, first to set downe that which they
maye meditate vpon in euerye misterie, leauing eche one to pause
therein, and to dilate the same, according to their capacitie and
deuotion: nowe for the ignorant, that knowe not howe to doo this,
without some [Avii^v] further helpe, I haue shewed thē the maner,
how to interteine thē-selues, and to discourse vpon eche point,
which soeuer they may thinke good to meditate vpon; out of which
maner of amplification they may gather these commodities folowing.

a. Rom. 1. b.

1. First, they shal better vnderstand the historye of that point,
whereon they purpose to meditate.

2. They maye conceaue the document or example, which sometimes is intermedled for their instruction.

3. They maye learne, howe otherwhiles to aske our Sauiour suche thinges, as the point whereon they meditate, may most fitly minister occasiō of; other-whiles to yeeld thanks for such graces and mercies as they maye be put in minde to haue beene done vnto them, and to this purpose may they apply the vocal prayer set downe at the end of euery misterye.

4. They maye with the reading of [Aviii] these amplifications, helpe thē-selues to auoide the distractions and wandring of minde, which other-whiles, yea, eftsons, happeth in time of meditation.

5. The Apostrophes and familier speeches which I haue nowe and thē intermedled in this methode and maner of dilatation, may serue to excite and kindle deuotion, being weake or wāting, as happeth many times to be.

6. After they haue read more then once the foresaid maner of amplifications vpon eche point, they shal perceaue them-selues so sufficiently instructed, as that of them-selues they may eyther alto-gether, or in part, be able to amplifie such articles as they are minded to meditate vpon; and when they found nothing suggested of their owne brayne and peculier deuotion, yet maye the readinge of these points that are here propoūded thē, with their amplificatiōs wel and [Aviiiᵛ] leisurly considered, serue for a sufficient meditation, whiles nothing els were graunted them. And of these, and such like fruites which the simple sort may suck and gather out of the fore-saide amplifications, the learned may in like wise helpe them selues ther-withal at some times, whē best shal like them; so that, as-wel to th'one as th'other they shal not be unprofitable.

Moreouer, this maner of distinguishing and entertaining a mans selfe vpon euerie article, may serue for al sortes of people; for who so mindeth to discourse vpō al the three pointes of the misterie, whereon he meditateth, wel may he so doo; and who fancied not to pause in eche point so long time, may make choise of that point that shalt best like him; seruing his turne, if he thinke good, with the meditating of one onely point, and the amplification therof, [Bj] if he list; which he may right easilye finde out, seing euerye point is so plainly distinguished a-part, as one hangeth not of an-other, but ech one is absolute in his owne conclusion. I thinke it good besides, to aduertise thee in this place, that the instructions which I haue geuen thee in the 6. 8. and 11. Chapters of, The exercise of a Christian life;[6] as also those aduises that I set thee downe in the Tretise I wrote of the meditation of the Passion, at the ende of the instructiō, may greatly helpe thee to the better meditating of these misteries; al the which documentes I here omitt for breuitie sake, referring thee onely to the foresaide places in the bookes aboue especified.

Finally, I thinke it meete to aduertise thee, that for-somuch as in the institution of the Rosarie it is ordeined that tenn *Aue Maries* and one *Pater noster* be recited vppon euery misterie, [Bjᵛ] these maye be saide in three sundrye maners. The first is, to recite them before thou enter into thy meditation. The second is, to say them in the very time of meditation. The third is, to saye them after a man hath finished his meditation. And this last way is, in mine opinion, the best, sith the soule doth commonly after meditation finde it self more supple, and better disposed to praye with attention and deuotion. Yet meane I not hereby to make a lawe, but that eche one may say them, at such time as best shal like them.

These particularities haue I thought good to touche, minding thereby to helpe nouices, and such as are smallye acquainted with this exercise, a labor that I haue willingly laide my hands to, as-wel, for that it was appointed me by those that haue authoritie to commaund me, as also, in regarde of the hope I haue conceued that it shal [Bij] benefite the brethren of our companie, for whose profite and commoditie, this pamphlet was principallye composed: whom I exhort and pray as earnestly as I can, to geue them selues diligently to this holy exercise of meditation, considering that for so smal paine they are promised so great a gaine, and so singuler consolation, as I am persuaded al those shalbe able to testifie, who with a willing and feruent desire shal for some time geue themselues to assaye and proue the same: For verily doo I hope, that such shal by experience finde his life to be the guide of their life, who is the way, *a* the truth, and the life; to whom, with the Father and the holy Ghost be eternal and euerlasting glory. Amen.

a. Ioh. 14. <.>

[Totivs Libri Svmma (Sig. Bijᵛ) and blank page (Sig. Biijʳ). Here follow the first two joyful mysteries, each illustrated with an appropriate woodcut, Sigs. Biijᵛ-Ciiijʳ. Sig. Ciiijᵛ is a woodcut of the Nativity.]

---

[6]This work is Entry I in this anthology.

[Cv]

The Third Ioyfvl
Misterie is of the Natiuitie of Iesus
Christe our Lord, whervpon thou maiest
meditate these pointes folowing.

The first is, howe our Ladye meaning to obey the Emperour
Caesar Augustus his proclamation, went frō Nazareth to Bethleem,
a where not finding any conuenient lodging, she withdrewe her selfe
into the publike and common Inne, or (if you thinke good) into the
houel and shoud that was there made with bowes for poore folkes.

a. Luc. 2. a.

Secondly, consider howe the houre of the glorious child-birth of
the most sacred mother being come, she brought forth the Sauiour
of the world, and with a wonderful great reuerence adored him,
swaddled him vp in suche poore cloutes as she had, and laide him in
a manger.

Thirdly, consider the Angels songes, b and the ioye and triumph
they made in this most happy child-birth, wherof one announced the
same to the Sheppardes that in that coast did watche ouer their
flocks; who speedily came to see and adore this celestial Infant.

b. Luc. 2. b.

[Cvᵛ] Tovching the first point, thou maiest amplifie thy meditation,
by weighing the circumstaunces that happen in the voiage which our
Lady vndertooke; wherby is plainly shewed, what pains and trouble
she endured therein, albeit, what-soeuer it was, she passed it ouer
with exceeding patience. First, the sharpnes of the season did
greatly augment her annoyes, sith this iorney was performed in the
verye hart of winter, when as we see it is verye painful trauailing.
Secondly, her pouertie, which forced her to suffer manye discom-
modities, especially, being great with childe, and so tender and delicate as she was. Thirdly, the lack of lodging, which could not be
prouided her in al the whole Citie of Bethleem, albeit (wel may we
beleue) that good Ioseph tooke great paines in seeking it very diligentlye; and howe seing them-selues thus refused, [Cvi] it coulde
not be, but that they felt great shame and confusion. O what a
soueraine solace and singuler cōfort should this be for poore folkes
that are in this world distressed, despised, and forsakē, if they considered, how the most woorthy, noble, and moste holy creatures,
which ought to haue been more honored & reuerēced then al the

whole world again (to witt, the Queene of heuen, and her most blessed Infant) were the most distressed, annoyed, and pained of al others.

Thov maiest pause in the second point, beholding with thy spiritual eyes, in what state the most blessed virgin found her-selfe the day of her most sacred deliueraunce; and here shalt thou see in her so vertuous a disposition, so holye a deuotion, so graue a modestie, so singuler a beautie, so great an eleuation of spirite in God, as no mans tonge can possiblye declare it.

[Cvi^v] Thou shalt finde, howe in counterchange of griefes *a* which other women feele in child-birth, she felt a strange and ineffable solace, a singuler ioy and diuine consolation; and being there-with wholly rapt and eleuate, the celestial bridegrome issued miraculously out of her wombe, as out of a most pretious *b* bride-chāber, without any alteration or detriment at al to her most perfect virginitie. O virgin-mother, and mother-virgin; A priuiledge neuer graunted to any other creature! O diuine excellencie, and dignitie due to thee alone, to be the mother of God, and mother of thine owne Father and *c* Creator! Who can possibly conceue what thy heart felt, when with thy bodily eyes thou beheldest the Prince of heauen lying naked in earth; and him shiuering for colde, who doth clothe and warme al other creatures? O with what reuerēce diddest thou prostrate [Cvii]thy selfe, to adore that infinite Maiestie, masked vnder the vaile of so great distresse and miserie! Oh, with what compassion diddest thou associate with thy teares those, which thy deere yonge sonne shed, feeling his so great annoiances! Oh, with what cordial loue endeuouredst thou to lul and lapp him vp in such poore swaddling cloutes as thou haddest, geuing him thy sacred brestes to suck vpon, which were at that time miraculouslye replenished with milke! Matters sufficient to melt anye flintie heart that would with leisure ponder and discusse them.

The Meditation of the thirde point wil furnish thee of fitt matter to moue compassion, if thou consider, howe this moste mightie monarche, this King *a* of al kinges, he whom neither the heauens nor earth can holde and comprehende, hath in such wise debased, humbled, and [Cvii^v]throwen him-selfe downe in a harde manger vpon a litle haye; he, whom the Angels doo adore, and in whose presence the powers of heauen doo quake againe, lieth quaking himself for colde betwixt two brute beastes. O diuine darling, what

a. Gen. 3. c.

b. Aug. initio. tract. 1. in Ioh. to. 9.

c. P sa. 18. a. Aug. in principio cap. 5. li. 2. de Synab. ad Catech. Tom. 9.

a. Coll. 2. b. 1. Tim. 6. c. Apoc. 17. d. & .19. c.

a. Ps. 23. b.
Ad. Tit. 2. d.
b. 2. Re. 6. a.
1. Par. 13. b.
c. Ioh. 1. a.

meaneth this geere? what humilitie and basenes is this, O Soueraine *a* King of glorye? what hast thou to doo with the crib, thou that hast thy throne aboue the *b* Cherubins? how art thou made thus dombe, O *c* eternal worde of the Father? whye weepest and wailest in such sort, thou, that art the ioye of al the holy Angels? verily, thou haste masked thy diuine nature with our humane nature, to be the King and Sauiour of Israel, and of the vniuersal world. The desire which thou hast to redeeme vs, moueth thee to doo these strange matters; the loue which made thee wel-care descend frō

a. Ber. ser. 3.
in Natius.
Domini.

heuē for our wal-fare, causeth thee nowe [Cviii]to be borne, and to *a* cloake, thy puissance with such penurie and extreme want of al thinges, that we shoulde thereby learne to meeke and humble our selues, and to detest al pride, al pamperinges and delicacies of the fleshe, louing the lowlines, the penance, and the pouertie, which thou diddest chuse and teach vs, and wouldest for this cause haue thy

b. Luc. 2. b.

natiuitie announced *b* to poore Sheppardes, of whom thou wast visited and adored, the which their visitation and adoration we ought attentiuely to ponder, and diligently to imitate.

[Cviii^v]   A Prayer.

What tongue can woorthely tel, O most woorthye Queene of Angels, the ineffable ioy and exultation which thou wert seased with in thy most sacred and virginal child-birth? When thou sawest the Redeemer of the worlde borne of thee, and adoring him with great reuerēce, didst swaddle him vp in poore cloutes, and laide him in a manger, where he was announced of the Angels, & visited of poore shepperds: I beseech thee, O most happy mother, by this his most holy natiuitie, that seing he was borne for vs, and geuen vnto vs, thou wilt obteine me of him, that he vouchsafe to be borne in my poore soule, with whom I maye be borne anewe, and leade henceforth such a new life, as maye continually be grateful to his diuine Maiestie. Amen.

[Here follow the remaining twelve mysteries with woodcuts, Sigs. Dj^r-Ovii^v. Then follow woodcuts and Latin litanies in honor of Mary, Sigs. Oviii^r-Qiii^r; directions for what one should do when he arises in the morning and retires at night, Sigs. Qiii^r-Qiiii^r; and the author's errata, Sig. Qiiii^v.]

XXI.

Instrvctions
for the ve of the beades,
conteining many matters of meditacion of mentall prayer, with
diuerse good aduises of ghostly
counsayle.
Where vnto is added a figure or forme of
the beades portrued in a Table.
Compiled by Iohn Bucke for the benefite of vnlearned. And Dedicated to the
honorable good Lady, Anne Lady
Hungarforde, sister to the Duchesse
of Ferria.

[Woodcut of Madonna surrounded by a rosary]
Imprinted at Lovain in the yere
of our Lordre. 1589.[1]

[The titlepage is followed by a woodcut of Mary and child; Sig.
Ai^r is blank and Sig Ai^v contains a coat of arms.]

[3] To the Richt Ver-
tuous Lady, Anne Lady Hun-
garfoorde, his honorable good
Maistres, Iohn Bucke Wisheth
al healthe.

For so muche as man borne in to this worlde haithe no long time
to liue Here, he being (as the Wyseman saithe) lent, not geuen to
life: And for that we must render an accompt, at the daye of Iudge-
mēt (before that dredefull Iudge, which is voyde of partialitie) not
onlie of woordes and woorkes, but of eache moment of time spent

---

[1]Pr. [Jan Maes.] Allison and Rogers, I, Entry 179. *STC* 4000.
John Bucke, the author, I have been unable to identify.
Anne Lady Hungarford was the daughter of Sir William Dormer of
Ascot and the sister of the Duchess of Feria. Her husband, Sir Walter Hungarford, in 1570 charged her with attempted murder and in 1560-68 accused her
of adultery. She was acquitted of these charges, and her husband was committed
to the Fleet for refusing to pay the court costs. In October of 1571, it is known
that she was living among the Catholics at Louvain. She fought vigorously
to keep her husband from disinheriting her children, one son and three
daughters. She died at Louvain in 1603 (*D. N. B.*, X, 260).

here, yea euen vnto the thoughtes of our hartes, euerie one in his
vocacion and degree: And for my part calling all this to the eyes of
my minde: seing also all my actions hitherto* to be verie base and
barrain in his sight, whiche is the true searcher of al thoughtes: I
began to think how I might employe my selfe in some woorke
acceptable to so bountifull and benigne a patrone, and lorde, as haith
[4] beside my creacion and redempcion, not onlie sanctified me and
preserued me from my infancie: but also brought me out of** that
darke Egiptiacal England, (the verie sea of heresie) and placed me
vnder so good and graciouse a ladie, in whom I dailie beholde
manie examples of true Religion, godlie*** fear, cōstant patience, and
Christian pietie. Therfore finding nothing more agreable to hys
diuine pleasure, than is the charitable trauail in mouing the deuociō
of others to the effectuall seruice of his Diuine Maiestie by prayer
and meditacion: and considering how great cōmoditie a litle direction in prayer may bring to the vnlearned and ignorāt, whose
weakenesse I wolde be glad anie waye to releue: I haue thought
**The first
parte of
this boo-
ke.**
good to put foorth suche spirituall exercises, as I my selfe haue
priuatlie vsed, with great comfort, in sayieng the Rosarie, Croune,
or Psalter of our blessed laidie the virgin Marie, vpon the beades.
And I haue also set doun sundry meditacions and consideracions to
**The se-
cōd part.**
be vsed otherwyse, touching aswel the passion of our Sauiour and
our redemption: as also the infinite benefites [5] and Graces most
plentifullie bestowed vpon euerie Christiā: to the ende that in thinking therof a good religiouse mynde may be more diligent and attentiue to note and marke what is sayd: more inflamed to deuocion:
and more moued with compunction and sorowe for synnes committed. And thies meditations a man may**** diuide in to seuen partes;
according to the dayes of the weeke: to the ende that a thankfull
hart Dailie beholding (as in a glasse) the bountifull guiftes of God
maye take occasion to hate synne, and to loue God so good a benefactor and patrone. And because many wel disposed parsones wolde
fayne walke accordīg to the wil of their lorde and Creator: yet doe
they wander astray by want of good instruction, rather than vpon
malice: I haue collected out of deuout authors certein lessons an

---

*hitherto] *ed.,* hithertho
**of] *ed.;* af
***godlie] *ed.;* goldie
****may] *ed.;* muy

directiōs sheweing, not onlie,* good meanes to auoyde synne, and
to frame the whole course of lyfe according to hys rule and commaundement, whiche sayeth; *Hoc fac, & viues.* Doe this, and thou
shault lyue: but also profitable signes and argumentes, whereby one
may** perceiue, [6] whether he standeth in the state of God his
grace and fauor, or no. Lastlie I haue added some rules to know
from whēce euell thoughtes do procede and meanes to auoyde them:
with a figure or portrature of the beades, conteining your Lady-
shippes vsuall Meditacion vpon them.

Thies with suche lyke being the sclēder fruit of my barrain wyt
hauing no better crop to put in to the barne, I haue published for
the benefit of the vnlearned, wiche can not skill of curiouse discourses
penned by great clerkes.

[Here continues, pp. 6-13, the dedication to her ladyship, praising
her vertuous life, comparing her to Paula in her charity, Job in her
patient suffering, and Lavinia in her kindness to the needy and
poor. The author assures her that her earthly afflictions are signs of
God's especial love for her since even the Blessed Virgin endured
great pain and trial.]

[14]   Certain Matters of
               Meditacion or mentall praeyer to be consi-
               *dered in reciting the Rosaire, Psalter, or****
               Croune of our Laidie the most blessed vir-
               gin Marie vpon the beades.

It is an auncient exercise of deuout Christianes in tyme of prayer,
and speciallie in the vse of the beades, to set befor the eyes of****
the Soule some conceit or Imaginacion of one or other matter conteined in the lyfe of our Sauiour, or of the blessed virgin Marie.*****
And this conceit well imprinted in mynde, wil kepe it from wauering
in the vain thoughtes,****** and will make it more attentiue and
hedefull: werby deuocion is soner kyndled: without whiche prayer
yeeldeth small fruit. Therfore when you are disposed to praey vpon
the beades: you may thynke vpon thre sortes of mysteries (wherof

---

*onlie] *ed.;* oulie
**may] *ed.;* muy
***or] *ed.;* ou
****of]*ed.;* oft
*****Marie] *ed.;* Matie
******thoughtes] *ed.;* thonghtes

fyue poinctes in every one are Ioyfull, fyue are dolorouse, and fyue
are gloriouse) in maner foloweing.

[Pages 15-18 contain the first two joyful mysteries.]

[18]   [Woodcut of the Nativity]

**The Na-
tiuitie of
Christ.**

3

The third Ioyefull mysterie is the natiuitie and byrthe of our
Sauiour. [19] Here thynk that thou seest swete Iesus new borne,
wrapped in poor clothes, layd in a cryb betwene two beastes in an
abiect place of a common Inne, for wāt of habilitie to hyre a better
lodging. And with this thought say the third *Pater noster,* and*
tenne *Aue Maries* foloweing attentiuelie and deuoutlie as before.

1

Then consider with what payn the most blessed virgin mirrour
of humilitie went from Nazareth to Bethleem in colde winter, yeeld-
ing obedience to the Emperour: And how the sonne of God wolde
before his byrthe shew obediēce with humilitie at all seasons: yea to
thy inferior if nede requyre or good occasiō.

2

Secondelie cōsider in what poor estate the lorde of all the worlde
wolde be borne and brought in to this worlde: and here learne to
cōtemne al worldlie pompe and vainglorious curiositie.

3

Thirdlie note here the loue of our Sauiour to mankynde, and
requite hym with loue again to the vttermost of all thy powers.

4

Fouerthlie beholde how the Angels from heauen preached to poor
Shepeheardes the comyng of our Redemer: And here learne [20] to
haue euer due regarde to the poor: and imitate thou those poor men
whiche with great zeale simplicitie and diligence sought our Sauiour,
to yeelde vnto hym all that honor and seruice which was requisit.
And after thies thoughtes prepare thy selfe to the fouerth Ioye
deuoutlie as before.

[Pages 20-37 contain the remaining twelve mysteries, followed
by seven short meditations on the benefits which God has bestowed
on mankind, pp. 38-49; a short meditation on the Passion, pp. 49-
52; a treatise on three kinds of meditation, pp. 52-55; meditations
on rejoicing with Christ, on firm resolution against sin, on the
misery of sin, on ascertaining God's favor of one's life, on repulsing
evil thoughts (pp. 74-75 missing in my copy), and on the heart of
man, pp. 55-78; a treatise on hope, pp. 78-82; prayers in honor of
Mary, pp. 82-84; and directions for using the attached picture of the
rosary as an aid to meditation, pp. 84-87.]

---

*and] *ed.;* ad

XXII.
The
Societie of the
Rosary.
Newly Augmented.

Gaude Maria *Virgo, cun-*
ctas haereses sola interemi-
sti in vniuerso mundo.

[Woodcut of Mary]

Dignare me laudare te
Virgo sacrata.
Da mihi virtutem
contra hostes tuos.[1]

[Henry Garnet, S. J.[2]]

[A2]

The Preface
to the Reader.

After the generall deluge and inundation* of the wholle worlde
in the time of Noë, Almightie God placed in the cloudes his Rainbow, as a token and obligation that he would no more destroy the

Gen. 6.

---

[1]n.p.d. [1596-97.] Pt. 2 contains "An Epistle Consolatory: of an Auncient
Pope To the Catholicks of Albania sore aggreeued with the Persecution of the
Heretickes of those daies." n.d. Pr. [secretly in England.] *STC* 19939a.
Allison and Rogers, I, Entry 355.
An earlier edition:
The Societie of the rosary. Wherin is conteined the begining, increase,
and profit of the same. n.p.d. [1593-94.] Anon. Pr. [secretly in England.]
This edition does not include the "An Epistle Consolatory. . . ." *STC*
21319. Allison and Rogers, I, Entry 354.

[2]Henry Garnet (1555-1606) was a convert to Catholicism. He entered the
Society of Jesus at Rome in 1575. His higher studies at the Roman College
were done under such eminent men as Suarez and St. Robert Bellarmine.
For a time he was English Penitentiary at St. Peter's and also professor of
Hebrew and mathematics at the Roman College. On May 8, 1586, Garnet
left Rome accompanied by Robert Southwell, S. J., bound for England. In
July these two eminent Jesuits landed in their homeland and began their arduous
apostolate. Garnet became the Superior of the Jesuits in England in 1587
upon the death of Fr. William Weston, S. J., a position which he held for
eighteen years. His daily life was one of disguise and constant danger. In 1605,
he was apprehended and committed to the Tower. In 1606, after twenty-three
examinations, he was condemned to death for high treason. On May 3, 1606,
he was hanged and later quartered in St. Paul's Churchyard (Gillow, II, 390-
395). For a detailed study of Garnet, see the *Records of the English Province*
of the Society of Jesus (ed. Henry Foley, 7 vols. [London, 1877-83], IV,
35-193).
*inundation] *ed.;* innudation

world with water. How generall a deluge of heresie and of all maner of iniquitie our miserable countrey hath these late yeeres susteined we yet feele by the experience of the calamitie therof: and it is to pitifull to remember how many soules haue already perished therby. Neither doe we see any other reliefe in so [A2ᵛ] great distresses: than to make our humble recourse vnto our mercifull Lord, and earnestly to desire of his soueraigne greatnesse: that shutting vp the deapth of hellish lakes, and the mighty cataracks of his heauie displeasure; these deadly fluddes may cease from the earth, and all creatures be restored to their former saftie. One singuler occasion of hope wee might haue of so greate a benefit: if it would please him but once to shew this signe of his Testamēt with mankind, his gloriouse rainbow, which discouering vnto the worlde most bewtifull coulers might signifie the caulme & faire weather, which were at hand: This rainbow I meane to be the glorious Virgin, a most beutifull signe of Gods frenship with men, and such a token of his singuler [A3] mercie, that when he hath often times loaded the skies with the heauie cloudes of his iminent vengence, he neuerthelesse looking vpon so glorious & beloued a creature, not appointed by him for wrath and anger, but chosen for a figure of mercy and peace, and therfore most worthely called the mother of mercy: forgetting our iniquities, and as it were in a maner his owne Iustice; withholdeth his seuere punishments, and in steede of brimstone and fire, which those cloudes should send vpon vs, leadeth vs *In nube diei, & tota nocte in illuminatione ignis* by the cloudes of his mercie in the day; and all the night by the comforte of his heauenly lights. I could here discourse at large how worthely this B. Virgin may be called a rainbow, & how ma-[A3ᵛ]ny excelent comparisons may be made therof vnto her: of the variety of her vertues, of the perfection of her greate excelencies figured in roūdness, of the statelines of that seate which God did choose in her for his owne person But sufficient it is for our purpose, that she is in speciall maner a rainbow against Heretickes: wher-as the Church generally singeth, she hath destroid all heresies in the wholle world, and therfore is a perticuler signe and aboade of the ceassing therof:[3] From this bow there goeth

Gen. 8.

Psal. 77.

Apoc. 4.

---

[3]The defeat of the Albigensian heretics at the Battle of Muret in 1213 and the naval victory of the Christian forces over the Turks at the Battle of Lepanto in 1571 are but two of the many victories of the Catholic Church over her enemies attributed to the intercession of Mary through the Rosary (*Catholic Encyclopedia*, XIII, 189).

none but chosē arrowes taken forth of the quiuer of God him selfe, yea arrowes of the saluatiō of our Lord, arrowes of saluation against *Sirta;* that is, arrowes of saluation both in tranquillity of the Church; and also against all the enimies of Israel, & [A4] the Church of God in the time of tentation and disturbance. Neither wanteth it a misterie, that this bow is bēt vpwards towards heauen: for it not only receiueth the strength from God, to whom it looketh: but wounding first the hart of God him-selfe, from thēce receiueth all comfort for his seruantes and confusion at the last for his wicked enimies.

Cant. 4.

This whē I consider, & waighing also with my selfe, how trew it is of her which is spoken of the wisdome of God, with which she was so aboundantlye endowed; that she preuenteth those which desire her for to shewe her selfe first vnto them: that she seeketh with great diligēce for those that are worthy of her, and sheweth her selfe in the waies pleasantly vnto them: and with all prouidēt [A4ᵛ] care runneth to meete thē. I fully perswade my selfe, that it is in our owne power to winne her, and to obtaine frō heauen a new rainbow: which being a signe of god, cannot signifie falsely, but most certainely fore-tell our comforte and reliefe. It is in our power I say: yet not except we desire her: she seeketh for vs but so, if we be worthy of her: she sheweth her selfe pleasant, but vnto those that she meeteth in the waies to seeke her: for whom she boūtifully prouideth all maner of good.

Sap. 6.

I present therefore vnto my most deare coūtry with the same loue and affection with which I would if so it pleased God presēt it my blood, a singuler meane of winning this Virgins fauour, and such a meane as by her selfe hath here tofore bene presented vnto [A5] the worlde, and now vndoubtedly by her self also not vnmindfull of her auncięt Dowry, is offered vnto our country the Society of the holy Rosary:[4] an auncient meanes euen from *S. Domincks* time of

---

[4]The invention of the beads as a counting device for prayers and also the practice of repeating one hundred and fifty Aves cannot be attributed to St. Dominic; both customs are notably earlier than the thirteenth century. Furthermore, the custom of meditating on the mysteries did not originate until two hundred years after St. Dominic's death. This rather widespread tradition associating St. Dominic with the devotion of the Rosary was probably begun about 1470-75 by a Dominican named Alan de Rupe. Alan, though a devout and zealous religious, was the victim of delusions and imaginary revelations (*Catholic Encyclopedia*, XIII, 186).

The Confraternity of the Holy Rosary was founded in 1470 at Douay, and by 1486 had members in England (*A Dictionary of Mary*, p. 254). The founder is generally believed to be Alan de Rupe (*Catholic Encyclopedia*, XIII, 188-189).

rooting out of heresie. Which albeit both in time past, and now of late yeres it hath ben embraced in our countrey, with great deuotion: yet neither hath it hitherto bene so generally vsed neither the nature and profit ther of so perfitly knowne, as for so greate a good were required. for (as scripture saith) A hidden wisdome, & an vnseene treasure, what profite is there in thē both? Wherfore I thought it my parte, knowing what opportunitie our countrey men may haue to be admitted vnto the participation of this treasure, diligently to search [A5ᵛ] out & breifly to set down what so euer either necessarily doth belōg or any waie might be profitable to the enioying of the same: fully perswading my selfe that as spirituall men in these Catholicke countreies are wont to say of thē selues; so the beades must be to our afflicted brethren, in steed of all maner of armour or weapons: for the weapons of our warfare are not carnall, but mighty to God, vnto the distruction of munitions, distroying Councelles, and all loftines extolling it selfe against the knowledge of God. Which perswasion of mine vnto those which shall duely weigh the perfection and excelencies of this most glorious Virgin, cannot any way be iudged false: for therfore is she called a well setled array of a pitched armie, because [A6]she mightily ouercometh, not only her owne, but also her deuout clients aduersaries. Which singuler protection we can no waie deserue more cōueniently: then by such seruice as her selfe hath elected and cōmended vnto vs, and of it selfe doth yeeld vs such commodities as in the treatise shall appeare. Yet this must I cōfesse, that I haue for the most part framed my selfe, vnto the simpler sorte: for such are they which most please our Lady, & in which she most delighteth: my intent hauing bene in this litle treatise, that as the beades are the vnlearned mans booke; so also such persons might here find whatsoeuer is necessary for their deuotion. And yet doubt I not, but any Catholicke minde will iudge the same worke not to be vnprofita-[A6ᵛ]ble vnto whosoeuer of neuer so greate knowledge with a certain spice of hereticall pride, will not contemne ordinarye Catholicke helpes of deuotion. Accept therfore (gentle Reader) this my present: & with conuenient diligēce and study vse the same. Which if thou doest: I doubt not, but how soeuer it may displease curiouse eies, it will not be displeasing to our B. Lady, nor without vnspeakable profite to our wholle countrey, thē the which two things next vnto Gods glory I desire nothing more. Fare-well.

Eccl. 20.

2. Cor. 1.

Cant. 6.

[Here follow a discourse on devotion to Mary, Sigs. Bi^r-C3^v, and a table of contents, Sigs. C4^r-C4^v.]

[1]

Of the Beginning,
Largenes & Pro-
fitte of this Societie.
Cap. 1.

Amongst diuerse companies or Societies, religiously instituted and moste deuoutlye folowed and reuerenced in the Church of God, one of the most auncient, generall, and profitable is, that which being instituted in the honour of the most blessed and immaculate Virgin Mary mother of God, and patronesse of all distressed mortalls, is cōmonly cal-[2]led the Society of the holy Rosary.

The first Founder and beginner therof was the glorious light of Gods Church S. Dominick who about 400. yeeres ago not being contented to haue instituted a noble order of religious persons, as well Freers as Nunnes, which in their seuerall houses & with most perfect rules seruing Almightie God, haue spreade their zeale and deuotion, ouer all the worlde: did also extend his charitable care and prouidēce euen to all sortes of people, and with his singuler wisdome and inflamed loue of soules, by the inspiration no doubt of the holye Ghost, and speciall reuelation of the same glorious Virgin, knit togither in one band of a mutuall Societie, all kind of deuout Christians. [3] For this deuout Saint, considering with S. Pavl, that he was debtour to the simple as-well as vnto the wise, and waying with himselfe that there were many seculer persons, whom either want of wil might withdraw, or necessitie of their estate and condicion might hinder from the strait path of Euangelicall perfection: found notwithstanding a means for thē to kindle and nourish deuotion, and with great facilitie to pray & obtaine by the most effectuall inter-cession of so great an aduocate all manner of good and perfecte giftes, from the only geuer and bestower therof the Father of lightes. From which so fruitefull meanes, should be excluded neither the husbādman in the fields, nor the trauailer in his iorney, nor the labourer with his toiling, nor [4]the simple by his vnskilfulnes nor the woman by her sex, nor the maried by their estate, not the yong by their ignorance, nor the aged by their impotencie, nor the sicke by their infirmitie, nor the poore for want of abilitie, nor the blind

*The
Anti-
quitie.*

*The
genera-
lity.
Rom. 1.*

for want of sight, yea the Religious them selues of both sexes, at all times and in all places, when they may want either bookes or other ordinary helpes of spirite, (although this be not one of the least among many others wherewith they abound) might hereby finde no smale increase of cōfort, feruour, and deuotion, in so much that wee see by experience, that there is not any deuout Christian, and which hath care of his soule, but in what estate soeuer he liue, if he haue conuenient opportunitie, he seeketh by giuing his name [5] vnto this holy cōfraternity, to become a cliēt or pupill of the most glorious Virgin

Wherin we may see the singuler profite and commoditie which redoūdeth vnto vs by the same. For if it be so generall a deuotion, in the wholle Church of God, as we haue said: then vndoubtedly we may say that one profitte which hereby we may reape, is the facilitie of an acceptable seruice of God, for that deuotion which repugneth to no estate or conditiō, but may so easely be performed, not requiring more knowledge, then to say the *Pater noster,* and *Aue Maria,* nor any more charge thē the price of a paire of Beades, nor any choice of place or situation of body, but as it shall like the partie, either to stand, site, lye walke, or kneele: especially ha-[6]uing no burden of conscience or charge of sinne if it be omitted: who seeth not thē how easie it is, and with what facilitie it may be obserued? yea who seeth not how great and carelesse a negligence, and how contemptuous a singularitie it were, to omit so generall a profession? This facilitie is also the greater for that there beeing diuers Societies of our Lady, euery one of which doth laudably endeuour to aduaunce the honor of so holye a creature, to theire owne singuler great gaine of deuotion, vertue and merite: in euery one are diuerse bondes either of rehearsing some certaine praiers euery day, or of ofte Confessing and Receiuing, or of some more stricte obseruance then is necessarie or easie and expedient for euery Christian: But in this of [7]the Rosary, that it may the rather be imbraced of all: though there be spirituall rewardes almost for euery godly action, in which euery man according to his deuotiō may exercise him self: yet is there no generall bond, but only to the rehearsing of the Beades thrice a weeke, as shall be shewed hereafter, and that without the incurring of any sinne by the omission therof, as hath bene saide before, yea and that also may be supplied by an other, who performeth the due exercise for his brother, being either sicke or

The profitte & commodity.

Diuers Societies of Our Lady.

One only necessarie bond in this Society.

otherwise hindered: as afterward shall appeare. But besides the facilitie there are other more singuler commodities herein. For secondly there is the speciall patronage and protectiō of the same most blessed and glorious Virgin. For although she be [8]worthely called a most louing aduocate of all faithfull Christians yet there no doubt doth her care more aboūd, where she hath most mercifully chosen & gathered, & knit togither such as she meaneth singulerly to tender, she hauing declared by sundry miracles, the familiar prouidēce which she carieth ouer this her familie. Thirdly in this deuotion of the Rosary is daily with great fruit remembred the principall pointes of the life of our Sauiour, and of his holy Mother, in so much that the daunger, of which the Prophet complaineth, when he saith that the wholle earth was brought to desolation, because there was not who did meditate or ponder in his hart: by this deuout exercise of Christian duety, is by all estates of men vtterly auoided: whilest [9]euery deuout Catholicke, dailye when he saieth his beades, doth as it were in a booke read and reuerentlye laieth before his eies, Christ our Sauiour incarnat in his Mother, sanctifying Iohn Baptist his holy Precursor, lying in a manger, offered vp to his Father in the Temple, teaching the Doctors, praying in the Garden, cruelly whipped crowned with thornes, carying his Crosse and exalted theron for our redemption, rising againe, ascending into heauen, sending his holy Spirite and gratious giftes vnto men, taking vp with childly affection his most holy Mother, euen corporally vnto heauen and exalting and crowning her ouer all his holy Saintes and Angells. Wherof what gratitude, what humilitie, what charitie, what spurres vnto all vertue [10]may be ingendered in Christian mindes, let euery one consider: it is not our purpose now to expoūd. And although this manner of remembring the life of Christ, may be practised by any one which is not of this Society: yet both this maner of deuiding & religiously honouringe these holy misteries, was first commended by S. Dominicke to this holy confraternitie, not without a speciall reuelation (as it is credibly thought) of the B. Virgin, and such vertuous practise will then be more acceptable, when it is performed with a relation, and respect, as of one of this so fauored a Societie.

4   Fourthlye this holy Societie hath many Indulgences or Pardons annexed vnto the saying of the Rosary: as shall hereafter appeare. Of the profit wherof as it is [11]not lawfull for any Catholicke to

The patronage of our Lady.

Godly meditation.

Hier. 12.

The 15. misteries of the Rosary.

Indulgences.

doubt, so were it to long here to intreate. Only this will I say : that although there be perhapps many greater Indulgences graunted vnto diuerse Graines,[5] then these of this confraternity, yet are not these to be neglected, but rather greatly to be esteemed for to causes. First for so many other commodities as are in this Societye : which cannot be obtained without saying once a weeke the Rosary, for respecte of this Society. Wherfore although one would for desire of greater Indulgence applye the saying of his Beades vnto other graines, yet is it verye expediēt thrise a weeke to apply his intention vnto the Society of the Rosary, saying his beades as a member therof, for than is he sufficiently disposed to receaue the [12]fruites of the same Societie, although he should neuer so often besides by saying the same seeke the Indvlgences of halowed graines. Secondly for that a sufficient cause beeing required for the valew of an Indulgēce as the Diuines do teach, these Indulgēces being confirmed by so diuers Popes, and hauing the valew of a cause from the influence of so diuers members, which in this Society euery where tend vnto one end of the seruice and honour of God and his blessed Mother, must of necessitie haue an vndoubted and more aboundant effect.

The participation of spirituall good.

5 Fifthly, there is in this confraternitie an inestimable treasure of the mutuall participation of all the good works done by the persons of the same, & of the wholle order of S. *Dominick* as wel Freers [13]as Nunnes. So that besids the generall influence which for the cōmuniō of Saints in the Church of God, is from one mēber of Christ his misticall body vnto another, by which one member reioiceth with another, suffereth with and for an other, and the aboundāce of one supplieth the want and pouertie of an other, so that both be in gods grace (without the which neither Indulgences may be obtained, nor the participation of good workes either giuen or receiued.) There is a more speciall benefite and participation in this Society by the particuler application of those which may by authoritie distribute so great a treasure of all that Fasting, Praying, Watching, Almes, & other works of Christian pietie, as are by so many so godly so farre dispersed [14]persons euery day and moment performed.

---

[5]*graines,* beads

6   Last of all, the benefitte of this Society lasteth after death also as shall be shewed also hereafter. For when the Soules departed, in the flames of Purgatorie yeldeth satisfaction for sinnes not perfectly remitted in this world, it may by the ordinary suffrages of Gods Church, be releeued, as vnto all Christians departed in Gods grace is common. But hee which for a soule departed of this Society offereth the vsuall deuotions of the same, besides the valew which such deuotions may haue of them selues commeth loden with the treasures and merittes of diuers other members of the Church to be applied for the releefe of the distressed soule. All which so great commodities shal [15]more plainly appeare in the summary following of the ordinances or statutes and graces of this Society. Which hath bene faithfully drawen forth of an Italian boke of the Rosary sette forth at Rome about 8. or 9. yeres sithēce by the Reuerend Generall of S. Dominicks order vnto whom especially the admission into this Society doth belong, although I vnderstand to my great comforte that there be diuerse within our Realme which haue either immediatelye from the same Generall or by some other lawfull meanes the like auctoritie.

The benefite after death.

[Here follows the substance of the book: the rules and ordinances of the Society, pp. 16-27; the blessing of the beads, pp. 27-29; the indulgences attached to the Rosary and a short defense of indulgences, pp. 30-37; a discussion of the Stations in Rome, pp. 37-46; a listing of the myteries of the Rosary and methods of saying the Dominican Rosary and other chaplets, pp. 46-168; a section entitled "Twenty Propositions to proue the Catholicke custome of saying the rosary," pp. 169-185; and explication of the basic prayers of the Rosary, the *Pater Noster* and *Ave,* pp. 186-196; and other diverse devotions, such as the examination of conscience, prayers for various occasions, directions for receiving Holy Communion, a listing of further indulgences, and Latin litanies in honor of the Virgin, pp. 196-232. Bound as part of this volume with separate pagination is "An Epistle Consolatory of an Auncient Pope. . . ," pp. 1-19.]

XXIII.

⁋ *A Methode, to meditate on the*
Psalter, or great Rosarie of our blessed Ladie:
With a Preface in the defence and comenda-
tion of it: And Meditations for
euery Morning and
Euening.
[Woodcut of Our Lady of the Rosary]
Printed at Antwerp. 1598.[1]
[Anonymous]

[Here begins the preface wherein the practice of saying the Rosary is defended, promarily by references to tradition, Sigs. A4ʳ-B8ʳ. Sigs. A2ᵛ, A3ᵛ, and B8ᵛ are blank.]

[C] Certaine obseruations
to be vsed in Praier, and
first the fiue parts therof
contained in a
verse.
1 Reuerently 2 Aduisedly 3 Deuoutly
Prepare, then reade, & meditate
4 heartily 5 humbly.
giue thankes and make request.
These are fiue partes of prayer much
praised and practised of
the best.

Prepare: If the basest Fidler dares not for feare of leesing his re-ward, or receiuing a worse turne presse to play in the bases pres-ence he commeth, without first tuning his instrument, howe [Cᵛ] much rather shoulde wee feare to presume to pray in gods presence who made, preserued, redeemed, and sanctified vs, & at which the angells and powers of heauen do tremble, without due preparatiō: And therefore wee haue placed a short iaculatorie praier at the beginning of euery Mystery, which you may vse in steede of a

---

[1]Imprint false; pr. [secretly in England.] Allison and Rogers, II, Entry 541. *STC* 17538.

better, with this *Prouiso,* that you do neuer leaue off to pronounce it, till you perceiue your tongue and heart doe concurre.

2   Then reade or remember the mysterie for helping of you, in the whiche I haue disposed two verses ouer euery picture.

3   And meditate eyther in all, [C2]or in some one or twoo of the points which I haue layd down, as your leisure and deuotion shall serue.

4   Giue thankes for thankfulnesse, for one benefite soliciteth another.

5   And make request, eyther for some particular thing, which your present necessitie requireth: or if you please, vse the two verses placed vnderneath the picturs of euery Mysterie.

[Here follows a listing of virtues which are to be demanded in petition, such as discretion, humility, firm faith, and others, Sigs. C2ʳ-C3ʳ. Following this section there is a short directive in verse urging the petitioner to be patient, to avoid distractions, etc., Sigs. C3ʳ-C4ʳ. Sig. C4ʳ is blank and Sig. C5ʳ contains a short introduction.]

[C5ʳ]   [The first joyful mystery]

Heere Gabriel the Archangel doth,   Matt. 1. 20.
  Our blessed Ladie greete: Luc. 1. 35.
Who with consent conceiued Christ,
  Our soueraigne Sauiour sweete.

[Woodcut of the Angel announcing to
Mary that she is to be the Mother of God]

God graunt the power and strength of God,
  My soule may dayly haile:
That it conceiuing Christ may bring
  Forth teares of good auaile.

[C6]   *Prepare*

Blessing your selfe with *in nomine,* Mother of God, pray for me
now and euer.

Then reade

The verses written ouer the picture

And meditate

1 On Gods great mercy and infinite charity, who vouchsafed so
humbly to incarnate himselfe to redeeme mankinde from the miserie
of orignall sinne, without any foregoing merit worthy of it.

2 On the exceeding loue which [C6ᵛ]our Ladie bare towardes
God from her very infancie, and the great care she had to performe
hir vow of Virginitie, and imitate her in loue and care to performe
all thy lawefull vowes and good purposes.

3 Of the greatnesse of the Ambassadour, importance of his em-
bassage, worthinesse of our Ladie, the entertainement she gaue the
Angell, their interparlie, and* the wonderful worke which was
wrought at the very instant of her consent, assuring thy selfe, that
God both can and will as effectually resigne thy will to his.

Giue thankes

[C7] For these, and all other benefites with *Alleluia* or *Laus tibi
Domine.*

And make request

Either for some gift of grace your present necessitie requireth,
or with the verses written vnder the picture. Then begin your
beades.

[Here follow the remaining fourteen mysteries, Sigs. C7ᵛ-G1ᵛ.
Hereafter follow verse meditations for evening and morning, Sigs.
G2ʳ-G4ᵛ.]

---

*and] *ed.;* and/and

XXIV.

The
Rosarie
of our Ladie.
Otherwise called
our Ladies
Psalter.
*With other godlie
exercises mentioned
in the Preface.*
Antverpiae.
Apud Ioannem Keerbergium.
Anno M. D. C.
Cum gratia et priuilegio.[1]
[Thomas Worthington[2]]

[The titlepage is very ornate, with saints and angels adoring the
Blessed Virgin and Christ Child on high.]

[★2]   The Preface,
*Containing diuers Annotations concerning the
Rosarie of our Ladie: and the other Exercises
here folowing: With the causes of composing and printing the same, in this forme; and
certaine commodities ensuing hereof.*

---

[1]Allison and Rogers, II, Entry 918. *STC* 17546.

[2]Thomas Worthington (1549-1626), after having been graduated from
Brasenose, Oxford, in 1570, went to Douay College in 1572-3 and received the
B. D. degree there in 1577. Soon after this, he was laboring successfully in
the English mission until 1584, when he was seized and committed to the
Tower; for over two months, he was confined to the "pit." On June 21, 1585
(*D. N. B.*, XXI, 957 suggests January 25, 1584-5) Thomas Worthington and
twenty other priests were released from the prison and exiled. Returning
to Rheims, the new site of the English College, he was soon appointed
Chaplain to Sir William Stanley's regiment in the Spanish service. In 1588,
Worthington was made a Doctor of Divinity by the University of Trier,
and in 1590, he returned to Rheims to teach divinity. In 1591, he went to
Brussels, where he once more resumed his duties as a chaplain. In 1599,
chiefly through the influence of Fr. Robert Persons, S. J., to whom he had
made a secret vow of obedience, Worthington became the President of the
English College. His close ties with the Jesuits, however, and several reforms
which did not please the secular priests caused him finally to lose his Presi-
dency. In 1613, he left Douay for Rome, where he was given a pension by
the cardinal-protector, was given a position with the Congregation of the
Index, and made an apostolic notary. While in Rome, he became a member

For so much (benigne Catholike reader) as euerie thing is better vnderstood, by the explication of his proper, or vsual name, it is first of al to be noted, that the name of Rosarie (which properly signifieth the place where roses doe growe, or be reserued) is here vsed for the forme of praier, which the renowmed religious father S. Dominicke,[3] about the yeare of our Lord 1200 (or as some thinke, a Religious Priest called Peter of Amiens[4] in Picardie, aboue an hundred yeares before) instituted, of certaine *Pater nosters, Aues* and *Credes,* together with certaine principal Mysteries to be meditated, in honour of our blessed Ladie, the virgin Marie, framed by the number of fiue, like to a Rose, that hath fiue leaues: Whereof it is called the Rosarie of Ovr Ladie.

Which name of Rosarie vsed sometimes largely, and sometimes strictly. Taken largely it containeth fifteene Decades or Tennes (that is to say, fifteene times one Pater noster with tenne Aues) and three Credes; and hath fifteene Mysteries applied thereunto, that is, to euerie Decade [★2ᵛ] one Mysterie. And the same is also called Ovr Ladies Psalter, because it hath so manie Aues, or salutations of our Ladie, as there be Psalmes in the Psalter of Dauid, which are an hundred and fiftie. But strictly taken (as it is cōmonly ment, when one is appointed for penance, or for pardon, or for other like cause to say a Rosarie) it containeth only fiue Decades, to witt, fiue Pater nosters and fiftie Aues, with one Crede. So that in the great Rosarie (or Ladie Psalter) be contained three particular Rosaries. And these three are resembled to three sortes of Roses, white, read, and damaske. For as these three colours doe signifie, ioye, payne, and glorie: so these three Rosaries do containe three sortes of Mysteries to be meditated, ioyful, sorowful and glorious.

This forme of praying, the first institutor of the Rosarie, did so accommodate to the vse of al faithfull persons, as it might be both a necessarie helpe to vnlerned people, and also a most profitable exercise to the most lerned in the world: as wel for the better auoiding

---

of the Oratory. In 1616, Worthington returned to England, where he resided with the Biddulphs at Biddulph Hall, Stafford, until his death (Gillow, V, 595-596). For an interesting account of Worthington's life, see *Records of the English Province of the Society of Jesus* (ed. Henry Foley, 7 vols. [London, 1877-1883], II, 104-110).

[3] For a note on St. Dominic's relationship to the Rosary, see p. 303, n. 4.

[4] Peter of Amiens (c. 1015-1115) is more commonly known as Peter the Hermit, an ascetic and preacher of the Crusades. He founded the monastery at Neufmoustier (*New Catholic Dictionary,* ed. Condé B. Pallen *et al* [New York, 1929], p. 752).

of idle, and hurtful distractions in the often repetition of the same prayers, as also for the more fruitful eleuating of the mind, meditating vpon the chiefest Mysteries of our faith, which concerne our Lord and Redeemer his coming into this world, [★3] and his going out of the same, and the happie effects of both.

For touching his coming into this world (whiche was so long and earnestly desired and expected) in the first Rosarie are to be meditated these fiue ioyful Mysteries.

[Here follows a listing of the five joyful, five sorrowful, and five glorious mysteries.]

[★3ᵛ] Thus much in general is euident by the tradition, and continual practise of al Catholike nations, for the space of foure or fiue hundred yeares at least: that is, since the time of S. Dominicke, or before. And of the same antiquitie and authoritie is the vse of Beades, which were inuēted for the better obseruing of the prescribed number of prayers, in saying the whole Rosarie. And considering, that no man can wel meditate vpon anie Mysterie, except he both particularly know, and perfectly remember, the special points therof, we can not doubt, but that Christian people were both taught the particular pointes of al the aboue mentioned fiftene Mysteries, and also had some forme or order prescribed, wherby they might the better remember the same pointes, euerie one in his place. Which instructions being, not commonly extant, and the vse of Beads also inhibited, and made dangerous to Catholikes, liuing amongst Heretikes in this age: for remedie of both these defects, a certaine Catho-[★4]like Priest, and prisoner for the Catholike Religion, in the towre of London and there also depriued, both of bookes and Beades, framed for him self a forme of meditation in saying the Rosarie, by noting so many particular pointes in euerie one of the fiftene Mysteries, that ech Mysterie seruing his owne decade, euerie *Pater noster, Aue* and *Crede* should haue their competent and particular pointes alotted. Wherby as wel the iust number of prayers, may without beades be exactly obserued, as also sufficient and apt matter be redely remembred, and the mind more eleuated to God, and idle distractions better auoided.

This priuat Exercise, albeit very vnperfect (as not purposed for the print, but rudely writtē,* and geuē to a priuat freind) yet

---

*writtē] *ed.;* writrē

did so content and please some wel disposed persons, that presently, without knowlege of the author, they caused it to be
printed, and so made common to manie. Wherby at last it came
into the handes of one, that knew better the authors meaning,
who finding manie faultes and defects in the edition, thought
good to correct and amend the same, and adorning it with Images[5] to set it forth anew, as wel to satisfie the good desires of such
as first did print it, as also for the like profite to others, who either
had it not, or vnderstood not the vse therof before.

[Here follow a description of other chaplets and a defense of
the Rosary devotion, Sigs. ★4ʳ★7ᵥ.]

[★7ᵛ] And so you see the maner of praying proposed [★8] in this
booke doth not hinder due attention, as the obiection pre-
supposeth, but greatly helpeth the same, and bringeth also other
spiritual commodities. Of which some may be here briefly noted.

For first, besides that the mind is hereby directed to the best
and most necessarie attention required in prayer, such also as be
not so wel instructed already, may by this forme of saying the
Rosaries and Corones here ensuing, learne many particular, and
most necessary points of Christian doctrine: which being once
knowen, can not but moue a true Christian hart to some, more or
lesse, cogitation and meditation of so great and singular benefites,
bestowed vpon vs by Almightie God. And the more one shal
meditate vpon the same, the more also shal his knowlege be stil
increased. So knowlege and meditation do mutually helpe and
increase ech other, but one without the other auaileth litle. For as
meditation without knowlege is erroneous: so knowlege without
meditation is drie and fruitles. But both together wil easely
inkindle the soul with the loue of God, and feede it with a spiritual refection, and sturre vp and inflame the desire to al possible
endeuour for the increase of Gods glorie, and health of their owne
and other mens soules. Likewise out of this varietie, and copie of
diuine Mysteries and benefites, the wel disposed may at al times
and occasions, choose suf-[★8ᵛ]ficient and fit pointes to meditate
vpon, in al their prayers vocal or mental. And finally, by diligent
vewing and beholding the pictures here placed, euerie one may
better conceiue and consider the Mysteries by them represented,

---

[5]Gillow indicates that the woodcuts are by Joan Collaert from designs by
M. de Vos (V, 596).

and be perhaps more moued to deuotion by sight therof, then by only reading. If any therfore wil vse this exercise, no doubt but for reward of their paines, they shal reape hereby no final fruite and increase of pietie. You at least (my deerely beloued in our Lord Iesus Christ) who haue not better meanes to further your deuotions withal, vse this helpe. And vouchsafe of your charitie to commend al vs, (who to do you good haue bestowed labour and cost, in setting forth this litle* worke) amongst your other deere frendes, vnto our B. Lord, and to his B. mother our Ladie, to our propre Angels, and special Patrons, and the whole Court of heauen, in your sweete deuotions. Amen. 25. of March. 1590.

Your owne al and euer in Christ,
T. W. P.[6]

[Here follow the half title and the first two joyful mysteries, pp. 1-9.]

[10] [Woodcut of the Nativity]

[11] *The Natiuitate of our Lord.*

After the holie virgin returned to Nazareth, from visiting her cosin, her husband Ioseph perceiuing her to be with child, is much trubled in mind, and doubtful what to do. For on one side he feareth the law, if he conceale, that his wiues conceiuing is not by him: On the other side, he knoweth the virgin, his spouse, to be of so godlie, chast, pure, and immaculate life, that he dare not accuse her, nor bring her into anie (be it neuer so smal) suspicion. She in the meane time being most hūble, and most modest, reueleth not, no not to her most deare husband, this so great a Mysterie, wrought in her by the powre of God. In fine Ioseph being iust, and holie, to auoide perplexitie, determineth secretly to leaue her: But while he thus thinketh, behold an Angel of our Lord appeareth to him in sleepe, saying: Ioseph sonne of Dauid, Feare not to tarie with Marie thy wife. For that which is conceiued in her, is of the Holie Ghost. And she shal bring forth a Sonne: And thou shalt cal his name Iesvs. For he shal saue his people from their sinnes.

---

*litle] *ed.;* litte
[6]T. W. P. is an abbreviation for Thomas Worthington, priest.

[12] 1. *Aue Maria.*

By cōmandement of Cesar Augustus, that al should be enrolled, euery one in the place whence they were descended: Ioseph with his spouse goeth to Bethleē, a citie of Dauid, because they were of his house and familie.

2. *Aue Maria.*

There by reason of their pouertie, and great concurse of people, not finding rowme in anie Inne, they take a poore lodging (as they may) in a stable.

3. *Aue Maria.*

In this place our Lord and Sauiour, King of al kings, the Sonne of God is borne, wrapped in clothes, and laid in a manger by an oxe and an asse, and is warmed by their breaths.

4. *Aue Maria.*

Forthwith an Angel appearing to Shepheards saith to them: Beholde, this day is borne to you a Saviovr, which is Christ our lord: in the citie of Dauid, and you shal find him swadled in clothes, and laid in a manger.

5. *Aue Maria.*

And sodenly, there was with the Angel an heauenlie armie, praising God, and singing: Glorie in the Highest to God: and in earth peace to men of good wil.

[13] 6. *Aue Maria.*

Then say the shepheards: Let vs go to Bethlehē, and see this thing which God hath done, and shewed to vs. And going with speede, they finde the child laid in a manger, and so returning glorifie God.

7. *Aue Maria.*

The eight day the childe is circūcised, and his name called Iesvs: that is Saviovr, according as the Angel had before signified to the virgin mother, and to Ioseph his supposed father.

8. *Aue Maria.*

Three Sages (*Kings or Princes*) knowing by the apparition of a glorious starre, that the king of Iewes (their expected Messias) is borne, come from the East to Ierusalem, to adore him.

9. *Aue Maria.*

King Herod and al Ierusalem with him are trubled, hearing these newes: yet there the Sages lerne of the hiegh Priests, that Christ should be borne in Bethlehem.

10. *Aue Maria.*

The Sages going towards Bethlehē see the starre againe, and it leadeth them euen to the house, where they finde the childe, and adore him; euerie one offering three giftes; Gold, Frankincense, and Myrrhe.

[Here follow the remaining twelve mysteries, pp. 14-102; meditations on the Crown of Our Lord and the Brigittene Rosary, pp. 103-113; and various prayers, Latin litanies, and the *Stabat Mater,* pp. 119-127. Page 128 contains the approbation of Matthias, Archbishop of Mechlin.]

BIBLIOGRAPHY

This bibliography does not include those works represented in the anthology.

Allen, William Cardinal. *An Apologie and true declaration of the institution and endeuours of the two English Colleges.* Mounts in Henault [actually Rheims], 1581.

Allison, A. F. "The Writings of Fr. Henry Garnet, S. J.," *Biographical Studies,* I(1951), 7-21.

Allison, A. F. and D. M. Rogers. *A Catalogue of Catholic Books in English Printed Abroad or Secretly in England, 1558-1640.* 2 pts. Bognor Regis, [England], 1956.

————. Review of *Elizabethan Recusant Prose, 1559-1582,* by A. C. Southern, *Library,* VI(June, 1951), 48-57.

Birt, Henry N. *The English Religious Settlement.* London, 1907.

Camm, Bede. *Forgotten Shrines.* London, 1910.

The Catholic Encyclopedia, ed. Charles Herbermann *et al.* 17 vols. New York, 1907-22.

Chambers, Robert. *Palestina.* Florence [actually London], 1600.

Chauncey, Maurice. *The Passion and Martyrdom of the Holy English Carthusian Fathers* (1570), ed. G. W. S. Curtis. London, 1935.

Cognet, Louis. *Post-Reformation Spirituality,* trans. P. Hepburne Scott. (*Twentieth Century Encyclopedia of Catholicism,* Vol. XLI.) New York, 1959.

De Backer, Augustin and Aloys. *Bibliothèque de la Compagnie de Jésus,* ed. Carlos Sommervogel. 2 pts. 10 vols. Bruxelles, 1890-1909.

De Guibert, Joseph. *The Theology of the Spiritual Life,* trans. Paul Barrett. New York, 1953.

A Dictionary of Mary, ed. and compiled Donald Attwater. New York, 1956.

The Dictionary of National Biography, ed. Leslie Stephen and Sidney Lee. 22 vols. London, 1908-09.

A Dictionary of Saints, ed. and compiled Donald Attwater. London, 1958.

Dictionary of the Bible, ed. John D. Davis. 4th ed. Grand Rapids, 1958.

A Dictionary of the Proverbs in England in the Sixteenth and Seventeenth Centuries, ed. Morris Tilley. Ann Arbor, 1950.

Dictionnaire de la théologie catholique, ed. A. Vacant *et al.* 15 vols. Paris, 1925.

Dictionnaire de Spiritualité ascétique et mystique, ed. Marcel Villers *et al.* 4 vols. Paris, 1932————. (This work is in progress; only entries A to E have been completed so far.)

Driscoll, J. P. "The Supposed Sources of Persons' 'The Christian Directory,'" *Recusant History,* V(1955), 235-243.

Firth, C. H. "Ballads and Broadsides," *Shakespeare's England,* ed. William Winter. 2 vols. New York, 1916, II, 511-538.

Foley, Henry, ed. *Records of the English Province of the Society of Jesus.* 7 vols. London, 1877-83.

Gillow, Joseph. *A Literary and Biographical History, or Bibliographical Dictionary of the English Catholics, from the Breach with Rome, in 1534, to the Present Time.* 5 vols. New York, 1885-1902.

Guillaume, Pierre. "Un précurseur de la Réforme catholique," *Revue d'histoire ecclésiastique,* XXV (1929), 260-274.

Hagedorn, Maria. *Reformation und Spanische Andachtsliteratur. Luis de Granada in England. (Kölner Anglistische Arbeiten,* Vol. XI.) Leipzig, 1934.

320

Hendriks, Laurence. *The London Charterhouse*. London, 1889.

Lercaro, Giacomo Cardinal. *Methods of Mental Prayer*, trans. T. F. Lindsay. Westminster, Maryland, 1957.

Lovasik, Lawrence. *Our Lady in Catholic Life*. New York, 1957.

Loyola, St. Ignatius. *The Spiritual Exercises*, trans. and ed. John Morris. 4th ed. rev. Westminster, Maryland, 1943.

Magee, Brian. *The English Recusants*. London, 1938.

Martz, Louis. *The Poetry of Meditation*. New Haven, 1954.

Milton, John. *John Milton: Paradise Regained, the Minor Poems, and Samson Agonistes*, ed. Merritt Hughes. New York, 1937.

More, Thomas. *Utopia*, trans. Ralph Robinson: ed. Phillip E. Hallett. London, 1935.

Muñoz, Luis. *La vida y virtudes del V. P. Luis de Granada*. Madrid, 1751.

New Catholic Dictionary, ed. Condé B. Pallen *et al.* New York, 1929.

Nouvelle biographie universelle, ed. Jean Chrétien Ferdinand. 46 vols. Paris, 1852-66.

Oechslin, Raphaël Louis. *Louis de Grenade ou la Rencontre avec Dieu*. Paris, 1954.

O'Shea, William. *The Worship of the Church; a Companion to Liturgical Studies*. Westminster, Maryland, 1957.

Oxford Dictionary of the Christian Church, ed. F. L. Cross. London, 1957.

Peers, E. A. *A Handbook to the Life and Times of St. Teresa and St. John of the Cross*. Westminster, Maryland, 1954.

Peers, E. A. *Spanish Mysticism*. London, 1924.

Pepler, Conrad. *The English Religious Heritage*. St. Louis, 1958.

Pollen, John H. *The English Catholics during the Reign of Queen Elizabeth*. London, 1920.

Pourrat, Pierre. *Christian Spirituality*, trans. W. H. Mitchell, S. P. Jacques, and D. Attwater. 4 vols. Westminster, Maryland, 1953-55.

Rivet, Mother Mary Majella. "The Influence of the Spanish Mystics on the Works of St. Francis de Sales." Unpublished Ph. D. dissertation, Catholic University of America, 1941.

Rollins, Hyder. "The Black-Letter Broadside Ballad," *PMLA*, XXXIV (1919), 258-339.

Rombaut, Edward. *Richard Verstegan: Een Polemist der Contra-Reformatie*. Brussels, 1933.

Roothaan, John. *How to Meditate*, trans. Louis Puhl. St. Meinrad, Indiana, 1957.

Roper, William. *The Life of Sir Thomas More, knighte*, ed. Elsie V. Hitchcock. London: The Early English Text Society, No. 197, 1935.

Simpson, Richard. *Edmund Campion. A Biography*. London, 1896.

Sitwell, Gerald. *Spiritual Writers of the Middle Ages*. (*Twentieth Century Encyclopedia of Catholicism*, Vol. XL.) New York, 1961.

Southern, A. C. *Elizabethan Recusant Prose, 1559-1582*. London, 1950.

Southwell, Robert. *The Complete Poems of Robert Southwell, S. J.*, ed. Alexander Grosart. (The Fuller Worthies Library) Blackburn, Lancashire, 1872.

Steele, Francesca. *The Convents of Great Britain*. London, 1902.

Stroud, Theodore S. "Father Thomas Wright: A Test Case for Toleration," *Biographical Studies*, I (1952), 189-219.

Symonds, Henry. *The Council of Trent and Anglican Formularies*. London, 1933.

Tade, George. "A Rhetorical Analysis of the *Spiritual Exercises* of St. Ignatius of Loyola." Unpublished Ph. D. dissertation, University of Illinois, 1955.

Tanquerey, Adolphe. *The Spiritual Life, a Treatise on Ascetical and Mystical Theology,* trans. Herman Branderis. Tournai, [Belgium], 1930.

Teresa of Avila. *Obras completas,* ed. M. Aguilar. Madrid, 1945.

Thurston, Herbert. "Catholic Writers and Elizabethan Readers. I—Father Persons' 'Christian Directory,'" *The Month,* LXXXII (December, 1894), 648-676.

————. "Our Popular Devotions. The Rosary," *The Month,* XCVI (1900), 620-637.

Underhill, John G. *Spanish Literature in the England in the Tudors.* New York, 1899.

Waugh, Evelyn. *Edmund Campion.* Boston, 1946.

White, Helen C. *English Devotional Literature, 1600-1640. (University of Wisconsin Studies in Language and Literature,* No. 29.) Madison, 1931.

————. "Some Continuing Traditions in English Devotional Literature," *PMLA,* LVII (December, 1942), 966-980.

————. *Tudor Books of Private Devotion.* Madison, 1951.